ACCESS 2003
PERSONAL TRAINER

CustomGuide, Inc.

O'REILLY®

Beijing • Cambridge • Farnham • Köln • Paris • Sebastopol • Taipei • Tokyo

Access 2003 Personal Trainer

by CustomGuide, Inc.

Copyright © 2005 O'Reilly Media, Inc. All rights reserved.
Printed in the United States of America.

Cover illustration © 2005 Lou Brooks.

Published by O'Reilly Media, Inc., 1005 Gravenstein Highway
North, Sebastopol, CA 95472.

O'Reilly books may be purchased for educational, business, or
sales promotional use. Online editions are also available for
most titles (*safari.oreilly.com*). For more information, contact
our corporate/institutional sales department: (800) 998-9938
or *corporate@oreilly.com*.

Editor	Michele Filshie
Production Editor	Philip Dangler
Art Director	Michele Wetherbee
Cover Designer	Emma Colby
Cover Illustrator	Lou Brooks
Interior Designer	Melanie Wang

Printing History

March 2005:   First Edition.

 This book uses RepKover™, a durable and flexible lay-flat binding.

ISBN: 0-596-00937-2
ISBN13: 978-0-596-00937-3
[C]

[03/07]

CONTENTS

Contents

About CustomGuide, Inc.

CustomGuide, Inc. (*http://www.customguide.com*) is a leading provider of training materials and e-learning for organizations; their client list includes Harvard, Yale, and Oxford universities. CustomGuide was founded by a small group of instructors who were dissatisfied by the dry and technical nature of computer training materials available to trainers and educators. They decided to write their own series of courseware that would be fun and user-friendly; and best of all, they would license it in electronic format so instructors could print only the topics they needed for a class or training session. Later, they found themselves unhappy with the e-learning industry and decided to create a new series of online, interactive training that matched their courseware. Today employees, students, and instructors at more than 2,000 organizations worldwide use CustomGuide courseware to help teach and learn about computers.

CustomGuide, Inc. Staff and Contributors

Jonathan High	President	Jeremy Weaver	Senior Programmer
Daniel High	Vice President of Sales and Marketing	Luke Davidson	Programmer
		Lisa Price	Director of Business Development
Melissa Peterson	Senior Writer/Editor	Soda Rajsombath	Office Manager and Sales Representative
Kitty Rogers	Writer/Editor		
Stephen Meinz	Writer/Editor	Megan Diemand	Sales Representative
Stan Keathly	Senior Developer	Hallie Stork	Sales Representative
Jeffrey High	Developer	Sarah Saeger	Sales Support
Chris Kanneman	Developer	Julie Geisler	Narrator

INTRODUCTION

About the Personal Trainer Series

Most software manuals are as hard to navigate as the programs they describe. They assume that you're going to read all 500 pages from start to finish, and that you can gain intimate familiarity with the program simply by reading about it. Some books give you sample files to practice on, but when you're finding your way around a new set of skills, it's all too easy to mess up program settings or delete data files and not know how to recover. Even if William Shakespeare and Bill Gates teamed up to write a book about Microsoft Access 2003, their book would be frustrating to read because most people learn by doing the task.

While we don't claim to be rivals to either Bill, we think we have a winning formula in the Personal Trainer series. We've created a set of workouts that reflect the tasks you really want to do, whether as simple as resizing or as complex as integrating multimedia components. Each workout breaks a task into a series of simple steps, showing you exactly what to do to accomplish the task.

And instead of leaving you hanging, the interactive CD in the back of this book recreates the application for you to experiment in. In our unique simulator, there's no worry about permanently damaging your preferences, turning all your documents purple, losing data, or any of the other things that can go wrong when you're testing your new skills in the unforgiving world of the real application. It's fully interactive, giving you feedback and guidance as you work through the exercises—just like a real trainer!

Our friendly guides will help you buff up your skills in record time. You'll learn the secrets of the professionals in a safe environment, with exercises and homework for those of you who really want to break the pain barrier. You'll have your Access 2003 skills in shape in no time!

About This Book

We've aimed this book at Access 2003. Some features may look different or simply not exist if you're using another version of the program. If our simulator doesn't match your application, check the version number to make sure you're using the right version.

Since this is a hands-on course, each lesson contains an exercise with step-by-step instructions for you to follow.

To make learning easier, every exercise follows certain conventions:

- This book never assumes you know where (or what) something is. The first time you're told to click something, a picture of what you're supposed to click appears in the illustrations in the lesson.

- When you see a keyboard instruction like "press Ctrl + B," you should press and hold the first key ("Ctrl" in this example) while you press the second key ("B" in this example). Then, after you've pressed both keys, you can release them.

Our exclusive Quick Reference box appears at the end of every lesson. You can use it to review the skills you've learned in the lesson and as a handy reference—when you need to know how to do something fast and don't need to step through the sample exercises.

Conventions Used in This Book

The following is a list of typographical conventions used in this book:

Italic

Shows important terms the first time they are presented.

`Constant Width`

Shows anything you're actually supposed to type.

Color

Shows anything you're supposed to click, drag, or press.

⋮ NOTE ⋮ *Warns you of pitfalls that you could encounter if you're not careful.*

TIP *Indicates a suggestion or supplementary information to the topic at hand.*

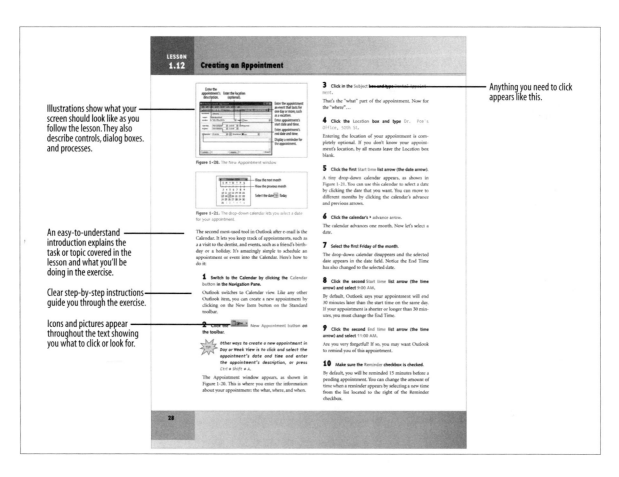

Illustrations show what your screen should look like as you follow the lesson. They also describe controls, dialog boxes, and processes.

An easy-to-understand introduction explains the task or topic covered in the lesson and what you'll be doing in the exercise.

Clear step-by-step instructions guide you through the exercise.

Icons and pictures appear throughout the text showing you what to click or look for.

Anything you need to click appears like this.

Using the Interactive Environment

Minimum Specs

- Windows 98 or better
- 64 MB RAM
- 150 MB Disk Space

Installation Instructions

Insert disc into CD-ROM drive. Click the "install" button at the prompt. The installer will give you the option of installing the "Interactive Content" and the "Practice Files." These are both installed by default. Practice files are also included on the CD in a directory called "Practice Files," which can be accessed without installing anything. If you select the installation item, the installer will then create a shortcut in your start menu under the title "Personal Trainer," which you can use to access your installation selections.

Use of Interactive Content

Once you've installed the interactive content, placing the disc in your drive will cause the program to launch automatically. Then, once it has launched, just make your lesson selections and learn away!

How to Contact Us

We have tested and verified the information in this book to the best of our ability, but you might find that features have changed (or even that we have made mistakes!). As a reader of this book, you can help us to improve future editions by sending us your feedback. Please let us know about any errors, inaccuracies, bugs, misleading or confusing statements, and typos that you find anywhere in this book.

To ask technical questions or to comment on the book, send e-mail to:

bookquestions@oreilly.com

The web site for *Access 2003 Personal Trainer* lists examples, errata, and plans for future editions. You can find this page at:

http://www.oreilly.com/catalog/accesspt/

For more information about this book and others, see the O'Reilly web site at:

http://www.oreilly.com

Please also let us know what we can do to make this book more useful to you. We take your comments seriously and will try to incorporate reasonable suggestions into future editions. You can write to us at:

O'Reilly Media, Inc.
1005 Gravenstein Highway North
Sebastopol, CA 95472
(800) 998-9938 (in the U.S. or Canada)
(707) 829-0515 (international or local)
(707) 829-0104 (fax)

Safari® Enabled

When you see a Safari® enabled icon on the cover of your favorite technology book, that means the book is available online through the O'Reilly Network Safari Bookshelf.

Safari offers a solution that's better than e-Books. It's a virtual library that lets you easily search thousands of top tech books, cut and paste code samples, download chapters, and find quick answers when you need the most accurate, current information. Try it free at *http://safari.oreilly.com*.

CHAPTER 1
THE FUNDAMENTALS

CHAPTER OBJECTIVES:

Start Microsoft Access, Lessons 1.1—1.3

Understand the Access program screen, Lesson 1.4

Give commands to Access, Lessons 1.5—1.8

Open and modify a database object or window, Lessons 1.9—1.10

Learn about tables, queries, forms, reports, and macros, Lessons 1.11—1.15

Preview and print a database object, Lesson 1.16

Select, cut, copy, and paste data, Lessons 1.17—1.18

Use editing, Help, and Zoom features, Lessons 1.19—1.23

Close a database and exiting Microsoft Access, Lesson 1.24

CHAPTER TASK: LEARN THE BASICS OF ACCESS 2003

Prerequisites

- **A computer with Windows 2000 or XP and Access 2003 installed.**
- **An understanding of basic computer functions (how to use the mouse and keyboard).**

Welcome to your first lesson on Microsoft Access! Microsoft Access is a powerful database program you can use to store all kinds of information—from a simple list of recipes to an inventory catalog with tens of thousands of products. Once information is stored in a Microsoft Access database, it's easy to find, analyze, and print.

Of all the programs in the Microsoft Office suite, Microsoft Access is the one that most intimidates people. "Mastering Microsoft Excel or Word was hard enough," they think. "How can I ever understand a complicated program like Access?" While it's true that Microsoft Access has many advanced features (there are computer consultants whose only job is programming Access databases), creating and working with a Microsoft Access database is probably a whole lot easier than you think.

With that in mind, this chapter is your introduction to Microsoft Access and the world of databases. In this chapter you will learn more about exactly what a database is, what it is used for, and how to perform simple database tasks, such as adding and deleting records. This chapter also takes you on a basic tour of various parts of a Microsoft Access database: Tables, Forms, Reports, and Queries. If you have worked with one of the other Microsoft Office applications, such as Microsoft Excel or Word, you will find that you already know a lot about the concepts covered in this chapter. And so, without further ado, turn the page and take your first step into the world of databases.

Figure 1-1. Similar to a file cabinet...

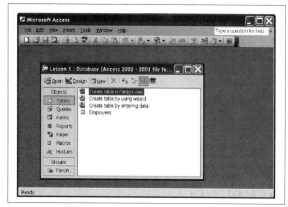

Figure 1-2. ...databases store and manage information related to a particular subject or purpose.

In its simplest form, a *database* is a collection of information that is organized into a list and stored in a manner similar to a file cabinet, as seen in Figure 1-1. Whenever you make a list of information, such as names, addresses, products, or invoices, you are, in fact, creating a database. Technically speaking, you don't even have to use a database program to create a database. You can make a list of information in all kinds of programs, such as Microsoft Excel, Word—even the meek and lowly Notepad program!

A database program, however, is much more powerful than a simple list you keep on paper or in a Microsoft Word document. A database program lets you:

- **Store Information:** A database stores lists of information that are related to a particular subject or purpose. It could be a list of aunt Mildred's home recipes, or business information, such as a list of hundreds of thousands of customers. A database also makes it easy to add, update, organize, and delete information.

- **Find Information:** You can easily and instantly locate information stored in a database. For example, you can find all the customers with the last name "Johnson" or all the customers who live in the 55417 zip code and are older than 65.

- **Analyze and Print Information:** You can perform calculations on information in a database. For example, you could calculate what percent of your total sales comes from the state of Texas. You can also present information in a professional-looking printed report.

- **Manage Information:** Databases make it easy to work with and manage huge amounts of information (see Figure 1-2). For example, with a few keystrokes you can change the area code for hundreds of customers in the (612) area code to a new (817) area code.

- **Share Information:** Most database programs (including Microsoft Access) allow more than one user to view and work with the same information at once. Such databases are called *multi-user databases*.

Databases usually consist of several parts. A Microsoft Access database may contain up to seven different database object types. The following table identifies the database objects you can use when creating a Microsoft Access database. Some objects you will use all the time (such as Tables), others you will hardly use (such as Modules). Table 1-1 lists various database objects and describes their uses.

Table 1-1. Database Objects

Object	Description
	Tables store a database's data in rows (records) and columns (fields). For example, one table could store a list of customers and their addresses while another table could store the customers' orders. A database must always contain at least one table where it can store information—all the other database objects are optional.
	Queries ask a question of data stored in a table. For example, a query might only display customers who are from Texas.
	Forms are custom screens that provide an easy way to enter and view data in a table or query.
	Reports present data from a table or query in a printed format.
	A special type of Web page designed for viewing and working with Microsoft Access data from an intranet or over the Internet.
	Macros help you perform routine tasks by automating them into a single command. For example, you could create a macro that automatically opens and prints a report.
	Like macros, modules automate tasks but by using a built-in programming language called Visual Basic or VB. Modules are much more powerful and complex than macros.

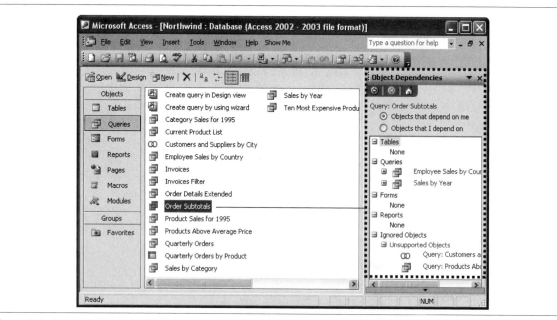

Figure 1-3. One of the most significant features of Access 2003 is its ability to display database object dependencies.

If you're upgrading from either Access 2000 or Access 2002 to Access 2003, you're in luck—in most respects, Access 2003 looks and works *almost* the same as both Access 2000 and Access 2002. One of the most significant features of Access 2003 is its ability to display database object dependencies, as shown in Figure 1-3. For example, you can see which queries, forms, and reports are based on a particular table. Table 1-2 shows what's new in Access 2003 (and if you're upgrading from Access 2000, what's new from Access 2002).

Table 1-2. What's New

New Feature	New in	Description
View object dependencies	2003	Perhaps the most useful and welcome feature in Access 2003 is its ability to let you view information on dependencies between database objects, which can dramatically save development time and reduce errors. For example, before deleting a query you can find out which forms, reports, and queries in the database use the query. You could then either change the record source of the dependent objects, or delete them, before deleting the original query. Macros, modules, and data access pages are not searched for dependencies, however.
Better security	2003	Microsoft has drastically increased the security settings in Access 2003 by setting the macro security level so that you are prompted every time you open a database containing Visual Basic for Applications (VBA) code in an Access database. Many databases contain macros and code—and while this new setting certainly increases security in Microsoft Access, most users will probably find it annoying. No problem—you can change the security level in Access to suit your own work environment and personal tastes. You can also automatically run macros based on whether they are digitally signed by a developer on a list of trusted sources.

Table 1-2. What's New (Continued)

New Feature	New in	Description
Propagating field properties	2003	Yet another helpful feature! In previous versions of Microsoft Access, whenever you modified a field's inherited property, such as its formatting property, you had to manually modify the property of corresponding controls in every form and report. Now, when you modify an inherited field property in Table design view, Access displays an option to update the property of all or some controls that are bound to the field.
Error checking in forms and reports	2003	Microsoft Access 2003 automatically checks for common errors in forms and reports. Error checking points out such errors as when the width of a report is greater than the page it will be printed on, and two controls being assigned to the same keyboard shortcut.
SharePoint Services support	2003	Microsoft's SharePoint Services makes it easy for users to collaborate and work together. Access 2003 can import, export, and link to information on a SharePoint Services list.
Office Online	2003	Access 2003 is better integrated with the Web with its new Office Online tools, which give you access to templates, articles, and tips on using Access 2003.
Streamlined User Interface	2002	Office XP has a new look and feel that improves the user's Office experience. This includes removing visually competing elements, visually prioritizing items on a page, increasing letter spacing and word spacing for better readability, and defining foreground and background colors to bring the most important elements to the front.
Smart Tags	2002	Perhaps the biggest new feature in Access 2003 is context-sensitive smart tags, a set of buttons that provide speedy access to relevant information by alerting you to important actions—such as formatting options for pasted information, formula error correction, and more.
Task Panes	2002	The Task Pane appears on the right side of the screen and lets you quickly perform searches, open or start a new database, and view the contents of the clipboard.
Multiple Undo and Redo	2002	You now have the ability to undo and redo multiple actions in Design View in all objects in your Microsoft Access databases and in views, stored procedures, and functions in your Microsoft Access projects.
Multiple Cut, Copy, and Paste Clipboard	2002	An improved Office XP Clipboard lets you copy up to 24 pieces of information at once across all the Office applications or the Web and store them on the Task Pane. The Task Pane gives you a visual representation of the copied data and a sample of the text, so you can easily distinguish between items as you transfer them to other documents.
PivotTable and PivotChart Reports	2002	Microsoft Access 2003 introduces PivotTable and PivotChart Views to tables, queries, and forms. PivotTables and PivotCharts summarize information into an organized and meaningful format and are great for analyzing data.
XML Support	2002	XML is quickly becoming the new standard for exchanging data between different programs. Access 2003 can now import and export information to and from XML file formats.

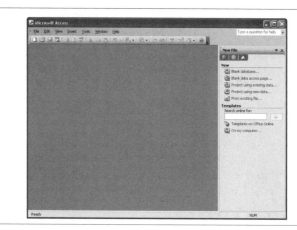

Figure 1-4. Microsoft Access 2003, as it appears when first started.

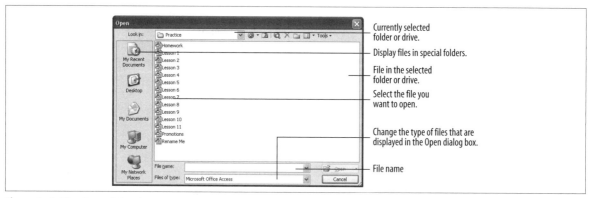

Figure 1-5. The Open dialog box.

You start Access 2003 the same as you would start any other Windows program—with the Start button. Because every computer is set up differently (some people like to rearrange and reorder their Program menu), the procedure for starting Access on your computer may be slightly different from the one listed here.

1 Make sure that your computer is on and the Windows desktop appears on the screen.

2 Click the Windows ⊞ start Start button, located in the bottom-left corner of the screen.

The Windows Start menu pops up.

3 Use the mouse to move the pointer over the words All Programs.

A menu pops up to the right of All Programs. The programs and menus you see listed depend on the programs installed on your computer, so your menu will probably look somewhat different from other users' menus.

4 On the All Programs menu, move the pointer over the words Microsoft Office 2003, then point to and click Microsoft Office Access 2003.

Once you click the Microsoft Access program, your computer's hard drive may whir for a moment while it loads Access. The Access program appears and the task pane displays options for opening an existing database or creating a new database, as shown in Figure 1-4.

You really can't do anything in Microsoft Access unless you open an existing database or create a new database. Most of the time you will open an existing database, and here's how to accomplish this simple task.

5 Click the Open button **on the toolbar.**

> **TIP** Other Ways to open a File are to Press Ctrl + 0, or select File → Open from the menu.

The Open dialog box appears, as shown in Figure 1-5. Now you have to tell Access where the database you want to open is located.

6 Navigate to the folder where your practice files are located.

7 Find and double-click the Lesson 1 **file.**

Access opens the Lesson 1 database and displays it in the database window. The special folders in the Open and Save As dialog boxes and their descriptions are outlined in Table 1-3.

Table 1-3. Special Folders in the Open and Save As Dialog Boxes

Heading	Description
	Displays a list of files that you've recently worked on.
	Displays all the files in the My Documents folder—the default location where Microsoft Office programs save their files.
	Displays the files and folders saved on your computer desktop.
	Displays a list of the disk drives and other hardware attached to your computer.
	Displays all the files and folders you can access on other computers.

QUICK REFERENCE

TO START MICROSOFT ACCESS:

1. CLICK THE WINDOWS START BUTTON.

2. SELECT ALL PROGRAMS → MICROSOFT OFFICE 2003 → MICROSOFT OFFICE ACCESS 2003.

TO OPEN A DATABASE:

• CLICK THE OPEN BUTTON ON THE TOOLBAR.

OR...

• SELECT FILE → OPEN FROM THE MENU.

OR...

• PRESS CTRL + O.

You might find the Access 2003 program screen a bit confusing and overwhelming the first time you see it. What are all those buttons, icons, menus, and arrows for? This lesson will help you become familiar with the Access program screen. There are no step-by-step instructions in this lesson—all you have to do is look at Figure 1-6 and then refer to Table 1-4 for details about each item. And, most of all, relax! This lesson is only meant to help you get acquainted with the Access screen—you don't have to memorize anything.

Don't worry if you find some of these objects confusing at first—they will make more sense after you've actually used them.

One more important note about the Access program screen: We have been examining the Database window in this lesson, but it is by no means the only screen that you will encounter in Microsoft Access. Just as there are sev-

eral different types of database objects in Microsoft Access, there are also dozens of different program screens—something that makes Access quite different from its Microsoft Office cousins Word and Excel. You will see some of these screens as we continue this chapter's tour of Microsoft Access.

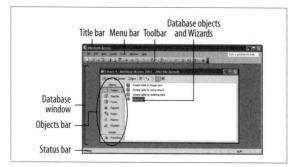

Figure 1-6. The Microsoft Access screen.

Table 1-4. The Access Program Screen

Element	What It's Used For
Title bar	Displays the name of the program you are currently using (in this case, Microsoft Access). The title bar appears at the top of all Windows programs.
Menu bar	Displays a list of menus you use to give commands to Access. Clicking a menu name displays a list of commands—for example, clicking the Edit menu name would display different formatting commands.
Toolbar	Toolbars are shortcuts—they contain buttons for the most commonly used commands (instead of having to wade through several menus). The toolbars in Access change depending on what you are working on. The database toolbar (the toolbar currently displayed) contains buttons for the Access commands that you will use most often, such as opening and printing databases.
Database window	The command center for a database, the Database window, allows you to view, create, edit, and modify database objects.
Objects bar	The Objects bar categorizes the different types of database objects. Each type of database object has its own icon—to view a type of object, click its icon on the Objects bar.
Database objects	Database objects are the basic components that make up a database. Database objects include tables, queries, forms, reports, pages, macros, and modules.
Status bar	Displays messages and feedback. The Status bar is especially important in Access since it can give you meaningful information and messages when you are entering information into a database.

Figure 1-7. The File menu.

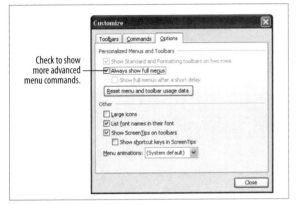

Check to show more advanced menu commands.

Figure 1-8. The Customize dialog box.

This lesson explains one of the best ways to give commands to Access—by using the *menus*. Menus for all Windows programs can be found at the top of a window, just beneath the program's title bar. In Figure 1-7, notice the words File, Edit, View, Insert, and Tools. The next steps will show you why they're there.

1 Click the word File on the menu bar.

A menu drops down from the word File, as shown in Figure 1-7. The File menu contains a list of file-related commands, such as New, which creates a new file; Open, which opens or loads a saved file; Save, which saves the currently opened file; and Close, which closes the currently opened file. Move on to the next step to try selecting a command from the File menu.

2 Click the word Open in the File menu.

The Open dialog box appears. You don't need to open a database quite yet, so…

3 Click the Cancel button to close the Open dialog box.

Notice that each of the words in the menu has an underlined letter somewhere in it. For example, the "F" in the File menu is underlined. Holding down the Alt key and pressing the underlined letter in a menu does the same thing as clicking it. For example, pressing the Alt key and then the F key would open the File menu. Move on to the next step and try it for yourself.

4 Press the Alt key and then press the F key.

The File menu appears. Once you open a menu, you can navigate to a different menu by using either the mouse or the Alt key and the letter that is underlined in the menu name.

If you open a menu and then change your mind, it is easy to close it without selecting any commands. Click anywhere *outside* the menu or press the Esc key.

5 Click anywhere outside the menu to close the menu without issuing any commands.

The menus in Access 2003 work quite a bit differently than in other Windows programs—even previous versions of Access! Microsoft Access 2003 displays its menu commands on the screen in three different ways:

- By displaying every command possible, just like most Windows programs, including earlier versions of Access.
- By hiding from view the commands you don't use as frequently (the more advanced commands).
- By displaying the hidden commands if you click the downward-pointing arrows at the bottom of the menu or keep the menu open for a few seconds.

6 Click the word Tools in the menu.

The most common menu commands appear in the Tools menu. Some people feel intimidated when confronted with so many menu options, so the menus in Office XP don't display the more advanced commands at first. To display a menu's advanced commands, either click the downward-pointing arrow at the bottom of the menu or keep the menu open for a few seconds.

7 Click the downward-pointing arrow at the bottom of the Tools menu.

The more advanced commands appear shaded on the Tools menu.

⁞ NOTE ⁞   *If there isn't a downward-pointing arrow at the bottom of the Tools menu, skip this step and move on to Step 8.*

If you're accustomed to working with earlier versions of Microsoft Office, you may find that hiding the more advanced commands is disconcerting. If so, you can easily change how the menus work. Here's how:

8 Select View → Toolbars → Customize from the menu and click the Options tab.

The Customize dialog box appears, as shown in Figure 1-8. This is where you can change how Access's menus work. There are two check boxes here that are important:

- **Always show full menus:** Clear this check box if you want to hide the advanced commands.
- **Show full menus after a short delay:** If this option is checked, Access waits a few seconds before displaying the more advanced commands on a menu.

9 Click Close.

See Table 1-5 below for the menus in Access and their descriptions.

Table 1-5. Menus Found in Microsoft Access

Menu Item	Description
File	File-related commands to open, close, print, and create new files.
Edit	Commands to copy, cut, paste, find, and replace text.
View	Commands to change how the screen is displayed.
Insert	Items that you can insert into a database, such as graphics and charts.
Format	Commands to format fonts, cell alignment, and borders.
Records	Commands to add, delete, sort, and filter information.
Tools	Tools such as the spell checker and macros. You can also change the default options for Microsoft Access here.
Window	Commands to display and arrange multiple windows (if you have more than one file open).
Help	Provides help with using Microsoft Access.

QUICK REFERENCE

TO OPEN A MENU:

• CLICK THE MENU NAME WITH THE MOUSE.

OR...

• PRESS ALT AND THEN THE UNDERLINED LETTER IN THE MENU.

TO DISPLAY A MENU'S HIDDEN COMMANDS:

• CLICK THE DOWNWARD-POINTING ARROW AT THE BOTTOM OF THE MENU.

OR...

• OPEN THE MENU AND WAIT A FEW SECONDS.

TO CHANGE HOW MENUS WORK:

1. SELECT VIEW → TOOLBARS → CUSTOMIZE FROM THE MENU AND CLICK THE OPTIONS TAB.

2. CHECK OR CLEAR EITHER THE ALWAYS SHOW FULL MENUS AND/OR SHOW FULL MENUS AFTER A SHORT DELAY OPTIONS, THEN CLICK CLOSE.

3. CHECK ALWAYS SHOW FULL MENUS TO SHOW MORE ADVANCED MENU COMMANDS.

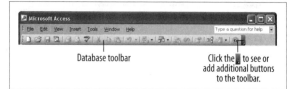

Figure 1-9. The Database toolbar.

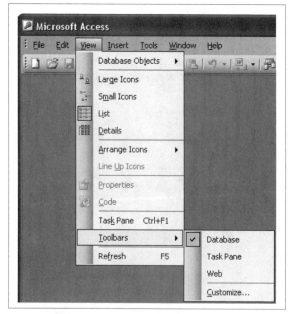

Figure 1-10. Selecting a toolbar to view.

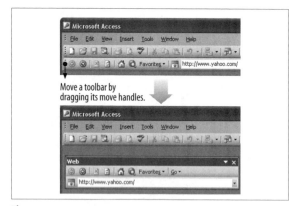

Figure 1-11. Moving a toolbar.

In this lesson we move on to another very common way of giving commands to Access—using toolbars. Toolbars are shortcuts—they contain buttons for the most commonly used commands. Instead of wading through several menus to access a command, you can click a single button on a toolbar. Access displays different toolbars,

depending on what you are working on. For example, when you view the Database window, Access displays the Database toolbar, which contains database-related commands.

This lesson explains how to use toolbars and also how to hide, display, and move toolbars.

1 Position the mouse pointer over the New button on the toolbar (but don't click the mouse yet!).

A ScreenTip appears over the button, briefly identifying what the button is—in this case, "New." If you don't know what a button on a toolbar does, simply move the pointer over it, wait a second, and a ScreenTip will appear over the button, telling you what it does.

2 Click the New button on the toolbar.

The Task Pane toolbar appears on the right side of the screen.

3 Click the Close button to close the Task Pane toolbar.

When you first start Access, one toolbar—the Database toolbar—appears by default, as shown in Figure 1-9. As you work with Access, you may want to display other toolbars, such as the Web toolbar or the Formatting toolbar to help you accomplish your tasks. This lesson explains how to move Access toolbars to different positions on the screen or remove them altogether.

4 Select View → Toolbars from the menu.

Another way to hide or display a toolbar is to right-click any toolbar and select the toolbar you want to hide or display from the shortcut menu.

A list of available toolbars appears, as shown in Figure 1-10. Notice that a check mark appears next to the Database toolbar. This indicates the toolbar is already selected and appears on the Access screen.

5 Select Web from the toolbar menu.

The Web toolbar appears. Toolbars don't have to be at the top the screen—you can move a toolbar anywhere you want.

6 Move the pointer to the move handle, ⋮ , at the far left side of the Web toolbar. Click and drag the toolbar to the middle of the screen, then release the mouse button.

The Web toolbar is torn from the top of the screen and floats in the middle of the window, as shown in Figure 1-11. Notice a title bar appears above the Web toolbar. You can move a floating toolbar by clicking its title bar and dragging it to a new position. If you drag a floating toolbar to the edge of the program window, it becomes a docked toolbar.

7 Click the Web toolbar's title bar and drag the toolbar up until it docks at the top of the screen.

The Web toolbar is reattached to the top of the Access screen.

8 Right-click any of the toolbars and select Web from the Toolbar shortcut menu.

The Web toolbar disappears.

QUICK REFERENCE

TO DISPLAY A TOOLBAR BUTTON'S DESCRIPTION:

- POSITION THE POINTER OVER THE TOOLBAR BUTTON AND WAIT A SECOND. A SCREENTIP WILL APPEAR AND TELL YOU WHAT THE BUTTON DOES.

TO VIEW OR HIDE A TOOLBAR:

- SELECT VIEW → TOOLBARS FROM THE MENU AND SELECT THE TOOLBAR YOU WANT TO DISPLAY OR HIDE.

OR...

- RIGHT-CLICK ANY TOOLBAR OR MENU AND SELECT THE TOOLBAR YOU WANT TO DISPLAY OR HIDE FROM THE SHORTCUT MENU.

TO MOVE A TOOLBAR TO A NEW LOCATION ONSCREEN:

- DRAG THE TOOLBAR BY ITS MOVE HANDLE (IF THE TOOLBAR IS DOCKED) OR TITLE BAR (IF THE TOOLBAR IS FLOATING) TO THE DESIRED LOCATION.

Filling Out Dialog Boxes

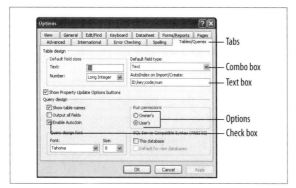

Figure 1-12. The Options dialog box.

Some commands are more complicated than others. Opening a database is a simple process—you only need to select File → Open from the menu or click the Open button on the Database toolbar. Other commands are more complex, such as changing the default options for Access. Whenever you want to do something relatively complicated, you must fill out a *dialog box*. Filling out a dialog box is usually quite easy. If you have worked at all with Windows, you have undoubtedly filled out hundreds of dialog boxes. Dialog boxes usually contain several types of controls, including:

- Text boxes
- List boxes
- Check boxes
- Combo boxes (also called drop-down lists)

It is important that you know the names of these controls, because this book will refer to them in many lessons throughout this guide. This lesson will give you a tour of a dialog box and explain each of these controls to you, so that you will know what they are and how to use them.

1 Select the word Tools on the menu bar.

The Tools menu appears. Notice that the Options menu in the Tools menu is followed by ellipses (…). The ellipses indicate that there is a dialog box behind the Options menu.

2 Select Options from the Tools menu.

The Options dialog box appears, as shown in Figure 1-12. Some dialog boxes have so many options that they are organized and grouped on separate sheets. Such dialog boxes have several sheet tabs near the top of the dialog box. To view a sheet, simply click its sheet tab.

3 Click the Tables/Queries tab.

The Tables/Queries tab appears in front of the dialog box, as shown in Figure 1-12. This is a more complex sheet in the dialog box and contains several different types of components that you can fill out.

Remember: The purpose of this lesson is to learn how to fill out dialog boxes—not how to change the default options for Access (we'll get to that later). The next destination on our dialog box tour is the text box.

Look at the "Text" text box, located in the Default field sizes section of the dialog box. Text boxes are the most common dialog box components and are nothing more than the fill-in-the-blank you're familiar with if you've filled out any type of paper form. To use a text box, you first select the text box by clicking it or pressing the Tab key until the insertion point appears in the text box, and then simply enter the text you want into the text box.

4 Click the Text text box and replace the 50 with 70.

You've just filled out the text box—nothing to it. The next stop in our dialog box tour is the *combo box*. There's a combo box located directly below the Text text box you just typed in. A combo box lists several (or many) options in a small box. You must first click a combo box's downward-pointing arrow in order to display its options. Sometimes a combo box will contain so many options that they can't all be displayed at once, and you must use the combo box's *scroll bar* to move up or down the list.

5 Click the Number combo box down arrow.

A list of numbering options appears below the combo box.

6 Select Byte from the combo box.

Sometimes you need to select more than one item from a dialog box—in such cases you use the *check box* control when you're presented with multiple choices.

7 In the Query design section click the Output all fields check box.

The last destination on our dialog box tour is the *button*. Buttons are found in every dialog box and are used to execute or cancel commands. The two buttons you'll see the most are:

- **OK:** Applies and saves any changes you have made and then closes the dialog box. Pressing the Enter key usually does the same thing as clicking the OK button.

- **Cancel:** Closes the dialog box without applying and saving any changes. Pressing the Esc key usually does the same thing as clicking the cancel button.

8 Click the Cancel button to cancel the changes you made and close the Options dialog box.

QUICK REFERENCE

TO USE A TEXT BOX:

- *SIMPLY TYPE THE INFORMATION DIRECTLY INTO THE TEXT BOX.*

TO USE A COMBO BOX:

- *CLICK THE DOWN ARROW TO LIST THE COMBO BOX'S OPTIONS. CLICK AN OPTION FROM THE LIST TO SELECT IT.*

TO CHECK OR UNCHECK A CHECK BOX:

- *CLICK THE CHECK BOX.*

TO VIEW A DIALOG BOX TAB:

- *CLICK THE TAB YOU WANT TO VIEW.*

TO SAVE YOUR CHANGES AND CLOSE A DIALOG BOX:

- *CLICK THE OK BUTTON OR PRESS ENTER.*

TO CLOSE A DIALOG BOX WITHOUT SAVING YOUR CHANGES:

- *CLICK THE CANCEL BUTTON OR PRESS ESC.*

Keystroke and Right Mouse Button Shortcuts

Figure 1-13. Right-click any object to display a list of things that you can do to the object.

You are probably starting to realize that there are several ways to do the same thing in Access. For example, to open a database, you can use the menu (select File → Open) or the toolbar (click the Open button). This lesson introduces you to two more methods of executing commands: Right mouse button shortcut menus and keystroke shortcuts.

You know that the left mouse button is the primary mouse button, used for clicking and double-clicking, and it's the mouse button that you will use over 95 percent of the time. So what's the right mouse button for? Whenever you *right-click* something, it brings up a shortcut menu that lists everything you can do to the object. Whenever you're unsure or curious about what you can do with an object, right-click it. A shortcut menu will appear with a list of commands related to the object or area you right-clicked.

Right mouse button shortcut menus are an especially effective way to give commands in Access because you don't have to wade through several levels of unfamiliar menus when you want to do something. For this lesson, assume you want to modify the Employees table.

1 Position the pointer over the ▦ Employees table and click the right mouse button.

TIP

Right-click an object to open a shortcut menu that lists the major things you can do to the object.

A shortcut menu appears where you clicked the mouse, as shown in Figure 1-13. Notice one of the items listed on the shortcut menu is Print. This is the same Print command that you can select from the menu by clicking File → Print. Using the right mouse button shortcut method is slightly faster and usually easier to remember than using the menus in Access. If you open a shortcut menu and then change your mind, you can close it without selecting anything. Here's how:

2 Move the pointer anywhere outside the shortcut menu and click the left mouse button to close the shortcut menu.

Remember that the options listed in the shortcut menu will vary, depending on what or where you right-clicked.

3 Position the pointer over the Database toolbar and click the right mouse button.

A shortcut menu listing all the toolbars you can view appears.

4 Move the pointer anywhere outside the shortcut menu and click the left mouse button to close the shortcut menu.

On to keystroke shortcuts. Without a doubt, keystroke shortcuts are the fastest way to give commands to Access, even if they are a little hard to remember. They're great time savers for issuing frequently used commands. To issue a keystroke shortcut, press and hold down the Ctrl key, press the shortcut key, and then release both buttons.

5 Press Ctrl + O (the "Ctrl" and "O" keys at the same time).

This is the keystroke shortcut to open a database and thus pressing Ctrl + O causes the Open dialog box to appear. Since you already have a database open you can close the dialog box without opening a new file.

6 Click Cancel to close the Open dialog box.

The Open dialog box closes.

> ⸻ NOTE ⸻ *Although we won't discuss it in this lesson, you can change or remap the default keystroke shortcuts for Access and assign them to execute other commands.*

Table 1-6 lists the shortcut keystrokes you're likely to use the most in Access.

Table 1-6. Common Keystroke Shortcuts

Keystroke	Description
Ctrl + O	Open a database.
Ctrl + W	Close a database.
Ctrl + P	Print current view.
Ctrl + Z	Undo.
F7	Check spelling.
Ctrl + +	New record.
Ctrl + -	Delete record.
Ctrl + C	Copies the selected text or object to the Windows clipboard.
Ctrl + X	Cuts the selected text or object from its current location to the Windows clipboard.
Ctrl + V	Pastes any copied or cut text or object in the Windows clipboard to the current location.
Ctrl + F	Find.
Ctrl + H	Find and replace.
Page down	Next screen.
Page up	Previous screen.

QUICK REFERENCE

TO OPEN A CONTEXT-SENSITIVE SHORTCUT MENU:

- RIGHT-CLICK THE OBJECT.

TO USE A KEYSTROKE SHORTCUT:

- PRESS CTRL + THE LETTER OF THE KEYSTROKE SHORTCUT YOU WANT TO EXECUTE.

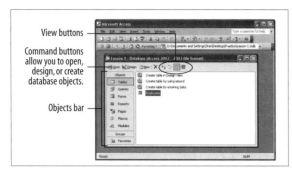

View buttons

Command buttons allow you to open, design, or create database objects.

Objects bar

Figure 1-14. The Database window.

Think of the Database window, as shown in Figure 1-14, as the mission control center for an Access database. You use the Database window to open, modify, and manage all the different types of objects in a database. The Database window contains buttons for each type of database object described in Table 1-7. To display a type of object, click the appropriate button.

1 Click the Forms icon on the Objects bar.

Access displays all the forms in the database. To open a database object, either select the object and click the Database window's Open button or double-click the object.

2 Double-click the Employees form.

The Employees form appears in its own window. We'll take a closer look at forms later on, so go to the next step and close the form window.

3 Close the Employees form by clicking its ☒ Close button.

You can modify any database object by opening it in Design View. *Design View* displays the structure of a database object and allows you to make changes to it. You don't have to know how to make changes to a

database object yet, but you will need to know how to open an object in Design View. Here's how:

4 Click the Employees form to select it.

5 Click the Design Design button on the Database window.

TIP *Another way to display an object in Design view is to open the object and click the View button on the toolbar.*

The Employees form opens in Design View. Now you can see the structure of the Employees form object and even make changes to the form (don't worry—we won't be covering that topic for quite a while!).

6 Close the Employees form by clicking its ☒ Close button.

When you work with database objects, you may find that you need to change how you view information on the screen. You can display database objects using one of four view modes: Large Icons, Small Icons, List, or Details. Figure 1-15 illustrates each of these four views. List View is the default view—and it's usually the best way to view database objects—but there are times when you may want to change views. For example you might want to use Details View to see when an object was created.

7 Click each of the four View buttons on the Database window to display each of the four views shown in Figure 1-15, then return to List view.

Table 1-7 lists the types of database objects, once more, for your viewing pleasure.

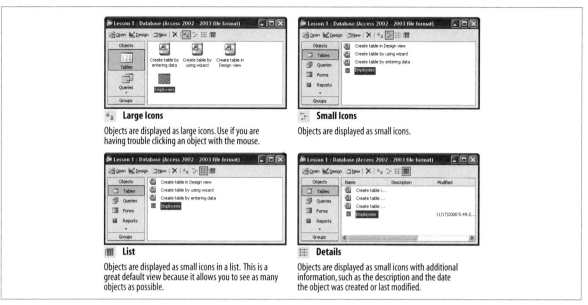

Figure 1-15. You can view database objects using four different views: Large Icons, Small Icons, List, and Details.

Table 1-7. Types of Database Objects

Object	Description
	Tables store a database's data in rows (records) and columns (fields). For example, one table could store a list of customers and their addresses while another table could store the customers' orders.
	Queries ask a question of data stored in a table. For example, a query might only display customers who are from Texas.
	Forms are custom screens that provide an easy way to enter and view data in a table or query.
	Reports present data from a table or query in a printed format.
	A special type of Web page designed for viewing and working with Microsoft Access data from an intranet or the Internet.
	Macros help you perform routine tasks by automating them into a single command. For example, you could create a macro that automatically opens and prints a report.
	Like macros, modules automate tasks but by using a built-in programming language called Visual Basic or VB. Modules are much more powerful and complex than macros.

QUICK REFERENCE

TO VIEW DIFFERENT TYPES OF DATABASE OBJECTS:

- IN THE DATABASE WINDOW, CLICK THE APPROPRIATE ICON IN THE OBJECTS BAR.

TO OPEN A DATABASE OBJECT:

- DOUBLE-CLICK THE OBJECT.

OR...

- CLICK THE DATABASE OBJECT AND CLICK THE OPEN BUTTON ON THE DATABASE WINDOW.

TO OPEN A DATABASE OBJECT IN DESIGN VIEW:

- CLICK THE DATABASE OBJECT AND CLICK THE DESIGN BUTTON ON THE DATABASE WINDOW.

OR...

- OPEN THE OBJECT AND CLICK THE VIEW BUTTON ON THE TOOLBAR.

TO CHANGE HOW DATABASE OBJECTS ARE DISPLAYED:

- CLICK THE APPROPRIATE VIEW BUTTON ON THE DATABASE WINDOW.

OR...

- SELECT VIEW ON THE MENU BAR AND SELECT THE DESIRED VIEW.

Figure 1-16. Use the Windows taskbar to view and move between open windows.

Open windows appear as icons on the taskbar. Click the window you want to work on.

Figure 1-17. Display two windows at the same time by selecting Window → Tile Horizontally from the menu.

One of the many benefits of working with Windows is that you can open and work with several windows at once. Working with multiple windows is particularly important in Access because each database object you open appears in its own window and you will often have to switch between those windows. The Database window always remains open—closing the Database window closes the current database.

This lesson explains how to open and work with more than one window. You will also learn some tricks on changing the size of a window, moving a window, and arranging a window.

1 Click the Tables icon on the Objects bar to display the tables in the current database.

Access displays all the tables in the current database.

2 Double-click the Employees table icon.

Remember that to open any database object, you can select the object and click the Open button in the Database window or just double-click the database object.

The Employees table appears in its own window. The Database window is still open too, although you may not be able to see it because it's behind the Employees table window.

One of the big changes in Access 2003 is that each open window appears as an icon on the Windows taskbar, as shown in Figure 1-16. To switch to a different document, click its icon on the taskbar.

3 Click the Lesson 1: Database icon on the Windows taskbar.

 Another way to switch between windows is to select Window *from the menu bar and then select the window you want to view.*

The Database window appears. The Employees table window is still open, but you can't see all of it because it is located behind the Database window.

Sometimes it can be helpful to view two or more windows on your screen at the same time. When you want to do this, you use the Window menu to select a tile option. Move on to the next step to try this for yourself.

4 Select Window → Tile Horizontally from the menu.

Both windows—the Database window and the Employees table window— appear on top of each other, as shown in Figure 1-17. Sometimes it's useful to look at more than one window at a time. Notice how the title bar for the Employees table window is a different color than the Database window? That's because the Database window is *active*, meaning it's the window or document you're currently working on. The other window, Employees table, is inactive.

5 Click anywhere in the Employees table window.

The Employees table window becomes active and the Database window becomes inactive.

To make working with several windows at once easier, you can change the size of the windows. You can *maximize* or enlarge a window so that it takes up the document window.

6 Click the Maximize button in the Employees table window title bar.

The Employees table window maximizes and fills the entire screen. You can change a maximized window back to its original size by clicking the Restore button, which replaces the Maximize button whenever a window is maximized.

7 Click the Restore button in the Employees table window title bar to restore the Employees table window to its previous size.

Make sure you click the lower Restore button—the Restore button for the Employees table window—and not the Restore button for the Access program. The window returns to its previous size.

You can also manually fine-tune a window's size to meet your own specific needs. A window must not be in a maximized state if you want to manually size it.

8 Position the mouse pointer over the top edge of the Employees table window until it changes to a ↕.

The arrows point in two directions, indicating that you can drag the window's border up or down.

⋮ NOTE ⋮ *The mouse is very picky about where you place the pointer, and sometimes it can be a little tricky finding the exact spot where the pointer changes.*

9 While the ↕ pointer is still over the top edge of the window, click and drag the mouse up a half-inch to move the window border, and release the mouse button.

Notice how the window border follows as you drag the mouse. When the window is the size you want, you can release the mouse button to resize the window. You just resized the window by adjusting the top edge of a window, but you can also adjust the left, right, and bottom edges of a window.

Sometimes when you have more than one window open at once, you may find that one window covers another window or other items on your screen. When this happens, you can simply move the window to a new location on the screen—just like you would move a report or folder to a new location on your desk.

10 Click and drag the title bar of the Employees table window to a new location on the screen. Release the mouse button to drop the window.

Remember that the title bar is at the top of the window or program and displays the name of the window or program.

11 Click on the Close button to close the Employees table window.

That's all there is to working with multiple windows!

QUICK REFERENCE

TO SWITCH BETWEEN MULTIPLE OPEN DOCUMENTS:

- CLICK THE DOCUMENT ON THE WINDOWS TASKBAR.

OR...

- SELECT WINDOW AND SELECT THE NAME OF THE DOCUMENT YOU WANT TO VIEW.

TO VIEW MULTIPLE WINDOWS AT THE SAME TIME:

- SELECT WINDOW FROM THE MENU BAR AND SELECT TILE HORIZONTALLY, TILE VERTICALLY, OR CASCADE FROM THE MENU.

TO MAXIMIZE A WINDOW:

- CLICK THE WINDOW'S MAXIMIZE BUTTON.

TO RESTORE A WINDOW:

- CLICK THE WINDOW'S RESTORE BUTTON.

TO MANUALLY RESIZE A WINDOW:

- CLICK AND DRAG ANY OF THE WINDOW'S BORDERS.

TO MOVE A WINDOW:

- DRAG THE WINDOW'S TITLE BAR TO THE LOCATION WHERE YOU WANT TO POSITION THE WINDOW.

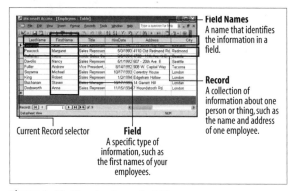

Figure 1-18. The structure of a table.

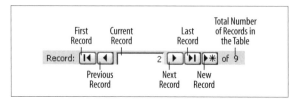

Figure 1-19. Record navigation buttons.

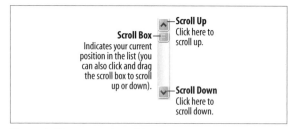

Figure 1-20. A vertical scroll bar.

Tables are the heart and soul of any database. Tables are where a database stores all of its information. All the other database objects—queries, forms, reports, pages, macros, and modules—are merely tools to analyze and manipulate the information stored in a table. Any of these other database objects are optional—but without tables, a database wouldn't be a database. Each table in a database stores *related information*. Most databases have more than one table: Each table is used to store a different type of information. For example, one table might contain a list of customers and their addresses, while another table might contain any orders placed by the customers, while yet another table might contain a list of products.

Tables are made up of groups of *fields*. A *field* is a specific type of information, such as a person's last name, address, or phone number. Together, the related fields for each individual person, place, or thing make up a single record. If your company has ten employees, your

employee table would have ten records—one for each employee.

Here's how to open and view a table:

1 Click the Tables icon in the Database window Objects bar.

Access lists all the tables in the current database.

2 Click the Employees table to select it and then click the Open button in the Database window.

Another ways to open a table is to select the table and click Open.

The Employees table opens in its own window, as shown in Figure 1-18. If you are working on a table, you will usually want to maximize the window so that you can see as much information as possible.

3 Click the table window's Maximize button.

The table window expands to fill the entire screen. Table information is displayed, entered, and modified in a *datasheet*. A datasheet is a grid that contains all the records in a table. Records are stored in rows and field names are stored in columns, as shown in Figure 1-18.

Let's take a closer look at the current table. First notice the ▶ that appears to the left of the first record in the table. This is the *record selector*, and it shows the record that you are currently working on.

Next, take a look at the *record navigation buttons* near the bottom of the screen, as shown in Figure 1-19. The record navigation buttons display the number of records in the current database and allow you to move between these records.

4 Click the ▶ Next Record button on the Record Navigation bar.

Other ways to move to the next record are to click anywhere in the record (if it is displayed on the screen), or to press the down arrow key

Access moves to the next record in the table. Notice that the ▶ record selector moves to the next record and that the Record Navigation bar indicates that you are currently viewing Record 2.

5 Click the Last Record button on the Record Navigation bar.

> **TIP** Another way to move to the last record is to press *Ctrl + End (when not editing the record).*

Tables will often contain too much information to display on the screen at once and you will have to use the vertical scroll bar to move up or down and/or the horizontal scroll bar to move left or right. Since the current database only contains nine records, Access can display all of them on the screen at once. However

you will still need to use the horizontal scroll bar in order to see all of the table's fields.

6 Click the Scroll Right button on the horizontal scroll bar at the bottom of the screen to scroll to the right.

The screen scrolls to the right, displaying previously hidden fields.

See Table 1-8 below for the ways to navigate a table. This ends the first half of our table tour. In the next lesson you'll learn how to add, edit, and delete a table's records.

Table 1-8. Table Navigation

To move to:	Navigation buttons	Keyboard	Mouse
The Next Record	Click the ▶ Next Record navigation button.	Press the ↓ (down arrow) key.	Click the record you want to select (if displayed).
The Previous Record	Click the ◀ Previous Record navigation button.	Press the ↑ (up arrow) key.	Click the record you want to select (if displayed).
The Last Record in the table	Click the ▶⎮ Last Record navigation button.	Press Ctrl + End (when not editing record).	N/A
The First Record in the table	Click the ⎮◀ First Record navigation button.	Press Ctrl + Home (when not editing record).	N/A

QUICK REFERENCE

TO OPEN A TABLE:

- CLICK THE TABLES ICON IN THE OBJECTS BAR AND DOUBLE-CLICK THE TABLE OR SELECT THE TABLE AND CLICK OPEN.

TO MOVE TO THE NEXT RECORD:

- CLICK THE NEXT RECORD NAVIGATION BUTTON, OR PRESS THE ↓ KEY, OR CLICK THE RECORD YOU WANT TO SELECT.

TO MOVE TO THE PREVIOUS RECORD:

- CLICK THE PREVIOUS RECORD NAVIGATION BUTTON, OR PRESS THE UP ARROW KEY, OR CLICK THE RECORD YOU WANT TO SELECT.

TO MOVE TO THE LAST RECORD IN A TABLE:

- CLICK THE LAST RECORD NAVIGATION BUTTON OR PRESS CTRL + END (WHEN NOT EDITING RECORD).

TO MOVE TO THE FIRST RECORD IN A TABLE:

- CLICK THE FIRST RECORD NAVIGATION BUTTON OR PRESS CTRL + HOME (WHEN NOT EDITING RECORD).

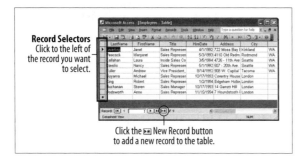

Record Selectors
Click to the left of
the record you want
to select.

Click the ⊞ New Record button
to add a new record to the table.

Figure 1-21. Adding a new record to a table.

You can easily add, change, or delete the records in your table. For example, you might want to add a record to store information about a new employee, change an existing record when an employee's address changes, or delete a record for an employee who no longer works for the company. This lesson explains how to do all three of these tasks. First, here's how to add a record to a table:

1 Click the New Record button on the Record Navigation bar, as shown in Figure 1-21.

 TIP Other ways to add a new record are to press Ctrl + +, or click the New Record button on the datasheet toolbar.

The ▶ record selector jumps to the blank row at the end of the table and the blinking insertion point (|) appears in the first LastName field.

2 Enter your last name in the LastName field.

If you make a mistake you can press the Backspace key to correct it.

Once you have finished entering data into a field you can press Tab or Enter to move to the next field or Shift + Tab to move to the previous field.

3 Press Tab to move to the next field and enter your first name.

Getting the hang of this data entry stuff? Move on to the next step and finish entering the new record.

4 Complete the record by entering your own information into each respective field (enter today's date for the hire date). Remember to press Tab to move to the next field.

 TIP When you have finished adding or editing a record, move to any other record to save your changes.

Finished entering all that information? Super! When you enter data, you don't have to click a Save button to save the information—Access automatically saves the information as you enter it. Neat, huh?

You can also make changes to the records in a table at any time. To edit a record, simply click the field you want to edit and make the changes. Let's try it!

5 Position the mouse over the left edge of the Title cell in your record (the Ⅰ pointer changes to a ⟨⟩) and then click to select the cell.

When a cell has been selected, anything you type will replace the original contents.

6 Type Inside Sales Coordinator.

The text "Inside Sales Coordinator" replaces the original contents of the Title field in your record. You might want to glance at Table 1-9, which lists several keys that are very important for editing and changing the contents of a field.

7 When you have finished making the change, press Tab.

You can permanently delete records that you no longer need from a table. Here's how:

8 Place the insertion point anywhere in the record you just added.

9 Click the ⨯ Delete Record button on the toolbar.

TIP Other ways to delete a record are to click the row selector for the record you want to delete and press Delete, or right-click the row selector of the record you want to delete and select Delete Rows from the shortcut menu.

The record disappears and a warning dialog box appears, asking you to confirm the deletion.

10 Click Yes to confirm the deletion and then close the table.

Congratulations! While it may not seem like you have gone over very much, you have just learned the ins and outs of data entry with Access—the most important (and boring) database task of all!

Table 1-9. Helpful Editing Keys

Key(s)	Description
Tab or Enter	Moves to the next field in the table. If you're at the last field or cell in a table, pressing Tab or Enter will save your changes and move to the first field in the next record.
Esc	The Esc or Escape key is the "Wait, I've changed my mind" key. Press Esc to cancel any changes you've made to a record.
↑, ↓, ←, or →	Use the arrow keys to move between fields and records. If you are editing a field, pressing the left and right arrow keys will move the insertion point one character to the left or right.
Delete	Nothing surprising here. The Delete key deletes or erases whatever is selected—text, cell contents, even entire records. If you're working with text, the Delete key erases characters to the right of the insertion point.
Backspace	Use the Backspace key to fix your typing mistakes—it erases characters to the left of the insertion point.

QUICK REFERENCE

TO ADD A NEW RECORD:

1. CLICK THE NEW RECORD NAVIGATION BUTTON.

   OR...

   CLICK THE NEW RECORD BUTTON ON THE TOOLBAR.

   OR...

   PRESS CTRL + +.

2. ENTER THE RECORD INFORMATION FOR THE FIELD, PRESSING TAB TO MOVE TO THE NEXT FIELD AND SHIFT + TAB TO MOVE TO THE PREVIOUS FIELD.

TO EDIT A RECORD:

• CLICK THE FIELD YOU WANT TO EDIT AND MAKE THE CHANGES.

TO DELETE A RECORD:

• PLACE THE INSERTION POINT ANYWHERE IN THE RECORD AND CLICK THE DELETE RECORD BUTTON ON THE TOOLBAR.

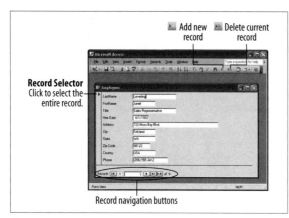

Figure 1-22. The Employees form.

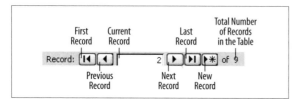

Figure 1-23. Record navigation buttons are displayed at the bottom of most forms.

Adding, viewing, and modifying information in a database should be straightforward and easy. Information in a table is often difficult to understand and manage. Access solves this problem by using *forms* to display table and query information. The forms in Access are actually quite similar to the ordinary paper type of form you fill out with a pen or pencil. Access forms have several major advantages over the traditional paper type of forms—they save you time, effort, and paper, not to mention no worries about trying to read poor penmanship!

Forms can include fill-in-the-blank fields, check boxes, lists of options—even information and prompts to help users complete the form. Forms can also contain buttons that allow you to perform other actions, such as running macros to print reports or labels. Forms can even validate data entry by automatically checking your entries for errors.

This lesson will give you a brief overview of the ins and outs of working with forms.

1 Click the Forms icon in the Objects bar.

Access lists all the forms in the current database.

2 Double-click the Employees form.

The Employees form opens in its own window, as shown in Figure 1-22. You should already be familiar with some of the items on the form, such as the record navigation buttons located at the bottom of the window, as shown in Figure 1-23. As with tables, the record navigation buttons are used to move between records.

3 Click the ▶ Next Record button on the Record Navigation bar.

Access moves to the next record. The Employees form displays information from the Employees table, one record at a time.

4 Practice using the form navigation buttons to move through the various records in the Employees table.

You can usually add new records to a form's underlying table. The procedure for adding a new record with a form is virtually the same as adding a new record to a table.

5 Click the New Record button on the Record Navigation bar.

TIP   Other ways to add a new record are to press Ctrl + +, or click the New Record button on the datasheet toolbar.

A blank form appears, ready for your information.

6 Enter your last name in the LastName field.

Just as with tables, once you have finished entering data into a form's field, you can press Tab or Enter to move to the next field or Shift + Tab to move to the previous field.

7 Press Tab to move to the next field and enter your first name.

8 Complete the record by entering your own information into each respective field (enter today's date for the hire date). Remember to press Tab to move to the next field.

When you enter data, you don't have to click a Save button to save the information-Access automatically saves the information as you enter it. When you have finished entering the record, you can close the form, click the New Record button to enter another record, or use the record navigation buttons to view another record.

The simple form used in this exercise contains only fill-in-the-blank style text fields. Some forms are more complex and may contain lists, combo boxes, check boxes—even sub-forms! If you are unfamiliar with these controls you might want to review the dialog box lesson, presented earlier in this chapter.

You can also delete records using a form. The procedure for deleting records in a form is no different than it is for deleting them from a table.

9 Make sure the record you just added appears in the form and click the Delete Record button on the toolbar.

The record disappears and a warning dialog box appears, asking you to confirm the deletion.

10 Click Yes to confirm the deletion and then click on the Close button to close the form.

Access deletes the record from the Employees table.

QUICK REFERENCE

TO OPEN A FORM:

- CLICK THE FORMS ICON IN THE OBJECTS BAR AND DOUBLE-CLICK THE FORM OR SELECT THE FORM AND CLICK OPEN.

TO MOVE BETWEEN RECORDS:

- USE THE RECORD NAVIGATION BUTTONS NEAR THE BOTTOM OF THE SCREEN.

TO DELETE A RECORD:

- PLACE THE INSERTION POINT ANYWHERE IN THE RECORD AND CLICK THE DELETE RECORD BUTTON ON THE TOOLBAR.

TO ADD A NEW RECORD:

- CLICK THE NEW RECORD NAVIGATION BUTTON.
  OR...
- CLICK THE NEW RECORD BUTTON ON THE TOOLBAR.
  OR...
- PRESS CTRL + +.

Tour of a Query

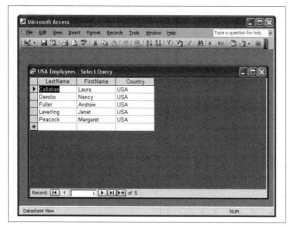

Figure 1-24. The USA Employees query displays only the last name, first name, and country for employees from the USA.

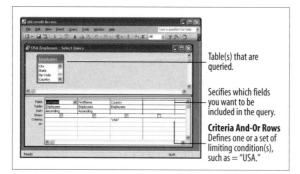

Table(s) that are queried.

Secifies which fields you want to be included in the query.

Criteria And-Or Rows
Defines one or a set of limiting condition(s), such as = "USA."

Figure 1-25. The USA Employees query in Design view.

Webster's definition of a query is:

Que-ry

1. A question; an inquiry.

2. A doubt in the mind; a mental reservation.

3. A notation, usually a question mark, calling attention to an item in order to question its validity or accuracy.

In its simplest form, a query in Access is no different than this definition—well, the first one, anyway. Queries ask a question of the information in a table and then retrieve and display the results. For example, if you wanted to know which employees had worked for the company for more than five years, you could create a query to examine the contents of the HireDate field to find all the records in which the hire date is more than five years old. Access would retrieve the information that meets your criteria and display it in a datasheet.

Here's how to open and run a query:

1 Click the Queries icon in the Objects bar.

Access lists all the queries in the current database.

2 Double-click the USA Employees query.

> **TIP** *Another way to open a query is to select the query and click Open.*

The USA Employees query opens in its own window, as shown in Figure 1-24. This query asks the Employees table "Which employees are from the USA?" and then displays the results in a datasheet. The information displayed in the USA Employees query isn't a duplication of the data in the Employees table—it's just another way of looking at it.

You have probably already noticed that the layout of the USA Employees query doesn't look any different than a table—records appear in rows, fields appear in columns, and the record navigation buttons appear at bottom of the window. Some queries even allow you to add, edit, and delete records to and from the underlying tables (as is the case with this query).

So how do queries work their magic? Let's take a "behind-the-scenes" look at the USA Employees query in *Design view*.

3 Click the View button on the toolbar.

Access displays the USA Employees query in Design view, as shown in Figure 1-25. In Design view you can see a query's underlying tables, which fields are included in the query, and the criteria used to specify which records to display.

Here you can see that the underlying table for this query is the Employees table, which appears in the upper portion of the Design view window. You can also see that three field names—LastName, First-Name, and Country—appear in the *design grid* below. These are the fields that are included in the query. Notice that "USA" appears in the Criteria row below the Country field. The query displays only the records that meet the criteria entered in this row. This query filters only those employees whose Country field equals "USA."

Let's try changing this query's criteria and see what happens…

4 Select the "USA" text in the criteria box and replace it with UK.

Now the query will display only employees from the UK. Let's return to *Datasheet view* and see the new query results. To switch back to Datasheet view, simply click the View button on the toolbar.

5 Click the View button on the toolbar.

Access displays the results of the query in Datasheet view. This time, instead of displaying employees from the USA, the query uses the new criteria and displays employees from the UK.

6 Click on the Close button to close the USA Employees query.

Because you made changes to the USA Employees query, a dialog box appears asking if you want to save your changes.

7 Click No.

The USA Employees query used in this exercise is about as simple as queries can get. Queries can ask much more detailed and complex questions of tables, such as "What were the totals of last month's sales, by region?" or "Which sales representatives had higher than average sales?" or "Which customers have purchased our meteorite-protection coverage option for their car insurance?" For now though, you have a good understanding of what queries are and what they can do for you.

QUICK REFERENCE

TO OPEN A QUERY:
* CLICK THE QUERIES ICON IN THE OBJECTS BAR AND DOUBLE-CLICK THE QUERY OR SELECT THE QUERY AND CLICK OPEN.

TO DISPLAY A QUERY IN DESIGN VIEW:
* OPEN THE QUERY AND CLICK THE VIEW BUTTON ON THE TOOLBAR.

OR...

* CLICK THE QUERIES ICON IN THE OBJECTS BAR, SELECT THE QUERY, AND CLICK DESIGN.

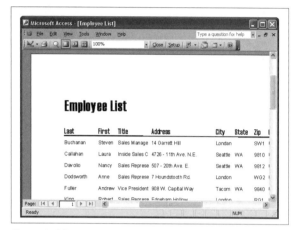

Figure 1-26. Printed reports present information in an organized fashion.

Managers like paper. Don't try explaining anything to them—they'll want to see it in printed hardcopy first. Fortunately, with a *report,* you can print database information from tables and queries and satisfy the demands of even the most paper-hungry supervisor. Although you can print table and query information directly from their datasheets, reports give you many more formatting and display options. Reports can be a simple list of records in a table or a complex presentation that includes calculations, graphics—even charts!

Reports are the most static of all the database objects. Unlike tables and forms, which allow user interaction, reports just sit there, waiting to be printed.

This lesson is your report primer. You won't get a chance to actually create a report in this lesson, but you will get a chance to look at an existing report. Here's how to open a report:

1 Click the Reports icon in the Objects bar.

Access lists all the reports in the current database.

2 Double-click the Employee List report.

TIP *Another way to open a report is to select the report and click Open.*

The Employee List report opens in its own window, as shown in Figure 1-26. Reports open in Print Preview mode by default so that you can see how they will look when printed.

You can enlarge the report by clicking the area you want to magnify with the ⌕ pointer.

3 Move the ⌕ pointer over an area of the report that contains data and click the mouse button.

Access magnifies the selected area. Once you have seen an enlarged area, you can zoom back out to see the overall page.

4 Move the ⌕ pointer over any area of the report and click the mouse button.

The report returns to the previous preview size.

If a report contains more than one page you can use the vertical scroll bar or the Page Up and Page Down keys to scroll through the pages of the report.

Reports wouldn't be very valuable if they couldn't be printed. To print a report, simply click the Print button on the toolbar. We'll skip printing the report for now, unless you want to see for yourself that the report will print when you click the Print button.

5 Click the Close button to close the report.

QUICK REFERENCE

TO OPEN A REPORT:
- CLICK THE REPORTS ICON IN THE OBJECTS BAR AND DOUBLE-CLICK THE QUERY OR SELECT THE QUERY AND CLICK OPEN.

TO ZOOM IN PRINT PREVIEW:
- CLICK THE AREA YOU WANT TO ZOOM (EITHER IN OR OUT) WITH THE MAGNIFYING GLASS POINTER.

TO PRINT A REPORT:
- CLICK THE PRINT BUTTON ON THE TOOLBAR.

OR...
- SELECT FILE → PRINT FROM THE MENU.

OR...
- PRESS CTRL + P.

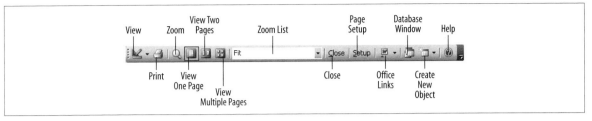

Figure 1-27. The Print Preview toolbar.

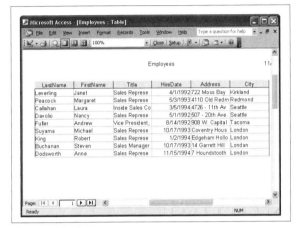

Figure 1-28. The Print Preview screen.

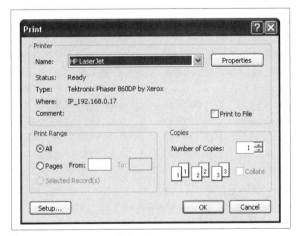

Figure 1-29. The Print dialog box.

Most database objects—tables, queries, forms, reports, and pages—and the information they contain can be printed. Sometimes it's a good idea to preview a database object onscreen to see if something needs to be changed before sending it to the printer. You can preview a database object by clicking the Print Preview button on the toolbar.

1 Click the Tables icon in the Objects bar.

Access lists all the tables in the database.

2 Double-click the Employees table.

The Employees table appears in its own window.

3 Click the [icon] Print Preview button on the toolbar.

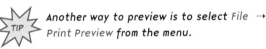
TIP *Another way to preview is to select* File → *Print Preview* from the menu.

The datasheet is previewed on the screen, as shown in Figure 1-28. You can enlarge the datasheet by clicking the area of the datasheet you want to magnify with the [icon] pointer.

4 Move the [icon] pointer over an area of the datasheet that contains data and click the mouse button.

Access magnifies the selected area. Once you have seen an enlarged area, you can zoom back out to see the overall page again.

5 Move the [icon] pointer over any area of the datasheet and click the mouse button.

The datasheet returns to the previous preview size.

6 Select File → Print from the menu.

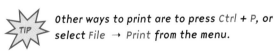
TIP *Other ways to print are to press* Ctrl + P, *or select* File → *Print* from the menu.

The Print dialog box appears, as shown in Figure 1-29. The Print dialog box allows you to specify printing options such as which pages to print and the number of copies you want printed. Table 1-10 describes the options listed in the Print dialog box.

Normally, you would click the dialog box's OK button to print; however, we are going to save the paper and close the Print dialog box without printing.

7 **Click** Cancel.

Table 1-10. Print Dialog Box Options

Print option	Description
Name	Used to select what printer to send your file to when it prints (if you are connected to more than one printer). The currently selected printer is displayed.
Properties	Clicking on the Properties button displays a dialog box with options available to your specific printer such as the paper size you want to use, if your document should be printed in color or black and white, etc.
Print Range	Allows you to specify which pages you want printed. There are several options: **All:** Prints the entire document. **Pages:** Prints only the pages of the file that you specify. Select a range of pages with a hyphen (like 5-8) and separate single pages with a comma (like 3,7). **Selected Record(s):** Prints only the text you have selected (before using the print command).
Number of Copies	Specify the number of copies you want to print.

QUICK REFERENCE

TO PRINT PREVIEW:

- CLICK THE PRINT PREVIEW BUTTON ON THE TOOLBAR.

OR...

- SELECT FILE → PRINT PREVIEW FROM THE MENU.

FOR ADVANCED PRINTING OPTIONS:

- SELECT FILE → PRINT FROM THE MENU.

- REFER TO TABLE 1-10 FOR INFORMATION ON VARIOUS PRINTING OPTIONS.

TO PRINT:

- CLICK THE PRINT BUTTON ON THE TOOLBAR.

OR...

- SELECT FILE → PRINT FROM THE MENU.

OR...

- PRESS CTRL + P.

Selecting Data

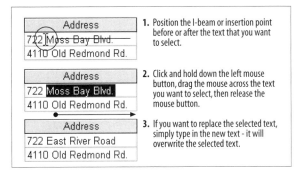

1. Position the I-beam or insertion point before or after the text that you want to select.

2. Click and hold down the left mouse button, drag the mouse across the text you want to select, then release the mouse button.

3. If you want to replace the selected text, simply type in the new text - it will overwrite the selected text.

Figure 1-30. How to select text using the mouse.

Figure 1-31. To select multiple records, position the pointer over the area to the left of the first record you want to select, then click and drag down until all the records you want to select are highlighted.

Often, before you can do anything in Access, you must select the data that you want to work with. Many common tasks, such as editing, formatting, copying, cutting, and pasting all require you to know how to select information in Access. The procedure for selecting text in Access is no different than selecting text in any other Microsoft Office program, so hopefully this lesson will be an easy review for you.

1 If it isn't already open, open the Employees table.

2 In the first record ("Janet Leverling") find and click the Address field, then click and drag the mouse across the words Moss Bay Blvd. as shown in Figure 1-30. When you're finished, release the left mouse button.

TIP You can also select text using the keyboard by pressing and holding the Shift key while using the arrow keys to select the text you want.

The words "Moss Bay Blvd." should be highlighted in black, as shown in Figure 1-30. Selecting text with the

mouse can be a little tricky, especially if you don't have much experience using the mouse. While text is selected, anything you type replaces the existing selected text.

3 Type East River Road.

TIP To replace text, select the text you want to replace, then type the new text with which you want to replace it.

The phrase "East River Road" replaces the selected text "Moss Bay Blvd."

You can also select an entire record or even groups of records in a table. Here's how.

4 Click the record selector for the Janet Leverling record (will change to →) to select the record.

NOTE When you are editing a record, the record selector changes to a pencil icon and the pointer changes to an I-beam insertion point.

To select multiple records, position the pointer to the left of the first record and then drag the → mouse pointer down until you have highlighted all the records you want to select.

5 Position the pointer over the ▶ record selector for the Janet Leverling record (will change to →), then click and drag the → pointer down to include the Andrew Fuller record.

You have highlighted the first few records in the table, as shown in Figure 1-31.

The procedure for selecting a field or column is almost the same as selecting a row—just click the field name that you wish to select.

6 Position the mouse over the FirstName field (changes to ↓) and click to select the column.

The FirstName field is selected.

7 Click anywhere in the datasheet to deselect the text.

The FirstName field is no longer selected.

That's all there is to selecting data in Access. It can't be stressed enough how important it is that you know how to select text and records. Knowing how to select text will make you more proficient and skillful at editing and formatting data.

Table 1-11 describes several shortcut techniques you can use to select data in Microsoft Access.

Table 1-11. Data Selection Shortcuts

To select	Do this	Visual Reference
A word	Double-click anywhere in the word.	FirstName / Title — Janet, Sales Representative; Margaret, Sales **Representative**; Laura, Inside Sales Coordinator
A cell	Position the mouse over the left edge of the cell you want to select (changes to) and click to select the cell.	FirstName / Title — Janet, Sales Representative; Margaret, **Sales Representative**; Laura, Inside Sales Coordinator
A record or row	Position the mouse over the record selector (→ changes to →) and click to select the record.	FirstName / Title — Janet, Sales Representative; **Margaret, Sales Representative**; Laura, Inside Sales Coordinator
A field or column	Position the mouse over the name of the field you want to select (changes to ↓) and click to select the field.	FirstName / **Title** ↓ — Janet, **Sales Representative**; Margaret, **Sales Representative**; Laura, **Inside Sales Coordinator**
The entire table	Click the empty box ( ) to the left of the field names.	FirstName / Title — **Janet, Sales Representative; Margaret, Sales Representative; Laura, Inside Sales Coordinator**

QUICK REFERENCE

TO SELECT TEXT:

1. MOVE THE INSERTION POINT TO THE BEGINNING OR END OF THE TEXT YOU WANT TO SELECT.

2. CLICK AND HOLD THE LEFT MOUSE BUTTON AND DRAG THE INSERTION POINT ACROSS THE TEXT, THEN RELEASE THE MOUSE BUTTON ONCE THE TEXT IS SELECTED.

TO REPLACE TEXT:

• REPLACE TEXT BY FIRST SELECTING IT AND THEN TYPING THE NEW TEXT YOU WANT.

TO SELECT CELLS, RECORDS, FIELDS, AND TABLES:

• REFER TO TABLE 1-11.

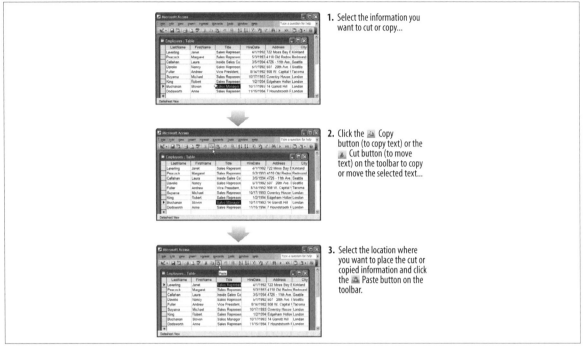

Figure 1-32. The procedure for selecting, copying, and pasting information in a table.

You already know how to select database data. Once you have selected some text, a cell, a record—just about any database object—you can cut it, removing it from its original location, and then paste it in another location. Copying is similar to cutting, except the information is copied instead of removed. Whenever you cut or copy something, it is placed in a temporary storage area called the *Clipboard*. The Clipboard is available in any Windows program, so you can cut and paste between different programs.

In Microsoft Access you can cut, copy, and paste any of the following items:

*   Text
*   Records
*   Database objects (such as tables, queries, forms, pages, and reports)
*   Controls (such as text boxes and labels on forms and reports)

This lesson will give you some practice copying and pasting text and objects in Access.

1 **If it isn't already open, open the Employees table.**

First you have to select the information you want to cut or copy.

2 **Find and select the Title field for the Steven Buchanan record (it should contain "Sales Manager"), as shown in Figure 1-32.**

You want to copy the text "Sales Manager" to the Clipboard so you can paste it to a different record. There are several different ways to copy something—we'll look at all of them. Try out each method and then use the method you like best.

3 **Click the 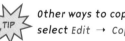 Copy button on the toolbar.**

> *TIP* Other ways to copy are to press Ctrl + C, or select Edit → Copy from the menu.

Nothing appears to have happened, but Access has just copied the selected "Sales Manager" text to the Windows Clipboard. Now you must move the cell pointer to the destination where you want to paste the copied text.

4 Find and select the Title field for the Janet Leverling record (it should contain "Sales Representative").

This is where you want to paste the copied text. There are several ways to paste information from the Windows Clipboard. Here's one of them:

5 Click the Paste button on the toolbar.

> **TIP** Other ways to paste are to select *Edit → Paste* from the menu, or press *Ctrl + V*.

The copied text is pasted into the selected Title field, replacing its original contents. Access still keeps the copied information in the Clipboard so you can paste it again in other locations. Try pasting the copied information in another record.

6 Find and select the Title field for the Andrew Fuller record (it should contain "Vice President, Sales"). Click the Paste button on the toolbar.

The copied information is pasted in the selected field.

Now that you're familiar with copying, let's try *cutting* some text.

7 Find and select the HireDate field for the Robert King record (it should contain "1/2/1994").

This time we'll cut or move the information in this cell instead of copying it.

8 Click the Cut button on the toolbar.

> **NOTE** *The Cut button may not operate if you select the text using the ⇧ pointer. Instead, place the insertion point before or after the text you want to select, click and hold down the left mouse button as you drag across the text, and then release the mouse button. Or place the insertion point and then select the text by using the arrow keys with the Shift key.*

9 Find and select the HireDate field for the Anne Dodsworth record (it should contain "11/15/1994"). Click the Paste button on the toolbar.

Access pastes the copied HireDate in the selected field.

You can also copy, cut, and paste text between two different Windows programs—for example, you could copy information from an Excel worksheet and paste it in an Access table. The cut, copy, and paste commands (the toolbar buttons, menus, and/or keyboard shortcuts) you learned in Access will work with most Windows applications.

If you are entering a lot of records that are nearly identical, you can also copy and paste entire records to create records quickly. After copying and pasting, you can edit the new record quickly to make a few changes. To copy a record, select the record's row selector, copy the record, select an empty row for the new record, and then paste the copied record.

QUICK REFERENCE

TO CUT AND PASTE:

1. SELECT THE INFORMATION YOU WANT TO CUT.

2. CLICK THE CUT BUTTON ON THE TOOLBAR.

   OR...

   SELECT EDIT + CUT FROM THE MENU.

   OR...

   PRESS CTRL + X.

3. SELECT THE DESTINATION WHERE YOU WANT TO PASTE THE INFORMATION.

4. CLICK THE PASTE BUTTON ON THE TOOLBAR.

   OR...

   SELECT EDIT + PASTE FROM THE MENU.

   OR...

   PRESS CTRL + V.

TO COPY AND PASTE:

1. SELECT THE INFORMATION YOU WANT TO COPY.

2. CLICK THE COPY BUTTON ON THE TOOLBAR.

   OR...

   SELECT EDIT + COPY FROM THE MENU.

   OR...

   PRESS CTRL + C.

3. SELECT THE DESTINATION WHERE YOU WANT TO PASTE THE INFORMATION.

4. CLICK THE PASTE BUTTON ON THE TOOLBAR.

   OR...

   SELECT EDIT + PASTE FROM THE MENU.

   OR...

   PRESS CTRL + V.

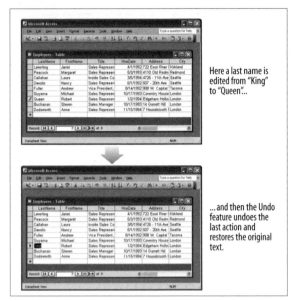

Here a last name is edited from "King" to "Queen"...

...and then the Undo feature undoes the last action and restores the original text.

Figure 1-33. Undoing a record edit.

You may not want to admit this, but you're going to make mistakes when you use Access. You might accidentally delete a record you didn't mean to delete or paste something you didn't mean to paste. Fortunately, Access has a wonderful feature called *Undo* that does just that. Your mistakes disappear! This lesson explains how to undo both single and multiple mistakes and how to redo your actions in case you change your mind.

It's important to note that the Undo feature in Access isn't nearly as powerful as it is in other Microsoft Office programs. In Microsoft Access 2003, Undo will only reverse the last action or command you made. If you make a mistake and don't catch it right away, chances are you won't be able to use Undo to correct it. If that weren't bad enough, Access can't even undo many actions! For example, if you delete a record and then decide you want to use Undo to retrieve the record, you're out of luck. (To its credit, Access *does* warn you whenever you delete a record that you will not be able to use Undo to bring it back.) Hopefully Microsoft will fix these problems in the next version of Access.

Here's how to use Undo:

1 If it isn't already open, open the Employees **table.**

First we need to make a "mistake" that we can undo…

2 Find the Robert King record. Select the LastName field for Robert King and type Queen.

Don't remember how to edit a record? Click the left edge of Robert King's LastName cell to select it and type "Queen." Press Tab when you're finished.

The Robert King is now Robert Queen. Whoops! Somebody's played a joke on you—better change Robert's last name back to "King" before he sees it. Here's how you can undo your "mistake."

3 Click the Undo button **on the toolbar.**

> *Other ways to undo are to press* Ctrl + Z, or select Edit → Undo *from the menu.*

Poof! The LastName field changes back to the original "King," as shown in Figure 1-33. That's all there is to using Undo in Access.

QUICK REFERENCE

TO UNDO YOUR LAST ACTION:

• CLICK THE UNDO BUTTON ON THE TOOLBAR.

OR...

• SELECT EDIT → UNDO FROM THE MENU.

OR...

• PRESS CTRL + Z.

Figure 1-34. The Spelling dialog box.

Figure 1-35. The "spelling check is complete" dialog box.

Spell checking used to be a feature only available in word-processing programs—but no more! You can use the spell checker in Access to find and correct any spelling errors that you might have made in your tables and forms. The spell checker in Access is shared and used by the other programs in the Microsoft Office suite, so any words you add to the custom spelling dictionary in one Microsoft Office program will be available to the other Microsoft Office programs.

Unfortunately, spell checking in Access is not nearly as useful as it is in a word processor. Most databases contain names, addresses, and information that the spell checker may not recognize. When this happens, click either Ignore to ignore the word or Add to add the word to the custom spelling dictionary.

1 If it isn't already open, open the Employees table.

Access will start checking the spelling of the words in a table where the cursor is located and will stop whenever it encounters a word that is not found in its dictionary. Before we start spell check, let's move to the very beginning of the table.

2 Press Ctrl + Home to move to the very beginning of the table.

3 Click the Spelling button on the toolbar.

> **TIP** *Other ways to spell check are to press F7, or select Tools → Spelling from the menu.*

The Spelling dialog box appears, as shown in Figure 1-34. Because it can't find the word "Leverling" in its dictionary, Access flags it as a possible spelling error. Obviously, Access is going to have problems checking the spelling of the LastName field. Instead of having to click "Ignore" for each and every last name Access doesn't recognize, you can tell Access to ignore the entire LastName field.

> **TIP** *Access also automatically corrects common spelling errors as you type. For example, it will change "hte" to "the," "adn" to "and," and so on. This feature is called AutoCorrect.*

4 Click Ignore 'LastName' Field to ignore all text in the LastName field.

Access ignores the LastName field and continues looking for spelling errors in the table. The next "mistake" it finds is in the word "Edgeham" in the address field. The Address field is obviously going to continue to be a problem, so…

5 Click Ignore 'Address' Field to ignore all text in the Address field.

The spell checker moves on and selects the word "Londan" as the next misspelled word in the table. Finally, a legitimate misspelling! Access lists a possible suggestion for the correct spelling of the word.

6 Click London in the Suggestions list and click Change.

Access makes the spelling correction for you.

The remaining words in the Employees table are spelled correctly, so you can safely ignore them.

7 Continue with the spell checker, ignoring the remainder of the flagged words, if any.

When the spell checker can't find any more incorrectly spelled words, Access will indicate the spelling check is complete by displaying the dialog box shown in Figure 1-35.

8 Click OK.

After that exercise, you're probably wondering if you should even bother using spell checking at all. That depends largely on what type of information is in your table. Spell checking can be very useful for identifying and correcting errors in certain types of fields, memos, and notes. Spell checking is nearly useless for last name fields, address fields, and other similar types of information.

QUICK REFERENCE

TO CHECK YOUR SPELLING:

• CLICK THE SPELLING BUTTON ON THE TOOLBAR.

OR...

• SELECT TOOLS → SPELLING FROM THE MENU.

OR...

• PRESS F7.

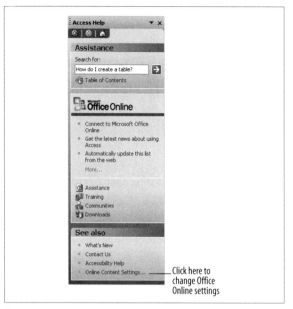

Figure 1-36. Asking a question in the Access Help task pane.

Click here to change Office Online settings

Figure 1-37. Offline Help search results.

Figure 1-38. Possible topic answers for your question.

When you don't know how to do something in Windows or a Windows-based program, don't panic—just look up your question in the Help files. The Access Help files can answer your questions, offer tips, and provide help for all of Access's features. Many Access users forget to use Help, but this is unfortunate, because the Help files know more about Access than most reference books do!

You can make the Access Help files appear by pressing the F1 key. Then all you have to do is ask your question in normal English. This lesson will show you how you can get help using the Access Help files.

1 Press the F1 key.

The F1 key is the help key for all Windows-based programs.

The Access Help task pane appears, as shown in Figure 1-36.

2 Type How do I create a table? in the Search for: text box.

You can ask Access Help questions in normal English, just as if you were asking a person instead of a computer. The program identifies keywords and phrases in your questions like "create" and "table."

⩘ NOTE ⩘ *Microsoft has totally changed the way Help works in Office 2003 with Office Online. Instead of searching for help in the files already stored on your computer, Office Online searches for the topic in their online database. The purpose of this feature is to provide current, up-to-date information on search topics. In their efforts to provide information on more advanced topics, however, they sometimes forgot the most basic and important ones.*

3 Click the ➡ Start searching button.

Office Online presents you with a list of topics that it thinks may be relevant for your question. You have to select the Help topic that you're looking for.

⩘ NOTE ⩘ *If you don't see a useful topic, you can change your settings to perform Help searches without Office Online. Here's how:*

4 Go to the "See also" section at the bottom of the Access Help task pane. Click the Online Content Settings option. Uncheck the Search online content when connected option and click OK. Click the Search list arrow in the Search area at the bottom of the task pane. Select Offline Help from the list and click the ➡ Start searching button.

The Offline Help search results appear, as shown in Figure 1-37.

5 Click the About creating a table (MDB) help topic.

Another window appears with several help options, as shown in Figure 1-38. See Table 1-12 for descriptions of the help buttons.

6 Click the word fields (shown in blue hypertext).

Access displays the definition of "fields." You can click on any word in blue hypertext to see its definition.

7 Click the Microsoft Office Access Help task pane's Close button to close the window.

The Help task pane closes.

Table 1-12. Help Buttons

Button	Description
⊞	Tiles the Access program window and the Help window so you can see both at the same time.
⇐	Moves back to the previous help topic.
⇒	Moves forward to the next help topic.
🖨	Prints the current help topic.

QUICK REFERENCE

TO GET HELP:

1. PRESS THE F1 KEY.

2. TYPE YOUR QUESTION IN THE ACCESS HELP TASK PANE AND CLICK THE START SEARCHING BUTTON OR PRESS ENTER.

3. CLICK THE HELP TOPIC THAT BEST MATCHES WHAT YOU'RE LOOKING FOR (REPEAT THIS STEP AS NECESSARY).

TO TURN OFF OFFICE ONLINE:

1. CLICK THE ONLINE CONTENT SETTINGS OPTION IN THE ACCESS HELP TASK PANE.

2. UNCHECK THE SEARCH ONLINE CONTENT WHEN CONNECTED OPTION AND CLICK OK.

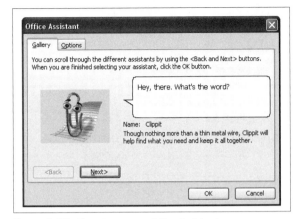

Figure 1-39. Choosing a new Office Assistant.

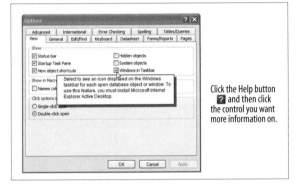

Click the Help button **?** and then click the control you want more information on.

Figure 1-40. Click the Help button to display help on what a dialog box control does.

If you find that Clippit's (the cartoon paperclip) antics are getting old, you can choose a different Office Assistant at any time. People have different tastes and personalities, and that's why Microsoft allows you to select from eight different Office Assistants. Of course, if you really hate the Office Assistant, you can always completely shut it off too.

The other topic covered in this lesson is how to use the Help button. During your journey with Access you will undoubtedly come across a dialog box or two with a number of confusing controls and options. To help you find out what the various controls and options in a dialog box are there for, many dialog boxes contain a Help (**?**) button that explains the purpose of each of the dialog box's controls. This lesson will show you how to use the Help button, but first, let's start taming the Office Assistant.

The Office Assistant must be somewhere on your computer's screen in order to change it, so…

1 If necessary, select Help → Show the Office Assistant from the menu.

The Office Assistant appears.

2 Right-click the Office Assistant and select Choose Assistant from the shortcut menu.

The Office Assistant dialog box appears, as shown in Figure 1-39.

3 Click the Back or Next button to see the available Office Assistants.

The Office Assistant you select is completely up to you. They all work the same—they just look and act differently.

4 Click OK when you find an Office Assistant you like.

If you find the Office Assistant annoying (like a lot of people do) and want to get rid of it altogether, you can close it the same way you did at the end of the last lesson.

5 Right-click the Office Assistant.

A shortcut menu appears.

6 Select Hide from the shortcut menu.

You can always bring the Office Assistant back whenever you require its help by pressing the F1 key. Now let's move on to how to use the Help button to discover the purpose of confusing dialog box controls.

7 Select Tools → Options from the menu and click the View tab.

The Options dialog box appears, as shown in Figure 1-40. Notice the Help button located in the dialog box's title bar just to the left of the dialog box's Close button.

8 Click the Help button (**?**).

The mouse pointer changes to a **?**, indicating you can point to anything on the dialog box to find out what it does. The Windows in Taskbar check box is rather confusing, isn't it? Move on to the next step and we'll find out what it's there for.

9 Click the Windows in Taskbar **check box with the** pointer.

A brief description of the Windows in Taskbar check box appears.

10 Click the Close button **to close the Options dialog box.**

QUICK REFERENCE

TO CHANGE OFFICE ASSISTANTS:

1. IF NECESSARY, SELECT HELP → SHOW THE OFFICE ASSISTANT FROM THE MENU.

2. RIGHT-CLICK THE OFFICE ASSISTANT AND SELECT CHOOSE ASSISTANT FROM THE MENU.

3. CLICK THE NEXT OR BACK BUTTONS UNTIL YOU FIND AN OFFICE ASSISTANT YOU LIKE, THEN CLICK OK.

TO HIDE THE OFFICE ASSISTANT:

• RIGHT-CLICK THE OFFICE ASSISTANT AND SELECT HIDE FROM THE SHORTCUT MENU.

TO SEE WHAT A CONTROL IN A DIALOG BOX DOES:

1. CLICK THE DIALOG BOX'S HELP BUTTON (LOCATED RIGHT NEXT TO THE CLOSE BUTTON).

2. CLICK THE CONTROL YOU WANT MORE INFORMATION ON WITH THE QUESTION MARK POINTER.

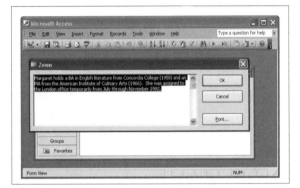

Figure 1-41. In its current state, the Notes field is not wide enough to display its contents.

Figure 1-42. Press Shift + F2 to display the Zoom box, making the contents of any cell easier to view and edit.

When you are viewing and working with data, sometimes a column will not be wide enough to display all the text in a cell or field, as shown in Figure 1-41. This is especially true for notes and memo fields, which may contain several paragraphs of text. Don't worry—you can summon the *Zoom box* to make the contents of any cell easier to view and edit.

1 If it isn't already open, open the Employees table.

Most of the information in this table fits nicely into its designated column. Move on to the next step and take a look at the Notes field, however.

2 Scroll to the right using the horizontal scroll bar until you can see the Notes field.

The Notes field is not wide or tall enough to display all its information. Move to the next step to see how the Zoom box can display the contents of a Notes cell.

3 Click the Notes field for any record, then zoom into that cell by pressing Shift + F2.

The Zoom box appears and displays the contents of the selected cell, as shown in Figure 1-42. You can edit the cell information in the Zoom box. When you're finished viewing or editing the cell, simply click OK to close the Zoom box. The cell will display any changes you made to the data.

4 Click OK to close the Zoom box and then click the Close button to close the Employees table window.

QUICK REFERENCE

TO ZOOM INTO A CELL:
* SELECT THE CELL YOU WANT TO ZOOM AND PRESS SHIFT + F2.

Closing a Database and Exiting Access

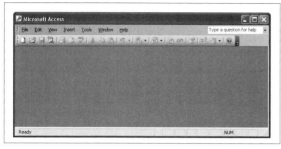

Figure 1-43. Access without an opened database.

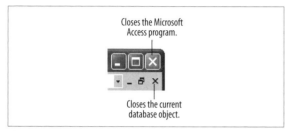

Closes the Microsoft
Access program.

Closes the current
database object.

Figure 1-44. The Access program and database object
window Close buttons.

Because the tasks covered in this lesson are so simple—closing an open database and exiting the Access program—you're at what is undoubtedly the easiest lesson in the guide.

Whenever you close the Database window, you close the current database.

1 Click the Database window's 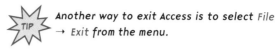 Close button.

TIP *Another way to exit Access is to select* File → Exit *from the menu.*

If any of your Access windows are maximized, you may see two Close buttons on your screen, as shown in Figure 1-43. Make sure you click the lower Close button to close the database window. (The Close button located in the far, upper right-hand corner of the screen closes the Microsoft Access program.) The current database closes, but the Access program does not, as shown in Figure 1-44. You can close a database when you're finished working on it but may still want to remain in the Access program—perhaps to open and work on another database. You have finished both this lesson and this chapter, so you want to exit, or close the Access program.

2 Click the Close button on the Microsoft Access title bar.

The Access program window closes, and you return back to the Windows desktop.

That's it! You've just completed your first chapter and are well on your way towards mastering Microsoft Access. You've already learned some very important things: how to start Access; enter records; open and work with tables, forms, queries, and reports; and print a database object. You will use these skills all the time in your long and illustrious relationship with Microsoft Access.

QUICK REFERENCE

TO CLOSE A DATABASE:

• CLICK THE DATABASE WINDOW'S CLOSE BUTTON.

OR...

• SELECT FILE → CLOSE FROM THE MENU.

TO EXIT MICROSOFT ACCESS:

• CLICK THE ACCESS PROGRAM CLOSE BUTTON.

OR...

• SELECT FILE → EXIT FROM THE MENU.

Chapter One Review

Lesson Summary

Starting Access and Opening a Database

To Start Microsoft Access: Click the Windows Start button and select All Programs → Microsoft Office 2003 → Microsoft Office Access 2003.

To Open a Database: Click the Open button on the toolbar, or select File → Open from the menu, or press Ctrl + O.

Understanding the Access Screen

Be able to identify the main components of the Access program screen.

Using Menus and Toolbars

Menus: Either click the menu name with the mouse pointer or press the Alt key and the letter that is underlined in the menu name.

Toolbars: Simply click the toolbar button you want to use.

To Display a Toolbar Button's Description: Position the pointer over the toolbar button and wait a second. A ScreenTip will appear above the button.

Filling Out Dialog Boxes

Be able to identify and use text boxes, list boxes, combo boxes, check boxes, and sheet tabs.

Keystroke and Right Mouse Button Shortcuts

Keystroke Shortcuts: Press Ctrl and the letter that corresponds to the shortcut command at the same time.

Right Mouse Button Shortcut Menus: Whenever you're unsure or curious about what you can do with an object, click it with the right mouse button to display a list of commands related to the object.

Opening and Modifying Database Objects

To View Different Types of Database Objects: From the Database window, click the appropriate icon in the Objects bar.

To Open a Database Object: Double-click the object or click the database object and click the Open button on the Database window.

To Open a Database Object in Design View: Click the database object and click the Design button on the Database window or open the object and click the View button on the toolbar.

To Change How Database Objects are Displayed: Click the appropriate View button on the Database window or select View on the menu bar and select the desired view.

Working with Multiple Windows

To Switch between Multiple Windows: Click the corresponding icon on the Windows taskbar or select Window and select the name of the window you want to view.

To View Multiple Windows at the Same Time: Select Window from the menu bar and select Tile Horizontally, Tile Vertically, or Cascade from the menu.

To Maximize a Window: Click the window's Maximize button.

To Restore a Window: Click the Window's Restore button.

To Manually Resize a Window: Position the mouse pointer over the edge of the window, hold down the mouse button, and drag the mouse to resize the window, then release the mouse button.

To Move a Window: Drag the window's title bar to the location where you want to position the window.

Tour of a Table

To Move to the Next Record: Click the Next Record navigation button, or press the ↓ key, or click the record you want to select.

To Move to the Previous Record: Click the Previous Record navigation button, or press the ↑ key, or click the record you want to select.

To Move to the Last Record in a Table: Click the Last Record navigation button or press Ctrl + End (when not editing record).

To Move to the First Record in a Table: Click the First Record navigation button or press Ctrl + Home (when not editing record).

Adding, Editing, and Deleting Records

To Add a New Record: Do any of the following:

- Click the New Record navigation button.
- Click the New Record button on the toolbar.
- Press Ctrl + + and then enter the record information for the field, pressing Tab to move to the next field and Shift + Tab to move to the previous field.

To Edit a Record: Click the field you want to edit and make the changes.

To Delete a Record: Place the insertion point anywhere in the record and click the Delete Record button on the toolbar.

Tour of a Form

To Move between Records: Use the record navigation buttons near the bottom of the screen.

To Add a New Record: Do any of the following:

- Click the New Record navigation button.
- Click the New Record button on the toolbar.
- Press Ctrl + + and then enter the record information for the field, pressing Tab to move to the next field and Shift + Tab to move to the previous field.

To Delete a Record: Place the insertion point anywhere in the record and click the Delete Record button on the toolbar.

Tour of a Query

To Display a Query in Design View: Open the query and click the View button on the toolbar. You can also select the query and click Design.

Tour of a Report

To Zoom in Print Preview: Click the area you want to zoom (either in or out) with the pointer.

To Print a Report: Click the Print button on the toolbar, or select File → Print from the menu, or press Ctrl + P.

Previewing and Printing a Database Object

To Preview: Click the Print Preview button on the toolbar or select File → Print Preview from the menu.

To Print: Do any of the following:

- Click the Print button on the toolbar.
- Select File → Print from the menu.
- Press Ctrl + P.

For Advanced Printing Options: Select File → Print from the menu and select your printing options from the Print dialog box.

Selecting Data

To Select Text: Move the insertion point to the beginning or end of the text you want to select, click and hold the left mouse button and drag the insertion point across the text, then release the mouse button once the text is selected.

To Replace Text: Replace text by first selecting it and then typing the new text you want.

To Select a Word: Double-click anywhere in the word.

To Select a Cell: Position the mouse over the left edge of the cell you want to select and click to select the cell.

To Select a Record or Row: Position the mouse over the record selector and click to select the record.

To Select a Field or Column: Position the mouse over the name of the field you want to select and click to select the field.

To Select the Entire Table: Click the empty box to the left of the field names.

Cutting, Copying, and Pasting Data

To Cut: Cut text or objects by selecting the text or object and using one of four methods to cut:

1. Click the Cut button on the toolbar.
2. Select Edit → Cut from the menu.
3. Press Ctrl + X.
4. Right-click and select Cut from the shortcut menu.

To Copy: Copy text or objects by selecting the text or object and using one of four methods to copy:

1. Click the Copy button on the toolbar.

2. Select Edit → Copy from the menu.

3. Press Ctrl + C.

4. Right-click and select Copy from the shortcut menu.

To Paste: Paste text or objects by selecting the text or object and using one of four methods to paste the data:

1. Click the Paste button on the toolbar.

2. Select Edit → Paste from the menu.

3. Press Ctrl + V.

4. Right-click and select Paste from the shortcut menu.

Using Undo

To Undo Your Last Action: Click the Undo button on the toolbar, or select Edit → Undo from the menu, or press Ctrl + Z.

Checking Your Spelling

To Check Your Spelling: Click the Spelling button on the toolbar, or select Tools → Spelling from the menu, or Press F7.

Getting Help from the Office Assistant

You can ask the Office Assistant (the cute animated character) your Help questions in conversational English.

This is the easiest and most common method of getting help.

Press F1 to open the Office Assistant, type your question in normal English, and click Search.

Changing the Office Assistant and Using the Help button

To Change Office Assistants: If necessary, select Help → Show the Office Assistant from the menu. Right-click the Office Assistant and select Choose Assistant from the menu, click the Next or Back buttons until you find an Office Assistant you like, then click OK.

To Hide the Office Assistant: Right-click the Office Assistant and select Hide from the shortcut menu.

To See What a Control in a Dialog Box Does: Click the dialog box's Help button (located right next to the Close button) and click the control you want more information on with the pointer.

Using the Zoom Box

To Zoom into a Cell: Select the cell you want to zoom and press Shift + F2.

Closing a Database and Exiting Access

To Close a Database: Click the Database window Close button or select File → Close from the menu.

To Exit Microsoft Access: Click the Access program Close button or select File → Exit from the menu.

Quiz

1. What are the columns in a Microsoft Access table called?
   A. Rows.
   B. Records.
   C. Fields.
   D. Cells.

2. Right-clicking something in Access:
   A. Deletes the object.
   B. Opens a shortcut menu listing everything you can do to the object.

   C. Selects the object.
   D. Nothing—the right mouse button is there for left-handed people.

3. Which of the following is NOT a type of Microsoft Access database object?
   A. Tables.
   B. Queries.
   C. Forms.
   D. Workbooks.

4. Which of the following database objects asks a question of information in a database and then displays the results?

A. Tables.

B. Queries.

C. Forms.

D. Reports.

5. Which of the following database objects makes it easy to view, edit, and enter database information?

A. Tables.

B. Queries.

C. Forms.

D. Reports.

6. Design View lets you view and modify the structure of any database object. (True or False?)

7. You can display a database object in Design View by: (Select all that apply.)

A. Selecting the database object and pressing Ctrl + V.

B. Selecting the database object and clicking the Design button on the Database window.

C. Opening the database object and selecting Tools → Design View.

D. Opening the database object and clicking the View button on the toolbar.

8. You must click the Save button on the toolbar to save a record. (True or False?)

9. The symbol that appears to the left of every record is:

A. The *New Record Pointer*, which indicates the records that have not yet been saved.

B. The *Record Delete Button*, which is used to delete records.

C. The *Record Selector*, which is used to select records.

D. The *Record Edit Indicator*, which indicates the record is being edited.

10. Which of the following statements is NOT true? (Select all that apply.)

A. You can display any database field in a Zoom box by pressing F2.

B. Microsoft Access is a spelling genius and even recognizes the names of people, places, and products.

C. In Microsoft Access, the Tab key moves to the next field and Shift + Tab moves to the previous field.

D. You can add and edit information in tables, forms, and some queries.

11. Which of the following is NOT a selection technique?

A. To select a word, double-click the word.

B. To select a row, click the record selector box.

C. To select a column, double-click anywhere in the column.

D. To select an entire table, click the empty box to the left of the field names.

12. How can you print three copies of a table?

A. Select File → Print from the menu and type 3 in the Number of copies text box.

B. Press Ctrl + P + 3.

C. Select File → Properties from the menu and type 3 in the Copies to print text box.

D. Click the Print button on the Standard toolbar to print the document, then take it to Kinko's and have 2 more copies made.

Homework

1. Start Microsoft Access and open the Homework database.

2. Open the Science Test Answers table.

3. Without counting by hand, how many records are currently in the Science Test Answers table?

4. Use the record navigation buttons to navigate between the records in the Science Test Answers table.

5. Add a new record to the table: Click the New button on either the table navigation button area or on the toolbar.

6. Enter the following information into the new record:

Grade	Score	Class	Answer
5th	C-	Science	Litter: a nest of young puppies

7. Change the score of the previous record from a C- to a D+.

8. Select the previous record by clicking its record selector, then delete the record by pressing the Delete key, and click Yes to confirm the deletion.

9. Close the Science Test Answers table and click No to the Save Changes message.

10. Click the Forms icon in the Objects bar and open the Test Answers form.

11. Enter the following information into a new record:

Grade	Score	Answer
8th	D	Germinate: To become a naturalized German

12. Close the Test Answers form.

13. Click the Queries icon in the Objects bar and open the Sort by Grades query.

14. Click the View button on the toolbar to display the Sort by Grades query in Design View.

15. Close the Sort by Grades query and exit Microsoft Access.

Quiz Answers

1. C. The columns in a Microsoft Access table are its fields.

2. B. Right-clicking an object displays a shortcut menu for the object.

3. D. You'll find workbooks in Microsoft Excel but not in Microsoft Access.

4. B. Queries ask a question of information in a table and display the results.

5. C. Forms display table and query information in an organized format, making it easy to view, add, and edit records.

6. True. Design View lets you view and modify the structure of any Microsoft Access database object.

7. B and D. Either of these procedures will display a database object in Design View.

8. False. Microsoft Access automatically saves database records—you don't have to click the Save button on the toolbar.

9. C. This is the Record Indicator and is used to select records.

10. A and B. You need to press the Shift key along with F2 to zoom and Spell Checker is usually not suitable for checking the spelling of typical table information.

11. C. To select a column, position the mouse over the name of the field you want to select and click to select that field.

12. A. You print by selecting File → Print from the menu.

CHAPTER 2

CREATING AND WORKING WITH A DATABASE

CHAPTER OBJECTIVES:

How to plan a database, Lesson 2.1
Create a database from scratch and use the Database Wizard, Lessons 2.2—2.3
Create a table from scratch and using the Table Wizard, Lessons 2.4, 2.6
Modify a table and understand data types, Lesson 2.5
Create and modify a query, Lessons 2.7—2.8
Create queries that sort and filter database information, Lesson 2.9
Developing AND and OR operators, Lesson 2.10
Create a form using the Form Wizard, Lesson 2.11
Create reports and mailing labels using the Report Wizard, Lessons 2.12—2.13
Learn about database object and file management, Lessons 2.14—2.15
Compacting and repairing a database, Lesson 2.16
Converting an Access database, Lesson 2.17

CHAPTER TASK: CREATE AND MODIFY A SIMPLE ACCESS DATABASE

Prerequisites

- **How to start Access.**
- **How to use menus, toolbars, dialog boxes, and shortcut keystrokes.**
- **How to open and modify database objects.**

Stop typing lists of information in Microsoft Word or Excel! In this chapter, you will learn how to create databases that can store names, addresses, and any other type of information that you can think of. You will be pleasantly surprised to find that creating a database isn't all that difficult. Microsoft Access even comes with a Database Wizard that takes you step by step through the process of creating a database.

Because there are so many components that constitute a database, this chapter will cover a lot of ground—but thankfully not in great detail. In this chapter, you will learn to create and modify the major database objects: tables, forms, queries, and reports. You will even learn some basic database management tasks, such as how to delete and rename database objects and how to repair and compress a database.

If all you need is a simple, easy-to-use database, look no farther than this chapter—more than likely, everything you need to know about creating databases is here.

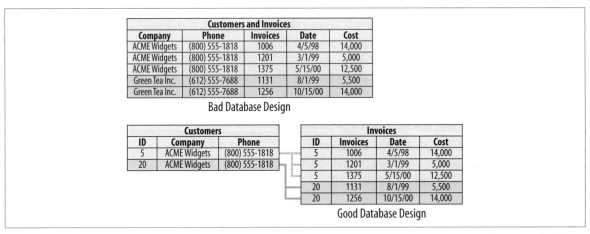

Name	Address
John Smith	408 W. Park, Lincoln, NE 68522
Angie Johnson	100 E. Central, Minneapolis, MN 55413
George Ecks	503 3rd Street, Houston, TX 77338

Bad Table Design

First	Last	Address	City	State	Zip
John	Smith	408 W. Park	Lincoln	NE	68522
Angie	Johnson	100 E. Central	Minneapolis	MN	55413
George	Ecks	503 3rd Street	Houston	TX	77338

Good Table Design

Figure 2-1. Break up information as much as possible: The same information stored in a poorly designed table and in a well-designed table.

Customers and Invoices

Company	Phone	Invoices	Date	Cost
ACME Widgets	(800) 555-1818	1006	4/5/98	14,000
ACME Widgets	(800) 555-1818	1201	3/1/99	5,000
ACME Widgets	(800) 555-1818	1375	5/15/00	12,500
Green Tea Inc.	(612) 555-7688	1131	8/1/99	5,500
Green Tea Inc.	(612) 555-7688	1256	10/15/00	14,000

Bad Database Design

Customers

ID	Company	Phone
5	ACME Widgets	(800) 555-1818
20	ACME Widgets	(800) 555-1818

Invoices

ID	Invoices	Date	Cost
5	1006	4/5/98	14,000
5	1201	3/1/99	5,000
5	1375	5/15/00	12,500
20	1131	8/1/99	5,500
20	1256	10/15/00	14,000

Good Database Design

Figure 2-2. Use multiple tables so that you don't duplicate information: The same information stored in a badly designed table and in a well-designed table.

Although you can always make changes to a database, a little planning ahead before you create a database can save you lots of time and headaches later on.

Consider Figure 2-1: In the first table, you can only sort by the name or address field. If you sort the name field, the sort is performed by the first name. If you sort the address field, the sort is performed by the street—you cannot sort by city, state, or zip code. You couldn't create a query or filter that only displays people from a particular state because the states are not stored in their own field. The fields are not flexible.

Now take a look at the second table in Figure 2-1. Here you can sort records by first name, last name, address, city, state, and zip code. You can also query and filter records using any of these fields.

Here are some guidelines for creating a well-designed database (see also Table 2-1):

- **Determine the Purpose of the Database:** The best way to do this is to write down a list of the reports and lists that you want to come *out* of the database. This may seem a little backward at first, but if you think about it, these reports are really the reason you're creating the database. Make a list of the reports and lists you want to see and then sketch some samples of these reports and lists—be as detailed as possible. This will help determine the tables and fields to include in your database.

- **Determine the Fields You Need:** This should be an easy step once you have determined the purpose of your database and have sketched some sample reports and lists. Think about the data type for each type of your fields—Will the field store text information? Numbers? Dates? Write down the data type next to each field.

- **Determine the Tables You Need:** Each table in the Database should be based on only one subject. By breaking each subject into its own table you avoid redundant information and make the database more organized. The second database in Figure 2-2 is broken down into two tables, Customers and Invoices, so there isn't any duplicated data. When you brainstorm, try to break down your information as much as possible. If your tables contain fields like Item 1, Item 2, Item 3, Item 4, and so on, you should probably break the information up into its own table.

- **Determine the Primary Key:** Each record in a table should have a *primary key* that uniquely identifies it. When you think about a primary key field, think *unique*—each primary key value must be the only one of its kind in a table. A customer ID or invoice number would be two good examples of fields that could be used as a table's primary key.

- **Determine the Relationship between Tables:** In Figure 2-2, the ID field links the Customers and Invoices tables together. One of the linked fields should be the table's *primary key.*

- **Sketch a Diagram of Your Database:** Create a diagram of your database. Draw a box for each of your tables and write the table's field names inside that box. Draw a line between the related fields in the tables. For example, in Figure 2-2, each record in the Customers table is related to one or more records in the Invoices table.

Table 2-1. Guidelines for Good Database Design

Guideline	Why?
Each field or column should contain the same type of information	This makes the table more meaningful, more organized, and easier to understand.
Try to break up information as much as possible	This gives you more power to sort, filter, and manipulate the list. See Figure 2-1 for an example.
Use multiple tables so that you don't duplicate information in the same table	Organize your information into several tables—each one containing fields related to a specific subject—rather than one large table containing fields for a wide range of topics. See Figure 2-2 for an example.
Don't use duplicate field names	Duplicate field names can cause problems when entering and sorting information.

Creating a Database Using the Database Wizard

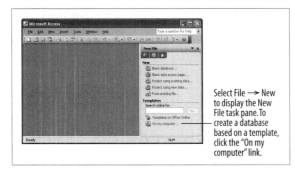

Figure 2-3. The New File task pane appears each time you start Access.

Select File → New to display the New File task pane. To create a database based on a template, click the "On my computer" link.

Click the Databases tab and then select a template from the list.

Figure 2-4. The Databases tab of the Templates dialog box.

If you're just getting started with Microsoft Access, the easiest way to create a database is by using one of the built-in database templates. A database template saves you time and effort, providing you with ready-to-use tables, forms, queries, and reports. There are templates available for the most common types of databases, such as contact management, inventory, and order taking. You can also modify a database created by the Database Wizard to better suit your needs.

This lesson explains how to use the Database Wizard to create a database by using a database template.

1 Start Microsoft Access and select File → New from the menu.

The Microsoft Access program appears with the New File task pane displayed, as shown in Figure 2-3. The New File task pane gives you quick access to any database you have worked on recently and allows you to create a new database.

2 Click the On my computer link in the task pane, and then click the Databases tab.

TIP

Another way to use the Database Wizard is to click the New button on the toolbar, click General Templates, and click the Databases tab. Or you can select File → New from the menu, click General Templates, and click the Databases tab.

The Templates dialog box appears with the Databases tab in front, as shown in Figure 2-4. Here you need to select the type of database you want to create. For this exercise we'll create a Contact Management database.

3 Double-click the Contact Management icon.

Access prompts you to type in a file name for your new database.

4 Type My Contacts and click Create.

The first screen of the Database Wizard appears and describes the database it will create for you.

5 Click Next to continue.

The next screen of the Database Wizard appears. This dialog box displays the standard tables and fields that the Database Wizard is building for you. Click a table on the left side of the dialog box to view its fields on the right side. If you want, you can remove the fields from the database by unchecking them. For this exercise we will leave the standard fields as they are.

6 Click Next to accept the Database Wizard's standard tables and fields.

Now you have to decide what your new database should look like. Access provides you with several aesthetic styles to choose from. Click a style to see a sample of what it looks like.

7 Browse the various styles by clicking each of them, then select the style you like best and click Next.

Another screen appears with more aesthetic decisions to make. Here you need to select the font you want to use in your reports. You can preview each of the font styles by clicking them.

8 Select the font style that you like best and click Next.

You're just about done. The next step in the Database Wizard asks you to enter a title for your new database. This title will appear on the heading of all the reports in your database. You can even add a graphic or logo to your reports by checking the "Yes, I'd like to include a picture" box, clicking the Picture button, and selecting the picture or graphic file.

9 Type ACME Client List and click Next.

That's it—you've finished giving the Database Wizard all the information it needs to create the database.

10 Click Finish to create the new database.

Access chugs along and creates the new database for you. When it's finished, the Main Switchboard dialog box will appear. The switchboard comes in very handy, making it easy to access the database's tables, forms, and reports.

11 Explore the tables, forms, and reports in the new database by clicking the various buttons on the switchboard form.

Move on to the next step when you have seen enough of the new database.

12 Close the new database by clicking Exit this database in the Main Switchboard dialog box.

That's it! You've created your first database using the Database Wizard. The database created by the Database Wizard may not be exactly what you're looking for, but you can always modify its tables, queries, forms, reports, and pages to better suit your needs. A lot of people create databases using the Database Wizard to serve as the foundation for a more customized database.

QUICK REFERENCE

TO CREATE A DATABASE USING THE DATABASE WIZARD:

1. CLICK THE NEW BUTTON ON THE TOOLBAR.
   OR...
   SELECT FILE → NEW FROM THE MENU.

2. CLICK THE ON MY COMPUTER LINK IN THE TASK PANE.

3. CLICK THE DATABASES TAB IN THE TEMPLATES DIALOG BOX.

4. DOUBLE-CLICK THE TYPE OF DATABASE YOU WANT TO CREATE.

5. FOLLOW THE ONSCREEN INSTRUCTIONS AND SPECIFY WHAT YOU WHAT TO APPEAR IN YOUR DATABASE.

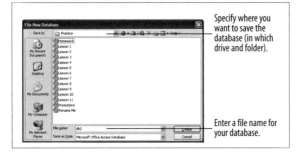

Figure 2-5. The New File task pane.

Click the "Blank database" link to create a new blank database.

Specify where you want to save the database (in which drive and folder).

Enter a file name for your database.

Figure 2-6. The File New Database dialog box.

Can't find a suitable database in the Database Wizard? Then you'll have to create a blank database and start from scratch. The advantage of creating a blank database is that it gives you the most flexibility and control over your database design. The disadvantage of creating a blank database is that you have to create every table, form, report, and query yourself.

Here's how to create a blank database.

1 Click the ☐ New button on the toolbar.

> **TIP**
>
> *Other ways to create a new database are to press Ctrl + N, or select File → New from the menu.*

The New File task pane appears, as shown in Figure 2-5.

2 Select Blank Database from the task pane.

The File New Database dialog box appears, as shown in Figure 2-6. Before you can put anything into your new database, you must first give it a file name and save it.

3 Navigate to the drive and folder where you want to save the new database, then type My First Database in the **File name** box and click **Create**.

Access creates a new database and saves it with the "My First Database" file name. The "My First Database: Database" window appears when it's finished. If you click the various database object tabs, you will notice that there aren't any database objects in the database yet. You will have to create all of the database objects yourself—something we will be covering in the next several lessons.

QUICK REFERENCE

TO CREATE A NEW BLANK DATABASE:

1. CLICK THE *NEW BUTTON* ON THE TOOLBAR.

    OR...

    SELECT *FILE → NEW* FROM THE MENU.

    OR...

    PRESS *CTRL → N.*

2. SELECT *BLANK DATABASE* FROM THE TASK PANE.

3. NAVIGATE TO THE DRIVE AND FOLDER WHERE YOU WANT TO SAVE THE NEW DATABASE, THEN TYPE A NAME FOR YOUR NEW DATABASE IN THE *FILE NAME* BOX AND CLICK *CREATE.*

Creating a Table Using the Table Wizard

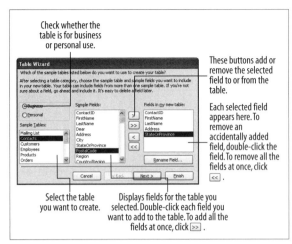

Check whether the table is for business or personal use.

These buttons add or remove the selected field to or from the table.

Each selected field appears here. To remove an accidentally added field, double-click the field. To remove all the fields at once, click ⟨<<⟩.

Select the table you want to create.

Displays fields for the table you selected. Double-click each field you want to add to the table. To add all the fields at once, click ⟨>>⟩.

Figure 2-7. The Table Wizard lets you create a table by adding ready-made fields to it.

If you're new to Access, the easiest way to add a table to an existing database is with the *Table Wizard*. The Table Wizard asks you a series of questions about which fields you want to appear in your table, and then it does all the dirty work of creating a new table for you. The Table Wizard can create a variety of different tables to store mailing lists, inventory, catalogs, and more.

1 Make sure that you have a blank database open.

If you don't have a blank database open, you can create one by clicking the New button on the toolbar, double-clicking Blank Database, entering a name for your database, and clicking Create.

2 Click the Tables icon in the Objects bar if it is not already selected.

Access lists all the tables in the current database.

3 Double-click Create table by using wizard.

The Table Wizard dialog box appears, as shown in Figure 2-7. This is definitely one of the more confusing dialog boxes in Access. The list in the far left of the dialog box contains the sample tables from which you can choose. See Table 2-2 for useful sample tables and their descriptions.

Start the Table Wizard by selecting the sample table you want to use.

4 Click Contacts from the Sample Tables list.

The Table Wizard displays the ready-made fields that you can incorporate into your table in the Sample Fields list. To add a field to your table, double-click the field or select the field and click the ⟨>⟩ button. Click the ⟨>>⟩ button to add all the sample fields to your table.

5 Double-click ContactID in the Sample Fields list.

The ContactID field appears in the "Fields in my new table" list. If you accidentally add a field to the "Fields in my new table" list, you can remove it by double-clicking it or by selecting it and clicking the ⟨<⟩ button.

6 Add the following fields to your table by double-clicking them: FirstName, LastName, Address, City, StateOrProvince, and PostalCode.

You can easily change the field names in your new table if you don't like the default names given to them by the Table Wizard. Here's how to rename a field:

7 Select StateOrProvince from the "Fields in my new table" list and click Rename Field.

The Rename field dialog box appears. From here, renaming a field is pretty much self-explanatory.

8 Replace the StateOrProvince text with State and click OK.

Once you have finished adding the fields to your table, you can move on to the next step in the Table Wizard.

9 Click Next.

The Table Wizard asks you to give your table a name and asks if you want to have Access set a primary key for you. You will learn more about primary keys later on, so for now let's accept the Table Wizard's default settings and create the table.

⸰ NOTE ⸰ *If other tables exist in your database, another screen will appear, asking you how this table relates to the other tables in your database.*

10 Click **Finish** to create the new table.

The Table Wizard builds the table using the fields you selected, then opens the new table—ready for your data input.

11 Close the Contacts table.

Table 2-2. Useful Sample Tables from the Table Wizard

Sample Table	Description
Employees	Tracks such employee data as addresses and phone numbers.
Orders	Tracks customer orders.
Contacts	Stores details about your customers and prospects.
Customers	Stores all your customer or client information.
Products	Maintains a list of products that your company sells.
Order Details	Tracks what was purchased in each order—used with the Orders table.
Time Billed	Tracks how much time to bill a client.
Expenses	Tracks expenses—useful for reimbursements or for billing customers.
Tasks	Tracks to-do items.

QUICK REFERENCE

TO CREATE A NEW TABLE USING THE TABLE WIZARD:

1. IN THE DATABASE WINDOW, CLICK THE TABLES ICON IN THE OBJECTS BAR AND THEN DOUBLE-CLICK CREATE TABLE BY USING WIZARD.

2. SELECT THE TYPE OF TABLE YOU WANT TO CREATE.

3. FOLLOW THE ONSCREEN INSTRUCTIONS AND SPECIFY WHAT YOU WANT TO APPEAR IN YOUR DATABASE.

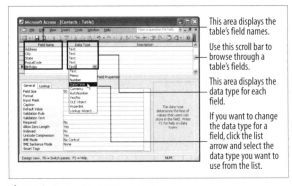

This area displays the table's field names.

Use this scroll bar to browse through a table's fields.

This area displays the data type for each field.

If you want to change the data type for a field, click the list arrow and select the data type you want to use from the list.

Figure 2-8. A table in Design view.

Once you have created a table, you can modify it later in *Design view*. Design view allows you to change the structure of a table by adding, deleting, and modifying its fields.

Because there are so many different types of data, Access offers several different types of fields. A field's data type determines the type of information that can be stored in a field. Table 2-3 lists the various data types available in Access. A field's data type restricts what type of information you can enter in a field. For example, you cannot enter text into a number field.

In this lesson you will modify a table by adding a new field and then determining the field's data type.

1 Click the Contacts table and click the Design button in the Database window.

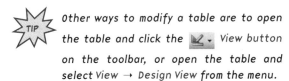

> **TIP**
> Other ways to modify a table are to open the table and click the ▼ View button on the toolbar, or open the table and select View → Design View from the menu.

The Contacts table appears in Design view, as shown in Figure 2-8, which allows you to add, delete, or modify the table's structure and fields.

Here's how to change a field name in Design view:

2 Scroll down, if necessary, and select the Postal-Code field in the Field Names column. Replace the text "PostalCode" with ZipCode.

That's how easy it is to change a field name. Now try adding a new field to the table.

3 Press Tab three times.

The cursor should be located in the blank Field Name box below the ZipCode field. To add a field in Design view, simply type a new field name in any blank Field Name box.

4 Type Birthday and press Tab.

By default, the Text data type is assigned to all new fields. Here's how to change a field's data type:

5 If it is not already selected, click the Data Type box next to the Birthday field.

A list arrow appears on the right side of the box.

6 Click the list arrow and select Date/Time from the list.

The new Birthday field will now only accept date and time information. The new Date/Time data type also makes your database more flexible and powerful because now you can sort birthdays by date or even use them in a calculation—for example, to determine a person's age.

Once you have finished modifying a table, you have to save your changes.

7 Click the Save button on the toolbar to save your changes.

> **TIP**
> Other ways to save a database object are to press Ctrl + S, or select File → Save from the menu.

You've finished modifying the table, so…

8 Close the Contacts table.

Table 2-3. Data Types

Data Type	Example	Description
Text	Legal Name: John Doe	Stores text, numbers, or a combination of both, up to 255 characters long. Text fields are the most common of all data types.
Memo	Notes: Sally displays a high amount of…	Stores long text entries—up to 64,000 characters long (the equivalent of 18 pages of text!). Use memo fields to store notes or anything else that requires a lot of space.
Number	Age: 31	Stores numbers that can be used in calculations.
Date/Time	Birthday: April 7, 1969	Stores dates, times, or both.
Currency	Price: $84.95	Stores numbers and symbols that represent money.
AutoNumber	Invoice Number: 187001	Automatically fills in a unique number for each record. Many tables often contain an AutoNumber field that is also used as their primary key.
Yes/No	Employed?: Yes	Stores only one of two values, such as Yes or No, True or False, etc.
OLE Object	Photo: 	Stores objects created in other programs such as a graphic, Excel spreadsheet, or Word document.
Hyperlink	Web Site: www.amazon.com	Stores clickable links to files on your computer, on the network, or to Web pages on the Internet.
Lookup Wizard	Purpose of Trip: 	A wizard that helps you create a field whose values are selected from a table, query, or a preset list of values.

QUICK REFERENCE

TO DISPLAY A TABLE IN DESIGN VIEW:

- OPEN THE TABLE AND CLICK THE VIEW BUTTON ON THE TOOLBAR.

OR...

- IN THE DATABASE WINDOW, CLICK THE TABLES ICON IN THE OBJECTS BAR, SELECT THE TABLE, AND CLICK THE DESIGN BUTTON.

TO CHANGE THE DATA TYPE FOR A FIELD:

1. DISPLAY THE TABLE IN DESIGN VIEW.

2. CLICK THE FIELD'S DATA TYPE BOX, CLICK THE LIST ARROW, AND SELECT THE DATA TYPE FROM THE LIST.

TO SAVE CHANGES TO A DATABASE OBJECT:

- CLICK THE SAVE BUTTON ON THE TOOLBAR.

OR...

- SELECT FILE → SAVE FROM THE MENU.

OR...

- PRESS CTRL + S.

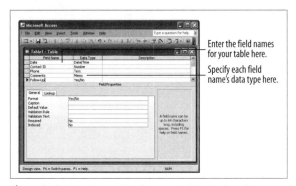

Enter the field names
for your table here.

Specify each field
name's data type here.

Figure 2-9. Creating a table from scratch in Design view.

The Table Wizard is helpful if you're new at building tables, but the more you start using Access, the less you will probably want to use the Table Wizard. That's because you will know exactly what type of tables and fields your database needs and how to create them.

This lesson explains how to build your own tables from scratch. The most straightforward way to build a table is in Design view, where adding fields to a table and specifying their data types is not much different than basic data entry.

1 Click the Tables icon in the Objects bar if it isn't already selected, then double-click Create table in Design view.

The new blank table appears in Design view. Now all you have to do is add the fields you want included in the table. The table you will create in this exercise will track telephone calls made to customers. Let's add the first field.

2 Type Date in the first blank Field Name box.

Since this field will store the date the call was made, you need to change the data type of the field to Date/Time.

3 Click the Data Type box next to the Date field.

A list arrow appears on the right side of the box.

4 Click the ☑ list arrow and select Date/Time from the list.

The Date field will now only accept date and time information. Let's add the next field to the table…

5 Press Tab two times and type Contact ID.

In case you were wondering, the *Description* box you just tabbed past is used to provide users with online prompts and instructions. Anything you enter in a field's Description box will appear in the Status bar whenever a user selects that field. We'll discuss the Description box in greater depth later on.

The Contact ID field will indicate the contact that was called. Since the Contact ID field will always be a number, you need to change its data type to numeric. A faster way of changing a field's data type is to type the first letter of the data type in the Data Type box. For example, typing a 'D' would change the data type to Date. Table 2-4 lists these keyboard shortcuts.

6 Press Tab.

The Data Type box should be selected. Try typing in the data type this time, instead of using the list arrow.

7 Type N in the Data Type box.

"Number" appears in the Data Type box.

8 Complete the table by entering the following field names and data types:

Field Name	Data Type
Phone	Text
Comments	Memo
FollowUp	Yes/No

Make sure that you press Tab after each field. If you make a mistake, you can either click the field you want to edit or press Shift + Tab to move back to the previous field. Your table should look like the one in Figure 2-9.

Once you have finished modifying a table, you have to save your changes.

9 Click the Save button on the toolbar to save your changes.

Access asks you to give your new table a name.

10 Type Phone Calls and click OK.

Access asks if you want to create a primary key now.

11 Click No and then close the current table and database.

Table 2-4. Data Type Shortcuts

Data Type	Shortcut	Data Type	Shortcut
Text	T	AutoNumber	A
Memo	M	Yes/No	Y
Number	N	OLE Object	O
Date/Time	D	Hyperlink	H
Currency	C	Lookup Wizard	L

QUICK REFERENCE

TO CREATE A TABLE FROM SCRATCH:

1. IN THE DATABASE WINDOW, CLICK THE TABLES ICON IN THE OBJECTS BAR AND THEN DOUBLE-CLICK CREATE TABLE IN DESIGN VIEW.

2. TYPE A FIELD NAME IN THE FIELD NAME COLUMN.

3. PRESS TAB, CLICK THE LIST ARROW IN THE DATA TYPE BOX, AND SELECT A DATA TYPE FOR THE FIELD.

4. REPEAT STEPS 2 AND 3 AS NECESSARY TO ADD NEW FIELDS TO THE TABLE.

5. CLOSE THE TABLE WINDOW.

6. CLICK YES TO SAVE THE TABLE, ENTER A TABLE NAME, AND THEN CLICK OK.

7. CLICK NO WHEN ACCESS ASKS IF YOU WANT TO CREATE A PRIMARY KEY NOW.

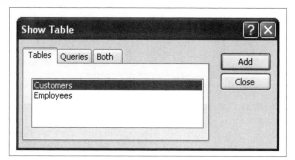

Figure 2-10. The Show Table dialog box.

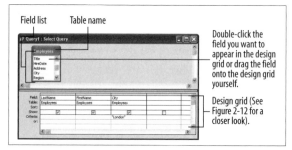

Figure 2-11. The Query window in Design view.

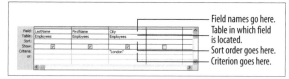

Figure 2-12. The design grid.

Most of the time the fastest and easiest way to create a query is in Design view. Here's how:

1 Open the Lesson 2 database.

Here's how to create a simple query:

2 In the Database window, click the Queries icon in the Objects bar and double-click Create query in Design view.

The Show Table dialog box appears, as shown in Figure 2-10. Here you have to select the table or query you want to use.

3 Click Employees and click Add.

When you have finished adding the tables and/or queries to your new query, you can close the Show Table dialog box.

4 Click Close.

The Query window appears in Design view, as shown in Figure 2-11. Notice that the window is split. The top half contains a box labeled Employees, which displays all the fields in the Employees table. The bottom half of the screen contains a design grid, which is where you will add the fields you want to appear in your query.

You can add fields to the design grid in two ways:

- By double-clicking the field in the field list.
- By clicking and dragging the field down to the design grid.

5 Double-click LastName and FirstName in the Employees field list.

Access adds the LastName and FirstName fields to the design grid.

Often you will have to use the field list's scroll bar to scroll up or down the list in order to find a field.

6 Scroll down in the field list and double-click the City field.

Now you need to specify any criteria for the query. You enter the criteria in the design grid's Criteria row. For this exercise you want to see only the records whose City fields contain "London"—move on to the next step to add this criteria to the query.

7 Click in the City column's Criteria row and type London.

If you want to use a field in the query, but you don't want it to be displayed in the query results, uncheck the "Show" box for that field. Your design grid should look like Figure 2-12.

8 Click the Show box for the City field to uncheck it.

The query will still use the criteria you specified for the City field, but it won't display the City field in the query results. You've created a simple query. Here's how to save it:

9 Click the Save button on the toolbar, type London Query and click OK.

OK—let's run our new query!

10 Click the Run button on the toolbar.

> **TIP** Other ways to run a query are to open the Query from the Database window, or click the ▦ ▾ Datasheet View button on the toolbar. You can also select Query → Run from the menu.

11 Access displays the results of the query.

Notice that while the City field is part of the query, it is not displayed because you unchecked its "Show" box back in Step 8.

Table 2-5 shows a smattering of criteria operators and examples to get you started.

Table 2-5. Common Criteria Operators

Operator	Example	Description
=	="MN"	Finds records equal to MN.
	"MN"	Finds records not equal to MN.
<	<10	Finds records less than 10.
< =	<=10	Finds records less than or equal to 10.
>	>10	Finds records greater than 10.
> =	>=10 AND 5	Finds records greater than or equal to 10 and not equal to 5.
BETWEEN	BETWEEN 1/1/99 AND 12/31/99	Finds records between 1/1/99 AND 12/31/99.
LIKE	LIKE "S*"	Finds text beginning with the letter "S." You can use LIKE with wildcards such as *.

QUICK REFERENCE

TO CREATE A QUERY IN DESIGN VIEW:

1. IN THE DATABASE WINDOW, CLICK THE QUERIES ICON IN THE OBJECTS BAR AND THEN DOUBLE-CLICK CREATE QUERY IN DESIGN VIEW.

2. SELECT THE TABLE YOU WANT TO ADD TO THE QUERY AND CLICK ADD.

3. REPEAT STEP 2 AS NECESSARY FOR ADDITIONAL TABLES OR QUERIES, AND CLICK CLOSE.

4. IN THE FIELD LIST, DOUBLE-CLICK EACH FIELD YOU WANT TO INCLUDE IN THE QUERY.

OR...

DRAG THE FIELD FROM THE FIELD LIST ONTO THE DESIGN GRID.

5. IN THE DESIGN GRID, ENTER ANY DESIRED SEARCH CRITERIA FOR THE FIELD IN THE CRITERIA BOX.

6. UNCHECK THE FIELD'S SHOW BOX IF YOU DON'T WANT IT TO BE DISPLAYED IN THE QUERY RESULTS.

7. CLOSE THE QUERY WINDOW.

8. CLICK YES TO SAVE THE QUERY, ENTER A QUERY NAME, AND THEN CLICK OK.

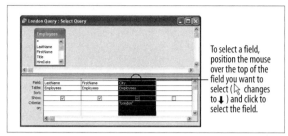

To select a field, position the mouse over the top of the field you want to select (↖ changes to ↓) and click to select the field.

Figure 2-13. Selecting a field in Query Design view.

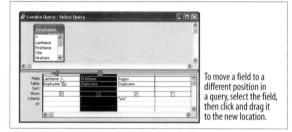

To move a field to a different position in a query, select the field, then click and drag it to the new location.

Figure 2-14. Moving a field in query mode.

As with any database object, you can modify any existing query. This lesson explains how to add and remove a field from a query and how to rearrange the fields in a query.

1 Click the Design button in the Database window.

The London Query appears in Design view. Here's how to remove a field from a query:

2 Position the mouse over the top of the City field (↖ changes to ↓) and click to select the entire field, as shown in Figure 2-13.

Once you have selected a field, you can delete it.

3 Press Delete to delete the selected City field from the query.

Now let's add a new field to the query.

4 Double-click the Region field in the Employees field list.

Access adds the Region field to the design grid. Now let's add some criteria to the new field so that only employees from Washington are displayed.

5 Click the Region column's Criteria row and type WA.

You can also rearrange the order of field names in a query. Here's how:

6 Select the FirstName field, then click and drag the selected field in front of the LastName field, as shown in Figure 2-14.

Let's see the results of the modified query.

7 Click the Run button on the toolbar to view the results of the query. Close the query without saving any changes.

QUICK REFERENCE

TO ADD A FIELD TO A QUERY:

- IN THE FIELD LIST, DOUBLE-CLICK EACH FIELD YOU WANT TO INCLUDE IN THE QUERY.

  OR...

- DRAG THE FIELD FROM THE FIELD LIST ONTO THE DESIGN GRID.

TO DELETE A QUERY FIELD:

- CLICK THE TOP OF THE FIELD YOU WANT TO DELETE AND PRESS DELETE.

TO REARRANGE FIELDS:

- POSITION THE POINTER OVER THE FIELD AND THEN CLICK AND DRAG THE FIELD TO A NEW LOCATION.

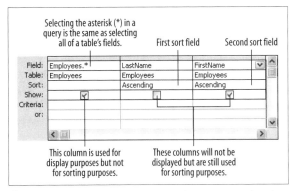

Selecting the asterisk (*) in a query is the same as selecting all of a table's fields.

First sort field

Second sort field

Field:	Employees.*	LastName	FirstName
Table:	Employees	Employees	Employees
Sort:		Ascending	Ascending
Show:	☑	☐	☑
Criteria:			
or:			

This column is used for display purposes but not for sorting purposes.

These columns will not be displayed but are still used for sorting purposes.

Figure 2-15. Creating a sort that sorts by LastName, then by FirstName.

Tables normally display records in the order they were entered. Instead of working with a table's jumbled record order, you can create a simple query that sorts the table information and presents it in an ordered, easy-to-read display. You can sort records alphabetically, numerically, or chronologically (by date) in ascending (A to Z) or descending (Z to A) order. You can also sort by multiple fields—for example, you could sort by LastName and then by FirstName. This lesson will show you how you can use a query to sort information in a table.

1 In the Database window, double-click Create query from Design view. Click Employees, click Add, and then click Close.

Notice that an asterisk (*) appears at the top of the Employees field list. Selecting a table's asterisk (*) in a query selects all of its fields at once.

2 Double-click the asterisk (*) in the Employees field list.

Access adds the asterisk to the design grid. Now you have to add the fields you want to use to sort the query.

3 Double-click LastName and FirstName in the Employees field list to add them to the design grid.

You are going to use the LastName and FirstName fields to sort the query. To sort a query, click the Sort row for the field you want to use to sort the query and select either Ascending or Descending.

4 Click in the LastName field's Sort box. Click the list arrow and select Ascending from the list. Repeat this step for the FirstName field.

The LastName and FirstName fields will already be displayed with all the other fields in the table because you added the asterisk (*) to the design grid. Because you don't want the LastName and FirstName fields to appear twice, you can uncheck their "Show" boxes.

5 Uncheck the Show box for the LastName and First-Name fields.

Your query should look like Figure 2-15. The query will still use the LastName and FirstName fields for sorting purposes, but it won't display these field names in the query results.

6 Save your query as AZ Query and then click the Run button on the toolbar to view the results. Close the query when you're finished.

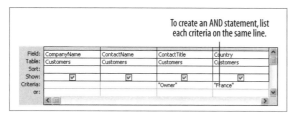

Figure 2-16. Creating an AND statement.

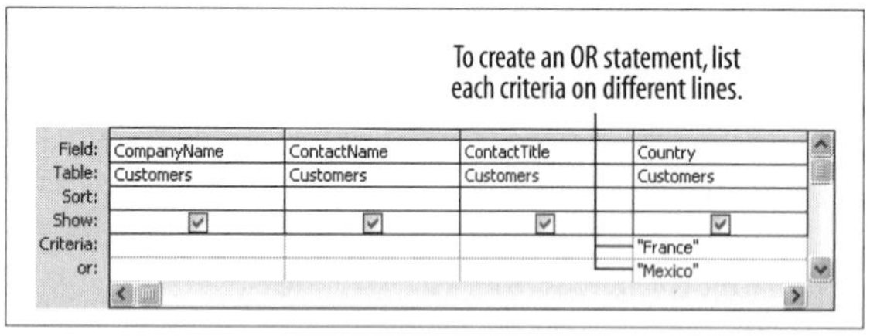

Figure 2-17. Creating an OR statement.

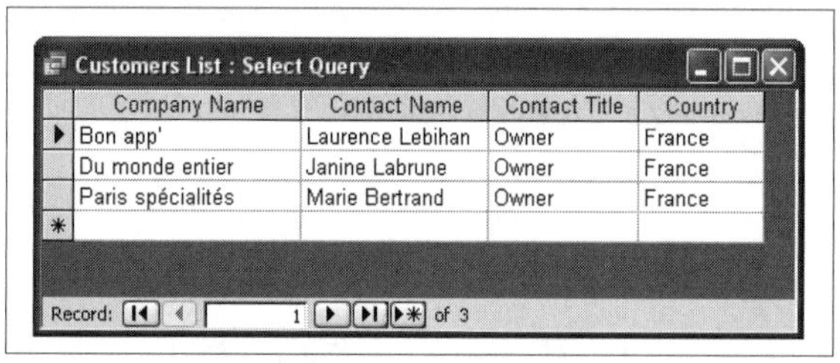

Figure 2-18. The results of the AND query.

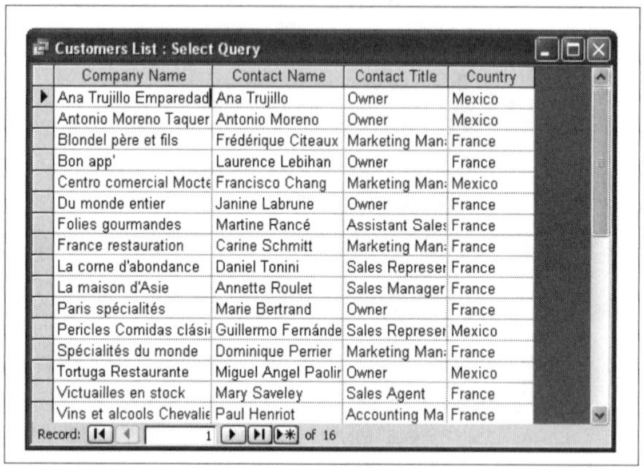

Figure 2-19. The results of the OR query.

The longer you work with Access, the more you will want to analyze your data. Before long you will want to create queries that match two or more conditions, such as "Which people have bought our products *AND* live in Michigan?" You might also want to create a query that matches only one of several conditions, such as "Which people have bought our beach balls OR water rafts?"

Toward that goal, this lesson introduces AND and OR operators. Here's the rundown on the two:

- **AND** narrows your query, making it more restrictive. For example, you could filter for employees who are from Washington *AND* who have been with the company for more than five years. To create an AND query, enter the criteria for the fields on the same Criteria row of the design grid.

- **OR** relaxes your query, so that more records match. For example, you could filter for employees who are from California *OR* Minnesota. To create an OR query, enter the criteria for the fields on different Criteria rows of the design grid.

The terms AND and OR operators may sound like they belong to the frighteningly technical world of programming, but if you already have a basic understanding of queries, they are remarkably easy to use.

1 Open the Customers List **query in Design view.**

Remember: To open any database object in Design view, simply select the object and click the Design button in the Database window.

The Customers List query appears in Design view. For this exercise you want to find which of your customers are from France *AND* own their own business. You will need to create an AND query because the ContactTitle field must equal "Owner" and the Country field must equal "France." To create an AND query, simply list each criteria on the same line, as shown in Figure 2-16.

2 Click the ContactTitle **column's Criteria row and type** Owner.

This will retrieve records whose ContactTitle equals "Owner." Next you have to enter the country criteria.

3 Click the Country **column's Criteria row and type** France.

Because you entered the Country criteria in the same Criteria row as the ContactTitle criteria, Access will treat it as an AND statement. (Which of my customers is an owner *AND* is from France?)

Move on to the next step to view the results of your first AND query.

4 Click the  View button **on the toolbar.**

Access displays the results of the query, as shown in Figure 2-18. Notice that the results match your queries' AND criteria—all the records have "Owner" in the ContactTitle field and "France" in the Country field.

Next we'll modify the query and create an OR statement.

5 **Switch to Design view by clicking the** View button **on the toolbar.**

You're back in Design view. First let's remove the Owner criteria from the query.

6 **Delete the** "Owner" **criteria from the ContactTitle Criteria row.**

This time you want to find which of your customers are from France *OR* are from Mexico. You will need to create an OR query to find these records. To create an OR query, simply list each criteria on its own line, as shown in Figure 2-17.

7 **In the** Country **column, click the** second Criteria row **and type** Mexico.

Because you entered each criteria in a different row, Access will treat it as an OR statement. (Which customers are from France *OR* are from Mexico?)

Move on to the next step to view the results of your OR query.

8 **Click the** View button **on the toolbar.**

Access displays the results of the query, as shown in Figure 2-19. Notice that the results match your queries' OR criteria—all the records have either "France" OR "Mexico" in the Country field.

9 Click the Save button on the toolbar to save your work and close the query window.

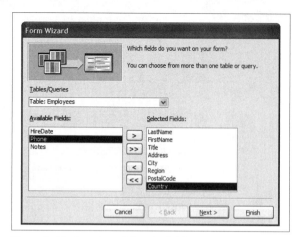

Figure 2-20. Step One: Select the fields you want to appear in your form.

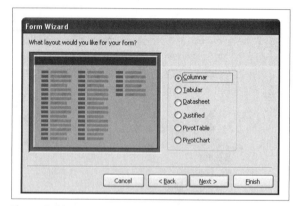

Figure 2-21. Step Two: Select a layout for the form.

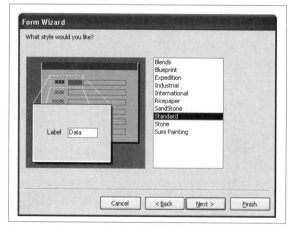

Figure 2-22. Step Three: Select a style for the form.

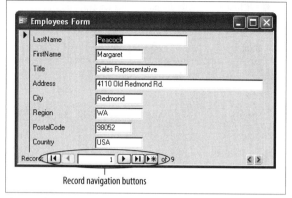

Record navigation buttons

Figure 2-23. The completed form.

You will usually want to use the Form Wizard to create your forms. It's almost always easier to create and modify a form created by the Form Wizard than it is to create one from scratch. This lesson will show you how to use the Form Wizard to create a form.

1 Click the Forms icon in the Objects bar, then double-click Create form by using wizard.

The Form Wizard appears, as shown in Figure 2-20. Anytime you create a form, you have to tell Access which table or query you want to use for your form.

2 Click the Tables/Queries list arrow and select Table: Employees.

Now that you have specified the table, you need to tell the Wizard which fields you want to display on the form. To add a field, double-click the field or select the field and click the [>] button. Click the [>>] button to add all the fields to your form.

3 Double-click the LastName field in the "Available Fields" list.

The LastName field appears in the "Selected Fields" list. If you accidentally add a field to the "Selected Fields" list, you can remove it by double-clicking it or by selecting it and clicking the [<] button.

4 Add the following fields to your table by double-clicking them: FirstName, Title, Address, City, Region, PostalCode, and Country.

Compare your Form Wizard dialog box to the one in Figure 2-20 when you're finished.

5 Click Next.

If you had selected fields from more than one table, the Form Wizard would ask how you would like to organize the data on your form. The Form Wizard doesn't ask us this question, however, since we are creating a form based on a single table.

Next the Form Wizard asks how you want to display the data on the form, as shown in Figure 2-21. You have six layout choices:

- **Columnar:** Displays one record at a time in an easy-to-read format.
- **Tabular:** Displays many records at a time.
- **Datasheet:** Displays many records at a time and looks exactly like a table in Datasheet view.
- **Justified:** Displays one record at a time in a format similar to a tax return— interesting, but it usually creates complicated forms that are difficult to work with.
- **PivotTable:** New in Access 2003, PivotTables dynamically summarize and analyze information into an easy-to-understand report. PivotTables are especially useful for seeing the bottom line in a large amount of information.
- **PivotChart:** Also new in Access 2003, PivotCharts dynamically summarize and analyze information, but by using a chart instead of a table.

The Form Wizard will select the layout option it thinks is best for your data. Keep in mind, however, the Form Wizard isn't always right.

For this exercise, we will use the default Columnar option.

6 Click Next.

Now the Form Wizard offers several interesting color styles that you can use in your form, as shown in Figure 2-22. Simply click a style to preview it.

 Some of the color styles can slow down the performance of your forms. Try to stick with either the Standard or Stone styles.

7 Click and preview each of the styles. When you're finished, click the Standard style and click Next.

The final window of the Form Wizard appears—you have to give your form a name.

8 Type Employees Form in the text box and click Finish.

After a few moments, your new form appears on screen, as shown in Figure 2-23. You don't have to worry about saving your new form—the Form Wizard does this for you automatically as part of the form creation process.

9 Use the form's record navigation buttons to browse through the records in the underlying Employees table. Close the form when you're finished.

QUICK REFERENCE

TO CREATE A FORM USING THE FORM WIZARD:

1. IN THE DATABASE WINDOW, CLICK THE FORMS ICON IN THE OBJECTS BAR AND THEN DOUBLE-CLICK CREATE FORM BY USING WIZARD.

2. SELECT THE TABLE OR QUERY YOU WANT TO USE TO CREATE YOUR FORM AND SELECT THE FIELDS THAT YOU WANT TO APPEAR ON THE FORM. CLICK NEXT WHEN YOU'RE FINISHED.

3. SELECT THE TYPE OF FORM YOU WANT TO CREATE AND CLICK NEXT.

4. SELECT A FORMAT FOR YOUR FORM AND CLICK NEXT.

5. GIVE YOUQR FORM A NAME AND CLICK FINISH.

Creating a Report with the Report Wizard

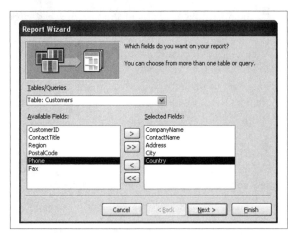

Figure 2-24. Step One: Select the fields you want to appear in your report.

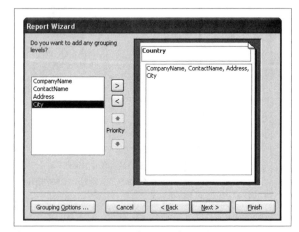

Figure 2-25. Step Two: Select how you want your fields to be grouped.

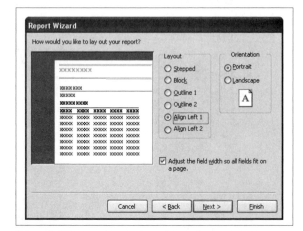

Figure 2-26. Step Three: Select a layout for your report.

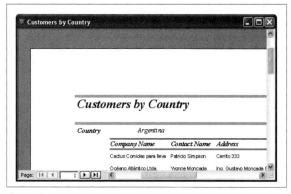

Figure 2-27. The new report.

Even more so than the Form Wizard, the fastest and easiest way to create a report is with the Report Wizard. It's almost always easier to create and modify a report created by the Report Wizard than it is to create one from scratch.

1 Click the Reports icon in the Objects bar and double-click Create report by using wizard.

The Report Wizard appears, as shown in Figure 2-24. Anytime you create a report you have to tell Access which table or query you want to use for your report.

2 Click the Tables/Queries list arrow and select Table: Customers.

Now that you have specified the table, you need to tell the Wizard which fields you want to display on the report. To add a field, double-click the field or select the field and click the > button. Click the >> button to add all the fields to your report.

3 Double-click the CompanyName field in the "Available Fields" list.

The CompanyName field appears in the "Selected Fields" list. If you accidentally add a field to the "Selected Fields" list, you can remove it by double-clicking it or by selecting it and clicking the < button.

4 Add the following fields to your table by double-clicking them: ContactName, Address, City, and Country.

Compare your Report Wizard dialog box to the one in Figure 2-24 when you're finished.

5 Click Next.

The Report Wizard asks you if and how you want to group the data in your report, as shown in Figure 2-25. For example, you can group all the customers from the same country together in your report. Grouping can help organize and summarize the information in your report. To use a specific field to group data, double-click the field you want to use. For this exercise, we'll group our report data using the Country field.

6 Double-click the Country field in the list.

The Country field appears on top of the sample report to show how Access will group the data in the report. If you change your mind, simply double-click the grouping field at the top of the sample report to remove it.

7 Click Next.

Next the Report Wizard asks if you want to sort the records in your report. Simply select the field you want to use to sort the records. You can click the button to the right of each list to toggle between ascending and descending sort orders.

8 Select CompanyName from the list and click Next.

Now the Report Wizard asks how you want to display the data on the report. Click a layout option to see it previewed onscreen. You can also specify the page orientation here.

⸭ NOTE ⸭ *If you're trying to get a lot of fields onto your report, consider using Landscape orientation. Landscape orientation lays the page along its longest side.*

9 Select the Align Left 1 option, as shown in Figure 2-26, and click Next.

Now the Report Wizard offers several interesting styles that you can use in your report. Click a style to preview it onscreen.

10 Select Corporate style and then click Next.

You need to give your new report a name.

11 Type Customers by Country in the text box and click Finish.

After a few moments, your new report appears on the screen, as shown in Figure 2-27. You don't have to worry about saving your new report—the Report Wizard does this for you automatically as part of the report creation process.

12 Close the report.

QUICK REFERENCE

TO CREATE A REPORT USING THE REPORT WIZARD:

1. IN THE DATABASE WINDOW, CLICK THE REPORTS ICON IN THE OBJECTS BAR AND THEN DOUBLE-CLICK CREATE REPORTS BY USING WIZARD.

2. SELECT THE TABLE OR QUERY YOU WANT TO USE TO CREATE YOUR REPORT AND SELECT THE FIELDS THAT YOU WANT TO APPEAR ON THE REPORT. CLICK NEXT WHEN YOU'RE FINISHED.

3. SELECT A FIELD BY WHICH TO GROUP THE REPORT AND CLICK NEXT (OPTIONAL).

4. SPECIFY THE FIELD(S) YOU WANT TO USE TO SORT THE REPORT AND CLICK NEXT (OPTIONAL).

5. SELECT A FORMAT FOR THE REPORT AND CLICK NEXT.

6. GIVE YOUR REPORT A NAME AND CLICK FINISH.

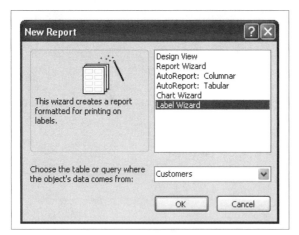

Figure 2-28. Select the table or query to use for your labels.

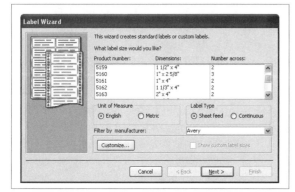

Figure 2-29. Select the product number for your Avery labels.

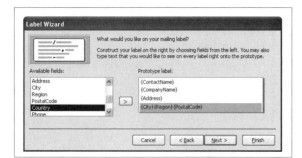

Figure 2-30. Select the fields and enter the text you want to see on your labels.

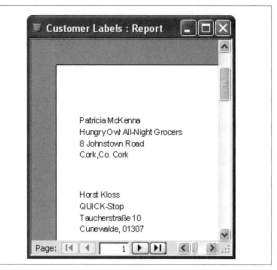

Figure 2-31. The completed labels.

For bulk mailings, nothing beats a good stack of mailing labels. The Access Label Wizard helps you quickly create labels for any number of uses: mailing labels, name tags—even labels for your floppy disks! The Label Wizard supports a huge variety of label sizes and brands (as long as they're from Avery).

In this lesson, you will use the Label Wizard to create a set of mailing labels.

1 Click the Reports icon in the Objects bar.

Access lists all the reports in the current database.

2 Click the Database window's ![New] New button.

The New Report dialog box appears, as shown in Figure 2-29.

3 Select Label Wizard from the list but DON'T CLICK OK YET.

Any time you create a report you have to tell Access which table or query contains the fields you want to use in your report.

4 Select Customers from the table or query drop-down list and click OK.

The first screen of the Label Wizard appears, as shown in Figure 2-28. If you're using Avery labels, the Label Wizard lists the various types of labels by product number. Simply scroll down and find the number that matches the one on your label box. If you're not using Avery labels, you may have to click the Customize button and tell the Label Wizard how to set up your nonstandard labels.

⋛ NOTE ⋛ *Save yourself time and headaches and always make sure to buy Avery or Avery-compatible labels.*

5 Make sure that the Unit of Measure is set to English, and then select 5161 from the list and click Next.

The next window of the Label Wizard lets you change the font used in your label. You can format the font type, size, weight, and color. If you're satisfied with the default font (Arial 8 point), you can simply click Next.

6 Click Next to accept the default font.

It's time to tell the Label Wizard which fields you want to use, as shown in Figure 2-30. You've done this before: Double-click a field to add it or select the field and click the ⟨ > ⟩ button.

7 Double-click the ContactName field in the "Available fields" list.

The ContactName field appears in the Prototype label. OK, there's a slight twist to the Label Wizard. The Label Wizard creates labels *exactly* how you tell it to. So if you want to place fields on separate rows, you need to press Enter to move to the next row.

Use the backspace key to delete a field from the Prototype label if you make a mistake.

8 Press Enter, double-click the CompanyName field in the "Available fields" list, press Enter, double-click the Address field, and press Enter.

If you want a character or text to appear on your labels, you'll need to type it in. For example, in the next step you will have to type in the comma and space between the City field and the Region field.

9 Double-click the City field, type a , (comma) followed by a Space, double-click the Region field, press Spacebar, and double-click the PostalCode field.

When you're finished, compare your prototype label to the one in Figure 2-30, then move on to the next step.

10 Click Next.

This window lets you sort your labels by any field. Simply double-click the field you want to use to sort the labels.

11 Double-click the PostalCode field and then click Next.

The final window of the Label Wizard appears. All you have to do now is give your new report a name.

12 Type Customer Labels in the text box and click Finish.

After a few moments, your labels appear on the screen, as shown in Figure 2-31. You don't have to worry about saving your new labels—the Label Wizard does this for you automatically as part of the report creation process.

⋛ NOTE ⋛ *Depending on your computer's printer setup, Access may warn you that some data may not be displayed. Go ahead and click OK.*

13 Close the report.

QUICK REFERENCE

TO CREATE LABELS:

1. IN THE DATABASE WINDOW, CLICK THE REPORTS ICON IN THE OBJECTS BAR, CLICK THE NEW BUTTON ON THE TOOLBAR, SELECT LABEL WIZARD FROM THE LIST AND CLICK OK.

2. SELECT THE TABLE OR QUERY YOU WANT TO USE TO CREATE YOUR LABELS AND CLICK OK.

   SELECT THE FONT YOU WANT TO USE FOR YOUR LABELS AND CLICK NEXT.

3. SELECT THE PRODUCT NUMBER FOR YOUR LABELS AND CLICK NEXT.

4. SELECT THE FIELDS THAT YOU WANT TO APPEAR ON THE REPORT AND ENTER ANY TEXT. CLICK NEXT WHEN YOU'RE FINISHED.

5. DOUBLE-CLICK THE FIELD YOU WANT TO USE TO SORT THE LABELS AND CLICK NEXT.

6. GIVE YOUR REPORT A NAME AND CLICK FINISH.

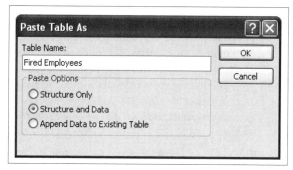

Figure 2-32. The Paste Table As dialog box.

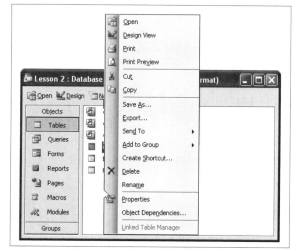

Figure 2-33. Right-click any database object to open a shortcut menu that lists different commands related to the object.

Not only can you view, open, and modify database objects (tables, queries, forms, etc.) from the Database window, you can also use it to cut, copy, paste, delete, and rename database objects.

1 Make sure you have the Database window open and click the Tables icon in the Objects bar.

One reason to copy a database object is that it's often easier to copy and use the design of an existing database object than it is to create a whole new object from scratch. For example, you might copy an Employees table so that you could create a new table using its structure.

You can use standard cut, copy, and paste procedures on any Microsoft Access database object in the Database window. That's right—the same cut and paste stuff you already know how to do with text works with tables, queries, forms, pages, and reports!

2 Select the Employees table and click the Copy button on the toolbar.

On the surface nothing appears to happen—but Microsoft Access has copied the Employees table to the Windows clipboard. Move on to the next step and paste the copied Employees table.

3 Click the Paste button on the toolbar.

The Paste Table As dialog box appears, as shown in Figure 2-32. First you have to specify a name for the new table.

4 Type Fired Employees in the Table Name box.

You have several options when you paste a table object—you can paste the:

- **Structure Only:** Pastes only the structure or design of the table.
- **Structure and Data:** Pastes the structure of the table and its data.
- **Append Data to an Existing Table:** Adds the copied records to an existing table in the database.

For this exercise we only want to paste the structure of the Employees table.

5 Select the Structure Only option and click OK.

Access pastes the copied Employees table as a new Fired Employees table.

⁞ NOTE ⁞ *You can also copy objects from one database to another using simple copy and paste commands. Copy the database object, start another session of Microsoft Access, and open the destination database. Click the Paste button to paste the copied object into the other database.*

6 Double-click the Fired Employees table.

Notice that there aren't any records in the Fired Employees table because you specified that you only wanted to copy the structure of the Employees table.

7 Close the Fired Employees table.

You can also rename a database object from the Database window. Here's how:

8 Right-click the Fired Employees table, select Rename from the shortcut menu, type Previous Employees and press Enter.

The "Fired Employees" table is now named "Previous Employees." Finally, here's how to delete any database object.

9 Select the Previous Employees table and press the Delete key. Confirm the deletion by clicking Yes.

Whenever you're unsure or curious about what you can do with a database object, try right-clicking it. A shortcut menu, as shown in Figure 2-33, will appear with a list of commands related to the database object. Table 2-6 contains some of the commands you'll see on the database object shortcut menu.

Intermediate and advanced Access users use a standard naming convention to make it easy to identify database objects. You are strongly encouraged to use the following naming convention as well, as it makes it easier to refer to database objects in expressions, macros, and VB procedures.

Object	Prefix	Example
Table	tbl	tblSales
Query	qry	qrySales
Form	frm	frmSales
Report	rpt	rptSales
Page	dap	dapSales
Macro	mcr	mcrSales
Module	bas	basSales

Table 2-6. Object Shortcut Menu Commands

Commands	Description
Open	Opens the selected object.
Design View	Opens the selected object in Design view so that it can be modified.
Print	Sends the selected object to the default printer.
Print Preview	Displays how the selected object will appear when it is printed.
Cut	Cuts/moves the selected object to the Windows clipboard.
Copy	Copies the selected object to the Windows clipboard.
Save As	Saves the selected object to a new object within the current database.
Export	Exports the selected object to another Access database or to a different file format.
Send To	Sends the selected object to an e-mail recipient via Microsoft Outlook.
Add to Group	Adds the selected object to Favorites or a new group.
Create Shortcut	Creates a shortcut on the Windows desktop to the selected object.
Delete	Deletes the selected object.
Rename	Renames the selected object.
Properties	Displays the properties and settings for the selected object.

QUICK REFERENCE

TO CUT/COPY AND PASTE A DATABASE OBJECT:

1. SELECT THE DATABASE OBJECT.

2. CLICK THE *CUT* BUTTON ON THE TOOLBAR.

   OR...

   CLICK THE *COPY* BUTTON ON THE TOOLBAR.

3. CLICK THE *PASTE* BUTTON ON THE TOOLBAR, ENTER A NAME FOR THE NEW OBJECT, AND CLICK OK.

TO RENAME AN OBJECT:

• RIGHT-CLICK THE OBJECT, SELECT *RENAME* FROM THE SHORTCUT MENU, AND ENTER A NEW NAME FOR THE OBJECT.

TO DELETE AN OBJECT:

• SELECT THE OBJECT AND PRESS THE *DELETE* KEY.

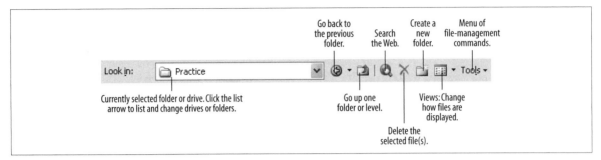

Figure 2-34. The Open dialog box's toolbar.

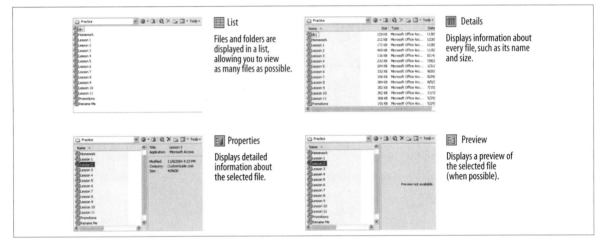

Figure 2-35. The Views list button lets you change how files are displayed in the Open dialog box.

File management includes moving, copying, deleting, and renaming the files you've created. Although it's a little easier to work with and organize your files using Windows Explorer or My Computer, you can also perform a surprising number of file-management chores right from inside Microsoft Access 2003—especially with its new and improved Open dialog box and Save As dialog box.

1   **Click the** Open button **on the toolbar.**

The Open dialog box appears. (See Figure 2-34 for the Open Dialog box's toolbar.) The Open dialog box is normally used to open files, but you can also use it to perform several file-management functions. There are two different ways to access file-management commands from inside the Open dialog box:

- Select a file and then select the command you want from the dialog box's Tools menu.

- Right-click a file and select the command you want from the shortcut menu.

2   **Right-click the** Rename Me **file.**

A shortcut menu appears with a list of available file-management commands for the selected file.

3   **Select** Rename **from the shortcut menu, type** Home Budget**, and press** Enter**.**

You have just changed the name of the selected file from "Rename Me" to "Home Budget." Instead of right-clicking the file, you could have selected it and then selected Rename from the Tools menu. Move on to the next step to learn how to delete a file.

4   **Click the** Home Budget **file to select it and press the** Delete **key.**

A dialog box appears, asking you to confirm the deletion of the Home Budget file.

5 Click Yes.

The Home Budget file is deleted. If you work with and create numerous files, you may find it difficult to remember what you named a file. To find the file(s) you're looking for, it can help to preview your files without opening them.

6 Click the Views button list arrow and select Details.

The Open dialog box changes the display of Access files in the Practice folder from List view to Details

view. (Figure 2-35 shows and describes the different views.) Change back to List mode to display as many files in the window as possible.

7 Click the Views button list arrow, select List to display the files in List view, and then close the dialog box by clicking Cancel.

Table 2-7 outlines some commands you can choose from the shortcut menu.

Table 2-7. File Shortcut Menu Commands

Command	Description
Select	Opens the selected file.
Open	Inactive command.
New	Inactive command.
Send To	Depending on how your computer is set up, it lets you send the selected file to a printer, to an email recipient, to a fax, or to a floppy drive.
Cut	Used in conjunction with the Paste command to move files. Removes the selected file from its current folder or location.
Copy	Used in conjunction with the Paste command to copy files. Copies the selected file.
Create Shortcut	Creates a shortcut—a quick way to a file or folder without having to go to its permanent location.
Delete	Deletes the selected file or files.
Rename	Renames the selected file.
Properties	Displays the properties of the selected file, such as when the file was created or last modified, or how large the file is.

QUICK REFERENCE

BASIC FILE MANAGEMENT IN THE OPEN DIALOG BOX:

1. OPEN THE OPEN DIALOG BOX BY SELECTING FILE → OPEN FROM THE MENU.

2. RIGHT-CLICK THE FILE AND REFER TO TABLE 2-7 FOR A LIST OF THINGS YOU CAN DO TO THE

SELECTED FILE, OR SELECT THE FILE AND SELECT A COMMAND FROM THE TOOLS MENU.

TO CHANGE HOW FILES ARE DISPLAYED:

• CLICK THE VIEWS BUTTON LIST ARROW AND SELECT A VIEW.

Compacting and Repairing a Database

Figure 2-36. Use the Compact and Repair Database command to clean up the database.

1 Select Tools → Database Utilities → Compact and Repair Database **from the menu, as shown in Figure 2-36.**

Your computer's hard disk will click and hum as Access compacts the database and repairs any errors it finds. The amount of time it takes to repair or compact a database depends on how large your database is, how long it's been since you've last compacted and repaired it, and how fast your computer is.

That's all there is to compacting and repairing a database!

Cars require maintenance to keep them running at their peak performance, and databases are no different. Your Access databases require some routine maintenance to prevent and/or correct problems and to keep them running at top performance. This lesson covers the two database utility commands:

- **Compact Database:** When you delete a database object or record, it leaves behind an empty hole previously occupied by the object. This isn't a big deal unless, over time, you have deleted lots of database objects and records. Compacting a database rearranges how the database is stored and reduces its file size.

- **Repair Database:** Over time, normal wear and tear causes errors to appear in your database, thus affecting its performance. Usually these errors are very minor and can easily be fixed by repairing the database.

Microsoft has combined compact and repair into a single command in Access 2003. If you have been busy adding, editing, and deleting records for a while or if your database seems buggy, sluggish, or is generating error messages, it would be a good idea to run the Compact and Repair Database command. Here's how to compact and repair a database:

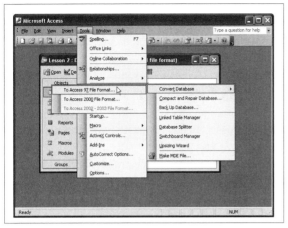

Figure 2-37. Using the Convert Database command.

Unlike other programs in the Microsoft Office XP suite, Access 2003 saves its files in a different format than previous Access 97 and 2000 databases. Because of this, you will need to convert older Access 97 and 2000 databases to the new Access 2003 format. This lesson explains how to do just that.

1 Make a backup copy of the Access database you're going to convert.

Ninety-nine percent of the time you won't encounter any problems when you convert a database, but it doesn't hurt to play it safe. Remember Murphy's Law: Anything that can go wrong usually does. Once you feel comfortable working with the converted Access 2003 database, you can erase the backup.

Once you've made your backup, move on to the next step.

2 Close the Microsoft Access database you're going to convert.

You're ready to convert the database!

3 Select Tools → Database Utilities → Convert Database → To Access 2003 File Format from the menu, as shown in Figure 2-37.

The Database To Convert From dialog box appears. Here you need to browse to and select the old Access database file you want to convert.

4 Browse to and double-click the old Access database file you want to convert.

Next you need to type a new name for the Microsoft Access 2003 database file.

⌗ NOTE ⌗ *You cannot convert an Access database into a file with the same name and location as the original database.*

5 Type a name for the new Microsoft Access database file and click Save.

6 Click OK to acknowledge the warning about version incompatibility.

Microsoft Access converts the database to Access 2003 format.

7 Close the Microsoft Access program.

QUICK REFERENCE

TO CONVERT AN OLD ACCESS DATABASE TO ACCESS 2003:

1. CLOSE ANY OPEN DATABASES AND SELECT TOOLS → DATABASE UTILITIES → CONVERT DATABASE AND SELECT THE APPROPRIATE FILE FORMAT FROM THE MENU.

2. BROWSE TO AND DOUBLE-CLICK THE ACCESS DATABASE FILE YOU WANT TO CONVERT.

3. TYPE A NAME FOR THE ACCESS 2003 DATABASE FILE AND CLICK SAVE.

4. CLICK OK TO ACKNOWLEDGE THE WARNING ABOUT VERSION INCOMPATIBILITY.

TO CONVERT AN ACCESS 2003 DATABASE TO AN OLD VERSION OF ACCESS:

1. OPEN THE DATABASE YOU WANT TO CONVERT AND SELECT TOOLS → DATABASE UTILITIES → CONVERT DATABASE AND SELECT THE APPROPRIATE FILE FORMAT FROM THE MENU.

2. BROWSE TO AND DOUBLE-CLICK THE ACCESS DATABASE FILE YOU WANT TO CONVERT.

3. TYPE A NAME FOR THE CONVERTED DATABASE FILE AND CLICK SAVE.

4. CLICK OK TO ACKNOWLEDGE THE WARNING ABOUT LOSING FUNCTIONALITY.

Lesson Summary

Planning a Database

Know how to plan a good database design.

Creating a Database Using the Database Wizard

To Create a Database Using the Database Wizard: Click the New button on the toolbar or select File → New from the menu. Click the On my computer link in the task pane, click the Databases tab in the Templates dialog box, then double-click the type of database you want to create. Follow the onscreen instructions and specify what you what to appear in your database.

Creating a Blank Database

To Create a New Blank Database: Click the New button on the toolbar, or select File → New from the menu, or press Ctrl + N. Select Blank Database from the task pane, then navigate to the drive and folder where you want to save the new database. Type a name for your new database in the File name box and click Create.

Creating a Table Using the Table Wizard

To Create a New Table Using the Table Wizard: In the database window, click the Tables icon in the Objects bar, double-click Create table by using wizard, then select the type of table you want to create. Follow the onscreen instructions and specify what you what to appear in your database.

Modifying a Table and Understanding Data Types

To Display a Table in Design View: Open the table and click the View button on the toolbar, or, in the database window, click the Tables icon in the Objects bar, select the table, and click the Design button.

To Change the Data Type for a Field: Display the table in Design view, click the field's Data Type box, click the list arrow, and select the data type.

To Save Changes to a Database Object: Click the Save button on the toolbar, or select File → Save from the menu, or press Ctrl + S.

Creating a New Table from Scratch

To Create a Table from Scratch: In the database window, click the Tables icon in the Objects bar and then double-click Create table in Design view. Type a field name in the Field Name column, press Tab, click the list arrow in the Data Type box, and select a data type for the field. Repeat the preceding steps as necessary to add additional fields. When you're finished, close the table window, click Yes to save the table, enter a table name, and then click OK.

Creating a Query in Design View

To Create a Query in Design View: In the database window, click the Queries icon in the Objects bar and then double-click Create query in Design view. Select the table you want to add to the query and click Add—repeat as necessary to add additional tables or queries. When you're finished, click Close. In the field list, double-click each field you want to include in the query or drag the field from the field list onto the design grid. In the design grid, enter any desired search criteria for the field in the Criteria box and uncheck the field's Show box if you don't want it to be displayed in the query results. Close the query window, click Yes to save the query, enter a query name, and then click OK.

Modifying a Query

To Add a Field to a Query: In the field list, double-click each field you want to include in the query or drag the field from the field list onto the design grid.

To Delete a Query Field: Click the top of the field you want to delete and press Delete.

To Rearrange Fields: Position the pointer over the field and then click and drag the field to a new location.

Sorting a Query Using Multiple Fields

To Sort a Query Using Multiple Fields: Open/display the query in Design view, and, if necessary, add the field you want to use to sort the query to the design grid. Click the Sort box list arrow for the first field you want to use to sort the query and select a sort order. Repeat for each additional field you want to use to sort the query, bearing in mind that the fields will be sorted from left to right.

Developing AND and OR Operators

To Create AND/OR Criteria: Open/display the query in Design view, enter your criteria in the appropriate field's first Criteria box. Enter additional criteria as follows: AND: Enter additional criteria for one or more fields in the appropriate field's Criteria box. All AND criteria should appear on the same row. OR: Enter additional criteria for one or more fields in the appropriate field's Criteria box, using a different row for each OR criteria.

Creating a Form with the Form Wizard

To Create a Form Using the Form Wizard: In the database window, click the Forms icon in the Objects bar and then double-click Create form by using wizard. Select the table or query you want to use to create your form, select the fields that you want to appear on the form, and click Next when you're finished. Select the type of form you want to create and click Next. Select a format for your form and click Next. Give your form a name and click Finish.

Creating a Report with the Report Wizard

To Create a Report Using the Report Wizard: In the database window, click the Reports icon in the Objects bar and then double-click Create reports by using wizard. Select the table or query you want to use to create your report and select the fields that you want to appear on the report. Click Next when you're finished. Select a field to group the report by and click Next (optional), then specify the field(s) you want to use to sort the report and click Next (also optional). Select a format for the report and click Next. Give your report a name and click Finish.

Creating Mailing Labels with the Label Wizard

To Create Labels: In the database window, click the Reports icon in the Objects bar, click the New button on the toolbar, select Label Wizard from the list and click OK. Select the table or query you want to use to create your labels, and click OK. Select the font you want to use for your labels and click Next. Select the product number for your labels and click Next. Select the fields that you want to appear on the report, enter any text, and click Next when you're finished. Double-click the field you want to use to sort your labels and click Next. Give your report a name and click Finish.

Database Object Management

To Cut/Copy and Paste a Database Object: Select the database object, click the Cut button or Copy button on the toolbar, click the Paste button on the toolbar, enter a name for the new object, and click OK.

To Rename an Object: Right-click the object, select Rename from the shortcut menu, and enter a new name for the object.

To Delete an Object: Select the object and press the Delete key.

File Management

Basic File Management in the Open Dialog box: Open the Open dialog box by selecting File → Open from the menu, right-clicking the file, and selecting the desired command.

To Change How Files Are Displayed: Click the Views button list arrow and select a view.

Compacting and Repairing a Database

To Compact and Repair a Database: Select Tools → Database Utilities → Compact and Repair Database from the menu.

Converting an Access Database

To Convert an Access Database: Close the database you want to convert and select Tools → Database Utilities → Convert Database and select the appropriate file format from the menu. Browse to and double-click the Access database file you want to convert. Type a name for the converted Access database file and click Save. Click OK to acknowledge the warning message.

Quiz

1. Which of the following is NOT a step in planning a database?

    A. Determine the fields you'll need and their data type.

    B. Determine the tables you'll need.

    C. Use the Database Planning Wizard to help determine the structure of your database.

    D. Determine the purpose of the database: the information you want to put into it and the reports you want to come out of it.

2. Which of the following statements is NOT true?

    A. The Database Wizard steps you through the process of creating a database and provides you with ready-to-use tables, forms, queries, pages, and reports.

    B. Datasheet View lets you view and modify the structure of any database object.

    C. The Table Wizard asks you a series of questions about what you want to appear in a table and then creates the table for you.

    D. You can add criteria to a query to determine which records are displayed.

3. Which of the following is NOT a data type?

    A. Text.

    B. Number.

    C. Picture/Graphic.

    D. Date/Time.

4. You can add a field to a query without displaying it in the query results. (True or False?)

5. Which of the following statements is NOT true? (Select all that apply.)

    A. To add a field to a query, double-click the field from the field list.

    B. Selecting the asterisk (*) in a query is the same as selecting all of a table's fields.

    C. You can only specify one set of criteria for each query—for example, to display customers from

Texas AND from Minnesota you would have to create two separate queries.

    D. You can sort a query's records by clicking the Sort box list arrow for the field you want to use to sort the query and select a sort order.

6. The fastest and easiest way to create a form or report is with the Form Wizard or the Report Wizard. (True or False?)

7. Microsoft Word is required in order to print mailing labels with Microsoft Access. (True or False?)

8. Which two of the following statements are NOT true? (Select all that apply.)

    A. Just as you can with files, you can cut, copy, paste, rename, and delete Microsoft Access database objects.

    B. Whenever you don't know how to do something to a database object, right-click the object. A shortcut menu listing everything you can do to the object will appear.

    C. When entered in the criteria row of a query design grid, the expression "MN" would display only those records equal to "MN."

    D. Avery labels are a nonstandard product and should never be used for mailing labels.

9. What is the maximum length a text field can be?

    A. 512 characters.

    B. There is no limit to how long a text field can be.

    C. 50 characters.

    D. 255 characters.

10. What is the memo data type field used for?

    A. To add an electronic Post-It® Note reminder to any record.

    B. For long text entries of one or more sentences.

    C. For short text entries of no more than 255 characters.

    D. To store objects created in other programs such as a graphic or Microsoft Word document.

11. Which of the following criterion would find records whose Personality field does not equal "Nice"?

    A. Nice.

    B. NOT Nice.

    C. IS NOT Nice.

    D. "Nice".

12. What happens when you add the asterisk (*) from any Field List to a query?

    A. The query uses the records from the table without displaying them.

    B. The query sorts the table's records in the order you specify.

    C. The query will include every field from the table.

    D. The table will not include any fields from the table.

13. You want to sort a query by a table's Last Name field. In order to do this, the Last Name field MUST appear in the displayed results of the query. (True or False?)

14. Where do reports and forms get their information from? (Select all that apply.)

    A. Tables.

    B. Queries.

    C. Forms.

    D. Modules.

15. What is the first step in creating a form or report with the Form Wizard or Report Wizard?

    A. Selecting how the form or report should be formatted.

    B. Selecting the underlying table or query on which you want to base the form or report.

    C. Reading several screens of mostly useless information and clicking Next.

    D. Selecting the fields that you want to appear in the form or report.

Homework

1. Start Microsoft Access.

2. Create a new blank database named Homework 2.

3. Create a new table in Design View that contains the following fields:

Field Name	Data Type
Last	Text
First	Text
Phone	Text
Age	Number

4. Save the table as Phone Numbers.

5. Use the Forms Wizard to create and save a columnar form named InsuranceClaim, using the Phone Numbers table as the data source.

6. Use the Reports Wizard to create and save a tabular report named InsuranceClaim, using the Phone Numbers table as the data source.

Quiz Answers

1. C. Since there isn't a Database Planning Wizard, you can't use it to help determine the structure of a database.

2. B. Design View lets you view and modify the structure of any database object. Datasheet View lets you view the records in a table, query, or form in a grid format.

3. C. There isn't a Picture/Graphic field in Microsoft Access, although OLE fields can store pictures and graphics in addition to other files created with external programs.

4. True. You can include a field in a query without displaying it in the query results by unchecking its Show box.

5. C. You can specify additional AND / OR criteria in a query by entering them in the appropriate AND / OR criteria rows.

6. True. Once you create a form or report using the Form Wizard or the Report Wizard, you can modify it to better suit your needs.

7. False. The Label Wizard, included with Microsoft Access, makes creating mailing labels a snap.

8. C and D. The expression "MN" would display only those records that are *not* equal to "MN," and Avery is the standard of the label industry.

9. D. A text field can have a maximum length of 255 characters.

10. B. The memo data field type is used for long text entries of one or more sentences.

11. D.

12. C. Adding the asterisk (*) from a Field List is the same as adding every field from the table.

13. False. You can sort the results of a query without displaying the field you used to sort the query.

14. A and B. Reports and forms get their information from tables and queries.

15. B. The first step in creating a form or report with the Form Wizard or Report Wizard is to select the underlying table or query for the form or report.

CHAPTER 3

FINDING, FILTERING, AND FORMATTING DATA

CHAPTER OBJECTIVES:

Find and replace database information, Lesson 3.1

Sort table information in ascending or descending order, Lesson 3.2

Filter information by selection, Lesson 3.3

Filter information by form, Lesson 3.4

Create an advanced filter, Lesson 3.5

Adjust the row height and column width in a datasheet, Lesson 3.6

Change the appearance of a datasheet, Lessons 3.7—3.8, 3.11

Freeze a field and hide columns, Lessons 3.9—3.10

CHAPTER TASK: FILTER AND SORT INFORMATION IN A TABLE AND CHANGE THE APPEARANCE OF A DATASHEET

Prerequisites

- **How to use menus, toolbars, dialog boxes, and shortcut keystrokes.**
- **How to open and modify database objects.**
- **How to add and edit database records.**

As databases grow larger and larger, finding a specific record or group of records becomes harder and harder. Fortunately, Microsoft Access is equipped with an arsenal of Find, Sort, and Filter commands that can track down and organize a table's information in record time.

In this chapter you will learn how to use these commands. First, you'll learn how to use the Find command to look up a specific record. Next, you'll learn how to sort information in a table—in ascending or descending order. Then, you'll learn all about filters: How they can find and display only records that meet your criteria, such as customers from the state of Texas.

Once you've learned how to organize and sort all that information, you'll learn how to make it look more professional. This chapter explains how to format a datasheet to change its font and appearance. You will also learn how to freeze and hide columns in a datasheet—an important task if you need to view large amounts of information.

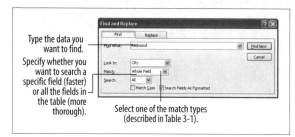

Type the data you want to find.

Specify whether you want to search a specific field (faster) or all the fields in the table (more thorough).

Select one of the match types (described in Table 3-1).

Figure 3-1. The Find tab of the Find and Replace dialog box.

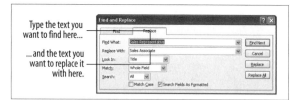

Type the text you want to find here...

...and the text you want to replace it with here.

Figure 3-2. The Replace tab of the Find and Replace dialog box.

Finding specific records or information in a large database would be like finding a needle in a haystack if it weren't for the Find feature. Find allows you to quickly search tables, queries, and forms for specified text—a critical database task. Select a field to search through all records in the current field only. This is usually quicker, especially if the field is indexed. Or select the datasheet or form to search through all fields in all records.

The Find and Replace feature is very useful. Imagine you are working on a huge database that tracks the feeding patterns of squirrels. You're almost finished when you realize that you've mistakenly referred to one of the species of squirrels you're tracking—flying squirrels—not by their proper scientific name "Sciuridae Glaucomys" but by the scientific name for the common gray squirrel "Sciuridae Sciurus." Yikes! It will take hours to go back and find every instance of "Sciuridae Sciurus" in your database and replace it with "Sciuridae Glaucomys." Or it could take you less than a minute if you use Access's Find and Replace function.

1 Start Microsoft Access, open the Lesson 3 database, and double-click on the Employees table.

First you need to put the cursor in the field that contains the data you want to look for. For this exercise we'll search the City field.

2 Click anywhere in the City field.

Here's how to open the Find and Replace dialog box.

3 Click the Find button on the toolbar.

TIP Other ways to find information are to press Ctrl + F, or select Edit → Find from the menu.

The Find and Replace dialog box appears with the Find tab in front, as shown in Figure 3-1. You tell Access what you're looking for in the Find What box.

4 In the Find What text box type Redmond.

Also important are the following options:

- **Look In combo box:** Allows you to search only the current field (which is faster) or all the fields in the entire table (which is slower).

- **Match combo box:** See Table 3-1 for a description of the Match combo box and its options.

- **Search combo box:** Allows you to search up or down from the insertion point or search the whole document.

- **Match Case check box:** Finds only text that has the same pattern of uppercase and lowercase characters as the text you specified.

- **Search Fields as Formatted check box:** Check to search based on the format rather than the value.

5 Click the Find Next button.

Access jumps to the first (and only) occurrence of the word "Redmond" that it finds in the table.

6 Click Cancel.

The Find and Replace dialog box closes. You can also replace information in a database.

7 Click anywhere in the Title field and select Edit → Replace from the menu.

TIP Another way to find and replace information is to press Ctrl + H.

The Find and Replace dialog box appears with the Replace tab in front, as shown in Figure 3-2.

8 In the Find What **text box type** Sales Representative.

You want to replace every occurrence of the phrase "Sales Representative" with the phrase "Sales Associate."

9 Select the Replace With **text box by clicking it or by pressing the** Tab **key and type** Sales Associate.

10 Click Replace All.

Access finds all the occurrences of the phrase "Sales Representative" in the table and replaces them with the words "Sales Associate."

TIP

Think before you use the Replace All button—you might not want it to replace every instance of a label or value! You can find and replace each individual occurrence of a label or value by clicking Find Next and Replace.

11 Click Yes **to acknowledge the warning and then click** Cancel.

The Find and Replace dialog box disappears and you're back to your datasheet. Notice how all the occurrences of the phrase "Sales Representative" have been replaced by the phrase "Sales Associate."

Table 3-1. Using the Match List Options

Match	Description
Whole Field	Finds only data that is exactly the same.
	Example: John finds John, but not Johnson, or Sue and John.
Any Part of Field	Finds data anywhere in the field.
	Example: John finds John, Johnson, and Sue and John.
Start of Field	Finds data only at the beginning of the field.
	Example: John finds John and Johnson, but not Sue and John.

QUICK REFERENCE

TO FIND INFORMATION:

1. CLICK THE FIND BUTTON ON THE TOOLBAR.

    OR...

    PRESS CTRL + F.

    OR...

    SELECT EDIT → FIND FROM THE MENU.

2. ENTER THE TEXT YOU WANT TO SEARCH FOR IN THE FIND WHAT TEXT BOX.

3. CLICK THE FIND NEXT BUTTON.

4. REPEAT STEP 3 UNTIL YOU FIND THE TEXT YOU'RE LOOKING FOR.

TO FIND AND REPLACE INFORMATION:

1. SELECT EDIT → REPLACE FROM THE MENU.

    OR...

    PRESS CTRL + H.

2. ENTER THE TEXT YOU WANT TO SEARCH FOR IN THE FIND WHAT TEXT BOXENTER THE TEXT YOU WANT TO REPLACE THE WORD WITH IN THE REPLACE WITH TEXT BOX.

3. CLICK THE FIND NEXT BUTTON.

4. CLICK THE REPLACE BUTTON TO REPLACE THE TEXT.

5. REPEAT STEPS 4 AND 5 IF THERE IS MORE THAN ONE OCCURRENCE THAT YOU WANT TO REPLACE.

    OR...

    CLICK REPLACE ALL TO SEARCH AND REPLACE EVERY OCCURRENCE OF TEXT IN THE TABLE.

Employees : Table

Employee ID	Last Name	First Name	Title	Birth Date
1	Davolio	Nancy	Sales Representative	08-Dec-48
2	Fuller	Andrew	Vice President, Sales	19-Feb-52
3	Leverling	Janet	Sales Representative	30-Aug-63
4	Peacock	Margaret	Sales Representative	19-Sep-37
5	Buchanan	Steven	Sales Manager	04-Mar-55
6	Suyama	Michael	Sales Representative	02-Jul-63
7	King	Robert	Sales Representative	29-May-60
8	Callahan	Laura	Inside Sales Coordinator	09-Jan-58
9	Dodsworth	Anne	Sales Representative	27-Jan-66

Record: 1 of 9

Figure 3-3. A table is normally displayed in the order its records were entered.

Employees : Table

Employee ID	Last Name	First Name	Title	Birth Date
5	Buchanan	Steven	Sales Manager	04-Mar-55
8	Callahan	Laura	Inside Sales Coordinator	09-Jan-58
1	Davolio	Nancy	Sales Representative	08-Dec-48
9	Dodsworth	Anne	Sales Representative	27-Jan-66
2	Fuller	Andrew	Vice President, Sales	19-Feb-52
7	King	Robert	Sales Representative	29-May-60
3	Leverling	Janet	Sales Representative	30-Aug-63
4	Peacock	Margaret	Sales Representative	19-Sep-37
6	Suyama	Michael	Sales Representative	02-Jul-63

Record: 1 of 9

Figure 3-4. The table sorted by the Last Name field.

When you enter new records in a table, they are added at the end of the table in the order you enter them (see Figure 3-3). Working with information in such a jumbled order can be difficult if not impossible. Fortunately you can *sort*, or change the order of records in a table. You can sort records alphabetically, numerically, or chronologically (by date). Additionally, you can sort information in ascending (A to Z) or descending (Z to A) order. This lesson will show you several techniques you can use to sort information in your tables, queries, pages, and forms.

⋛ NOTE ⋚ *If you frequently sort a table the same way, you should consider creating and using a query that automatically sorts the table data for you. A query that sorts a table alphabetically by name would be a good example of such a query.*

1 If it isn't already open, find and open the Employees table.

First you need to put the cursor in the field you want to use to sort the table. You want to sort the list by the last name, so you would select the LastName field.

2 Click anywhere in the Last Name field.

Here's how to sort a table:

3 Click the ↓ Sort Ascending button on the toolbar.

Access sorts the table, ordering the records in ascending (A-Z) order by last name, as shown in Figure 3-4. You can also sort a list in descending (Z-A) order.

4 Click the ↓ Sort Descending button on the toolbar.

The list is sorted in descending (Z-A) order by the Last Name field.

Let's try sorting the table using a different field.

5 Click anywhere in the Birth Date field and click the Sort Ascending button on the toolbar.

Access sorts the table by the Birth Date field and we instantly discover that poor Margaret Peacock is the oldest employee in the company.

Table 3-2 shows examples of methods of sorting.

Table 3-2. Sort Examples

Order	Alphabetic	Numeric	Date
Ascending	A, B, C	1, 2, 3	1/1/99, 1/15/99, 2/1/99
Descending	C, B, A	3, 2, 1	2/1/99, 1/15/99, 1/1/99

QUICK REFERENCE

TO SORT RECORDS BY ONE FIELD:

1. CLICK ANYWHERE IN THE COLUMN YOU WANT TO USE TO SORT THE LIST.

2. CLICK EITHER THE **SORT ASCENDING** BUTTON OR **SORT DESCENDING** BUTTON ON THE TOOLBAR.

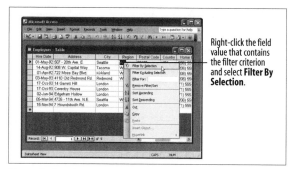

Figure 3-5. Filtering a table by selection.

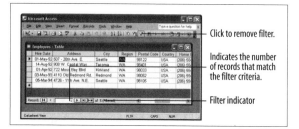

Figure 3-6. The table is filtered so that only records that have "WA" in the Region field are displayed.

Sometimes you may want to see only certain records in your table. By *filtering* a table, you display only the records that meet your criteria and hide the records that do not. For example, you could filter a client list to display only clients who live in California.

There are several filter methods:

- **Filter by Selection:** The fastest and easiest of the three filter commands. Simply find and select the value you want to use as the filter criteria, and then use Filter By Selection to find all records with the selected value.
- **Filter by Form:** Here you type your filter criteria into a blank form that contains all the field names in the table. Works well if you have more than one criteria.
- **Advanced Filter/Sort:** The most powerful and complicated filter method. Creating an advanced filter is really not any different from creating a query.

In this lesson, you will learn how to use the fastest and easiest way to filter a list with the nifty *Filter by Selection* feature.

1 If it isn't already open, find and open the **Employees** table.

The first step is finding a record and field that matches your criterion. For example, to find all the addresses from Minnesota you would put the cursor in any State field that contained MN.

2 Find the **Region** field and then right-click any **WA** value.

A shortcut menu appears, as shown in Figure 3-5. Notice that the shortcut menu actually contains four filter-related commands. You can read more about these commands in Table 3-3.

3 Select **Filter By Selection** from the shortcut menu.

 Another way to filter by selection is to select the record and field that matches your criterion and click the Filter by Selection *button on the toolbar.*

Access filters the table so that only records that contain "WA" in the Region field are displayed, as shown in Figure 3-6. Notice that the bottom of the table window tells you the number of records that match your filter criteria. Also the message (Filtered) indicates that the table is currently being filtered.

Here's how to remove a filter:

4 Click the Remove Filter button on the toolbar.

All the records in the table are displayed.

The opposite of Filter by Selection is *Filter Excluding Selection*, which filters all records that *don't* contain the criteria value. For example, to find all the addresses that *aren't* from Minnesota, you would put the cursor in any State field that contained MN.

5 Find the **City** field and then right-click any **London** value. Select **Filter Excluding Selection** from the shortcut menu.

This time Access displays all the records that do not contain London in the City field.

6 Click the **Remove Filter button** on the toolbar.

All the records in the table are displayed.

Table 3-3. Filter Shortcut Menu Commands

Command	Description
Filter by Selection	Finds and displays all records with the selected value.
Filter Excluding Selection	Finds and displays all records that *don't* contain the selected value.
Filter For	Finds and displays all records that match the text you enter.
Remove Filter/Sort	Removes the applied filter from the table.

QUICK REFERENCE

TO FILTER BY SELECTION:

1. FIND THE FIELD VALUE ON WHICH YOU WANT TO BASE THE FILTER.

2. RIGHT-CLICK THE FIELD VALUE AND SELECT FILTER BY SELECTION FROM THE SHORTCUT MENU.

   OR...

   CLICK THE FIELD VALUE, THEN CLICK THE FILTER BY SELECTION BUTTON ON THE TOOLBAR.

TO FILTER EXCLUDING THE SELECTION:

- RIGHT-CLICK THE FIELD VALUE YOU WANT TO EXCLUDE AND SELECT FILTER EXCLUDING SELECTION FROM THE SHORTCUT MENU.

TO REMOVE A FILTER:

- RIGHT-CLICK THE FILTERED TABLE AND SELECT REMOVE FILTER/SORT FROM THE SHORTCUT MENU.

OR...

- CLICK THE REMOVE FILTER BUTTON ON THE TOOLBAR.

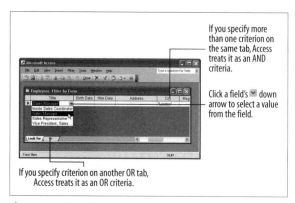

If you specify more than one criterion on the same tab, Access treats it as an AND criteria.

Click a field's ☑ down arrow to select a value from the field.

If you specify criterion on another OR tab, Access treats it as an OR criteria.

Figure 3-7. The Filter by Form window.

Filtering by Form makes it easy to create a filter that uses more than one criterion. The Filter by Form window enables you to enter your filter criterion by picking values that you want the filtered records to have.

If you look at Figure 3-7, you'll notice that several tabs appear at the bottom of the Filter by Form window. If you specify more than one criterion on the same Filter by Form tab, Access treats it as an AND criteria statement, meaning a record must match all the criteria in order to be displayed. For example, you could filter for employees who are from Washington *AND* who had been with the company for more than five years.

If you specify filter criterion on different tabs, Access treats it as an OR criteria statement, meaning a record has to match the criterion on one tab or the other to be displayed. For example, you could filter for employees from California *OR* Minnesota.

1 If it isn't already open, find and open the Employees table.

First you need to display the Filter by Form window.

2 Click the ☒ Filter by Form button on the toolbar.

The Filter by Form window, which looks like an empty replica of your table, appears as shown in Figure 3-7.

The Filter by Form window may already contain a value from a previous filter. If that's not a field that you want to use in your filter, you can press Delete to clear the old criteria.

3 Press Delete to delete any old filter criteria.

Next you have to select the field and value you want to use as your criteria.

4 Click the City field.

A down arrow appears in the field that the cursor is in. Click this down arrow to see a list of values used in that field.

5 Click the City list arrow and select London from the list.

This will display only records whose City field contains "London."

You can create an AND criteria statement by specifying more than one criterion on the same Filter by Form tab. For example you could filter for employees who are from London *AND* who have been employed since before 1994.

6 Click the Title field, click the Title list arrow and select Sales Manager from the list.

This will display only records for employees who are from London and whose title is Sales Manager.

7 Click the ▽ Apply Filter button on the toolbar.

Access applies the filter and displays only those records whose City field equals "London" *AND* whose Title field equals "Sales Manager." Only one record meets the filter criteria. Let's try modifying the query and adding an OR criteria statement.

8 Click the Filter by Form button on the toolbar.

If you have another set of criteria or rules to filter records by, click the Or tab at the bottom of the Filter by Form window.

9 Click the Or tab at the bottom of the Filter by Form window.

Access displays another blank Filter by Form window. Access will search for any criterion you enter on this tab in addition to your original criterion. You decide to filter for records whose City field equals "London" *AND* whose Title field equals "Sales Manager" *OR* whose Title field equals "Vice President, Sales."

10 Click the Title **field and select** Vice President, Sales **from the list.**

Notice that a new Or tab appears at the bottom of the Filter by Form window. You can use as many "Or" statements as you need to define all your filter criteria.

Let's see what records our modified filter will find.

11 Click the Apply Filter button **on the toolbar.**

Access applies the filter and displays records whose City field equals "London" *AND* whose Title field

equals "Sales Manager" *OR* whose Title field equals "Vice President, Sales." Two records meet the filter criteria.

12 Click the Remove Filter button **on the toolbar.**

Access once more displays all the records in the table.

Table 3-4 describes common criteria operators and examples you can use in your filters.

Table 3-4. Common Criteria Operators

Operator	Example	Description
=	="MN"	Finds records equal to MN.
	"MN"	Finds records not equal to MN.
<	<10	Finds records less than 10.
< =	<=10	Finds records less than or equal to 10.
>	>10	Finds records greater than 10.
> =	>=10 AND 5	Finds records greater than or equal to 10 and not equal to 5.
BETWEEN	BETWEEN 1/1/99 AND 12/31/99	Finds records between 1/1/99 AND 12/31/99.
LIKE	LIKE "S*"	Finds text beginning with the letter "S." You can use LIKE with wildcards such as *.

QUICK REFERENCE

TO FILTER BY FORM:

1. CLICK THE FILTER BY FORM BUTTON ON THE TOOLBAR.

2. CLICK THE EMPTY TEXT BOX BELOW THE FIELD YOU WANT TO FILTER, CLICK THE DROP-DOWN ARROW AND SELECT THE VALUE YOU WANT TO USE TO FILTER THE RECORDS.

3. REPEAT STEP 2 FOR EACH ADDITIONAL FIELD YOU WANT TO USE TO SPECIFY ADDITIONAL FILTER CRITERIA.

4. IF YOU WANT TO USE OR CRITERIA, CLICK THE OR TAB AT THE BOTTOM OF THE SCREEN TO SPECIFY THE ADDITIONAL FILTER CRITERIA.

5. CLICK THE APPLY FILTER BUTTON ON THE TOOLBAR.

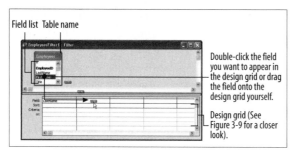

Field list Table name

Double-click the field you want to appear in the design grid or drag the field onto the design grid yourself.

Design grid (See Figure 3-9 for a closer look).

Figure 3-8. The Filter window.

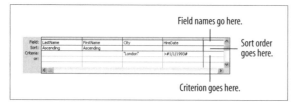

Field names go here.

Sort order goes here.

Criterion goes here.

Figure 3-9. A close-up of the Design grid.

The most powerful filter is the *Advanced Filter*. The Advanced Filter is so powerful that you can think of it as a baby query. In fact, the procedure for creating an Advanced Filter is virtually the same as it is for creating a simple query. The problem with Advanced Filters is that they can be difficult to set up the first few times—especially if you're new to Access.

Advanced Filters have many advantages. They have the ability to:

- **Sort by multiple fields:** You can sort records using several fields. For example, you could sort a table alphabetically by last name and then by first name.

- **Use complex filter criteria and expressions:** You can use advanced expressions and operators to search for data. For example you could filter for dates that fall *Between* 1/1/95 *And* 12/31/99.

- **Use multiple AND/OR statements:** You can use more than one criterion to sift through records. For example, you could filter for employees who are from Washington *AND* who have been with the company for more than five years.

This lesson explains how to get your own Advanced Filters up and running.

1 If it isn't already open, find and open the Employees **table.**

Here's how to create an Advanced Filter/Sort:

2 Select Records → Filter → Advanced Filter/Sort **from the menu.**

The Filter window appears, as shown in Figure 3-8. The Advanced Filter will probably contain criteria from a previous filter that will have to be removed.

3 Click the ✕ Clear Grid button **on the toolbar to clear the grid of any preexisting criteria.**

You're ready to create your Advanced Filter. Notice in Figure 3-8 that the window is split. The top half contains a box labeled Employees, which displays all the fields in the current table. The bottom half of the screen contains a design grid, which is where the filter information goes.

The first thing you need to do is select the fields that you want to use in your filter. You can add fields to the design grid in two ways:

- By double-clicking the field on the field list.

- By clicking and dragging the field down to the design grid yourself.

Because the field list doesn't have a lot of room, you will usually need to use the field list's scroll bar to scroll up or down the list.

4 Double-click the LastName **field in the field list.**

Access adds the Last Name field to the design grid.

5 Double-click the FirstName, City, HireDate, **and** Region **fields to add them to the design grid as well.**

You can use any field on the design grid to sort or filter the table. To sort by a field, click the Sort row in the column that contains the field that you want to sort and select Ascending or Descending from the list.

6 Click the LastName **column's Sort row and select** Ascending **from the drop-down list.**

This will sort the table by the LastName field in Ascending order. You can also sort by more than one field. For example, you could sort by LastName and then by FirstName. When you use several fields to sort a table, Access performs the sort in the order the fields appear in the design grid.

7 Click the FirstName column's Sort row and select Ascending.

Next you need to specify the criteria for the Advanced Filter. You type the criteria in the design grid's Criteria row.

8 Click the City column's Criteria row and type London.

If you specify more than one criterion on the same Criteria row, Access treats it as an AND criteria statement, meaning a record must match all the criteria in order to be displayed. For example, you could filter for employees who are from Washington *AND* who were hired after January 1, 1993.

9 Click the HireDate column's Criteria row and type >1/1/93.

This criteria will display only records whose Hire-Date is greater than, or after, 1/1/93. Because it's on the same Criteria row as the City field's "London" criteria, the filter will display only those records whose City field equals "London" and whose Hire Date is after 1/1/93.

If you specify filter criterion on the Or rows, Access treats it as an OR criteria statement, meaning a record has to match the criterion on one row or the other to be displayed. For example you could filter for employees from California *OR* Minnesota.

10 Click the Region column's Or row and type WA.

Your completed design grid should look similar to the one shown in Figure 3-9. You're ready to try the Advanced Filter.

11 Click the Apply Filter button **on the toolbar to apply the filter.**

The Advanced Filter window closes, and Access applies the filter and displays the records that meet your criteria.

12 Click the Remove Filter button **to remove the filter.**

QUICK REFERENCE

TO CREATE AN ADVANCED FILTER:

1. SELECT RECORDS → FILTER → ADVANCED FILTER/SORT FROM THE MENU.

2. DOUBLE-CLICK EACH FIELD YOU WANT TO INCLUDE FROM THE FIELD LIST.

   OR...

DRAG THE FIELD FROM THE FIELD LIST ONTO THE DESIGN GRID.

3. IN THE DESIGN GRID, ENTER ANY DESIRED SEARCH CRITERIA FOR THE FIELD IN THE CRITERIA ROW.

4. CLICK THE SORT BOX LIST ARROW FOR THE FIELD AND SELECT A SORT ORDER (OPTIONAL).

5. CLICK THE APPLY FILTER BUTTON ON THE TOOLBAR.

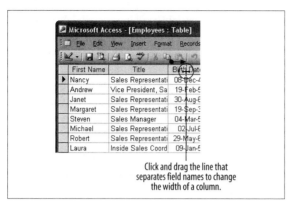

Figure 3-10. Adjusting the width of a column.

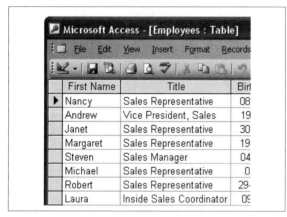

Figure 3-11. The resized column.

Click and drag the line that separates records to change the height of a row.

Figure 3-12. Adjusting the height of a row.

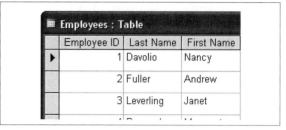

Figure 3-13. The resized row.

Access is usually pretty smart about how wide to make the columns of a table or query so hopefully you won't have to do much resizing. Sometimes, however, you will discover that some of the columns or rows are not large enough to display the information they contain. This lesson explains how to change the width of a column and the height of a row.

1 If it isn't already open, find and open the Employees **table.**

Most of the columns in this table are wide enough to display all their information. The Title column, however, needs to be slightly wider.

2 Carefully position the pointer over the right edge of the Title **field until it changes to a ↔.**

Once the pointer is positioned over the column line and appears as a ↔, you can adjust the column width to make it narrower or wider.

3 Click and hold the mouse button and drag the line to the right about a half-inch, as shown in Figure 3-10, then release the mouse button.

Access resizes the width of the Title column, as shown in Figure 3-11.

You can also have Access automatically adjust the width of a field or column so that it can hold the widest entry. This neat feature is called *AutoFit*. To use AutoFit, simply double-click the right edge of the column or field you wish to adjust.

4 Scroll to the right until the Address field is displayed. Double-click the right edge of the Address field name to automatically adjust its width.

AutoFit automatically adjusts the width of the Address field so that it is wide enough to display its longest entry.

Unless you are working with a table that contains several memo fields with lots of text, you will probably want to stick with the default row height. The procedure for adjusting the height of a row is almost the same as adjusting the width of a column—simply click and drag the bottom of any record's row heading.

5 Move the pointer to the record selection area and carefully position the pointer between any two records, until it changes to a ✛.

Once the pointer appears as a ✛ you can adjust the row height to make it smaller or wider.

6 Click and hold the mouse button and drag the line down until the row height doubles, as shown in Figure 3-12, then release the mouse button.

The height of all the rows in the table is doubled, as shown in Figure 3-13.

Splendid! In just one lesson you've learned how to adjust the width of columns and the height of rows in a datasheet.

QUICK REFERENCE

TO ADJUST THE WIDTH OF A COLUMN:

- DRAG THE COLUMN HEADER'S RIGHT BORDER TO THE LEFT OR RIGHT.

OR...

- RIGHT-CLICK THE COLUMN HEADER(S), SELECT COLUMN WIDTH FROM THE SHORTCUT MENU, AND ENTER THE COLUMN WIDTH.

OR...

- SELECT THE COLUMN HEADER(S), SELECT FORMAT → COLUMN WIDTH FROM THE MENU, AND ENTER THE COLUMN WIDTH.

TO ADJUST THE HEIGHT OF A ROW:

- DRAG THE ROW HEADER'S BOTTOM BORDER UP OR DOWN.

OR...

- RIGHT-CLICK THE ROW HEADER(S), SELECT ROW HEIGHT FROM THE SHORTCUT MENU, AND ENTER THE ROW HEIGHT.

OR...

- SELECT THE ROW HEADER(S), SELECT FORMAT → ROW HEIGHT FROM THE SHORTCUT MENU AND ENTER THE ROW HEIGHT.

TO AUTOMATICALLY ADJUST THE WIDTH OF A COLUMN OR ROW:

- DOUBLE-CLICK THE RIGHT BORDER OF THE COLUMN OR BOTTOM BORDER OF A ROW.

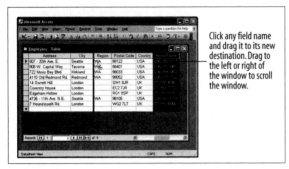

Click any field name and drag it to its new destination. Drag to the left or right of the window to scroll the window.

Figure 3-14. Moving a column to a new location in the datasheet.

When you first created a table, hopefully, you thought about its field order, so that most of the time your data will appear in the order you want. Sometimes, however, you may want to temporarily change the column order of a table.

This lesson explains how to move a field to a different location on the datasheet.

1 If it isn't already open, open the Employees table.

For this exercise, imagine that you have to call all the people listed in the Employees table. The only problem is that you can't view both the employee name fields and Home Phone fields at the same time. To fix this problem, you decide to move the Home Phone field next to the employee name fields.

Here then, is how to move a field or column:

2 Scroll to the right until you find the Home Phone field. Click the Home Phone field name and hold down the mouse button.

Now you have to drag the column to its new destination. If the destination is too far to the left or right to appear on the screen, drag the column to the left or right of the window—the datasheet will scroll in that direction.

3 Drag the Home Phone column to the far left of the window to scroll the datasheet to the left.

Make sure you keep holding down the mouse button! As you move the column, a bar moves between the columns, showing where the column will go when you release the mouse button, as shown in Figure 3-14.

4 Drag the column to the left of the Region field and release the mouse button to drop the column.

The Home Phone column and all its data moves next to the Region field.

QUICK REFERENCE

TO MOVE A COLUMN:

1. CLICK THE FIELD NAME OF THE COLUMN YOU WANT TO MOVE.

2. DRAG THE SELECTED COLUMN TO ITS NEW LOCATION.

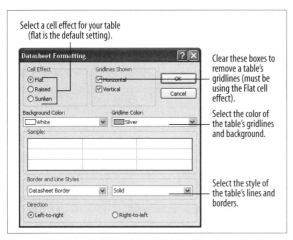

Figure 3-15. The Datasheet Formatting dialog box.

Select a cell effect for your table (flat is the default setting).

Clear these boxes to remove a table's gridlines (must be using the Flat cell effect).

Select the color of the table's gridlines and background.

Select the style of the table's lines and borders.

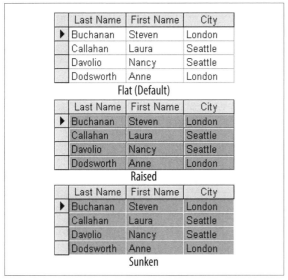

Flat (Default)

Raised

Sunken

Figure 3-16. Examples of the three cell effect options: Flat, Raised, and Sunken.

Unless you are the type of person who likes to frequently change their Windows desktop wallpaper or rearrange your bedroom furniture on a monthly basis, you can safely skip this lesson. Changing the appearance of cells in a table is purely cosmetic and is probably one of the *least* important things to know about Access.

Are you still there? Okay, here's how to give a table a three-dimensional look:

1 If it isn't already open, open the Employees table.

2 Select Format → Datasheet from the menu.

The Datasheet Formatting dialog box appears, as shown in Figure 3-15. You can select one of the 3-D effects from the Cell Effect area. See Figure 3-16 for an illustration of each of these cell effects.

You can also change the color of a table's *gridlines* (the lines that separate the rows and columns) and background as well as the border and line styles. Unless you have a compelling reason for doing so, you should normally leave these settings as they are.

If you don't want gridlines at all, set the Cell Effect to Flat and uncheck both of the "Gridlines Shown" boxes.

3 Select the Cell Effect options you want.

The Sample area of the dialog box displays how the Cell Effect settings will appear.

4 Click OK when you're finished changing the Cell Effect settings.

The datasheet changes according to your settings.

QUICK REFERENCE

TO CHANGE A DATASHEET'S GRIDLINE EFFECTS:

1. SELECT FORMAT → DATASHEET FROM THE MENU.

2. SELECT THE CELL EFFECT OPTION YOU WANT AND CLICK OK.

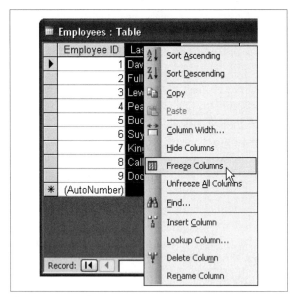

Figure 3-17. Freeze a field by right-clicking the field name and selecting Freeze Columns from the shortcut menu.

This field is frozen and will remain on the screen at all times.

Figure 3-18. Information in the frozen field remains on the screen as you scroll and move through the table.

Most tables have so much information that it won't all fit on the same screen. When this happens, you have to scroll through the datasheet to add, delete, modify, and view information. The problem with scrolling and viewing information in a large table is that it can be confusing when you can't see such important information as names or product numbers.

To overcome this problem, you can *freeze* a field so it stays in the same place while you scroll around the rest of the table.

1 If it isn't already open, open the Employees table.

Here's how to freeze a field.

2 Right-click the Last Name field name and select Freeze Columns from the shortcut menu, as shown in Figure 3-17.

The Last Name field is now frozen and will always remain visible as you move through the rest of the table. Try scrolling the table window to see for yourself.

3 Scroll the table to the right to view all its data.

Notice how the frozen Last Name field stays on the screen as you scroll the table, allowing you to always be able to see the last name for each record, as shown in Figure 3-18. Now you're ready to unfreeze the Last Name field.

4 Select Format → Unfreeze All Columns from the menu.

All the fields in the table are now unfrozen.

QUICK REFERENCE

TO FREEZE A COLUMN:
- RIGHT-CLICK THE COLUMN FIELD NAME YOU WANT TO FREEZE AND SELECT FREEZE COLUMNS FROM THE SHORTCUT MENU.

TO UNFREEZE A COLUMN:
- SELECT FORMAT → UNFREEZE ALL COLUMNS FROM THE MENU.

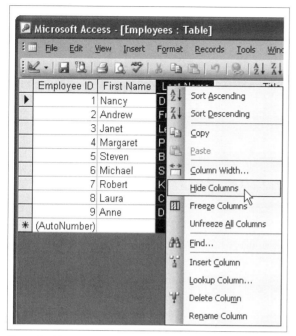

Figure 3-19. Hide a field by right-clicking the field name and selecting Hide Columns from the shortcut menu.

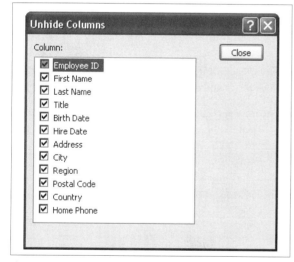

Figure 3-20. The Unhide Columns dialog box lets you check and uncheck the columns you wish to hide or display.

A hidden column or field is still in your table—you just can't see it. You can temporarily hide a column when you want to reduce the amount of information that is displayed on the screen. The procedure for hiding and unhiding a column is almost the same as freezing a column. Here it is:

1 If it isn't already open, open the Employees table.

Here's how to hide a field.

2 Right-click the Last Name field name and select Hide Columns from the shortcut menu, as shown in Figure 3-19.

The Last Name field is temporarily hidden from view.

You can select and hide several columns at once by clicking the first field name and then dragging to the last field name, but you will have to select Format → Hide Columns from the menu. You can't right-click any of the columns to display the shortcut menu without deselecting the columns.

When you want to make your hidden columns reappear try this:

3 Select Format → Unhide Columns from the menu.

The Unhide Columns dialog box appears, as shown in Figure 3-20. To redisplay a column, simply click the check box next to the field you want to see again.

4 Click the Last Name check box and click Close.

Poof! The Last Name field is redisplayed.

QUICK REFERENCE

TO HIDE A COLUMN:

- RIGHT-CLICK THE COLUMN FIELD NAME YOU WANT TO HIDE AND SELECT HIDE COLUMNS FROM THE SHORTCUT MENU.

TO UNHIDE A COLUMN:

- SELECT FORMAT → UNHIDE COLUMNS FROM THE MENU.

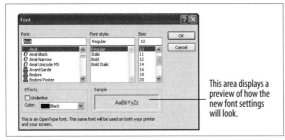

Figure 3-21. The Font dialog box.

This area displays a preview of how the new font settings will look.

Being a practical business program, Access displays its tables in a no-nonsense, easy-to-read font. You can change the font used to display table data. You can make the text appear darker and heavier (**bold**), slanted (*italics*), larger, and in a different typeface or color. Most people are satisfied with the default font used in tables, and if you're one of them, you may want to skip this lesson.

One very important note about changing a table's font: The font settings you make apply to the *entire table*, not just a particular cell, column, or row.

Here's how to change the font used in a table:

1 If it isn't already open, open the Employees table.

Once you have the table in Datasheet view you can change its font.

2 Select Format → Font from the menu.

The Font dialog box makes its entrance, as shown in Figure 3-21. To select a new font, simply find and click it from the Font list.

3 Scroll down the Font list until you find Times New Roman. Click the Times New Roman font.

The table data will now be displayed using the Times New Roman font.

⸱ NOTE ⸱ *When selecting fonts always try to use a TrueType font. TrueType fonts are the universal font standard used by Windows and they look great when printed. TrueType fonts have a double-T icon next to them.*

Next try changing the font size. Font sizes are measured in points (pt.) which are 1/72 of an inch. The larger the number of points, the larger the font. Here's how to change font size:

4 Select 11 from the Size list.

Notice that the Sample area of the Font dialog box displays what your new font setting will look like.

You've finished making changes to the font settings so move on to the next step.

5 Click OK to save your font-change settings and close the Font dialog box.

The Font dialog box closes and Access displays the table with the new font settings. Don't like your new font settings? Don't worry—you can always close a table without saving your layout changes.

6 Click on Close to close the Employees table, then click No so you don't save any of your layout changes.

There are several other font formatting options available in the Font dialog box. The purpose of this lesson isn't to go through all of them, but to explain how to use the Font dialog box. You can experiment with the different font formatting options to see what they do. Table 3-5 explains the different options in the Font dialog box.

Table 3-5. Font Formatting Options

Option	Description
Font	Displays and allows you to change the font from those installed on your computer.
Font style	Formats the style of the font: Regular (no emphasis), Italic, Bold, and Bold Italic.
Size	Displays and allows you to increase or decrease the size of the font.
Color	Displays and allows you to change the font color.
Underline	Allows you to add underlining to your fonts.

QUICK REFERENCE

TO OPEN THE FONT DIALOG BOX:

- SELECT FORMAT → FONT FROM THE MENU.

Chapter Three Review

Lesson Summary

Finding and Replacing Information

To Find Information: Click the Find button on the toolbar, or press Ctrl + F, or select Edit → Find from the menu. Enter the text you want to search for in the Find What text box, and then click the Find Next button until you find what you are looking for.

To Find and Replace Information: Select Edit → Replace from the menu, or press Ctrl + H. Enter the text you want to search for in the Find What text box, enter the text you want to replace the word with in the Replace With text box. Click the Find Next button to move to the first occurrence of the text and click the Replace button to replace the text or click the Find Next button to move to the next occurrence of the text. Repeat if there is more than one occurrence that you want to replace or click Replace All to search for and replace every occurrence of text in the table.

Sorting Records

To Sort Records by One Field: Click anywhere in the column you want to use to sort the list, and click either the Sort Ascending button or Sort Descending button on the toolbar.

Filtering by Selection

To Filter by Selection: Find the field value on which you want to base the filter, right-click the field value, and select Filter by Selection from the shortcut menu, or click the field value, then click the Filter by Selection button on the toolbar.

Filter Excluding the Selection: Right-click the field value you want to exclude and select Filter Excluding Selection from the shortcut menu.

To Remove a Filter: Right-click the filtered table and select Remove Filter/Sort from the shortcut menu, or click the Remove Filter button on the toolbar.

Filtering by Form

To Filter by Form: Click the Filter by Form button on the toolbar, click the text box for the field you want to filter, click the drop-down arrow, and select the value you want to use to filter the records. Repeat this step for each additional field you want to use to specify additional fil-

ter criteria—if you want to use Or criteria, click the Or tab at the bottom of the screen to specify the additional filter criteria. Click the Apply Filter button on the toolbar.

Creating an Advanced Filter

To Create an Advanced Filter: Select Records → Filter → Advanced Filter/Sort from the menu, and then double-click each field you want to include from the field list, or drag the field from the field list onto the design grid. In the design grid, enter any desired search criteria for the field in the Criteria row. Click the Apply Filter button on the toolbar.

Adjusting Row Height and Column Width

To Adjust the Width of a Column: Drag the column header's right border to the left or right. You can also right-click the column header(s), select Column Width from the shortcut menu, and enter the column width, or you can select the column header(s), select Format → Column Width from the menu, and enter the column width.

To Adjust the Height of a Row: Drag the row header's bottom border up or down. You can also right-click the row header(s), select Row Height from the shortcut menu, and enter the row height or select the row header(s), select Format → Row Height from menu and enter the row height.

To Automatically Adjust the Width of a Column or Row: Double-click the right border of the column or bottom border of a row.

Rearranging Columns

To Move a Column: Click the field name of the column you want to move, then drag the selected column to its new location.

Changing Gridline and Cell Effects

To Change a Datasheet's Gridline Effects: Select Format → Datasheet from the menu, select the Cell Effect option you want, and click OK.

Freezing a Field

To Freeze a Column: Right-click the column field name you want to freeze and select Freeze Columns from the shortcut menu.

To Unfreeze a Column: Select Format → Unfreeze All Columns from the menu.

Hiding a Column

To Hide a Column: Right-click the column field name you want to hide and select Hide Columns from the shortcut menu.

To Unhide a Column: Select Format → Unhide Columns from the menu.

Changing the Datasheet Font

To Open the Font Dialog Box: Select Format → Font from the menu.

Quiz

1. Which of the following is NOT a command to find specific words or phrases in a database?

   A. Click the Find button on the toolbar.

   B. Select Edit → Find from the menu.

   C. Click the Find button on the record navigation button area.

   D. Press Ctrl + F.

2. The only way to find and replace information in Microsoft Access is with an Update Query. (True or False?)

3. Which of the following is NOT true? (Select all that apply.)

   A. Filter by Selection finds all records that match a selected value.

   B. Filter Excluding Selection finds all records that do not match a selected value.

   C. Filter by Form lets you enter your filter criteria in a blank form and works well so long as you do not need to use multiple AND/OR criteria.

   D. An Advanced Filter is similar to creating a simple select query.

4. The criteria BETWEEN 1/1/99 AND 12/31/99 would:

   A. Display records between the dates 1/2/99 and 1/1/00.

   B. Display records whose dates equaled 1/1/99 or 12/31/99.

   C. Display records between the dates 1/1/99 and 12/31/99.

   D. Do nothing – this criteria has not been entered using the proper syntax.

5. In an Advanced Filter, which of the following are ways you can add fields to the design grid? (Select all that apply.)

   A. Select the field from the Add Field List on the toolbar.

   B. Double-click the field in the field list.

   C. Select Edit → Add Field from the menu, select the field from the list, and then click OK.

   D. Drag and drop the field from the field list to the design grid.

6. The only way you can rearrange the order of fields in a datasheet is by reordering the fields in table Design View. (True or False?)

7. Which of the following statements is NOT true?

   A. Bill Gates has more money than I do.

   B. When you *freeze* a field it stays in the same place while you scroll around the rest of the datasheet.

   C. You can temporarily hide a field or column if you want to reduce the amount of information that is displayed on the screen.

   D. To hide a field, select the field and click the Hide Column button on the toolbar.

8. How do you freeze a column or field in Microsoft Access?

A. Click anywhere in the column and click the Freeze button on the toolbar.

B. Place an ice cube on the column.

C. Right-click the column and select Freeze Columns from the shortcut menu.

D. Click anywhere in the column and select Edit → Freeze Column from the menu.

9. How do you filter by selection?

A. Find and double-click the value on which you want to base the filter.

B. Find the value on which you want to base the filter, right-click the field value, and select Filter by Selection from the shortcut menu.

C. Find and select the value on which you want to base the filter and select Tools → Filter by Selection from the menu.

D. This feature is found in Microsoft Excel, not Access.

10. What is a fast way to adjust the width of a column?

A. Double-click the left side of the column heading.

B. Double-click the right side of the column heading.

C. Right-click the left side of the column heading.

D. Select Tools → Adjust Column Width from the menu.

Homework

1. Start Microsoft Access and open the Homework database.

2. Open the Customers table in Datasheet View.

3. Click anywhere in the LastName field and find any customers with the last name "Eller."

4. With the cursor in the FirstName field, use the Find and Replace command to replace every instance of the first name "John" with the first name "Jack."

5. Use the Sort command to sort the Customers table by the LastName field, in ascending order.

6. Use the Filter by Selection command to display only records from the state of Texas (TX). **Hint:** Right-click any TX value in the State field and select Filter by Selection from the shortcut menu.

7. Remove the filter.

8. Use the Filter by Form command to display only those records from "TX" or "MN."

9. Create an Advanced Filter to display records for customers from "TX" or "MN" and who were born before 1/1/1950.

10. Close Microsoft Access.

Quiz Answers

1. C. There are buttons to add and navigate records in the record navigation area, however, there isn't a Find button.

2. False. An Update Query can find and replace information in Microsoft Access (more about that later) but so can the Find and Replace command, which you can use by selecting Edit → Replace or pressing Ctrl + H.

3. C. Filter by Form is great for using multiple AND/ OR criteria.

4. C. Displays records between the dates 1/1/99 and 12/31/99.

5. B and D. Both of these are ways to add fields to the design grid in an Advanced Filter.

6. False. You can rearrange the order of fields in a datasheet by simply selecting them and then dragging and dropping them to the new desired location.

7. D. To hide a field, simply right-click the column and select Hide Columns from the shortcut menu.

8. C. You can freeze a column by right-clicking the column and selecting Freeze Columns from the shortcut menu.

9. B. You can filter a selection by finding the value on which you want to base the filter, right-clicking the field value, and selecting Filter by Selection from the shortcut menu.

10. B. Double-clicking the right side of a column automatically adjusts its width.

CHAPTER 4

WORKING WITH TABLES AND FIELDS

CHAPTER OBJECTIVES:

Understand and modify a table's field properties, Lesson 4.1

Index a field and add a primary key to a table, Lessons 4.2—4.3

Insert, delete, and reorder fields, Lesson 4.4

Change a field's data type, Lesson 4.5

Format fields and adjust how information is displayed, Lessons 4.6—4.11

Set a default value and requirements for a field, Lessons 4.12—4.13

Specify data validation options for a field, Lesson 4.14

Create an input mask, lookup field, or value list, Lessons 4.15—4.17

CHAPTER TASK: MODIFY A TABLE'S FIELDS AND JOIN TWO RELATED TABLES

Prerequisites

- **How to use menus, toolbars, dialog boxes, and shortcut keystrokes.**
- **How to open and modify database objects.**
- **How to add and edit database records.**

Tables are by far the most important part of any database. Tables are where a database stores all of its information. All the other database objects—queries, forms, reports, pages, and macros—are merely tools to analyze, manipulate, and display the information stored in a table. Any of these other database objects are optional—but without tables, a database wouldn't be a database.

If you are interested in creating your own databases, this may be one of the most important chapters in the entire book. Why? Because, at their heart, the most useful and efficient databases use well-structured tables to store their information.

This chapter explains just about everything you will ever need to know about tables and fields: how to link two or more related tables, how to create indexes for faster performance, and how to create a *primary key field*, which uniquely identifies each record in a table. This chapter also explains how to change all the properties and settings for your tables' fields, such as how they are formatted and what kind of information they can store.

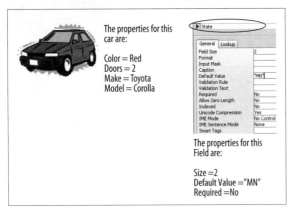

The properties for this car are:

Color = Red
Doors = 2
Make = Toyota
Model = Corolla

The properties for this Field are:

Size = 2
Default Value = "MN"
Required = No

Figure 4-1. A comparison of a car's properties with a field's properties.

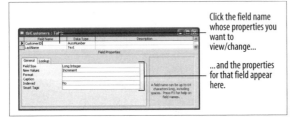

Click the field name whose properties you want to view/change...

...and the properties for that field appear here.

Figure 4-2. You need to be in Design view in order to view and change a table's field properties.

A *property* is an attribute that defines an object's appearance, behavior, or characteristics. For example, a car's properties would include its color, make and model, and shape. A property for a numeric field might be the number of decimal places displayed or the maximum number of characters a field can hold. See Figure 4-1, which illustrates the comparison.

Just about every object in Access—every heading on a report, every label on a form, every field in a table—has its own set of properties that you can view and change. This property concept might seem a little confusing at first, but it's something you have to learn if you want to become proficient at using Microsoft Access. Because you can almost always change object properties, you can also sometimes think of an object's properties as its settings.

Over half of this chapter is devoted to working with a table's field properties, so consider this your introduction to field properties and to properties in general.

1 **Start Microsoft Access, if necessary, and open the Lesson 4 database.**

To view and modify the Field Properties for a table, you first need to open the table in Design view.

2 **In the Database window, select the tblCustomers table and click the Design button.**

> **TIP**
>
> *Other ways to switch to Design view are to open the table and click the View button on the toolbar, or open the table and select View → Design View from the menu.*

As you can see in Figure 4-2, the table design window is broken into two sections. The top section contains the table's field names and the bottom section displays the properties for the selected field. Simply click the field name whose properties you want to view.

3 **Click the LastName field.**

The lower Field Properties section of the window displays the properties for the LastName field. To change a field property, simply click the property box you want to change and enter the new settings—simple.

Table 4-1 describes all the field properties. Don't worry if some of them seem confusing—you will get a lot of practice adjusting each and every one of these properties in this chapter. It's important to note that certain types of fields have their own sets of properties. For example, number fields have a Decimal Places property while text fields do not.

Table 4-1. Important Field Properties

Field Property	Description
Field Size	**Text fields:** The maximum number of characters (up to 255) that can be entered in the field. The default setting is 50.
	Number / Currency fields: Stores the number as a Byte, Integer, Long Integer, Single, Double, or Replication ID. The default setting is Long Integer.
Format	How the data in the field will be displayed on the screen.
Input Mask	Creates a format or pattern in which data must be entered.
Decimal Places	The number of decimal places in Number and Currency fields.
Caption	A label for the field that will appear on forms. If you don't enter a caption, Access will use the field name as the caption.
Default Value	A value that Access enters automatically in the field for new records.
Validation Rule	An expression that limits the values that can be entered in the field.
Validation Text	The error message that appears when an incorrect or restricted value is entered in a field with a validation rule.
Required	Specify whether or not a value must be entered in the field. The default is No.
Allow Zero Length	Specify whether or not the field allows zero-length text strings (a string containing no characters). Zero-length text strings are useful if you must enter data in a field, but no data exists. For example, if a Social Security field requires data, but you don't know the social security number, you would enter a zero-length text string in the field. To enter a zero-length text string type "" in the cell. The cell will appear empty. The default is No.
Indexed	Specify whether or not you want to index the field to speed up searches and sorts performed on the field. The default is No.

QUICK REFERENCE

TO DISPLAY A TABLE IN DESIGN VIEW:

• OPEN THE TABLE AND CLICK THE VIEW BUTTON ON THE TOOLBAR.

OR...

• IN THE DATABASE WINDOW, CLICK THE TABLES ICON IN THE OBJECTS BAR, SELECT THE TABLE, AND CLICK THE DESIGN BUTTON.

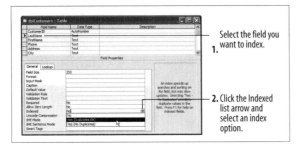

Figure 4-3. Adding an Index to a table's LastName field.

Just like an index in a book, when you index a field, it helps Access find and sort information quickly—especially in large tables. You can index any field in a table to dramatically speed up queries and sorts. When you sort or query a large table using an indexed field, Access finds or sorts the information by consulting the index instead of sifting through the entire table.

Here are some more important notes about indexes:

- Since indexes speed up searching and sorting, you should index the fields you frequently use to search or sort. For example, if you often search for specific last names, you should create an index for the LastName field.
- Don't index *too* many of a table's fields. The more fields you index, the slower your searches and sorts will be—defeating the entire purpose of an index. Only index the fields you use to search and sort data.
- Any field can be indexed *except* memo, OLE, and hyperlink fields.
- Primary key fields are indexed automatically (we'll discuss primary keys more in future lessons).
- If you choose, indexes can prevent duplicate entries in your table (for example, if you don't want to allow two customers to have the same social security number).

This lesson will give you some practice adding indexes to your tables.

1 Make sure you have the tblCustomers table open in Design view.

Indexing a field is a fairly simple operation. First you need to click the name of the field you want to index. The LastName field is a great index candidate because it is frequently used to find and sort information.

2 Click the LastName field.

The blinking cursor should appear in the LastName field. Here's how to index the selected field.

3 In the Field Properties section, click the Indexed list arrow, as shown in Figure 4-3.

The Indexed list gives you three choices:

- **No:** The field is not indexed. This is the default setting.
- **Yes (Duplicates OK):** The field is indexed and Access will allow records in this field to have the same value.
- **Yes (No Duplicates):** The field is indexed and Access won't allow records in this field to have the same value (for example, if you don't want to allow two customers to have the same social security number).

Most of the time you will want to choose the "Yes (Duplicates OK)" option, since some people may have the same last name.

4 Select the Yes (Duplicates OK) option from the list.

Most of the time Access creates the index in a matter of seconds. If you have a huge table with thousands of records, it will take longer to create the index.

Let's try indexing another field. Since you do a lot of sorting by Zip Codes, let's index the ZipCode field as well.

5 Click the ZipCode field and then click the Indexed list arrow.

Since people can (and do) live in the same Zip Code, you want to select the "Yes (Duplicates OK)" option.

6 Select the Yes (Duplicates OK) option from the list.

You don't need to index any of the other fields in this table since you don't use them as frequently in your sorts and queries. You do need to save the changes you've made to your table, however.

7 Click the Save button on the toolbar to save the changes you've made to the table.

If you need to remove an index from a field, select the field, click the Indexed list arrow, and select the "No" option. Access will delete the field's index.

QUICK REFERENCE

TO INDEX A FIELD:

1. MAKE SURE THE TABLE IS OPEN IN DESIGN VIEW AND THEN CLICK THE FIELD YOU WANT TO INDEX.

2. CLICK THE INDEXED BOX.

3. CLICK THE LIST ARROW AND SELECT ONE OF THE FOLLOWING:

- YES (DUPLICATES OK) IF YOU WANT TO ALLOW MULTIPLE RECORDS TO HAVE THE SAME DATA IN THIS FIELD.

- YES (NO DUPLICATES) IF YOU WANT TO ENSURE THAT NO TWO RECORDS HAVE THE SAME DATA IN THIS FIELD.

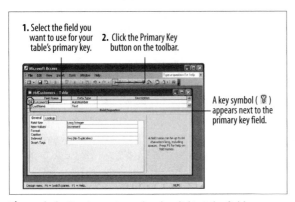

1. Select the field you want to use for your table's primary key.

2. Click the Primary Key button on the toolbar.

A key symbol (🔑) appears next to the primary key field.

Figure 4-4. Create a primary key by clicking the field you want to use as the primary field and then clicking the Primary Key button on the toolbar.

A *primary key* is a special kind of indexed field that uniquely identifies each record in a table. When you think about primary key fields, think *unique*—each primary key value must be the only one of its kind in a table. A customer ID or invoice number would be two good examples of fields that could be used as a table's primary key.

Here are some things you need to know about primary keys:

- A table can have only *one* primary key.
- The values in the primary key fields must be unique. For this reason, many people use an *AutoNumber field* as their primary key. AutoNumber fields automatically add a new, unique number to each record in a table.
- Every table you create should have a primary key because it helps keep your data organized and easy to work with. In fact, if you create a table without a primary key, Access will ask if you want to add one. If you answer Yes, Access will create an AutoNumber field at the beginning of the table and set it as the primary key.
- The primary key field is automatically indexed.
- Yes/No, OLE, and hyperlink fields can't be used as the primary key.
- The primary key is normally a single field, but two or more fields can act together as the primary key, so long as their combined values are unique. Such multi-field keys are usually difficult and confusing to work with, however.
- Primary keys are especially important in creating relationships between tables.

So what makes a good primary key field? The most important consideration for a primary key is its *uniqueness*. A primary key field must always be different in every record, so you might be able to use a Customer ID, Invoice Number, or Social Security Number field as your table's primary key.

If a table doesn't have a unique field that is suitable as the primary key (and most tables don't), you can add an AutoNumber field to your table. The AutoNumber field will automatically add a new, unique number to each of the records in a table.

This lesson explains how to add a primary key to a table.

1 Make sure the tblCustomers table is open in Design view.

First you need to click the name of the field you want to use as your primary key. If your table doesn't have a natural primary key field, you will need to add one. AutoNumber fields make great primary keys.

For this exercise we'll use the CustomerID AutoNumber field as the table's primary key.

2 Click the CustomerID field.

Now you can set the CustomerID field as the table's primary key.

3 Click the 🔑 Primary Key button on the toolbar.

Another way to set the primary key is to right-click the field you want to use as the primary key and select Primary Key from the shortcut menu.

A key symbol (🔑) appears next to the CustomerID field, as shown in Figure 4-4, indicating that it is the table's primary key. Notice that Access also sets the Indexed field to "Yes (No Duplicates)." Access automatically indexes the CustomerID field so that sorts and queries using the field will be faster and so that you cannot enter duplicate values in the field.

4 Click the Save button on the toolbar to save the changes you've made to the table.

QUICK REFERENCE

TO ADD A PRIMARY KEY TO A TABLE:

1. DISPLAY THE TABLE IN DESIGN VIEW, AND CLICK THE FIELD THAT YOU WANT TO SET AS THE PRIMARY KEY. IF SUCH A FIELD DOESN'T EXIST, YOU WILL HAVE TO CREATE IT.

   AUTONUMBER FIELDS MAKE GREAT PRIMARY KEYS.

2. CLICK THE PRIMARY KEY BUTTON ON THE TOOLBAR.

   OR...

   RIGHT-CLICK THE FIELD YOU WANT TO USE AS THE PRIMARY KEY AND SELECT PRIMARY KEY FROM THE SHORTCUT MENU.

tblCustomers : Table

Field Name	Data Typ
LastName	Text
MI	Text
FirstName	Text
Phone	Text
Address	Text
City	Text
State	Text
ZipCode	Text
DOB	Text
SSN	Text

General | Lookup

Field Size	255
Format	
Input Mask	
Caption	

tblCustomers : Table

Field Name	Data Typ
LastName	Text
MI	Text
FirstName	Text
Phone	Text
Address	Text
City	Text
State	Text
ZipCode	Text
DOB	Text
SSN	Text

General | Lookup

Field Size	255
Format	
Input Mask	
Caption	

1. Select the row you want to move by clicking its row selector...

2. ...and then drag the row to a new location.

Figure 4-5. The procedure for changing the order of fields in a table.

You can insert, delete, and reorder fields in your tables in Design view. Remember that in Design view, for tables, each row corresponds to a field. You add a field by inserting a new row and delete a field by deleting its corresponding row.

1 If necessary, open the Lesson 4 database.

In order to be able to insert, delete, or reorder fields, you must be in Design view.

2 If necessary, select the tblCustomers table and click the Design button in the document window.

The table appears in Design view. To insert a new field, you must first click the row selector of the field that will appear below the new field you want to insert.

3 Click the ▓ row selector for the Phone field. Press Insert to add a blank field.

Now all you have to do is give the new row a name and specify its data type.

4 Click the Field Name box for the new row and type MI.

You've added a new field. Now let's see how to rearrange the order of fields in a table.

5 Click the ▓ MI row selector to select the MI field.

Now you can move the selected MI row.

6 Click and drag the ▓ MI row selector down below the City row, as shown in Figure 4-5.

Finally, here's how to delete a field:

7 With the MI field still selected, press Delete to delete the selected field.

Access deletes the MI field from the tblCustomers table.

Great! In a very short lesson you've learned three new table skills.

QUICK REFERENCE

TO INSERT A ROW:

1. CLICK THE ▓ ROW SELECTOR FOR THE FIELD THAT WILL BE BELOW THE NEW FIELD YOU WANT TO INSERT.

2. PRESS INSERT.

TO CHANGE THE ORDER OF FIELDS IN A TABLE:

1. CLICK THE ▓ ROW SELECTOR FOR THE FIELD YOU WANT TO MOVE.

2. CLICK AND DRAG THE SELECTED ROW TO THE DESIRED LOCATION.

TO DELETE A FIELD FROM A TABLE:

• CLICK THE ▓ ROW SELECTOR FOR THE FIELD AND PRESS DELETE.

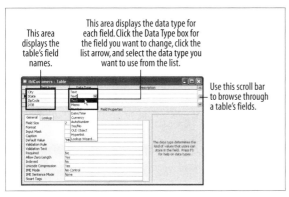

This area displays the table's field names.

This area displays the data type for each field. Click the Data Type box for the field you want to change, click the list arrow, and select the data type you want to use from the list.

Use this scroll bar to browse through a table's fields.

Figure 4-6. A field's data type determines what type of information the field can store.

Because there are so many different types of data, Access offers several different types of fields. A field's *data type* determines the type of information that can be stored in a field, as shown in Figure 4-6. Table 4-2 lists the various data types available in Access. A field's data type helps prevent data-entry errors because it restricts what type of information you can enter in a field. For example, you cannot enter text in a number data-type field.

If you've been working with Access for a while, you probably already know some of this stuff. Just consider this lesson a quick review.

1 Make sure the tblCustomers table is open in Design view.

First you need to select the field whose data type you want to change.

2 Click the DOB field.

The blinking cursor should appear in the DOB field name. Since the DOB field stores the employee's date of birth, it should be a Date/Time field instead of a Text field. Here's how to change a field's data type:

3 Click the Data Type box next to the DOB field.

A list arrow appears on the right side of the DOB Data Type box.

4 Click the list arrow and select Date/Time from the list.

The DOB field will now only accept date and time information. The new Date/Time data type also makes your database more flexible and powerful because now you can sort birthdays by date or use a person's birthday in a calculation—for example, to determine a person's age.

Once you have finished modifying a table, you have to save your changes.

5 Click the Save button on the toolbar to save your changes.

> **TIP** Other ways to save a database object are to press Ctrl + S, or select File → Save from the menu.

Table 4-2. Data Types

Data Type	Example	Description
Text	Legal Name: John Doe	Stores text, numbers, or a combination of both, up to 255 characters long. Text fields are the most common of all data types.
Memo	Notes: Sally displays a high amount of…	Stores long text entries—up to 64,000 characters long (the equivalent of 18 pages of text!). Use memo fields to store notes or anything else that requires a lot of space.
Number	Age: 31	Stores numbers that can be used in calculations.
Date/Time	Birthday: April 7, 1969	Stores dates, times, or both.
Currency	Price: $84.95	Stores numbers and symbols that represent money.

Table 4-2. Data Types (Continued)

Data Type	Example	Description
AutoNumber	Invoice Number: 187001	Automatically fills in a unique number for each record. Many tables often contain an AutoNumber field that is also used as their primary key.
Yes/No	Employed?: Yes	Stores only one of two values, such as Yes or No, True or False, etc.
OLE Object	Photo: 	Stores objects created in other programs such as a graphic, Excel spreadsheet, or Word document.
Hyperlink	Web Site: www.amazon.com	Stores clickable links to files on your computer, on the network, or to Web pages on the Internet.
Lookup Wizard	Purpose of Trip: Airborne FedEx UPS	A wizard that helps you create a field whose values are selected from another table, query, or a preset list of values.

QUICK REFERENCE

TO CHANGE THE DATA TYPE FOR A FIELD:

1. DISPLAY THE TABLE IN DESIGN VIEW.

2. CLICK THE FIELD'S DATA TYPE BOX, CLICK THE LIST ARROW, AND SELECT THE DATA TYPE.

Using Field Descriptions

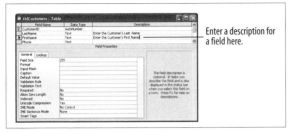

Enter a description for a field here.

Figure 4-7. A field's description lets you provide your database users with onscreen prompts and instructions.

The description for a field appears in the Status bar whenever the field is selected.

Figure 4-8. A field's description appears in the Status bar whenever you select the field.

Descriptions make your database fields easier to fill out and use by providing users with onscreen instructions and help. Whenever a user selects a field, anything typed in that field's Description box will appear in the Status bar. There really isn't anything to adding a description to a field—just type the text you want to appear in the field's Description box.

1 Make sure the tblCustomers table is open in Design view.

First you need to select the field where you want to add a description.

2 Click the Description box for the LastName field.

Now you can add a description to the LastName field that will appear in the Status bar whenever the Last-Name field is selected.

3 Type Enter the Customer's Last Name.

Let's add a description to the FirstName field as well.

4 Click the Description box for the FirstName field and type Enter the Customer's First Name.

Your table should look like Figure 4-7. Let's see how the new descriptions look.

5 Click the Save button on the toolbar to save your changes, then click the View button to display the table in Datasheet view.

You will need to scroll to the right to see the descriptions.

6 Click anywhere in the LastName field.

The Status bar displays the field's description, as shown in Figure 4-8.

QUICK REFERENCE

TO ADD A DESCRIPTION TO A FIELD:

• MAKE SURE THE TABLE IS DISPLAYED IN DESIGN VIEW, CLICK THE FIELD'S DESCRIPTION BOX, AND TYPE THE DESCRIPTION.

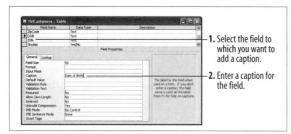

Figure 4-9. Adding a caption to a field.

Figure 4-10. The same fields with and without captions.

Think of the Caption property as a field's pseudonym or stage name. When you create forms and reports, Access uses the field's Field Name as the field's heading. When you add a caption to a field, however, it appears as the heading for the field instead of the field name. Captions are useful when you want to provide more detailed headings for your field names. For example, instead of displaying the rather ambiguous DOB field name, you could add a more meaningful "Date of Birth" caption to the DOB field to make your forms and reports easier to read and understand. The original DOB field name is not affected in any way.

This lesson explains how to add a Caption to a field.

1 Click the View button on the toolbar to open the table in Design view.

The tblCustomers table contains two unclearly labeled fields that could use captions: the DOB (date of birth) and SSN (social security number) fields. You probably already know the first step by now—click the name of the field where you want to add the caption.

2 Click the DOB field.

Now you can add a more meaningful caption to the DOB field that will appear as the field's heading.

3 Click the Caption box in the Field Properties section and type Date of Birth.

Your table should look like Figure 4-9. Now let's add a caption to the SSN field.

4 Click the SSN field, click the Caption box in the Field Properties section, and type Social Security No.

Let's see how the new captions look.

5 Click the Save button on the toolbar to save your changes, then click the View button to display the table in Datasheet view.

You will need to scroll to the right to see the captions. Figure 4-10 shows the same fields with and without captions.

Changing the Field Size

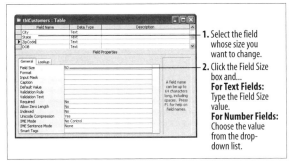

1. Select the field whose size you want to change.

2. Click the Field Size box and...
   For Text Fields: Type the Field Size value.
   For Number Fields: Choose the value from the drop-down list.

Figure 4-11. The Field Size property determines the maximum number of characters the field will accept.

The *Field Size* property determines the maximum size of information that can be stored in a text or number field. For example, if you set the size of a text field to 2, you could enter "MN" but not "Minnesota." There are several reasons why you would want to change the size of a field:

- Changing the field size reduces data-entry errors.
- Access can process smaller field sizes more quickly.
- Smaller field sizes require less hard-drive storage space.

Field sizes work a little differently for text and number fields. In text fields, the Field Size property determines the maximum number of characters the field can accept, as shown in Figure 4-11. In numbers fields, the Field Size property determines what type of number the field will accept.

In this lesson you will change the size of a table's fields.

1 If necessary, open the Lesson 4 database and double-click the tblCustomers table.

In order to change the field size, you must be in Design view.

2 Click the View button on the toolbar.

The table appears in Design view. You probably already know the first step by now—click the name of the field whose property you want to change.

3 Click the State field.

Now change the State's field size.

4 Click the Field Size box in the Field Properties section and type 2.

The State field can now only accept a maximum of two characters. Users will now have to enter standard two-digit state abbreviations.

Let's try changing the size of another field.

5 Click the ZipCode field.

Notice that the ZipCode's field size is set at 50. We probably won't have any 50-digit Zip Codes for at least a few more years, so you can safely change the field size to a smaller number.

6 Click the Field Size box in the Field Properties section and type 11.

The ZipCode field will now accept no more than 11 digits.

⸱ NOTE ⸱   *Be very careful when you're changing the Field Size of a field that already contains data. Access will truncate or delete data that is larger than the new field size.*

7 Click the Save button on the toolbar to save your changes, click Yes to confirm the change, and close the table.

If you are working with a number field, the Field Size property determines the type and size of the number that a field will accept, as shown in Table 4-3.

Table 4-3. Available Number Field Sizes

Heading	Number Range	Decimal Places	Storage Size
Byte	0 to 255	None	1 byte
Integer	-32,768 to 32,767	None	2 bytes
Long Integer	-2.1×10^{38} to 2.1×10^{38}	None	4 bytes

Table 4-3. Available Number Field Sizes (Continued)

Heading	Number Range	Decimal Places	Storage Size
Single	-3.4×10^{38} to 3.4×10^{38}	7	4 bytes
Double	-1.8×10^{308} to 1.8×10^{308}	15	8 bytes
Replication ID	N/A	N/A	16 bytes

QUICK REFERENCE

TO CHANGE THE FIELD SIZE:

1. MAKE SURE THE TABLE IS DISPLAYED IN DESIGN VIEW.

2. SELECT THE FIELD WHOSE SIZE YOU WANT TO CHANGE.

3. CLICK THE FIELD SIZE BOX IN THE FIELD PROPERTIES SECTION.

4. FOR TEXT FIELDS: TYPE THE FIELD SIZE VALUE.

   FOR NUMBER FIELDS: CHOOSE THE VALUE FROM THE LIST.

Formatting Number, Currency, and Date/Time Fields

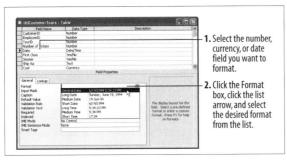

1. Select the number, currency, or date field you want to format.

2. Click the Format box, click the list arrow, and select the desired format from the list.

Figure 4-12. The Format property determines how values are displayed in a field.

A field's Format property changes how information appears in the field, not how the data is actually stored in the field. For example, a date field could be formatted to display the same value as 6/10/2000; Saturday, June 10, 2000; or 10-Jun-00. Each field type has its own set of formats. For example, number fields have a different set of formats than date/time or text fields.

This lesson explains how to format number, currency and date/time fields. There are two ways to format a number, currency and date/time field:

- By selecting a ready-made format from the Format list (the easy way).
- By typing a series of formatting characters in the Format box (the hard way).

Hopefully, the ready-made formats listed in Table 4-4 will be all you will ever need to format your fields. This lesson explains how to format number, currency, and date/time fields by selecting a ready-made format.

1 Double-click the tblCustomerTours table.

Let's take a look at how the number and date fields in this table are currently formatted. Notice that the Cost currency field has two decimal places and that the Date field displays its dates in the 1/1/2000 format.

⁝ NOTE ⁝ *If you haven't installed any Year 2000 updates, such as the Microsoft Office 97 Service Pack 2, your dates may be displayed in 1/1/00 format. If this is the case, you should visit the Microsoft Office Update Web site, located at www.officeup-date.com, and download Microsoft Office 97 Service Pack 2.*

2 Switch to Design view by clicking the ⬛ ⬝ View button on the toolbar.

Now you can change the formats of the fields in the tblCustomerTours table.

3 Click the Date field and click the Format box in the Field Properties section.

A list arrow appears in the Format box. You can format this field the easy way by clicking the arrow to select from a list of ready-made number formats, as shown in Figure 4-12.

4 Click the list arrow and select Medium Date.

The Date field will now display its dates in 1-Jan-00 format instead of the 1/1/2000 format.

You can also specify how many decimal places you want numbers in a field to display. To change the number of decimal places in a number field, you enter the number of decimal places you want displayed in the *Decimal Places* box.

5 Click the Cost field, click the Decimal Places list arrow, and select 0.

Now the Cost field will not display any decimal places, and Access will round any decimals equal to or greater than five to the next number.

⁝ NOTE ⁝ *Depending on the field property, the Property Update Options button may appear next to the Cost field. By default, the Decimal Places property only affects the number of decimal places that are displayed—not how many decimal places are stored. If you want to change this, click the Property Update Options button and select "Update Decimal Places everywhere Cost is used" from the menu.*

You'll need to save the table before you can view your new Format settings.

⁝ NOTE ⁝ *The Decimal Places property setting has no effect if the Format property is blank or is set to General Number.*

6 Click the Save button on the toolbar to save your changes.

Now let's see how the fields look with their new formats.

7 Switch to Datasheet view by clicking the View button on the toolbar.

Notice the Date field now displays dates in a 1-Jan-00 format and the Cost field no longer has any decimal places.

Below you will find a list of ready-made number, currency, and date/time formats that you can choose from. These standard formats should be all you'll ever need—if not, take a look at Lesson 4-10: *Formatting Number, Currency, and Date/Time Fields by Hand.*

Table 4-4. Number, Currency, and Date/Time Formats

Number Format	Example	Date/Time Format	Example
General Number	1234.567	General Date	6/10/2000 6:35:21 PM
Currency	$1,234.57	Long Date	Saturday, June 10, 2000
Euro	€1,234.57	Medium Date	10-Jun-00
Fixed	1234.57	Short Date	6/10/2000
Standard	1,234.57	Long Time	6:35:21 PM
Percent	123456.70%	Medium Time	6:35 PM
Scientific	1.23E+03	Short Time	18:35

QUICK REFERENCE

TO FORMAT NUMBER AND CURRENCY FIELDS:

1. MAKE SURE THE TABLE IS DISPLAYED IN DESIGN VIEW AND CLICK THE FIELD YOU WANT TO FORMAT.

2. CLICK THE FORMAT BOX IN THE FIELD PROPERTIES SECTION.

3. CLICK THE LIST ARROW AND SELECT A NUMBER FORMAT.

TO CHANGE THE NUMBER OF DECIMAL PLACES:

1. MAKE SURE THE TABLE IS DISPLAYED IN DESIGN VIEW AND THEN CLICK THE FIELD YOU WANT TO FORMAT.

2. CLICK THE DECIMAL PLACES BOX IN THE FIELD PROPERTIES SECTION.

3. CLICK THE LIST ARROW AND SELECT THE NUMBER OF DECIMAL PLACES YOU WANT TO DISPLAY.

Formatting Number, Currency, and Date/Time Fields by Hand

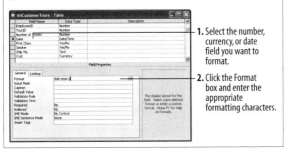

1. Select the number, currency, or date field you want to format.

2. Click the Format box and enter the appropriate formatting characters.

Figure 4-13. The Format property determines how values are displayed in a field. You can create your own custom number, currency, or date formats by entering the appropriate formatting characters.

If none of the ready-made number, currency, or date/time formats meet your needs, you can format your number, currency, and date/time fields the old-fashioned way—by hand. Formatting fields by hand is a laborious and confusing process—you tell Access how you want the field to be formatted by typing the appropriate formatting characters in the Format box. On the other hand, manually formatting a number, currency, or date/time field gives you complete flexibility on how the field displays its information.

In this lesson you will learn how to format number, currency, and date/time fields by hand.

1 Click the Design button on the toolbar to switch to Design view.

Now you need to click the field you want to format.

2 Click the Date field.

This time we will specify our own date/time format instead of using one of the Format Property box's ready-made data formats. Formatting number, currency, and date/time fields by hand isn't exactly a difficult process, but you will probably need to use Table 4-5 and Table 4-6 on the next page in order to know which formatting characters to enter.

3 Click the Format box in the Field Properties section and type ddd mmm d.

Your table should look like Figure 4-13. This will display the date in Sun Mar 8 format. Look at Table 4-5 for a description of the characters you just entered

4 Click the Save button on the toolbar to save your changes, and then switch to Datasheet view by clicking the View button on the toolbar.

Notice the Date field now displays its days using the Date format you specified.

5 Close the tblCustomerTours table.

Use the characters in the following table when you want to format number, currency, or date/time characters by hand. You can mix and match any of the following characters. For example, you could add "mmmm" (full name of month) to "yy" (last two digits of the year) to get "January 00."

Table 4-5. Date/Time Formatting Characters

Character	Description	Format	Display
:	Time separator	h:nn	8:45
/	Date separator	m/d/yy	10/8/00
-	Date separator	m-d-yy	10-8-00
d	Day in one or two numeric digits	m/d/yy	10/8/00
dd	Day in two numeric digits	m/dd/yy	10/08/00
ddd	First three letters of the weekday	ddd, m/d/yy	Sun, 3/8/00
dddd	Full name of the weekday	dddd, m/d/yy	Sunday, 3/8/00
m	Month in one or two digits	m/d/yy	3/15/00
mm	Month in two digits	mm/dd/yy	03/15/00
mmm	First three letters of the month	mmm-d-yy	Mar-15-00
mmmm	Full name of the month	mmmm d, yyyy	March 15, 2000

Table 4-5. Date/Time Formatting Characters (Continued)

Character	Description	Format	Display
yy	Last two digits of the year	m/d/yy	3/15/00
yyyy	Full year	mmmm d, yyyy	March 15, 2000
h	Hour in one or two digits	h:n	8:45
hh	Hour in two digits	hh:nn	08:45
nn	Minute in two digits	hh:nn	13:09
ss	Second in two digits	hh:nn:ss	10:45:07
AM/PM	Twelve-hour clock (uppercase)	hh:nn AM/PM	08:45 AM
am/pm	Twelve-hour clock (lowercase)	hh:nn am/pm	08:45 am

Table 4-6. Number Formatting Symbols

Character	Description	Data	Format	Display
#	Display a digit or nothing	50	#	50
0	Display a digit or 0	50	#.00	50.00
.	Display a decimal separator	50	#.	50.
,	Display thousands separator	5000	#,###	5,000
$	Display the $ currency symbol	50	$#.00	$50.00
%	Multiply the value by 100 and add a percent sign	0.5	#%	50%
E-, E+, e-, e+	Scientific notation	500000	#.00E+00	5.00E+05

QUICK REFERENCE

TO MANUALLY FORMAT A DATE/TIME, NUMBER, OR CURRENCY FIELD:

1. MAKE SURE THE TABLE IS DISPLAYED IN DESIGN VIEW AND CLICK THE FIELD YOU WANT TO FORMAT.

2. CLICK THE FORMAT BOX IN THE FIELD PROPERTIES SECTION.

3. ENTER THE APPROPRIATE FORMATTING CHARACTERS OR SYMBOLS FOR HOW YOU WANT THE DATE OR NUMBER TO BE FORMATTED.

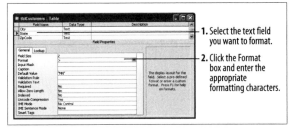

Figure 4-14. The Format property determines how values are displayed in a field. You can determine how text is displayed by entering the appropriate formatting characters.

Just like number, currency, and date/time fields, a text field's Format property changes how information appears in the field. The Format property only changes how data is displayed on screen, not how the data is actually stored in the field.

Unfortunately, unlike number fields, text fields don't have any ready-made settings built into them and must be formatted manually. Luckily, text fields don't have nearly as many formatting options as number, currency, and date/time fields. The most common of these text formatting characters are the *greater than symbol* (>), which makes all text in the field appear in uppercase, and the *less than symbol* ( ), which makes all text in the field appear in lowercase, regardless of how it was entered. In both cases, Access actually stores the data *exactly as it was typed*.

This lesson will give you some practice formatting text fields.

1 If necessary, open the Lesson 4 database.

Now let's open the tblCustomers table.

2 Double-click the tblCustomers table.

First let's enter a sample record using your own personal information.

3 Click the ⨀ New Record button on the Record Navigation bar, located at the bottom of the table window.

Access inserts a new blank record at the bottom of the table.

4 Press the Tab key and then enter your information into the new record. When you reach the State field, enter the state abbreviation in lowercase letters.

Move on to the next step when you have finished entering your record into the table.

5 Click the View button on the toolbar to display the table in Design view.

Access displays the tblCustomers table in Design view. First you have to click the name of the field you want to format.

6 Click the State field.

You can make sure that the contents of the State field are always capitalized by adding a greater than symbol (>) to the Format box.

7 Click the Format box in the Field Properties section and type a greater than symbol (>).

Your table should look like Figure 4-14. Access will display the contents of the State field in uppercase, even if it was entered in lowercase.

NOTE *Remember that the Format property only changes how data is displayed onscreen, not how the data is actually stored in the field.*

8 Click the Save button on the toolbar to save your changes.

Now let's see how the State field looks with its new format.

9 Switch to Datasheet view by clicking the View button on the toolbar.

Notice that the lowercase state abbreviation you entered back in Step 2 now appears in uppercase.

Table 4-7 contains formatting symbols for text fields.

Table 4-7. General and Text Formatting Symbols

Character	Description	Text	Format	Display
!	Aligns text from the right	Hello	!	Hello
<	Lowercase	Hello	<	hello
>	Uppercase	Hello	>	HELLO
"ABC"	Always displays quoted text	4	&" oz."	4 oz.
@	Character is required	5558000	@@@-@@@@	555-8000
*	Fill available space with next character	Alert	&*!	Alert!!!!!!!!!!
[color]	Displays value in color	Hello	[red]	Hello

QUICK REFERENCE

TO MANUALLY FORMAT A TEXT FIELD:

1. MAKE SURE THE TABLE IS DISPLAYED IN DESIGN VIEW AND CLICK THE TEXT FIELD YOU WANT TO FORMAT.

2. CLICK THE FORMAT BOX IN THE FIELD PROPERTIES SECTION.

3. ENTQR THE APPROPRIATE TEXT FORMATTING SYMBOLS.

Setting a Default Value

1. Select the field.

2. Enter its Default Value here.

A value that is automatically entered in this field for new records

Figure 4-15. A field's default value is automatically entered in the field whenever you add a new record.

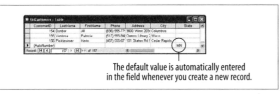

The default value is automatically entered in the field whenever you create a new record.

Figure 4-16. The default value for the State field automatically appears in a new record.

You can enter a *default value* to specify a value that is automatically entered in a field when a new record is created. For example, if most of your clients are from Texas, you could set the default value for the State field to "TX." When a user adds a record to the table, they can either accept the "TX" default value for the State field or enter their own value.

1 Switch to Design view by clicking the View button on the toolbar.

Since the majority of your customers are from Minnesota, you decide to add "MN" as the default value for the State field.

2 Click the State field.

Now you can add a default value to the State field

3 Click the Default Value box and type MN, as shown in Figure 4-15.

TIP

A common default value used in Date fields is the current date. To automatically add the current date, type =Date() in the field.

Let's see how the new default value works.

4 Click the Save button on the toolbar to save your changes, and then click the View button to display the table in Datasheet view.

You will need to add a new record in order to see any default values.

5 Click the ▶✳ New Record button on the Record Navigation bar.

Access adds a new blank record to the table. Notice that the State field already contains the "MN" default value, as shown in Figure 4-16. If the customer is from another state, you can simply replace the default value with your own data.

QUICK REFERENCE

TO ENTER A DEFAULT VALUE FOR A FIELD:

1. MAKE SURE THE TABLE IS DISPLAYED IN DESIGN VIEW AND CLICK THE FIELD YOU WANT TO ADD A DEFAULT VALUE TO.

2. CLICK THE DEFAULT VALUE BOX IN THE FIELD PROPERTIES SECTION.

3. ENTER THE DEFAULT VALUE YOU WANT TO APPEAR IN THE FIELD FOR NEW RECORDS.

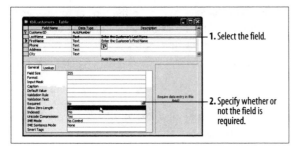

1. Select the field.

2. Specify whether or not the field is required.

Figure 4-17. The Required field property lets you specify whether or not a field must contain data.

In most tables, there are usually at least a few fields that absolutely must contain data in order for the record to be meaningful. For example, at the absolute minimum, a customer record needs to have the customer's first and last name—otherwise, why bother entering it? You can specify that a field *must* contain data to prevent users from leaving out important information when they are entering data.

This lesson explains how you can make sure that a field has a value for each record.

1 Switch to Design view by clicking the View button on the toolbar.

You decide to specify that the LastName field must contain data for each record.

2 Click the LastName field.

Here's how to prevent a user from leaving out data in a field.

3 Click the Required list arrow and select Yes, as shown in Figure 4-17.

Let's see how the new default value works.

4 Click the Save button on the toolbar to save your changes, click No to close the message about testing existing data, and then click the View button to display the table in Datasheet view.

You will need to add a new record in order to see any default values.

5 Click the New Record button on the Record Navigation bar.

Access adds a new blank record to the table.

6 Enter a new record with your own information. Leave the LastName field blank, however.

Let's see what happens…

7 When you have finished entering the record, click in any other record or press Ctrl + Enter to save the record.

Access displays a dialog box that states that the Last-Name field cannot contain a null value.

QUICK REFERENCE

TO REQUIRE DATA ENTRY FOR A FIELD:

1. MAKE SURE THE TABLE IS DISPLAYED IN DESIGN VIEW AND CLICK THE FIELD YOU WANT TO REQUIRE DATA ENTRY FOR.

2. CLICK THE REQUIRED BOX IN THE FIELD PROPERTIES SECTION.

3. CLICK THE LIST ARROW AND SELECT YES.

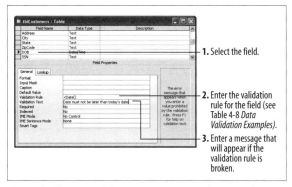

1. Select the field.

2. Enter the validation rule for the field (see Table 4-8 *Data Validation Examples*).

3. Enter a message that will appear if the validation rule is broken.

Figure 4-18. Data validation tests incoming data to make sure it conforms to a specified set of rules.

Figure 4-19. Access displays the error message you entered whenever the validation rule is broken.

Without a doubt, *data validation* is the most powerful tool you can use to prevent data-entry errors. With data validation, Access actually tests data to make sure that it conforms to what you want to appear in the table. If the incoming data doesn't meet your requirements, Access rejects it and displays an error message.

Data validation works best in number, currency, and date/time fields. You can create a validation rule for text entries, but doing so can be complicated—especially if you want to test a lot of text variables.

There are actually *two* boxes that relate to data validation. They are the:

- **Validation Rule box:** Used to specify the requirements for data entered into the field.

- **Validation Text box:** Used to specify the message that will be displayed to the user when data that violates the validation rule is entered.

Creating data validation rules can be a little tricky—you create a data validation using the same hard-to-remember operators that you use in filters and queries. Table 4-8 contains some data validations that you can modify and use in your tables.

1 If necessary, open the Lesson 4 database and double-click the tblCustomers table.

The tblCustomers table opens.

2 Switch to Design view by clicking the View button on the toolbar.

You decide to specify that the DOB field cannot be later than today's date. (We can't have any people with birthdays in the future, can we?)

3 Click the DOB field.

Before we get started, you need to make sure that the DOB field is a Date/Time field—you should have changed this in a previous lesson.

4 Verify that the DOB field's Data Type is set to Date/Time.

First you need to enter a validation rule.

5 Click the Validation Rule box and type Date( ).

The validation rule you just entered will prevent users from entering dates later than today's date in the DOB field. Next you have to specify the error message that Access will display if someone tries to break your validation rule by entering a future date.

6 Click the Validation Text box and type Date must not be later than today's date.

Your table should look similar to Figure 4-18. Let's test our new data validation rule.

7 Click the Save button on the toolbar to save your changes, click No to close the message about testing existing data, and then click the View button to display the table in Datasheet view.

Data validation rules apply to both new and existing records. Move on to the next step and try modifying a record so that it breaks our data validation rule.

8 Click the DOB field for any record. Change the date to a future date that falls after today, and then press Enter.

When you try to violate the validation rule, Access displays the Validation Text you entered back in Step 5, as shown in Figure 4-19.

9 Click OK and press Esc to cancel the change.

Consider the following table your data validation "cheat sheet." It contains samples of the most common types of validation rules. Feel free to copy, modify, or mix and match these examples to create your own validation rules.

Table 4-8. Data Validation Examples

Validation Rule	Description
<100	Must be less than 100.
<=100	Must be less than or equal to 100.
Between 1 and 10	Must be between 1 and 10.
0	Must not equal 0.
<1/1/95	Must be a date before 1/1/95.
>= Date( )	Must be today's date or later.
<= Date( )	Must be today's date or earlier.
"Business" Or "Pleasure" Or "Other"	Must be "Business" or "Pleasure" or "Other."
Like "??"	Must have two characters.
Like "####"	Must have four numbers.

QUICK REFERENCE

TO VALIDATE FIELD DATA:

1. MAKE SURE THE TABLE IS DISPLAYED IN DESIGN VIEW AND CLICK THE FIELD YOU WANT TO APPLY A VALIDATION RULE TO.

2. CLICK THE VALIDATION RULE BOX IN THE FIELD PROPERTIES SECTION.

3. ENTER AN EXPRESSION YOU WANT TO USE TO VALIDATE THE FIELD'S DATA (SEE TABLE 4-8).

4. CLICK THE VALIDATION TEXT BOX IN THE FIELD PROPERTIES SECTION.

5. TYPE THE TEXT THAT ACCESS WILL DISPLAY WHEN THE USER TRIES TO ENTER INCORRECT DATA FOR THE FIELD.

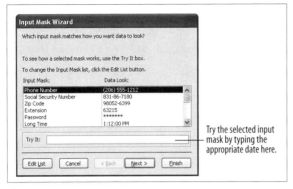

Figure 4-20. The first step of the Input Mask Wizard.

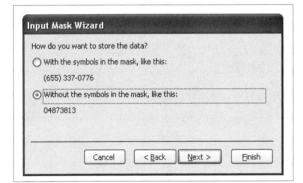

Figure 4-21. Specify how you want your text to be stored: with or without the input mask symbols.

An *Input Mask* limits the amount and type of information that can be entered in a field. You have probably already seen an example of an input mask on an ordinary paper form—the type of form that assumes you're too dimwitted to know how to write down your phone number or social security number and thus provides you with a guide like (___) ___ - _____ or ___-___-_____. Look familiar? That's an input mask, pure and simple.

There are two ways to create an input mask:

- Click the 🔲 Build button and have the Input Mask Wizard create the input mask for you (the fast and easy way). The only problem with the Input Mask Wizard is that it can only help you create input masks for phone numbers, social security numbers, Zip Codes, and date and time fields.

- Create the input mask yourself by typing a series of characters in the Input Mask box (the hard way). If you want to use this brutal method, refer to Table 4-9 to see what you have to enter in order to create an input mask.

In this lesson you will learn how to use the Input Mask Wizard to add an input mask to a field.

1 Switch to Design view by clicking the View button on the toolbar.

Now let's create an input mask for the Phone field in order to reduce data entry errors and to remind users to enter the area code.

2 Click the Phone field.

Now let's look at the Input Mask property…

3 Click the Input Mask box.

A 🔲 button appears next to the Input Mask box—click this button to start the Input Mask Wizard.

4 Click the 🔲 Build button to start the Input Mask Wizard.

The first step of the Input Mask Wizard appears, as shown in Figure 4-20. All you need to do here is select the input mask you want to choose.

If you want to try an input mask to see how it works, click the input mask you want to use and then type some sample text in the "Try It" box.

> ⸭ NOTE ⸭   *Depending on how Access is set up on your computer, an error message may appear when you click the Build button. Don't worry—all this means is that the Input Mask Wizard is not currently installed. Click OK to install it.*

5 Click the Phone Number input mask and then try typing a phone number in the Try It box. Click Next when you're finished.

The next step of the Input Mask Wizard appears. If you want, you can select a different placeholder to use than the default underscore (__) character.

6 Click Next.

The next step of the Input Mask Wizard is very important—specifying how Access should store your data (see Figure 4-21). You have two choices:

- **With the symbols in the mask:** This will store only the text you type in the field and the input mask symbols. For example, if you enter 5555555555 in a

Phone field, Access will save the input mask symbols with the text you enter, so (555) 555-5555 would be saved.

- **Without the symbols in the mask:** This will store only the text you type in the field. For example, if you enter 5555555555 in a Phone field, Access will display (555) 555-5555 but only store the numbers you typed (5555555555).

This may not seem like much of an issue, and it's not unless you want to export your table. Then you will have to work with the results of the decision you made here: the phone numbers will be in either 5555555555 or (555) 555-5555 format.

7 Select the **With the symbols in the mask** option and click **Next**.

That's it! You're ready to create your input mask!

8 Click **Finish** to create the input mask.

The Input Mask Wizard creates an input mask for the field.

Creating an input mask by hand is difficult, but it can be done. Create an input mask from scratch by entering the characters shown in the following table into the Input Mask box.

Table 4-9. Input Mask Characters

Character	Description	Character	Description
0	Numbers 0 to 9 required; plus and minus signs not allowed.	&	Character or space required.
9	Number or space optional; plus and minus signs not allowed.	C	Character or space optional.
#	Number or space optional; plus and minus signs not allowed.	<	Converts the following characters to lowercase.
. , : ; - /	Decimal point, thousands, date, and time separators.	>	Converts the following characters to uppercase.
A	Letter or number required.	!	Displays characters from right to left, rather than left to right.
a	Letter or number optional.	\	Displays the following input mask character. For example, * would display *.
L	Letters A to Z required.	Password	Displays an asterisk(*) for each character you type.
?	Letter or number optional.		

QUICK REFERENCE

TO CREATE AN INPUT MASK FOR A FIELD:

1. MAKE SURE THE TABLE IS DISPLAYED IN DESIGN VIEW AND CLICK THE FIELD YOU WANT TO CREATE AN INPUT MASK FOR.

2. CLICK THE INPUT MASK BOX IN THE FIELD PROPERTIES SECTION.

3. CLICK THE BUILD BUTTON TO START THE INPUT WIZARD AND SELECT AN INPUT MASK FROM THE PREDEFINED LIST.

OR...

MANUALLY CREATE THE INPUT MASK BY ENTERING THE APPROPRIATE CHARACTERS.

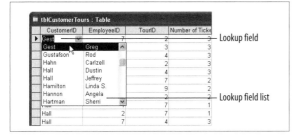

Figure 4-22. A lookup list displays values from a table or query.

Figure 4-23. Create a lookup list by selecting Lookup Wizard as the field's Data Type.

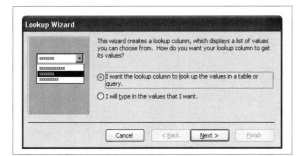

Figure 4-24. Select a source for the lookup field's values.

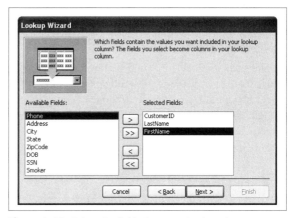

Figure 4-25. Select the fields that contain the values.

Lookup fields are definitely one of the coolest and most powerful features in Access. A lookup field lets you pick a field's entry from a list of values. There are two ways that a lookup field can get its list of values:

- From a list of values or options that you enter yourself. For example, you could add the values "FedEx," "UPS," and "AirBorne" to a Shipping field.

- From a list of values in a table or query. For example, instead of entering a CustomerID number, you could select the CustomerID from a list of names.

You can see an example of a lookup field in Figure 4-22. Instead of you having to type a hard-to-remember CustomerID number, the lookup field displays more meaningful information, such as the customer's name, yet still stores the CustomerID number in the field. Lookup fields will make more sense once you have actually worked with them, so let's jump right into this lesson's exercise.

1 Close the tblCustomers table without saving your changes, then open the tblCustomerTours table in Design view.

Let's use a lookup field to make the CustomerID field easier to view and add data to. Here's how to create a lookup field:

2 Click the Data Type box next to the CustomerID field, click the list arrow, and select Lookup Wizard, as shown in Figure 4-23.

The Lookup Wizard dialog box appears, as shown in Figure 4-24, and asks if you want your lookup field to get its values from another table or query or if you want to type a list of options yourself. Since you want your lookup field to get its values from the tblCustomers table, you will select the first option.

3 Click Next.

The next step in the Lookup Wizard is to select the table or query that contains the values for your lookup field. You want to look up customer names, so you would select the tblCustomers table.

4 Select the tblCustomers table and click Next.

Now you have to select the fields that contain the values you want to display in your lookup field. The Lookup Wizard displays the field names in tblCustomers table that you can add to your lookup field. To add a field to your lookup field, double-click the field or select the field and click the ⸢ > ⸣ button.

This step can be a little confusing at first. You need to add the field that contains the value you want to enter—the CustomerID field—but you also want to add several fields that will display more meaningful information in the value list, such as the LastName and FirstName fields.

5 Double-click the CustomerID, LastName, and FirstName fields to add them to the lookup field, as shown in Figure 4-25. Click Next when you're finished.

The next step in the Lookup Wizard dialog box is selecting a sort order for your list. You can sort records by up to four fields, in either ascending or descending order. We don't want to assign a sort order right now, so let's move on to the next step.

6 Click Next.

This next step allows you to adjust the width of the columns in your lookup list. To adjust the width of a column, drag its right edge to the width you want, or double-click the right edge of the column heading to get the best fit.

You can also indicate whether or not to include the primary key in the column by checking or unchecking the "Hide key column" check box. Any primary key fields will be hidden by default to make the lookup field less confusing. As you can see, your primary key field, CustomerID, is hidden.

⸢ NOTE ⸣ *If the table or query you are working with does not have a primary key, the "Hide key column" check box will not appear. The Lookup Wizard will instead include an additional step where you will be prompted to select the column that will act as the bound column.*

7 Click Next. Complete the Lookup Wizard by clicking Finish.

You've finished creating the lookup field! Let's test it out....

8 Click Yes to save your changes and then click the View button to display the table in Datasheet view.

The CustomerID field still contains CustomerID numbers, but now it searches for and displays the customer's LastName field—much easier to understand.

9 Click the CustomerID field for any record. Click the list arrow that appears in the field.

Out pops a list of all the customers in the tblCustomers table—neat, huh? All you have to do is click a customer's name to add their CustomerID number to the CustomerID field.

10 Press Esc to close the list without selecting any options.

QUICK REFERENCE

TO CREATE A LOOKUP FIELD:

1. DISPLAY THE TABLE IN DESIGN VIEW.

2. CLICK THE FIELD'S DATA TYPE BOX, CLICK THE LIST ARROW, AND SELECT LOOKUP WIZARD.

3. CLICK THE I WANT THE LOOKUP COLUMN TO LOOK UP THE VALUES IN A TABLE OR QUERY OPTION AND CLICK NEXT.

4. SELECT THE TABLE OR QUERY YOU WANT TO USE FOR THE LOOKUP LIST AND CLICK NEXT.

5. SELECT THE FIELDS YOU WANT TO ADD TO THE LOOKUP FIELD AND CLICK NEXT.

6. SELECT A SORT ORDER FOR YOUR LIST (OPTIONAL) AND CLICK NEXT.

7. ADJUST THE WIDTH OF THE COLUMNS THAT WILL APPEAR IN THE LOOKUP LIST AND INDICATE WHETHER OR NOT TO INCLUDE THE PRIMARY KEY IN THE COLUMN. CLICK NEXT.

8. IF PROMPTED, SELECT A COLUMN THAT WILL ACT AS THE BOUND COLUMN AND CLICK NEXT.

9. ENTER A LABEL FOR THE LOOKUP COLUMN AND CLICK FINISH.

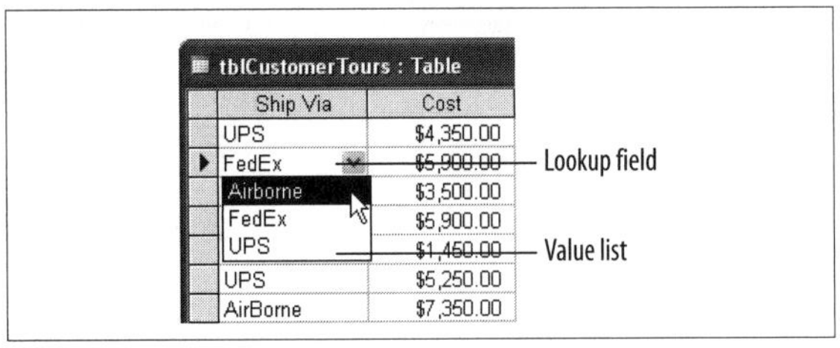

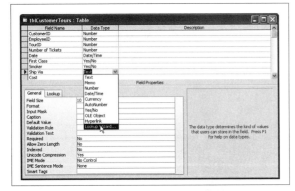

Figure 4-26. A value list displays a list of options that you specify.

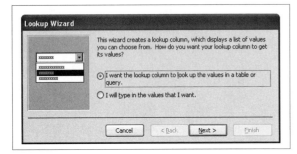

Figure 4-27. Create a value list by selecting Lookup Wizard for the field's Data Type.

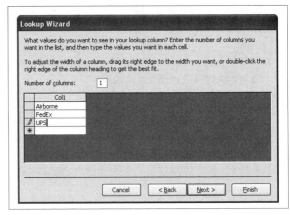

Figure 4-29. Enter the options you want to see in the value list.

Similar to its cousin the lookup list, a *value list* displays a list of values in a drop-down list. Unlike a lookup list, which displays data in a table or query, a value list displays a list of options that you manually enter, as shown in Figure 4-26. A value list is useful if you enter the same data in a field again and again. For example, if you ship a product using three different courier services, you could create a value list that displays the three courier services, such as AirBorne, FedEx, and UPS.

Although it's possible to change the options displayed in a value list, doing so is a rather cumbersome process. For that reason, you should only use value lists for values that will not change very often. If you want to display a lot of options, such as a list of state abbreviations or values that may change frequently, you should create a table to store those values and then display them with a lookup list instead. It's a lot easier to change values in a table than it is to change options in a value list.

This lesson will show you how to create a value list that contains several static options.

1 **If necessary, open the** Lesson 4 **database and double-click the** tblCustomerTours **table.**

The tblCustomerTours table appears.

Figure 4-28. Select a source for the lookup field's values.

2 Switch to Design view by clicking the View button on the toolbar.

Let's create a value list that will make it easier to enter data into the Ship Via field.

3 Click the Data Type box next to the Ship Via field, click the list arrow, and select Lookup Wizard, as shown in Figure 4-27.

The Lookup Wizard dialog box appears, as shown in Figure 4-28, and asks if you want your lookup field to get its values from another table or query or if you want to type a list of options yourself. Since you want to personally enter the options that appear in the value list, you will want to select the second option.

4 Click the I will type in the values that I want option and click Next.

The next step of the Lookup Wizard appears, as shown in Figure 4-29. This step is pretty easy—simply enter the options you want to be displayed in the value list.

5 Click in the Col1 box, type Airborne, press Tab, type FedEx, press Tab, and type UPS.

The value list will display these three values.

 NOTE *If you want to add a lot of options (ten or more) to your value list or if the values in the list will change, consider creating a table to store the values and display them with a lookup list instead. Adding the initial options to a value list is easy, but adding, changing, or deleting these values can be a burden.*

6 Click Next.

You've finished creating the value list!

7 Complete the Lookup Wizard by clicking Finish.

Let's see how our new value list works.

8 Click the Save button on the toolbar to save your changes and then click the View button to display the table in Datasheet view.

To display the value list for the Ship Via field, simply click the Ship Via field and click the list arrow.

9 Click the Ship Via field for any record. Click the list arrow that appears in the field.

Out pops the value list with the three couriers you entered in Step 5.

10 Select FedEx from the lookup list.

TIP *You can also select an option from a lookup field by typing the first few letters of the entry.*

> ## QUICK REFERENCE
>
> **TO CREATE A VALUE LIST:**
>
> 1. DISPLAY THE TABLE IN DESIGN VIEW.
>
> 2. CLICK THE DATA TYPE BOX OF THE FIELD YOU WANT TO CREATE THE VALUE LIST FOR, CLICK THE LIST ARROW, AND SELECT LOOKUP WIZARD.
>
> 3. CLICK THE I WILL TYPE IN THE VALUES THAT I WANT OPTION AND CLICK NEXT. SPECIFY THE NUMBER OF COLUMNS YOU WANT TO APPEAR IN THE VALUE LIST.
>
> 4. ENTER THE VALUES IN THE LIST. RESIZE THE COLUMN WIDTHS IF NECESSARY. CLICK NEXT WHEN YOU'RE FINISHED.
>
> 5. ENTER A LABEL FOR THE LOOKUP COLUMN AND CLICK FINISH.

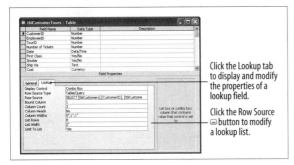

Click the Lookup tab to display and modify the properties of a lookup field.

Click the Row Source button to modify a lookup list.

Figure 4-30. You can display and modify the properties of a lookup field by clicking the Lookup tab in the Field Properties section.

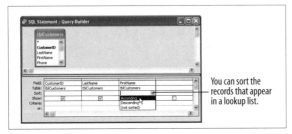

You can sort the records that appear in a lookup list.

Figure 4-31. The SQL Statement: Query Builder window lets you modify what appears in a lookup list.

Modifying an existing lookup field isn't nearly as straightforward as creating one. You can display and modify the properties for a lookup field by clicking on the Lookup tab in the Field Properties section. There are several reasons why you would want to modify a lookup field:

- To sort the records in a lookup list. For example, to sort the records in a lookup list alphabetically by last name.

- To add, change, or delete the static options in a value list. For example, you could add "U.S. Postal Service" to a Ship Via value list.

In this lesson you will learn how to view and modify an existing lookup field.

1 Switch to Design view by clicking the View button on the toolbar.

The CustomerID lookup field we created in an earlier lesson is cool, but what if the list of names isn't displayed in alphabetical order? Not a problem—you can change this by modifying the lookup field. Display and change the properties for a lookup field by clicking the Lookup tab in the Field Properties section.

2 Click the CustomerID field, then click the Lookup tab in the Field Properties section.

The properties for the CustomerID lookup field are displayed, as shown in Figure 4-30. You can learn more about these properties in Table 4-10.

3 Click the Row Source box.

That technical SELECT [tblCustomers].[CustomerID] stuff in the Row Source box is a *SQL* statement. SQL (Structured Query Language) is a language most database programs use to create queries; it tells lookup fields where to get their values. Fortunately, you don't have to know how to write SQL to modify a lookup field—you can use the familiar query grid to create the SQL statement for you.

4 Click the ⟨...⟩ Row Source button to display the SQL Statement: Query Builder window.

The SQL Statement: Query Builder window appears, as shown in Figure 4-31. Yep—it's the same query grid that you're already familiar with.

5 In the LastName field, click the Sort box list arrow and select Ascending, as shown in Figure 4-31.

This will sort the CustomerID lookup field by the LastName field.

6 Close the SQL Statement: Query Builder window and click Yes when you are prompted to save your changes.

Access updates the SQL statement for the CustomerID lookup field. You can also view, change, or delete options from a value list using the Lookup tab.

7 Click the Ship Via field.

The Row Source box contains the value list options.

8 Click the Row Source box.

The Row Source box contains the text "Airbone";"FedEx";"UPS". You can add options to the value list by typing them into the Row Source box—just make sure that the options are enclosed by quotation marks (") and separated by a semicolon (;).

9 Type ; "US Mail" **so that the Row Source reads** "Airbone;"FedEx";"UPS";"US Mail".

That's it—you've finished modifying the lookup fields in the tblCustomerTours table.

10 Save your changes, close the tblCustomerTours table and the database.

Table 4-10. Lookup Field Properties

Property	Description
Display Control	Determines whether the lookup field is a text box, combo box, or list box.
Row Source Type	Determines how Access provides data to the lookup field: from a table or query, from a list of values specified in the Row Source box, or from a list of field names in a table or query.
Row Source	Determines what is displayed in the lookup field. The Row Source property setting depends on the Row Source Type property setting.
Bound Column	The column in the lookup list that contains the value that is actually stored in the field. The bound column is the first column (1) by default.
Column Count	The number of columns that are displayed in the lookup field list.
Column Widths	The width of each column that is displayed in the lookup field list. Setting a column width to 0 hides the column.
Limit to List	Determines whether a field can accept a value that is not in the lookup list.

QUICK REFERENCE

TO MODIFY A LOOKUP LIST:

1. DISPLAY THE TABLE IN DESIGN VIEW.

2. CLICK THE LOOKUP LIST'S FIELD NAME BOX, THEN CLICK THE LOOKUP TAB IN THE FIELD PROPERTIES SECTION.

3. CLICK THE ROW SOURCE BUTTON TO DISPLAY THE SQL STATEMENT: QUERY BUILDER WINDOW.

4. MAKE THE DESIRED CHANGES AND THEN CLOSE THE SQL STATEMENT: QUERY BUILDER WINDOW.

Chapter Four Review

Lesson Summary

Understanding Field Properties

To Display a Table in Design View: Open the table and click the View button on the toolbar, or, in the Database window, click the Tables icon in the Objects bar, select the table, and click the Design button.

Indexing a Field

To Index a Field: Display the table in Design view. Click the field you want as an index, click the Indexed box, click the list arrow, and select one of the following: Yes (Duplicates OK) if you want to allow multiple records to have the same data in the field, or select Yes (No Duplicates) if you want to ensure that no two records have the same data in the field.

Adding a Primary Key to a Table

To Add a Primary Key to a Table: Display the table in Design view and click the field that you want to set as the primary key. If such a field doesn't exist, you will have to create it. Click the Primary Key button on the toolbar or right-click the field you want to use as the primary key and select Primary Key from the shortcut menu.

Inserting, Deleting, and Reordering Fields

To Insert a Row: Click the row selector for the field that will be below the new field you want to insert and press Insert.

To Change the Order of Fields in a Table: Click the row selector for the field you want to move and click and drag the selected row to the desired location.

To Delete a Field from a Table: Click the row selector for the field and press Delete.

Changing a Field's Data Type

To Change the Data Type for a Field: Display the table in Design view, click the field's Data Type box, click the list arrow, and select the data type.

Using Field Descriptions

To Add a Description to a Field: Display the table in Design view, click the field's Description box, and type the description.

Adding a Caption

To Add a Caption to a Field: Display the table in Design view, click the field you want to add a caption to, click the Caption box in the Field Properties section, and type the caption.

Changing the Field Size

To Change the Field Size: Display the table in Design view, click the field whose size you want to change, click the Field Size box in the Field Properties section, and either type the Field Size value (for text fields) or choose the value from the list (for number fields).

Formatting Number, Currency, and Date/Time Fields

To Format Number and Currency Fields: Display the table in Design view, click the field you want to format, click the Format box in the Field Properties section, click the list arrow, and select a number format.

To Change the Number of Decimal Places: Display the table in Design view, click the field you want to format, click the Decimal Places box in the Field Properties section, click the list arrow, and select the number of decimal places you want to display.

Formatting Number, Currency, and Date/Time Fields by Hand

To Manually Format a Date/Time, Number, or Currency Field: Display the table in Design view, click the field you want to format, click the Format box in the Field Properties section, and enter the appropriate formatting characters or symbols.

Formatting Text Fields

To Manually Format a Text Field: Display the table in Design view, click the text field you want to format, click the Format box in the Field Properties section, and enter the appropriate text formatting symbols.

Setting a Default Value

To Enter a Default Value for a Field: Display the table in Design view, click the field you want to add a default value to, click the Default Value box in the Field Properties section, and enter the default value you want to appear in the field for new records.

Requiring Data Entry

To Require Data Entry for a Field: Display the table in Design view, click the field you want to require data entry for, click the Required box in the Field Properties section, click the list arrow, and select Yes.

Validating Data

To Validate Field Data: Display the table in Design view, click the field you want to apply a validation rule to, click the Validation Rule box in the Field Properties section, and enter an expression you want to use to validate the field's data. Next, click the Validation Text box in the Field Properties section and type the text that Access will display when the user tries to enter incorrect data for the field.

Creating an Input Mask

To Create an Input Mask for a Field: Display the table in Design view, click the field you want to create an input mask for, and click the Input Mask box in the Field Properties section. Click the Build button to start the Input Wizard, then either select an input mask from the predefined list or manually create the input mask by entering the appropriate characters.

Creating a Lookup Field

To Create a Lookup Field: Display the table in Design view, click the field's Data Type box, click the list arrow, and select Lookup Wizard. Click the I want the lookup column to look up the values in a table or query option, click Next, then select the table or query you want to use for the look up list and click Next. Select the fields you want to add to the lookup field and click Next. Select a sort order for your list (optional) and click Next. Adjust the width of the columns that will appear in the lookup list and indicate whether or not to include the primary key in the list. If the table or query doesn't have a primary key, you will be prompted for the column that will act as the bound column. Click Next. Enter a label for the Lookup column, and click Finish.

Creating a Value List

To Create a Value List: Display the table in Design view, click the field's Data Type box, click the list arrow, and select Lookup Wizard. Click the I will type in the values that I want option and click Next. Specify the number of columns you want to appear in the value list, then enter the values in the list. Resize the column widths, if necessary, and click Next when you're finished. Enter a label for the Lookup column and click Finish.

Modifying a Lookup List

To Modify a Lookup List: Display the table in Design view, click the lookup list's field name box, then click the Lookup tab in the Field Properties section. Click the Row Source button to display the SQL Statement: Query Builder window, make the desired changes, and then close the SQL Statement: Query Builder window.

Quiz

1. Which of the following is NOT a field property?

   A. Field Size.

   B. Format.

   C. Color.

   D. Indexed.

2. Indexing a field dramatically speeds up queries and sorts performed on the field, therefore you should always index every field in a table. (True or False?)

3. Which of the following statements is NOT true?

   A. The Indexed property has three settings: No, Yes (Duplicates OK), and Yes (No Duplicates).

   B. Primary key fields are automatically indexed.

   C. The Yes (No Duplicates) index option prevents duplicate entries in your table.

   D. You can index any type of field: text, date/time, AutoNumber, number, currency, yes/no, memo, OLE object, and hyperlink fields.

4. Which of the following fields would NOT make a suitable primary key?

A. An AutoNumber field.

B. A customer's social security number.

C. An invoice number.

D. A date field.

5. Text entered in the field Description box will appear in a pop-up window whenever a user selects that field. (True or False?)

6. The Field Size property works differently, depending on whether the field is a text or number field. (True or False?)

7. Which of the following Format properties would display the full name of the month?

A. MONTH.

B. FULLMONTH.

C. mm.

D. mmmm.

8. Which of the following statements is NOT true?

A. The Default Value property is automatically entered in a field when a new record is created.

B. The Required property determines if a user must enter a value in a field or not.

C. A lookup field lets you pick a field's entry from a list of values, which often comes from another table or query.

D. (___) ___ - _____ is an example of a Required property.

9. What does adding a > into the Format box of a text field do?

A. Requires all characters entered in the field to be in uppercase.

B. Displays the characters in the field in uppercase.

C. Requires all characters entered in the field to be numbers.

D. Displays the characters in the field in a larger font.

10. Which of the following statements is NOT true?

A. The Default Value box lets you specify a value that is automatically entered in a field when a new record is created.

B. The Required box lets you specify if data entry is required for a field.

C. The maximum length of a memo field is 255 characters.

D. The Validation Rule box lets you test data to make sure that it conforms to what you want to appear in the table. For example, entering 100 would require that a number be less than 100.

11. You want to create a field that lets you add a customer's name by picking it from a drop-down list. Which of the following fields would let you do this?

A. A memo field.

B. A lookup field.

C. An OLE field.

D. A hyperlink field.

12. What is the corresponding text for the <#1/1/95# Validation Rule Setting?

A. Enter a date before 1995.

B. Enter a value less than 1,195.

C. Enter a value greater than 1,195.

D. Value must be less than 95 characters.

13. You can set a field as the primary key by selecting the field and clicking the Primary Key button on the toolbar. (True or False?)

Homework

1. Open the Homework database.

2. Open the Customers table in Design View.

3. Limit the Field Size of the LastName and FirstName fields to 15 characters.

4. Specify a format for the State field that will display all entries in uppercase.

5. Create an Input Mask for the SSN field so that users must enter information in a __ _-_ _-__ _ format and make the SSN field a required field.

6. Index both the LastName and FirstName fields (duplicates OK).

7. Make the SSN field the table's primary key.

8. Save your changes to the Customers table and close the Homework database.

Quiz Answers

1. C. There are Color properties for other database objects, but not for fields in a table.

2. False. Only index those fields that you frequently use to filter or sort information. Indexing too many fields in a table slows down filters and sorts, defeating the whole idea behind the index property.

3. D. This was a tricky question—you can't index memo, OLE object, or hyperlink fields.

4. D. Because the date isn't usually a unique value (the same date might appear more than once in the same table), it wouldn't normally make a good candidate for a table's primary key.

5. False. Text in the field Description box will appear in the Status bar when a user selects that field.

6. True. Text fields and Number/Currency fields have a different set of Field Size properties.

7. D. Another difficult question—"mmmm" would display the full name of the month.

8. D. (__ _) __ _ - ____ _ is a example of an Input Mask property, not a Required property.

9. B. Adding a to a text field's Format box displays all characters in uppercase.

10. C. Memo fields have a maximum length of 64,000 characters.

11. B. A lookup field lets you select a value from a drop-down list.

12. A.

13. True. This is the procedure for setting a field as a table's primary key.

CHAPTER 5

CREATING RELATIONAL DATABASES

CHAPTER OBJECTIVES:

Understand table relationships, Lesson 5.1

Create a relationship between two tables, Lesson 5.2

Understand and enforce referential integrity, Lessons 5.3—5.4

Understand relationship types, Lesson 5.5

CHAPTER TASK: JOIN TWO RELATED TABLES

Prerequisites

- **How to use menus, toolbars, dialog boxes, and shortcut keystrokes.**
- **How to open and modify database objects.**
- **How to add and edit database records.**

This chapter covers what many people agree is one of the most difficult database concepts—how to create and work with relational databases. A *relational database* contains two or more tables that are related to each other in some way. For example, a database might contain a Customers table and an Invoices table that contains the customer's orders.

In this chapter you will learn how to link tables in an existing database together in a one-to-many relationship to create a relational database. You will also learn how to enforce referential integrity between those tables to keep records in related fields valid and accurate.

Relational databases can be confusing at first, so we'll take things slowly and explain everything in great detail as we go. Let's get started!

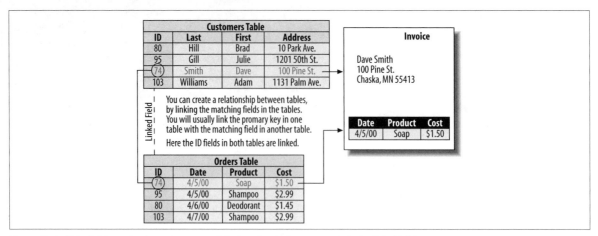

Figure 5-1. This database tracks customers and their orders in two separate but related tables.

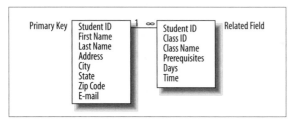

Figure 5-2. Sketch out a diagram of your database, including its tables and how they relate to each other.

There are two basic types of databases:

- **Flat File:** Think of a Rolodex when you think of a flat-file database. A flat-file database stores all of its information—names, addresses, etc.—in the same place, just like addresses are stored on a Rolodex card. Flat-file databases are incredibly simple to create and use, but they're not very powerful or well suited to many business tasks.

- **Relational:** A relational database contains multiple tables that are related through matching fields. Figure 5-1 illustrates the design of a relational database. The database in Figure 5-1 has two tables—one that stores customer names and addresses, and another that stores customer orders. The two tables are related or linked by a common field. Relational databases are very powerful, but developing one takes a lot of skill, a lot of practice, and a strong understanding of tables and fields.

Microsoft Access can create either type of database—flat file or relational. However, most Access databases tend to be of the relational type.

Still fuzzy about how relational databases work? To see an example of a relational database, look at the diagram illustrated in Figure 5-1. This database tracks customers and their orders. To store this information, the database uses two tables: Customers and Orders. Each table contains fields that store similar information. The Customers table contains only information about customers and their addresses. The Orders table contains only information about any orders that were placed—it doesn't contain any information about the customers. The two tables both have an ID field, and it's this ID field that relates or links the two tables.

Relational databases save storage space by cutting down on duplicate data. For example, the relational database shown in Figure 5-1 stores information in two related tables and eliminates the need to reenter a customer's name and address each time that customer places a new order.

Relational databases require *lots* of planning ahead. Before you attempt to create your database, you should sit down with a trusty pencil and a pad of paper and walk through the following steps:

- **Determine the Purpose of the Database:** Write down a list of the reports and lists that you want to come *out* of the database. This may seem a little backward at first, but these reports are the reason you're creating the database. Make a list of the reports and lists you want to see and then sketch some samples of these reports and lists—be as detailed as possible. This will help determine the tables and fields to include in your database.

- **Write Down the Fields You Need:** This should be an easy step once you have determined the purpose of your database and have sketched some sample reports and lists.

- **Organize and Group Related Fields into Separate Tables:** Each table in the database should be based on only one subject. By breaking each subject into its own table, you avoid redundant information and make the database more organized. The database in Figure 5-1 is broken down into two tables, Customers and Orders, so there isn't any duplicated data. When you brainstorm, try to break down your information as much as possible. If your table contains fields like Item 1, Item 2, Item 3, Item 4, and so on, you should probably break each item up into its own table.

- **Identify and Add the Fields Common to Each Table:** In Figure 5-1 the Customers table's ID field links to the Orders table's ID field. One of the linked fields should be the table's *primary key*. See Lesson 4.3 for more information about primary keys.

- **Sketch a Diagram of Your Database:** Create a diagram of your database similar to the one shown in Figure 5-2. Draw a box for each of your tables and write the table's field names inside that box. Draw a line between the related fields. Most table relationships are a *one-to-many* relationship. This means that a record in one table may be related to one or more records in another table. For example, in Figure 5-1, each record in the Customers table is related to one or more records in the Orders table. This makes sense since, hopefully, most customers will place more than one order. You should indicate the two sides of the relationship by drawing a "1" on the "one" side of the relationship line and an "∞" (infinity symbol) on the "many" side of the relationship line.

All this writing and planning may seem like a lot of work, but they're both critical steps in creating a sound database. Carpenters wouldn't start building a house without their blueprints, would they? No—and it's no different if you're going to create a good relational database.

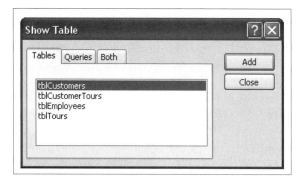

Figure 5-3. The Show Table dialog box.

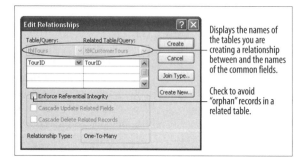

Figure 5-4. The Edit Relationships dialog box.

Figure 5-5. Click and drag the primary key field from one table to the matching field in the related table.

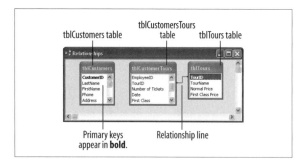

Figure 5-6. The Relationships window.

Once you begin to understand the difficult concept of relational databases, the process of actually linking the tables in a database is rather simple. You link related tables by connecting the table's common fields in Access's *Relationships window*, shown in Figure 5-6. The Relation-

ships window lets you view, create, and modify relationships among tables in a database.

Keep the following rules in mind when you link two tables together:

- **Linked fields should be (almost) identical.** Related fields must have the same data type and field size, and they must contain the same kind of information. Related fields don't *have* to have the same field name—but they should so that things don't get confusing. The most common problem people have when they try to link two tables is caused by fields with different data types and/or sizes.

- **The primary key in one table is usually linked with a matching field in the other table.** Notice that in Figure 5-6 the tblTours table's primary key, TourID, links to the TourID field in the tblCustomerTours table.

- **Fields related to an AutoNumber primary key field must be Number fields with the Long Integer Field Size.**

Now you're ready to create a relationship between the tables in your database. Here's how to do it:

1 Locate and click on the Lesson 5 database to open it.

To view and create relationships between tables, you need to display the Relationships window.

2 Click the Relationships button on the toolbar.

> **TIP** *Another way to define table relationships is to right-click any blank area in the Database window and select* Relationships.

The Relationships window appears. If any relationships exist between the tables in your database, each of these tables will appear in a small box with lines connecting the table's linked fields.

3 If the Show Table dialog box doesn't appear when you open the Relationships window, click the Show Table button on the toolbar.

First you have to add the tables that you want to relate using the Show Table dialog box, as shown in Figure 5-3. In this exercise you want to relate the tblCustomers, tblCustomerTours, and tblTours tables, so you will need to add these tables to the Relationships window.

4 Click the tblCustomers table and click Add.

The tblCustomers table appears in the Relationships window.

5 Click the tblCustomerTours and tblTours tables and then click Add to add them to the Relationships window.

You can close the Show Table window when you have finished adding all the tables that you want to relate to one another.

6 Click Close to close the Show Table dialog box.

You're ready to start relating the tables you added. Relating tables may sound difficult, but it's really nothing more than dragging and dropping the field you want to use to link one table to the other. Before you can drag and drop the matching field from one table to the other, you have to make sure that the linking fields in both tables are visible.

7 Drag the TourID field from the tblTours table to the TourID field in the tblCustomerTours table, as shown in Figure 5-5.

Dragging a field from one table to another in the Relationships window links the two tables using the selected field.

⁝ NOTE ⁝ *Okay, so dragging and dropping isn't quite that easy. Access is very picky about where you point, click, drag, and drop. You need to be very accurate and drag the pointer right next to the field you're linking to.*

The Edit Relationships dialog box appears, as shown in Figure 5-4. What's especially important here is the Enforce Referential Integrity check box. Referential integrity helps you avoid "orphan" records and maintains database accuracy. For example, checking the Referential Integrity box would ensure that you could not enter an invoice for a customer in an Invoice table unless that same customer existed in a Customers table. We'll discuss referential integrity more later in the chapter.

8 Click Create to create the relationship between the tblTours and tblCustomerTours tables.

The Edit Relationships dialog box closes and a line appears between the two tables' TourID fields, indicating that the tables are linked, as shown in Figure 5-6.

Congratulations! You've just linked two related tables together!

QUICK REFERENCE

TO DEFINE TABLE RELATIONSHIPS:

1. IN THE DATABASE WINDOW, CLICK THE RELATIONSHIPS BUTTON ON THE TOOLBAR.

   OR...

   RIGHT-CLICK ANY BLANK AREA IN THE DATABASE WINDOW AND SELECT RELATIONSHIPS.

2. IF NECESSARY, CLICK THE SHOW TABLE BUTTON ON THE TOOLBAR.

3. CLICK THE TABLE YOU WANT AND CLICK ADD.

4. REPEAT STEP 3 FOR EACH TABLE YOU WANT TO USE IN THE RELATIONSHIP.

5. CLICK CLOSE.

6. CLICK THE RELATED FIELD IN THE FIRST TABLE AND DRAG IT TO THE RELATED FIELD IN THE SECOND TABLE.

7. SPECIFY ANY REFERENTIAL INTEGRITY AND/ OR JOIN TYPE OPTIONS (OPTIONAL).

8. CLICK CREATE TO CREATE THE RELATIONSHIP.

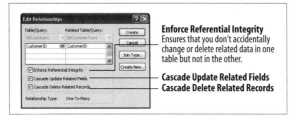

Figure 5-7. The Edit Relationships dialog box.

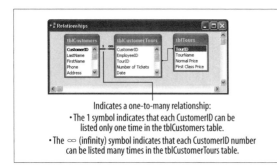

Indicates a one-to-many relationship:
- The 1 symbol indicates that each CustomerID can be listed only one time in the tblCustomers table.
- The ∞ (infinity) symbol indicates that each CustomerID number can be listed many times in the tblCustomerTours table.

Figure 5-8. The Relationships window. The relationship line between the tblCustomers table and the tblCustomerTours table indicates a one-to-many relationship.

When you create a relationship between two tables, it is usually a good idea to enforce *referential integrity*. So what does this technical-sounding phrase mean? Referential integrity keeps records in related fields valid and accurate. Referential integrity ensures that you don't accidentally change or delete related data in one table but not in the other. For example, say you were using two related Social Security fields to link two tables. Referential integrity would not allow you to change the Social Security number in one record without changing the Social Security number in the other related records.

Access is *very* picky about when you can set referential integrity. You can only use referential integrity when all of the following conditions are met:

- One of the linked fields is a primary key
- The related fields are the same data type and size. (If you are using an AutoNumber field, you can relate it to a Number field with a Long Integer Field size.)
- Both tables are in the same Access database.
- You can't have a record in a related table unless a matching record already exists in the primary table. Orphan data in a related table is the most common problem people encounter when attempting to establish referential integrity.

Once you have established referential integrity, the following rules are set:

- You can't add a record to a related table unless a matching record already exists in the primary table.
- You can't change the value of a primary key in the primary table if matching records exist in the related table (unless you select the Cascade Update Related Fields option).
- You can't delete a record from a primary table if matching records exist in a related table (unless you select the Cascade Delete Related Records option).

In this lesson you will learn how to enforce referential integrity. You should still have the Relationships window open from the previous lesson in order to complete this lesson.

First, let's establish a relationship between the tblCustomers table and the tblCustomerTours table…

1 Drag the CustomerID field from the tblCustomers table to the CustomerID field in the tblCustomerTours table.

The Edit Relationships dialog box appears, as shown in Figure 5-7. We want to enforce referential integrity so that you can't enter a CustomerID in the tblCustomerTours table unless that CustomerID number already exists in the tblCustomers table.

2 Check the Enforce Referential Integrity box.

This will enforce referential integrity between the tables. If you get an error message, it's because your tables and fields don't meet all the required conditions listed on the previous page.

There are two other very important boxes in the Edit Relationships dialog box:

- **Cascade Update Related Fields:** When you change data in the main field of one table, Access will automatically update the matching data in the related table.
- **Cascade Delete Related Records:** When you delete a record in the main table, Access will automatically delete any matching records in the related table.

These are both very powerful options—think twice before using them.

3 Check both the Cascade Update Related Fields box and the Cascade Delete Related Records box.

Now you can save the changes to the relationship.

4 Click Create to create the relationship between the tblCustomers and tblCustomerTours tables.

Access creates the relationship between the two tables and enforces referential integrity between them. Notice that the join line between the tblCustomers table and the tblCustomerTours table looks a little dif-

ferent. This relationship indicates that referential integrity is being enforced between the two tables and that the tables have a one-to-many relationship, as shown in Figure 5-8 (more about that later).

5 Click the Close button to close the Relationships window and click Yes to save the changes you made.

In the next lesson you will get to test the results of your new referential integrity settings.

QUICK REFERENCE

TO ENFORCE REFERENTIAL INTEGRITY:

1. IN THE DATABASE WINDOW, CLICK THE RELATIONSHIPS BUTTON ON THE TOOLBAR.

   OR...

   RIGHT-CLICK ANY BLANK AREA IN THE DATABASE WINDOW AND SELECT RELATIONSHIPS.

2. DOUBLE-CLICK THE JOIN LINE FOR THE RELATIONSHIP YOU WANT TO WORK WITH.

3. CHECK THE ENFORCE REFERENTIAL INTEGRITY BOX.

4. IF YOU WANT CHANGES TO THE PRIMARY FIELD OF THE PRIMARY TABLE COPIED TO THE RELATED FIELD IN THE RELATED TABLE, CHECK THE CASCADE UPDATE RELATED FIELDS BOX.

5. IF YOU WANT ACCESS TO AUTOMATICALLY DELETE ORPHAN RECORDS IN THE RELATED TABLE, CHECK THE CASCADE DELETE RELATED RECORDS BOX.

6. CLICK OK.

Figure 5-9. The Cascade Delete Related Records option automatically deletes orphan records in related tables. Here Access asks you to confirm the deletion of any related records.

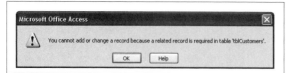

Figure 5-10. Because a record doesn't exist in the tblCustomers table, referential integrity will not let you add an orphan record.

In this lesson you will get to test the referential integrity rules you established in the previous lesson. You just went over it, but since this referential integrity stuff is a little tricky and confusing at first, let's review…

Once you have established referential integrity, the following rules are set:

- You can't add a record to a related table unless a matching record already exists in the primary table.
- You can't change the value of a primary key in the primary table if matching records exist in the related table (unless you select the Cascade Update Related Fields option).
- You can't delete a record from a primary table if matching records exist in a related table (unless you select the Cascade Delete Related Records option).

Think you have a better understanding of referential integrity yet? No? This lesson will give you a chance to work with some related tables where referential integrity has been set. You will also learn how to delete a relationship between two tables.

1 Open the tblCustomers table in Datasheet View.

First let's try deleting a record in the tblCustomers table.

2 Click on the record selector for the record with the CustomerID 1 (Antonio Rommero) and click the Delete Record button on the toolbar.

Because you enabled both referential integrity and cascaded deletes in the previous lesson, Access displays the dialog box shown in Figure 5-9. Access wants you to confirm your deletion, as deleting the customer record will delete any related data for the customer in the tblCustomerTours table.

3 Click Yes.

Access deletes the record from the tblCustomers table and any related tours for the customer in the tblCustomerTours table. If you hadn't enforced referential integrity between these tables, you would be left with one or more "orphan" records for Antonio Rommero in the tblCustomerTours table.

4 Close the tblCustomers table and open the tblCustomerTours table in Datasheet view.

Yikes! The tblCustomerTours table contains a lot of ID number fields, such as CustomerID and TourID. Unless you have a printed a list of these ID numbers (or have a super-human memory), you won't know which CustomerID to enter. (By the way, this is why you will want to use a lot of forms and queries in relational databases—to hide all the technical inner workings of a database from your hapless users.)

Anyway, let's try adding a new record to the tblCustomerTours table.

5 Click the New Record button on the Record Navigation bar.

Access adds a new blank record to the table.

6 Enter a new record using the information in the following tables.

Before you finish adding the record, it's very important that you remember that you deleted the CustomerID 1 record back in Steps 2 and 3. Since you enforced referential integrity between the two related CustomerID fields, move on to Step 7 to find out what happens when you try to add the record.

CustomerID	EmployeeID	TourID	Number of Tickets	Date
1	4	2	1	4/2/00

First Class	Smoker	Ship Via	Cost
0	0	FedEx	450

7 Finish adding the record by pressing Tab or clicking in any other record when you have finished entering the record's information.

Because a CustomerID 1 doesn't exist in the tblCustomers table, a dialog box appears, as shown in Figure 5-10, informing you that Access can't add the record because doing so would violate referential integrity.

8 Click OK to close the dialog box.

You can cancel the addition of the new record.

9 Press Esc to cancel the new record, then close the tblCustomerTours table.

Now that you have a better feel for how referential integrity works, let's look at the other two topics in this lesson—printing and deleting table relationships.

10 Click the [icon] Relationships button on the toolbar.

Sometimes you may want a printed hard copy of the Relationships window.

11 Select File → Print Relationships from the menu.

A report appears in Print Preview. You don't actually need to print anything for now, so…

12 Click the Close button to close the report without saving changes.

Sometimes you may want to delete the relationship between two tables. Access is very restrictive about letting you modify a related table, and often you must temporarily delete the relationship between two tables, modify one of the tables, and then re-connect them. Here's how to delete a table relationship.

13 Click the join line between the tblTours table and the tblCustomerTours table to select it and press Delete.

⋮ NOTE ⋮ *Clicking a tiny join line between two tables requires a lot of mouse dexterity—you probably will have to try several times before you get it.*

Access asks you to confirm the deletion. Let's leave the table relationship be for now.

14 Click No and click the Close button to close the Relationships window.

QUICK REFERENCE

TO PRINT THE RELATIONSHIPS WINDOW:

1. IN THE DATABASE WINDOW, CLICK THE RELATIONSHIPS BUTTON ON THE TOOLBAR.

   OR…

   RIGHT-CLICK ANY BLANK AREA IN THE DATABASE WINDOW AND SELECT RELATIONSHIPS.

2. SELECT FILE → PRINT RELATIONSHIPS FROM THE MENU.

3. MODIFY THE REPORT THAT APPEARS IN PRINT PREVIEW, IF NECESSARY, AND THEN CLICK THE PRINT BUTTON ON THE TOOLBAR.

TO DELETE A TABLE RELATIONSHIP:

1. OPEN THE RELATIONSHIPS WINDOW.

2. CLICK THE JOIN LINE THAT CONNECTS THE TABLES AND PRESS DELETE.

3. CLICK YES TO CONFIRM THE DELETION.

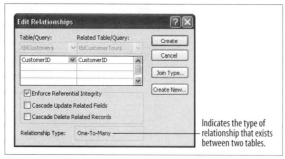

Figure 5-11. The Edit Relationships dialog box indicates the type of relationship that exists between two tables.

When you link two tables together, they form one of three possible relationships, as shown in Figure 5-11. This information is rather technical, but it's good to know if you're working with related or linked tables. There isn't a step-by-step exercise in this lesson—all you have to do is look over Table 5-1 to get a better understanding of table relationships.

Table 5-1. Types of Relationships

Relationship	Description
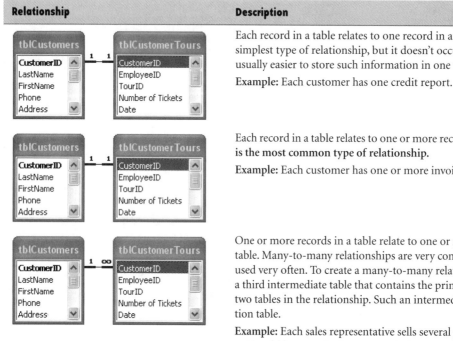	Each record in a table relates to one record in another table. This is the simplest type of relationship, but it doesn't occur very often because it's usually easier to store such information in one table instead of two. **Example:** Each customer has one credit report.
	Each record in a table relates to one or more records in another table. **This is the most common type of relationship.** **Example:** Each customer has one or more invoices.
	One or more records in a table relate to one or more records in another table. Many-to-many relationships are very confusing and thus aren't used very often. To create a many-to-many relationship, you usually need a third intermediate table that contains the primary keys from each of the two tables in the relationship. Such an intermediate table is called a junction table. **Example:** Each sales representative sells several products, and each product is sold by several sales representatives.

Chapter Five Review

Lesson Summary

Understanding Table Relationships

Make sure that you have a good understanding of table relationships.

Creating Relationships between Tables

To Define Table Relationships: In the Database window, click the Relationships button on the toolbar or right-click any blank area in the Database window and select Relationships. If necessary, click the Show Table button on the toolbar, click the table you want, and click Add. Repeat for each for table you want to use in the relationship and click Close when you're finished. Click the related field in the first table and drag it to the related field in the second table, specify any referential integrity and/or join type options (optional). Click Create to create the relationship.

Enforcing Referential Integrity

To Enforce Referential Integrity: In the Database window, click the Relationships button on the toolbar or right-click any blank area in the Database window and select Relationships. Double-click the join line for the relationship you want to work with and check the Enforce Referential Integrity box. If you want changes to

the primary field of the primary table copied to the related field in the related table, check the Cascade Update Related Fields box, or if you want Access to automatically delete orphan records in the related table, check the Cascade Delete Related Records box. Then Click OK.

Testing Referential Integrity and Printing and Deleting Table Relationships

To Print the Relationships Window: In the Database window, click the Relationships button on the toolbar or right-click any blank area in the Database window and select Relationships. Select File → Print Relationships from the menu. Modify the report that appears in Print Preview, if necessary, and then click the Print button on the toolbar.

To Delete a Table Relationship: Open the Relationships window, click the join line that connects the tables, and press Delete. Click Yes to confirm the deletion.

Quiz

1. You can use fields with different data types to link two tables. (True or False?)

2. Which of the following statements is NOT true?

   A. Click the Relationships button on the toolbar to display the table relationships in a database.

   B. Once you have added the required tables to the Relationships window, you can relate the tables by clicking the related field in the first table and dragging it to the related field in the second table.

   C. Referential integrity keeps records in related fields valid and accurate.

   D. For most people, table relationships are an easy-to-understand, straightforward concept.

3. You have created a relationship between a Customers table and a related Customer Orders table and have established referential integrity in this relationship without the Cascade Delete Related Records option. Can you delete a record in the Customers table if it has related records in the Customer Orders table? (Yes or No?)

4. If the Cascade Delete Related Records referential integrity option is selected, when you delete a record in the main table, Access will automatically delete any matching records in the related table. (True or False?)

5. How can you display the relationships in a database?

   A. Select View → Relationships from the menu.

   B. Click the Relationships button in the Database window.

   C. Click the Relationships button on the toolbar.

   D. Select Edit → Relationships from the menu.

6. How can you add a table to the Relationships window?

   A. Select Edit → Add Table from the menu.

   B. Click the Show Table button on the toolbar.

   C. Select the table from the Table list on the toolbar.

   D. Select Tools → Add Table from the menu.

Homework

1. Open the Homework database.

2. Open the Customers table in Design View. Set the SSN field as the table's primary key (if it isn't already). Save your changes and close the Customers table.

3. Using the Relationship window, establish a relationship between the Customers table and the Insurance Claims table, using the SSN field to join the two tables.

4. Enforce referential integrity for the Customers/Insurance Claims relationship.

5. Enable Cascade Update Related Fields and Cascade Delete Related Records for the Customers/Insurance Claims relationship.

6. Close the Relationships window.

7. Close the Homework database.

Quiz Answers

1. False. With the exception of AutoNumber and Number fields, related fields must always have the same data type in order to be used to join two tables.

2. D. If only this were true! The truth is, understanding how to create and work with table relationships is a concept that most users struggle with initially.

3. No. Referential integrity would prevent you from deleting a record in a primary table if it has records in a related table (unless the Cascade Delete Related Records option is selected).

4. True. The Cascade Delete Related Records option automatically deletes records in any related tables.

5. C. Click the Relationships button on the toolbar to display the relationships in a database.

6. B. You can add a table to the Relationships window by clicking the Show Table button on the toolbar.

CHAPTER 6

WORKING WITH QUERIES

CHAPTER OBJECTIVES:

Understand the various types of queries and their purposes, Lesson 6.2

Create queries based on more than one table, Lesson 6.3

Create queries that calculate and summarize information, Lessons 6.4, 6.7, 6.12

Use the Expression Builder to create expressions, Lesson 6.5

Use an IIf function, Lesson 6.6

Display only top or bottom values, Lesson 6.8

Create parameter queries that prompt the user for information, Lesson 6.9

Create queries that find duplicate and unmatched records, Lessons 6.10—6.11

Create action queries that delete, update, append, and export information, Lessons 6.13—6.16

CHAPTER TASK: CREATE A VARIETY OF QUERIES THAT ANALYZE AND MANIPULATE DATABASE INFORMATION

Prerequisites

- **How to use menus, toolbars, dialog boxes, and shortcut keystrokes.**
- **How to open and modify database objects.**
- **A basic understanding of queries: how to specify criteria and sort information.**

Queries are the stars of Microsoft Access. Queries make sense out of all the thousands of jumbled records and display exactly what you need to know. Queries discover things like what the average price of tea in China is or which customers bought the most parakeet food from your company. Queries can even make widespread changes to the records in your database without wearing out your mouse and keyboard! For example, a *delete query* can automatically delete a whole bunch of records that meet your criteria.

In this chapter you will learn how to harness the power of queries. First you will learn about all the different types of queries: simple select queries, parameter queries that prompt you for more information, crosstab queries that summarize records in an easy-to-understand format, and action queries that actually modify the records in your database.

All this power comes with a price tag: Many people find that queries are one of the more difficult database objects, and learning how to fully utilize queries isn't something you can learn in an afternoon. By the time you finish this chapter, however, you will have a good start towards understanding and mastering queries.

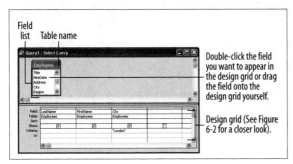

Field list

Table name

Double-click the field you want to appear in the design grid or drag the field onto the design grid yourself.

Design grid (See Figure 6-2 for a closer look).

Figure 6-1. The Query window in Design view.

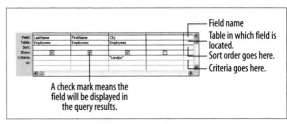

Field name

Table in which field is located.

Sort order goes here.

Criteria goes here.

A check mark means the field will be displayed in the query results.

Figure 6-2. A close-up of the design grid.

Before we start tackling the functions and types of queries, let's take a step back and review. This lesson is more of a "cheat sheet" than an exercise. Hopefully, it will help you remember what you already know about queries.

Figure 6-1 shows the Query window in Design view, Figure 6-2 shows a close-up of the design grid, and Table 6-1 outlines the Common Criteria Operators.

Table 6-1. Common Criteria Operators

Operator	Example	Description
=	="MN"	Finds records equal to MN.
	"MN"	Finds records not equal to MN.
<	<10	Finds records less than 10.
< =	<=10	Finds records less than or equal to 10.
>	>10	Finds records greater than 10.
> =	>=10	Finds records greater than or equal to 10.
BETWEEN	BETWEEN 1/1/99 AND 12/31/99	Finds records between 1/1/99 AND 12/31/99.
LIKE	LIKE "S*"	Finds text beginning with the letter "S." You can use LIKE with wildcards such as *.
NOT	NOT "MN"	Finds records not equal to MN.
IS NULL	IS NULL	Finds records whose fields are empty.
IS NOT NULL	IS NOT NULL	Finds records whose fields contain values.

QUICK REFERENCE

TO CREATE A QUERY IN DESIGN VIEW:

1. CLICK THE QUERIES ICON IN THE OBJECTS BAR, THEN DOUBLE-CLICK *CREATE QUERY IN DESIGN VIEW.*

2. SELECT THE TABLE OR QUERY YOU WANT TO USE AND CLICK ADD.

3. REPEAT STEP 2 AS NECESSARY FOR ADDITIONAL TABLES OR QUERIES. CLICK CLOSE WHEN YOU'RE FINISHED.

4. DOUBLE-CLICK EACH FIELD YOU WANT TO INCLUDE FROM THE FIELD LIST.

OR...

DRAG THE FIELD FROM THE FIELD LIST ONTO THE DESIGN GRID.

5. IN THE DESIGN GRID, ENTER ANY DESIRED SEARCH CRITERIA FOR THE FIELD IN THE *CRITERIA* ROW.

6. CLICK THE SORT BOX LIST ARROW FOR THE FIELD AND SELECT A SORT ORDER.

7. CLOSE THE QUERY WINDOW.

8. CLICK YES TO SAVE THE QUERY, ENTER A QUERY NAME, AND THEN CLICK OK.

Understanding the Different Types of Queries

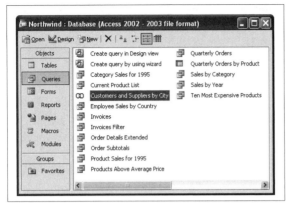

Figure 6-3. Each type of query has its own icon so that you can identify it. Table 6-2 describes the different types of queries.

We will cover most of these query types in this chapter, so here's a quick overview of the different types of queries you'll find in Microsoft Access. Each type of query has its own icon, as shown in Figure 6-3. Table 6-2 describes the different types of queries.

Up until now, when you thought of a query, you were actually probably thinking of a *select query*—a particular type of query. Select queries are by far the most common and useful type of query in Access; however, there are other types of queries that are also important.

QUICK REFERENCE

- REFER TO TABLE 6-2 TO BE ABLE TO IDENTIFY THE VARIOUS TYPES OF MICROSOFT ACCESS QUERIES AND WHAT EACH OF THEM DOES.

Table 6-2. Types of Queries

Query Type	Description
Select Query	The most basic and common type of query, select queries find and display the data you want from one or more tables or queries.
Parameter Query	Prompts the user for specific information every time the query is run.
Crosstab Query	Summarizes data in a table format that makes it easy to read and compare information.
While select queries display information that matches your criteria, the following action queries do something to the data that matches your criteria—such as change or delete it.	
Make_table Query	Creates a new table from all or part of the data in one or more tables. Useful for backing up and exporting information.
Append Query	Appends or adds selected records from one table to another table. Useful for importing information into a table.
Delete Query	Deletes selected records from one or more tables.
Update Query	Updates selected information in a table. For example, you could raise the prices on all trips to Europe by 15 percent.
Union Query	Combines fields from two or more tables or queries into one field and is written directly in SQL.

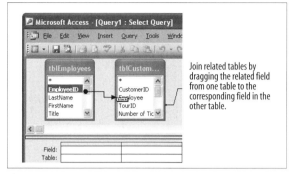

Figure 6-4. You can manually join two tables by dragging a field from one table's field list to the matching field in the other table's field list.

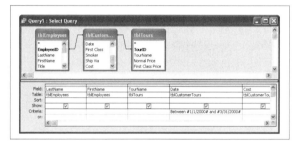

Figure 6-5. A multiple-table query in Design view.

In Access you will often need to look at and analyze information that comes from not one but several different tables. Since Access is a *relational database*, it's easy to establish a relationship between two or more tables and look at the information that goes together.

Just like it sounds, a *multiple-table* query blends together information from two or more related tables. Working with a multiple-table query usually isn't much different from working with a single-table query. You tell Access which tables you want to use in your query and specify the fields and criteria you want to see. The main difference between a multiple-table query and a single-table query is that with multiple-table queries, Access creates a link between related tables. When the query is displayed in Design view, this link (called a *join*) appears as a line that connects two or more tables.

When you create a multiple-table query, Access will usually link or join the tables automatically. Sometimes, however, you will have to manually join two tables in the query design window. You can manually join two tables by dragging a field from one table's field list to the matching field in the other table's field list, as shown in Figure 6-4. If the tables don't have any fields in common, you must add another table to act as a bridge between

them. This lesson will give you some experience creating a multiple-table query.

1 Open the Lesson 6 database.

You should know how to create a query by now…

2 Click the Queries icon in the Objects bar and then double-click Create query in Design view.

The query design window and Show Table dialog box both appear. You have to select the tables and/or queries you want to use.

3 Click the tblEmployees table and click Add.

A field list for the tblEmployees table appears in the top half of the query design window. You also want to add the tblCustomerTours table and the tblTours table to the query.

4 Add the tblCustomerTours table and tblTours table to the query.

When you have finished adding the tables and/or queries to your query, you can close the Show Table dialog box.

5 Click Close.

If two tables are related, Access will automatically connect their common fields with a join line. For example, Access automatically joined the tblTours table and the tblCustomerTours table because they are already related. If the tables aren't related you will have to manually join the tables by dragging a field from one table's field list to the matching field in the other table's field list.

You need to connect the tblEmployees table with the tblCustomerTours table.

6 Click EmployeeID in the tblEmployees field list and drag and drop it onto Employee in the tblCustomer-Tours field list.

Click EmployeeID in the tblEmployees field list and drag and drop it onto Employee in the tblCustomer-Tours field list.

⸱ NOTE ⸱ *You can remove a join from a query by clicking the join line (careful—there's not much there to click!) and pressing Delete.*

Next you need to specify the fields you want to appear in the query results. You can add fields to the query design grid in two ways:

- By double-clicking the field in the field list.
- By clicking and dragging the field down to the design grid yourself.

Because field lists don't have much room to display their contents, you may have to scroll up or down the list in order to find the field you want.

7 **Double-click the** LastName **and** FirstName **fields in the tblEmployees field list.**

Access adds the LastName and FirstName fields from the tblEmployees table to the design grid. Next add the fields for the tblTours and tblCustomerTours tables.

8 **Double-click the** TourName **field in the tblTours field list and the** Date **and** Cost **fields in the tblCustomerTours field list.**

Next you need to specify any criteria for the query. For this exercise, you want to see tours from the first quarter of the year.

9 **Click the** Date **column's** Criteria **row and type** Between 1/1/00 and 3/31/00.

You want to sort your query by date, so…

10 **Click the** Date **column's** Sort **box list arrow and select** Ascending.

That's it! You've just created a multiple-table query, as shown in Figure 6-5.

11 **Save the query as** qryFirstQuarterTours **and click** OK.

Let's run our new query!

12 **Click the** Run button **on the toolbar.**

Other ways to run a query are to open the query from the Database window, or click the View button *on the toolbar in Design view, or select* Query → Run *from the menu.*

Access displays the results of the query. The results show the names of the employees who sold tours and the names, dates, and costs of each tour.

Creating a Calculated Field

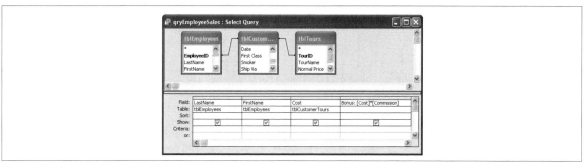

Figure 6-6. Creating a calculated field.

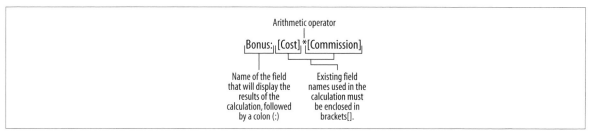

Figure 6-7. To enter fields in an expression, type the field name in brackets ([Order Total]).

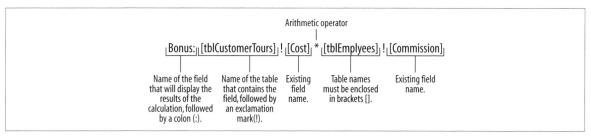

Figure 6-8. If a field name exists in more than one table, you will need to enter the name of the table that contains the field in brackets ([Customer Tours]) followed by an exclamation mark (!). Then type the field name in brackets ([Order Total]).

Normally, when you create a database, you should only have to enter the information you need and not worry about data or values that Access calculates based on information already in the database. A calculated field performs some type of arithmetic on one or more fields in a database to come up with a completely new field. For example, if your database has an Order Total field and a Tax Rate field, Access can calculate these two fields to find out the Sales Tax for each order: [Order Total] × [Tax Rate] = [Sales Tax].

You must create an *expression* (or formula) to perform a calculation. To enter fields in an expression, type the field name in brackets ([Order Total]), as described in Figure 6-7. If a field name exists in more than one table, you will need to enter the name of the table that contains the field in brackets ([Customer Tours]) followed by an

exclamation mark (!). Then type the field name in brackets, such as [Order Total], as described in Figure 6-8. For example if an Orders table and a Shipping table both contain a Date field, you would tell Access which of the two Date fields you want to use by typing the table name ([Orders]), an exclamation mark (!), and then the field name ([Date]) or, in other words, [Orders]![Date]. Yes, calculated fields can be a little confusing at first…

This lesson will show you how to add a calculated field to a query.

1 If necessary, open the Lesson 6 database.

Now let's open the qryEmployeeSales query in Design view.

2 Click the Queries icon in the Objects bar if necessary, click the qryEmployeeSales query, and then click the Design button.

Instead of creating a query from scratch, you can modify an existing query and save it with a different name.

3 Click the blank Field cell of the fourth column and type Bonus:[Cost]*[Commission], as shown in Figure 6-6.

You can also use the Expression Builder to help you create your calculated fields. Click the Builder button on the toolbar, double-click the field you want to use in the calculation, click the button that corresponds to the calculation you want, and then click or type any other fields or values you want to use.

The expression you entered will create a new calculated field named "Bonus" that will display the results of the Cost field in the tblCustomerTours table multiplied by the Commission field in the tblEmployees table.

Let's see the results of our calculated field.

4 Click the Run button on the toolbar.

Other ways to run a query are to open the query from the Database window, or click the View button on the toolbar in Design view, or select Query → Run from the menu.

Access displays the results of the query. The "Bonus" calculated field multiplies the Cost field by the Commission field in each record and displays the results.

Save your changes in a new query with a different name. Here's how:

5 Select File → Save As from the menu.

The Save As dialog box appears.

6 Type qryEmployeeBonus in the Save Query 'qryEmployeeSales' To: box and click OK.

Access saves your changes in a new query named "qryEmployeeBonus."

7 Close the query.

You're already familiar with some of the arithmetic operators used in expressions; including math symbols such as the plus sign (+) to perform addition between values, and the minus sign (-) to perform subtraction between values. Check out Table 6-3 below for a refresher on the various arithmetic operators.

Table 6-3. Arithmetic Operators

Operator	Description
*	Multiplication
+	Addition
-	Subtraction
/	Division
^	Exponentiation

QUICK REFERENCE

TO CREATE AN EXPRESSION OR CALCULATION IN A QUERY:

1. DISPLAY THE QUERY IN DESIGN VIEW.

2. CLICK THE FIELD ROW OF A BLANK COLUMN IN THE DESIGN GRID.

3. ENTER THE FIELD NAME FOR THE CALCULATED FIELD FOLLOWED BY A COLON (:).

4. ENTER THE EXPRESSION YOU WANT ACCESS TO CALCULATE, USING THE PROPER SYNTAX.

OR...

CLICK THE BUILD BUTTON ON THE TOOLBAR, DOUBLE-CLICK THE FIELD YOU WANT TO USE IN THE CALCULATION, CLICK THE BUTTON THAT CORRESPONDS TO THE CALCULATION YOU WANT, AND THEN CLICK OR TYPE ANY OTHER FIELDS OR VALUES YOU WANT TO USE. WHEN YOU'RE FINISHED, CLICK OK.

5. CLICK THE VIEW BUTTON OR RUN BUTTON ON THE TOOLBAR TO SEE THE RESULTS.

Working with Expressions and the Expression Builder

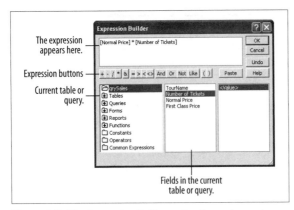

The expression appears here.

Expression buttons

Current table or query.

Fields in the current table or query.

Figure 6-9. The Expression Builder makes it easy to create expressions and calculations by letting you select the fields and operators you want to use in the expression.

You can add calculations to queries, forms, and reports by typing an *expression,* or a formula that tells Access exactly what to calculate. An expression can be any combination of values, identifiers (such as the value in a field), and operators that result in a value. Here's an example of an expression that calculates profit from two fields called Income and Expenses:

    Profit: [Income] – [Expenses]

You can also use constants in an expression, such as:

    Commission: [Sales] * .15

Number fields aren't the only types of fields that you can use in expressions—you can also perform calculations with dates, times, and text data.

The problem with creating expressions is you have to enter a formula so that Access understands it (and believe me, Access isn't very bright). For example, when you create an expression, some types of information must be enclosed between special characters so that Access knows what type of information it is—table names and field names must be enclosed in [brackets], text strings in "quotation marks," and so on. Table 6-4 has more information about how to use various elements in an expression.

If you know what you want an expression to do but not how to write it, you can try using the *Expression Builder.* The Expression Builder lets you pick the fields, mathematical symbols, and functions you can use to create an expression.

This lesson will give you some more experience writing expressions—both on your own and using the Expression Builder.

1 Click the qrySales **query and then click the** Design **button.**

First you need to insert a blank column at the beginning of the design grid. Here's how:

2 Position the mouse over the top of the Normal Price **field (until** ⤓ **changes to** ⬇**) and click to select the field. Press** Insert **to add a new column.**

A column is inserted before the Normal Price column. In the next step, you will learn how to create one of the most common database functions: how to combine the tblEmployees table's FirstName and LastName fields to display the full name.

3 Type Agent:[FirstName]&" "&[LastName] **in the Field row.**

The ampersand (&) symbol is used to combine or *concatenate* two or more text fields. The " " adds a space between the [FirstName] and [LastName] fields.

Next you need to enter an expression that calculates the cost of the tour by multiplying the Number of Tickets field by the Normal Price field. You will use the Expression Builder to help you write this expression.

4 Click a new blank field and click the Build **button on the toolbar.**

> **TIP**
>
> *Another way to use the Expression Builder is to right-click in any field and select* Build *from the shortcut menu.*

The Expression Builder appears, as shown in Figure 6-9. The Expression Builder contains an area where you can build the expression, buttons you can use to build the expression, and the fields and controls in the current query, report, or form.

5 Double-click Normal Price, **click the** * Multiplication button, **and double-click** Number of Tickets.

The completed expression appears in the expression box, as shown in Figure 6-9. You're finished writing the expression so you can close the Expression Builder.

6 Click OK.

The Expression Builder closes. Add a meaningful label to the new calculated field.

7 In the new calculated field, replace the Expr1: label with Total:

The edited expression should read Total:[Normal Price]*[Number of Tickets]. Let's see the results of the new query.

8 Click the Run button on the toolbar.

The query combines the FirstName and LastName fields in the new Agent field and displays the total sales price in the new Total field.

9 Click the Save button on the menu to save your changes and then close the query.

Microsoft Access is very strict about how you write your expressions. If your expressions aren't written in the correct syntax, they won't work. Use the following table as a guideline for adding fields, text, and constants to your expressions.

Table 6-4. How Types of Data Should Look in an Expression

Type of Data	How It Should Look
Text	"Minneapolis"
Date/Time	#20-Mar-99# (Access will add the # symbols)
Field Name	[Price]
Field Name in a Specific Table	[Products]![Price]
Concatenated (Combined) Text and Fields	[Last]& ", "&[First]
Calculated Field (Using Two Fields)	[SalePrice]-[Cost]
Calculated Field (Using a Field and a Constant)	[SalePrice]*0.1

QUICK REFERENCE

TO CREATE AN EXPRESSION WITH THE EXPRESSION BUILDER:

1. DISPLAY THE QUERY IN DESIGN VIEW.

2. CLICK THE FIELD ROW OF A BLANK COLUMN IN THE DESIGN GRID.

3. CLICK THE BUILD BUTTON ON THE TOOLBAR, DOUBLE-CLICK THE FIELD YOU WANT TO USE IN THECALCULATION, CLICK THE BUTTON THAT CORRESPONDS TO THE CALCULATION YOU WANT, AND THEN CLICK OR TYPE ANY OTHER FIELDS OR VALUES YOU WANT TO USE.

4. CLICK OK.

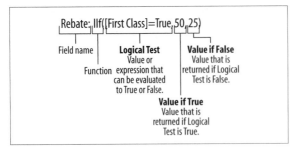

Figure 6-10. The syntax for the IIf function.

Figure 6-11. Here the IIf function evaluates the value in the First Class field and returns 50 if the First Class field is True and 25 if the First Class field is False.

Functions are used to create more complicated calculations or expressions than operators can. For example, the SUM function adds several values together, and the IPmt function calculates the loan payments based on an interest rate, the length of the loan, and the principal amount of the loan.

There are several hundred functions in Access, but all of them are used in a similar way: the name of the function, followed by the arguments in parenthesis. An *argument* in Access is the value a function uses to perform its calculation—not the heated disagreement you have over political views. For example, the argument in the formula πr^2 would be *r*, or the radius, used to find the area of a circle.

This lesson introduces a very useful database function: the *IIf* function. The IIf function is a *conditional function* or *logical function* because it evaluates a condition and returns one value if the condition is true and another value if the condition is false. For example, you could use the IIf function in an invoice to create a formula that would subtract a 5-percent discount from the invoice if the total were more than 500 dollars—otherwise, the IIf Function wouldn't subtract anything.

The IIf function contains three arguments, as shown in Figure 6-10. Since you can use the Expression Builder to help you create IIf function formulas, you really don't need to memorize the syntax of the function.

In this lesson you will use the IIf function to create a field that gives passengers a 50-dollar rebate if they fly first class and a 25-dollar rebate if they fly coach, as shown in Figure 6-11.

1 Click the qryRebate query and then click the Design button.

You need to create a calculated field that will determine how much of a rebate passengers should receive. Create this field in the first blank Field row.

2 Click the blank Field row in the fifth column and click the Build button on the toolbar.

The Expression Builder appears.

In the bottom-left of the window, the Expression Builder displays a list of several folders that contain information. For example, the Tables folder contains a list of all the tables in the current database. These folders are displayed in a *hierarchical* view. A plus symbol (⊞) or a minus symbol (⊟) next to a folder means a folder contains several subfolders. Normally, these subfolders are hidden. You can display the hidden folders within a folder by double-clicking the folder. To see the contents of a folder, simply select the folder—its contents will appear in the middle and left windows.

To use one of the built-in functions, double-click the Functions folder and select the Built-In Functions folder in the bottom-left window.

3 Double-click the Functions folder in the bottom-left window.

The Functions folder expands and displays its contents. The Built-In Functions folder contains several hundred functions that are included in Access.

4 Click the Built-In Functions folder.

When you select the Built-In Functions folder in the left window, the middle window displays the function categories you can use, and the right window displays the functions in the selected category. If you know the category of the function you want to use, you can select it in the middle window to narrow down your choices in the right window.

5 Scroll down the middle window and find and click the Program Flow function category.

The right window displays the Program Flow functions.

6 Double-click the IIf function in the right window.

Access adds IIf («expr», «truepart», «falsepart») to the expression box. Now that you know the proper syntax of the IIf function, you need to replace the argument names with the data values. You can double-click to select any argument name so that you can replace it with your own value.

7 Double-click the «expr» argument.

You need to specify the logical test—if the passenger flew first class or not.

8 Double-click the Tables folder in the left window, click the tblCustomerTours folder, and then double-click the First Class field in the middle window.

The Expression Builder adds the First Class field to the expression. Finish the rest of the logical test.

9 Type =True.

Your expression should read IIf ([tblCustomer-Tours]![First Class]=True, «truepart», «falsepart»). Now you have to replace the «truepart» and «falsepart» arguments with the values you want to use if the IIf statement is true or false.

10 Double-click the «truepart» argument and type 50, then double-click the «falsepart» argument and type 25.

11 Click OK.

The Expression Builder closes. We need to give the new calculated control a more meaningful name…

12 In the new calculated field, replace the Expr1: label with Rebate:

Let's see the results of the new query.

13 Click the Run button on the toolbar.

The IIf expression in the new Rebate field evaluates the First Class field and returns a 50-dollar rebate if the customer flew first class, and a 25-dollar rebate if not.

Save your changes.

14 Save your changes and close the query.

QUICK REFERENCE

TO CREATE AN IIF (IF…THEN) FUNCTION:

1. DISPLAY THE QUERY IN DESIGN VIEW.

2. CLICK THE FIELD ROW OF A BLANK COLUMN IN THE DESIGN GRID.

3. ENTER THE FIELD NAME FOLLOWED BY A COLON (:).

4. TYPE THE EXPRESSION USING THE SYNTAX IIF(«EXPR», «TRUEPART», «FALSEPART»)

OR…

CLICK THE BUILD BUTTON ON THE TOOLBAR. DOUBLE-CLICK THE FUNCTIONS FOLDER IN THE BOTTOM-LEFT WINDOW, CLICK THE BUILT-IN FUNCTIONS FOLDER, SCROLL DOWN THE MIDDLE WINDOW AND CLICK THE PROGRAM FLOW CATEGORY, THEN SCROLL DOWN THE RIGHT COLUMN AND DOUBLE-CLICK THE IIF FUNCTION. REPLACE THE PARTS OF THE PASTED IIF FUNCTION WITH THE FIELDS AND VALUES YOU WANT, THEN CLICK OK.

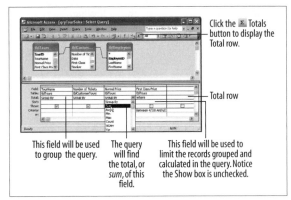

Click the **Σ** Totals button to display the Total row.

Total row

This field will be used to group the query.

The query will find the total, or *sum*, of this field.

This field will be used to limit the records grouped and calculated in the query. Notice the Show box is unchecked.

Figure 6-12. Using a query to find the total number of tickets and sales, grouped by the TourName field and the Number of Tickets field.

When you work with queries, you will often be less interested in the individual records and more interested in summarized information about groups of records. A query can calculate information about a group of records in one or more tables. For example, you could create a query that finds the total amount of tea your company sold to China in 1998 or how much all that tea cost. The *Total row* lets you group and summarize information in a query. The Total row normally is tucked away from view in the query design window—you can make the Total appear by clicking the Totals button on the toolbar or by selecting View → Totals from the menu. Once the Total row is displayed, you can tell Access how you want to summarize the fields.

1 Click the qryTourSales query and then click the Design button.

First you need to add the field that you want to group data by onto the design grid. You want to calculate the total sales and number of tickets sold for each tour package, so you will group the query by the Tour-Name field.

2 Double-click the TourName field in the tblTours field list.

The TourName field appears as the first field in the design grid. Next you need to add the fields you want to summarize.

3 Double-click the Number of Tickets and Cost fields in the tblCustomerTours field list.

To summarize your query, you must summon the *Total row*. To summon the Total row, click the Totals

button on the toolbar or select View → Totals from the menu.

4 Click the **Σ** Totals button on the toolbar.

TIP *Another way to display the Total row is to select View → Totals from the menu.*

The Total row appears in the design grid. "Group By" must remain in the TourName Total row to group the records by the TourName field. Next you need to select the fields you want to summarize and the calculation you want to perform on them.

5 Click the Total row in the Number of Tickets column and click the list arrow that appears.

A list of calculations appears, similar to those shown in Figure 6-12. All you have to do is simply select the calculation you want to perform on the field. Table 6-5 describes the available calculations.

6 Select Sum from the list.

This will total the values in the Number of Tickets field.

7 Click the Total row in the Cost column, click the list arrow, and select Sum from the list.

You can specify criteria to limit the records you want to be calculated—simply enter the criteria in the Criteria row of any grouped or calculated fields. If the field you want to use for the criteria isn't one of the grouped or calculated fields, you must use the "Where" option in the field's Total row. The "Where" option limits the records used in the calculation without being included in the query results.

You want to calculate only those records from the second quarter of the year.

8 Double-click the Date field in the tblCustomer-Tours field list.

Here's how to add criteria to the Date field.

9 Click the Total row in the Date column, click the list arrow, and select Where from the list.

The "Where" option is used only to limit records—its results cannot be displayed in the results of the query. Access automatically unchecks the "Show" check box.

10 Click the Date column's Criteria row and type Between 4/1/00 and 6/30/00.

You're ready to see the results of the new query.

11 Click the Run button on the toolbar.

Access displays the results of the query, which calculates the total sales and number of tickets sold for each tour package.

12 Save the query as qryTourTotals and then close the query.

Table 6-5. Total Options

Option	Description
Group By	Groups the values in the field so that you can perform calculations on the groups.
Sum	Calculates the total (sum) of values in a field.
Avg	Calculates the average of values in a field.
Min	Finds the lowest value in a field.
Max	Finds the highest value in a field.
Count	Counts the number of entries in a field, not including blank (Null) records.
StDev	Calculates the standard deviation of values in a field.
Var	Calculates the variance of values in a field.
First	Finds the values from the first record in a field.
Last	Finds the values from the last record in a field.
Expression	Tells Access that you want to create your own expression to calculate a field.
Where	Specifies criteria for a field to limit the records included in a calculation.

QUICK REFERENCE

TO CALCULATE OR SUMMARIZE A GROUP OF RECORDS:

1. DISPLAY THE QUERY IN DESIGN VIEW.

2. IF NECESSARY, CLICK THE TOTALS BUTTON ON THE TOOLBAR.

3. MOVE THE FIELD THAT YOU WANT TO GROUP DATA BY ONTO THE DESIGN GRID. MAKE SURE GROUP BY APPEARS IN THAT FIELD'S TOTAL ROW.

NOTE: THE FIELD(S) YOU WANT TO GROUP BY MUST APPEAR FIRST IN THE DESIGN GRID AND HAVE GROUP BY IN THEIR TOTAL ROW.

4. MOVE THE FIELD THAT YOU WANT TO PERFORM CALCULATIONS ON ONTO THE DESIGN GRID.

5. CHOOSE THE TYPE OF CALCULATION THAT YOU WANT TO PERFORM BY CLICKING THE FIELD'S TOTAL ROW, CLICKING THE LIST ARROW, AND SELECTING A CALCULATION FROM THE LIST.

Display Top or Bottom Values

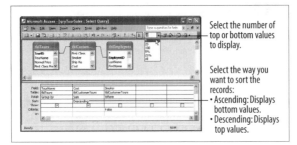

Figure 6-13. Telling Access to display only the top five values in a query.

qryTourSales : Select Query

TourName	Cost	Smoker
China	$18,900.00	0
China	$12,600.00	0
China	$12,600.00	0
China	$12,600.00	0
China	$12,600.00	0
China	$12,600.00	0
China	$12,600.00	0

Record: 1 of 7

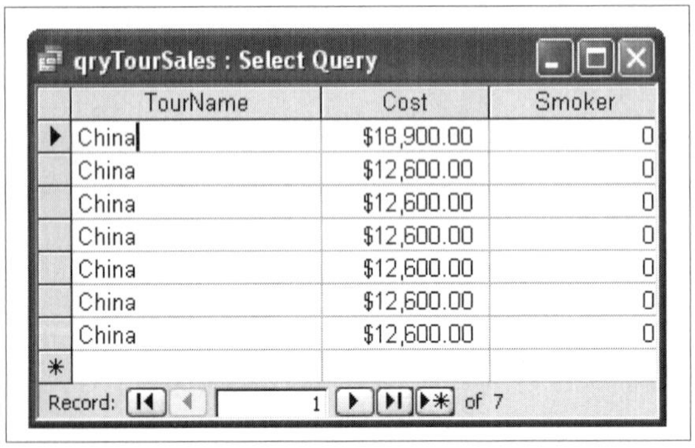

Figure 6-14. Access displays the top five values it finds in the query.

qryTourSales : Select Query

TourName	SumOfCost	Smoker
Western Canada	$75,625.00	0
African Safari	$81,795.00	0
Yucatan	$87,285.00	0
Europe 10 Days	$105,050.00	0
Historical USA	$131,950.00	0

Record: 1 of 5

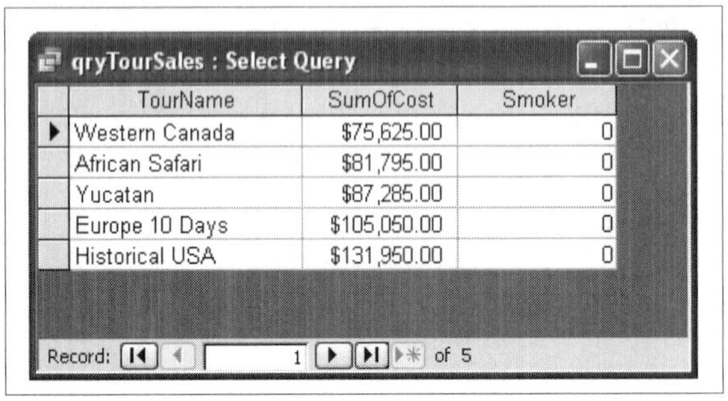

Figure 6-15. Access displays the five tours with the lowest total sales.

If all you care about is the highest or lowest values produced by a query, you can use the Top Values list in the Query Design toolbar to display only these records. For example, you could use the Top Values list to display the ten largest or smallest orders in the Invoices table.

This lesson explains how you can use the Top Values list to display the top or bottom values in a query.

1 Click the qryTourSales query and then click the Design button.

Move to the next step and add the fields you want to see in your query.

2 Double-click the TourName field in the tblTours field list, and the Cost and Smoker fields in the tblCustomerTours field list.

You want to create a query that retrieves the five most expensive nonsmoking tours. First you need to add the nonsmoking criteria to the query.

3 Click the Criteria row in the Smoker column and type False.

Now you need to sort the field that you want to display the top or bottom values for. The Sort row works a little differently when you're using top or bottom values:

- **Ascending:** Displays bottom values.
- **Descending:** Displays top values.

You want the query to display the top values in the Cost field, so…

4 In the Cost column, click the Sort box list arrow and select Descending.

Next you have to use the Top Values list to specify the number of top values you want to be displayed in your query results.

5 Click the Top Values list arrow on the toolbar and select 5, as shown in Figure 6-13.

This will display the five most expensive tickets. You're ready to run the query.

6 Click the Run button on the toolbar.

Access displays the results of the query, similar to Figure 6-14.

7 Click the View button on the toolbar to display the query in Design view.

You can also use the Top Values feature to display the top or bottom values from a calculation. Let's modify the query so that it calculates the total sales of nonsmoking tour sales.

8 If the Total row is not already displayed, click the Totals button on the toolbar.

The Total row appears. You need to specify which field you want to use to group the query, which field(s) you want to be calculated, and which fields are used to limit the number of records displayed in the query.

You want to group records using the TourName field, and since its Total row already displays Group By, you can leave it as it is. You will need to tweak the Total row for both the Cost and Smoker fields, however.

9 Click the Total row in the Cost column, click the list arrow, and select Sum from the list.

This will total the Cost field. The Smoker field is used as criteria to limit the records displayed to only nonsmokers—it shouldn't be included in the query results. Move on to the next step to tell Access this.

10 Click the Total row in the Smokers column, click the list arrow, and select Where from the list.

One more change before we run the query—this time instead of displaying the top values for the Cost field we want to display its bottom values.

11 In the Cost column, click the Sort box list arrow and select Ascending.

This will summarize the five tours with the lowest sales (for nonsmokers). Let's see the results…

12 Click the Run button on the toolbar.

Access displays the results of the query, as shown in Figure 6-15.

13 Save the query as qryBottomTours and then close the query.

Table 6-6 explains what each of the options in the Top Values list does.

Table 6-6. The Top Values List

Do This…	…to Display This
Click 5, 25, or 100 from the Top Values List	The top 5, 25, or 100 records
Type a number, such as 15 in the Top Values box	The top 15 (or specified number of) records
Click 5% or 25% from the Top Values List	The top 5 or 25 percent of records
Type a percentage, such as 20%, in the Top Values box	The top 20 percent (or specified percent) of records
Click All from the Top Values list	All of the records

QUICK REFERENCE

TO VIEW TOP OR BOTTOM VALUES:

1. DISPLAY THE QUERY IN DESIGN VIEW.

2. CLICK THE APPROPRIATE SORT FIELD AND SELECT EITHER:

ASCENDING: DISPLAYS BOTTOM VALUES.

DESCENDING: DISPLAYS TOP VALUES.

3. SELECT AN OPTION FROM THE TOP VALUES LIST ON THE TOOLBAR.

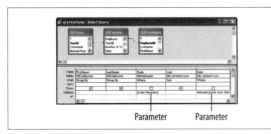

Figure 6-16. Enter a parameter by entering a message or prompt enclosed in [brackets] in the field's criteria row.

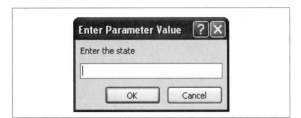

Figure 6-17. The parameter query prompts the user to enter the state.

	FirstName	LastName	SumOfCost
▶	Aaron	Burr	$243,210.00
	Bernardo	Fuentes	$265,330.00
	Joseph	Black	$70,105.00
	LeAnne	Norton	$145,520.00
	Shelia	Lindquist	$129,140.00

Figure 6-18. The results of the parameter query.

Getting tired of modifying a query every time you want to use a new criterion? A parameter query is your answer. A parameter query prompts the user for the query's criteria. For example, you could create a Regional Sales query that would ask for the name of the state that you want to filter by.

Creating a parameter query is easy. All you have to do is click the Criteria row for the field that you want to use as a parameter and type a message, enclosed in [brackets], that you want Access to display when you run the query, as shown in Figure 6-16.

1 Click the qryTourSales query and then click the Design button.

As always, you need to add the field that you want to group data by onto the design grid. This time we want

to create a query that summarizes total employee sales. Here are the fields that we will use in the query:

2 In the tblEmployees field list, double-click the FirstName, LastName, and State fields, and in the tblCustomerTours field list, double-click the Cost and Date fields.

Next you need to tell the query that you want to group and summarize the query.

3 If necessary, click the Totals button on the toolbar.

The Total row appears. You need to specify which field(s) you want to use to group the query, which field(s) you want to be calculated, and which field(s) you want to use to limit the number of records displayed in the query.

You want to group records using the FirstName, Last-Name, and State fields and find the total of the Cost field.

4 Click the Cost column's Total row, click the list arrow, and select Sum from the list.

This will total the Cost field. We will use the Date field as criteria to limit the records to those that fall between two dates. Instead of entering a criteria expression with two fixed date values, such as "Between 1/1/00 and 3/31/00," we will create two parameters that will prompt the user to enter the two date values each time they run the query.

5 Click the Date column's Criteria row and type Between [Enter start date] and [Enter end date].

You've just created two parameters—the [Enter start date] parameter and the [Enter end date] parameter.

Since the Date field is only being used as a criteria field, you need to select the "Where" option from its Total row.

6 Click the Date column's Total row, click the list arrow, and select Where from the list.

The "Show" check box automatically unchecks itself, indicating that the Date field will not appear in the query results.

Let's add one more parameter—one that prompts the user to enter the state where the tour was sold.

7 Click the State column's Criteria row and type [Enter the state].

This will prompt the user to enter the name of the state.

Since the State field is only being used as a criteria field, you need to select the "Where" option from its Total row.

8 Click the State column's Total row, click the list arrow, and select Where from the list.

Let's test our parameter query.

9 Click the Run button on the toolbar.

Access prompts you to enter the first parameter, as shown in Figure 6-17. You want to summarize records from Washington.

10 Type WA and click OK.

Access prompts you for the next parameter—the start date.

11 Type 1/1/00 and click OK.

Access prompts you for the last parameter—the end date.

12 Type 6/30/00 and click OK.

Access displays the results of the parameter query, as shown in Figure 6-18. The order of your query may be different if you put the FirstName field on the design grid before the LastName field.

13 Save the query as qryParameter and then close the query.

Some advanced Access developers use custom-made forms to provide parameter queries with their information. If developers bind a parameter to the controls on a form (such as [frmCustomers]![Name]), users can fill out one dialog box instead of having to fill out five or six pop-up dialog boxes.

QUICK REFERENCE

TO CREATE A PARAMETER QUERY:

1. DISPLAY THE QUERY IN DESIGN VIEW.

2. CLICK THE CRITERIA ROW FOR THE FIELD YOU WANT TO USE FOR YOUR PARAMETER CRITERIA AND ENTER THE TEXT OF THE PROMPT, SURROUNDED BY SQUARE BRACKETS [ ].

3. CLICK THE VIEW BUTTON OR RUN BUTTON ON THE TOOLBAR TO RUN THE QUERY.

4. ENTER A CRITERIA VALUE IN RESPONSE TO THE PROMPT AND CLICK OK.

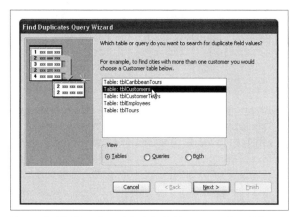

Figure 6-19. Step One: Select the table or query in which you want to search for duplicate values.

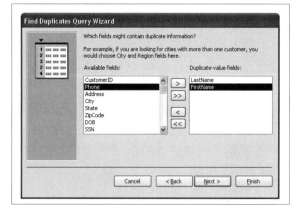

Figure 6-20. Step Two: Select the field or fields that contain the duplicate values.

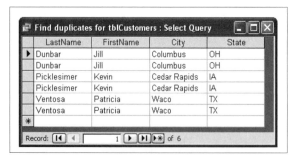

Figure 6-21. The query displays those records that have duplicate values in both the LastName and FirstName fields.

The Find Duplicates Query Wizard helps you find records that have the same value in one or more fields. So when would you need to use a Find Duplicates Query? Here are a few scenarios:

- To search for duplicate values in an Orders table to find out which customers have placed more than one order.

- To search for duplicate values in several fields to search for data-entry errors. For example, if you and another user accidentally entered the same customers into a table, you could search for duplicate values in the Last-Name and FirstName fields to find and delete the duplicated records.

Access provides a wizard to make creating a query that finds duplicate information in a snap.

"Arrr-rrgh!" you shout as you realize that you and another co-worker have just entered the same customers into a database. Fortunately, you can find the duplicated records by using the Find Duplicates Query Wizard.

1 If necessary, open the Lesson 6 database.

Now let's create a new query.

2 In the Database window, click the Queries icon in the Objects bar and click the New button.

The New Query dialog box appears.

3 Select the Find Duplicates Query Wizard and click OK.

The first step of the Find Duplicates Query Wizard appears, as shown in Figure 6-19. Choose the table or query that you want to sift through for duplicate records.

4 Select the tblCustomers table and click Next.

The second step of the Find Duplicates Query Wizard appears, as shown in Figure 6-20. Her you will tell Access which field or fields might contain the duplicate information.

Since you are trying to find duplicate customers, you decide to search the FirstName and LastName fields for duplicate values.

5 Double-click the LastName and FirstName fields.

The LastName and FirstName fields appear in the "Duplicate-value fields" list.

6 Click Next.

The next step of the Find Duplicates Query Wizard appears. You can select any field (other than the ones you specified in Step 4) that you want to be displayed in the query.

You decide to display the City and State fields so you can verify that the records are duplicates.

7 Double-click the City and State fields. Click Next when you're finished.

You're finished! Well, almost. You have to give your query a name, or you can accept the default name Access gives the query.

8 Click Finish.

Access saves the query with the name "Find duplicates for tblCustomers" and displays the results of the query, as shown in Figure 6-21.

9 Close the query.

QUICK REFERENCE

TO USE THE FIND DUPLICATES QUERY WIZARD:

1. IN THE DATABASE WINDOW, CLICK THE QUERIES ICON IN THE OBJECTS BAR AND CLICK THE NEW BUTTON.

2. SELECT FIND DUPLICATES QUERY WIZARD AND CLICK OK.

3. SELECT THE TABLE OR QUERY YOU WANT TO SEARCH AND CLICK NEXT.

4. DOUBLE-CLICK THE FIELD(S) THAT MAY CONTAIN THE DUPLICATE VALUES AND CLICK NEXT.

5. DOUBLE-CLICK ANY ADDITIONAL FIELDS THAT YOU WANT TO APPEAR IN THE QUERY RESULTS AND CLICK NEXT.

6. CLICK FINISH.

Finding Unmatched Records

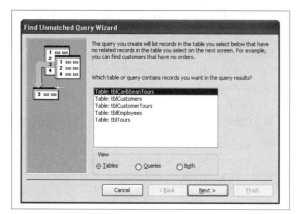

Figure 6-22. Select the table or query with the values you want to display in the query.

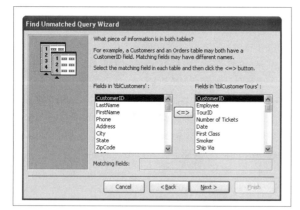

Figure 6-23. Specify the field that will join the records in the first table to the records in the second table.

Figure 6-24. The query displays those records in the Customers table that do not have any matching records in the tblCustomerTours table.

The Find Unmatched Query Wizard helps you find the records in one table that do not have matching records in another table. Some scenarios when you might need to create such a query include:

- To find customers who have never placed an order.
- To find products that have never been purchased.
- To find "orphan" records. If you haven't enforced referential integrity in your related tables, deleting a record in one table could leave one or more orphan records in a related table. For example, if you delete a customer record from a Customer table, you may leave several unmatched records for that customer in an Order table.

In this lesson you will use the Find Unmatched Query Wizard to create a query to find customers who have never booked a tour.

1 In the Database window, click the Queries icon in the Objects bar and click the New button.

The New Query dialog box appears.

2 Select the Find Unmatched Query Wizard and click OK.

The first step of the Find Unmatched Query Wizard appears, as shown in Figure 6-22. You need to choose the table or query whose values you want to display in the query. Since you want to find customers without any tour packages, you would select the tblCustomers table.

3 Select the tblCustomers table and click Next.

The second step of the Find Unmatched Query Wizard appears. Here you have to tell Access which table contains the related records. Let's select the tblCustomerTours table.

4 Select the tblCustomerTours table and click Next.

The third step of the Find Unmatched Query Wizard appears, as shown in Figure 6-23. Here you have to specify the related field to join the records in the first table to the records in the second table. Once you have selected the matching record in both tables, click the <=> button to join the two tables.

5 Verify that the CustomerID field is selected in both tables and click the <=> button.

The Matching fields area displays the fields used to join the tables (CustomerID = CustomerID).

6 Click Next.

Almost there! Now you have to specify which fields you want to see in the query.

7 Double-click the LastName, FirstName, City, and State fields.

The LastName, FirstName, City, and State fields should all appear in the "Selected fields" list.

8 Click Next.

Here you can give your query a name—or you can accept the default name that Access gives the query.

9 Click Finish.

Access saves the query with the name "tblCustomers Without Matching tblCustomerTours" and displays the results of the query, as shown in Figure 6-24.

10 Close the query.

QUICK REFERENCE

TO USE THE FIND UNMATCHED QUERY WIZARD:

1. IN THE DATABASE WINDOW, CLICK THE QUERIES ICON IN THE OBJECTS BAR AND CLICK THE NEW BUTTON.

2. SELECT FIND UNMATCHED QUERY WIZARD AND CLICK OK.

3. SELECT THE TABLE WHOSE VALUES YOU WANT TO DISPLAY AND CLICK NEXT.

4. SELECT THE TABLE THAT CONTAINS THE RELATED RECORDS AND CLICK NEXT.

5. SPECIFY THE RELATED FIELDS THAT JOIN THE TWO TABLES, THEN CLICK THE <=> BUTTON TO JOIN THE TWO TABLES AND CLICK NEXT.

6. DOUBLE-CLICK ANY ADDITIONAL FIELDS THAT YOU WANT TO APPEAR IN THE QUERY RESULTS AND CLICK NEXT.

7. CLICK FINISH.

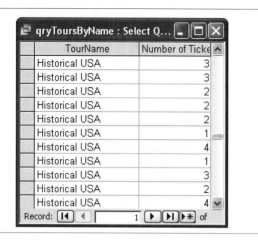

Figure 6-25. It's difficult to see the bottom line in a long list of records like this.

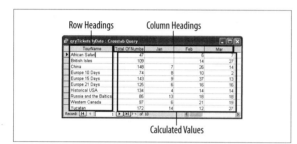

Figure 6-26. A crosstab query displays a summary view of Figure 6-24's information.

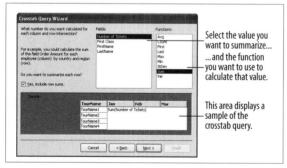

Figure 6-27. In the Crosstab Query Wizard, select the number to be calculated where the columns and rows intersect.

Figure 6-28. A crosstab query in Design view.

There are many ways that queries can help you summarize and analyze all that information in your database. A *crosstab query* displays summarized information in a table format that makes it easy to analyze and compare data. Look at the information displayed in Figure 6-25—difficult to see the bottom line, isn't it? Now look what happens when the same information is placed in a crosstab query, as shown in Figure 6-26. Which do you think is easier to understand?

You can create a crosstab query in Design View or by using the Crosstab Query Wizard. The Crosstab Query Wizard is usually much easier, but it does have some limitations:

- If you need to use more than one table or query in the crosstab query, you will first need to create a separate query that has the tables you want to use.

- You can't specify any limiting criteria when using the Crosstab Query Wizard. (But you can always modify the crosstab query in Design View and add the criteria yourself.)

In this lesson you will use the Crosstab Query Wizard to create a query that summarizes monthly ticket sales by tours.

1 In the Database window, click the Queries icon in the Objects bar and click the New button.

The New Query dialog box appears.

2 Select Crosstab Query Wizard and click OK.

The first step of the Crosstab Query Wizard appears. Here you need to select the table or query that contains the values you want. For this exercise you will use the ToursByName query as the source for the crosstab query.

3 Click the Queries option in the View section to display the queries in the database, select the qry-ToursByName query, and click Next.

The second step of the Crosstab Query Wizard is which field you want to use as the row headings for the crosstab. Let's use the TourName field for your row headings.

4 Double-click the TourName field and click Next.

The next step is determining which field you want to use for your column headings. Let's use the Date field as the column heading.

5 Double-click the Date field.

Because you selected a date field, the Crosstab Query Wizard asks by which interval you want to group the dates: date, month, quarter, year, or date/time. For this exercise you want the date column to group dates by months.

6 Double-click the Month option.

Probably the most important step in the Crosstab Query Wizard is determining which field you want to calculate where columns and rows intersect and the type of calculation you want to use to summarize the fields.

7 Select the Number of Tickets field from the Fields list and the Sum option from the Functions list, as shown in Figure 6-27.

This will calculate the total number of tickets sold for each tour, grouped by month.

8 Click Next.

You have to give your crosstab query a name.

9 Type qryTicketsByDate and click Finish.

Access saves the query with the name "qryTicketsByDate" and displays the results of the query, as shown in Figure 6-26. Let's modify the crosstab query and add some limiting criteria.

10 Click the View button to display the crosstab query in Design view.

The crosstab query appears in Design view as shown in Figure 6-28. Notice the Crosstab row, which you use to determine if a field should be a column heading, row heading, or value.

11 Double-click the First Class field in the qryTours-ByName list.

You only want to see tours for passengers without first class tickets.

12 Click the First Class column's Total row, click the list arrow and select Where from the list. Click the First Class column's Criteria row and type False.

13 Click the Run button on the toolbar.

Access displays the crosstab query, which only includes non-first class tickets.

14 Close the query without saving your changes.

QUICK REFERENCE

TO CREATE A CROSSTAB QUERY:

1. IN THE DATABASE WINDOW, CLICK THE QUERIES ICON IN THE OBJECTS BAR AND CLICK THE NEW BUTTON.

2. SELECT CROSSTAB QUERY WIZARD AND CLICK OK.

3. SELECT THE TABLE OR QUERY YOU WANT TO USE AND CLICK NEXT.

4. SELECT THE FIELD YOU WANT TO USE AS THE ROW HEADING AND CLICK NEXT.

5. SELECT THE FIELD YOU WANT TO USE AS THE COLUMN HEADING AND CLICK NEXT.

6. SELECT THE FIELD YOU WANT TO SUMMARIZE, THE TYPE OF CALCULATION YOU WANT TO USE TO SUMMARIZE THE FIELD, AND CLICK NEXT.

7. TYPE A NAME FOR THE CROSSTAB QUERY AND CLICK FINISH.

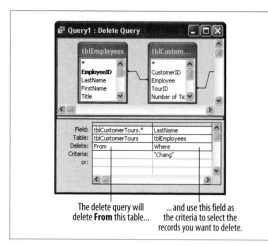

Figure 6-29. A delete query in Design view.

Figure 6-30. Access asks you to confirm the delete query.

Definitely the most dangerous of all queries is a *delete query*, a query that deletes a whole bunch of records at a time. Once you have deleted records using a delete query, you cannot undo the results—the records are gone forever! Creating a delete query is no different than creating a select query—with one very important difference: While a select query displays the records that match your criteria, a delete query deletes those records. For this reason, you should always preview the results of a delete query in Datasheet View to see which records will be deleted.

If you want to delete records from multiple tables—for example, a customer and all of that customer's orders—you need to do a few things first:

- Define relationships between the tables.
- Establish referential integrity for the join(s) between the tables and turn on the Cascade Delete Related Records option.

LeAnne Chang, one of North Shore Travel's managers, decides to open her own competing travel agency across the street, and being the vindictive person she is, takes all her customers with her. In this lesson you will create a delete query to delete all the tours sold by LeAnne Chang.

1 From the Database window, click the Queries icon in the Objects bar and click the New button.

The New Query dialog box appears.

2 Select Design View and click OK.

The query design window and Show Table dialog box both appear. You have to select the tables and/or queries you want to use in the delete query.

3 Click the tblEmployees table and click Add.

A field list for the tblEmployees table appears in the top half of the query design window.

4 Add the tblCustomerTours table and tblTours table to the query.

When you have finished adding the tables and/or queries, you can close the Show Table dialog box.

5 Click Close.

If the tables are related, Access automatically connects their common fields with a join line. If the tables aren't related, you will have to manually join them by dragging a field from one table's field list to the matching field in the other table's field list.

You need to connect the tblEmployees table with the tblCustomerTours table.

6 Click the EmployeeID field in the tblEmployees field list and drag and drop it onto the Employee field in the tblCustomerTours field list.

Now you need to tell Access that this is a delete query.

7 Click the Query Type button list arrow on the toolbar and select Delete Query from the list.

> **TIP** Another way to change the type of query is to select *Query* from the menu and select the type of query from the list.

Access converts the select query to a delete query and displays the Delete row in the query design grid. Now you have to tell Access what you want to delete.

8 Drag the asterisk (*) from the top of the tblCustomerTours field list into the design grid.

Notice that *From* appears in the Delete cell for the
asterisk field, indicating that the records will be
deleted from the tblCustomerTours table. Unless you
want the delete query to delete each and every record
in the tblCustomerTours table, you will need to add
some limiting criteria. You decide to use the last name
Chang as the limiting criteria.

9 Drag the LastName field from the tblEmployees
field list into the design grid.

This time *Where* appears in the Delete cell for the
LastName field, indicating that the LastName field
will be used as the criteria to select which records will
be deleted from the tblCustomerTours table.

10 Click the LastName column's Criteria row and
type Chang.

Access will add the "quotation marks" around the text
string Chang for you, as shown in Figure 6-29. That's
all there is to creating a delete query.

⸱ NOTE ⸱ *Before you run a delete query, you should
always preview the results in Datasheet
view first. Click the View button on the
toolbar to display the delete query in
Datasheet view.*

11 Click the View button on the toolbar to preview
the results of the delete query in Datasheet view.

The delete query displays the results of the delete
query. Let's switch back to Design view.

12 Click the View button on the toolbar to return to
Design view.

Let's run the delete query and delete the selected
records.

13 Click the Run button on the toolbar.

Ever-cautious Access asks if you really want the delete
query to delete the records, as shown in Figure 6-30.

14 Click Yes.

Access silently deletes all 75 tour records for LeAnne
Chang.

15 Close the query without saving your changes
and open the qryToursByName query.

Notice that all the tours for LeAnne Chang are gone.

16 Close the qryToursByName query.

QUICK REFERENCE

TO CREATE A DELETE QUERY:

1. IN THE DATABASE WINDOW, CLICK THE
   QUERIES ICON IN THE OBJECTS BAR AND
   CLICK THE NEW BUTTON.

2. SELECT DESIGN VIEW AND CLICK OK.

3. ADD THE APPROPRIATE TABLES AND
   QUERIES AND CLICK CLOSE.

4. CONNECT ANY UNRELATED TABLES.

5. CLICK THE QUERY TYPE BUTTON LIST
   ARROW ON THE TOOLBAR AND SELECT
   DELETE QUERY.

   OR...

   SELECT QUERY → DELETE QUERY FROM
   THE MENU.

6. DRAG THE TABLE FROM WHICH YOU WANT
   TO DELETE RECORDS AND THE FIELD YOU
   WANT TO USE AS THE CRITERIA ONTO THE
   DESIGN GRID.

7. CLICK THE VIEW BUTTON TO VIEW THE
   RESULTS OF THE DELETE QUERY.

8. IF YOU'RE SATISFIED THAT THE
   APPROPRIATE RECORDS WILL BE DELETED,
   CLICK THE RUN BUTTON ON THE TOOLBAR
   AND CLICK YES TO CONFIRM THE
   DELETION.

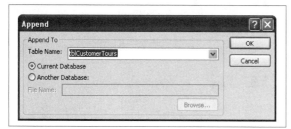

Figure 6-31. The Append dialog box asks where you want to add the query's records.

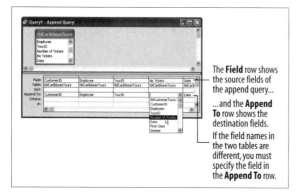

The **Field** row shows the source fields of the append query...

...and the **Append To** row shows the destination fields.

If the field names in the two tables are different, you must specify the field in the **Append To** row.

Figure 6-32. An append query in Design view.

An append query takes a group of records from one or more tables or queries in your database and adds them to another existing table. Append queries are especially useful for importing information into a table. For example, you could use an append query to import several dozen customer records from an Excel spreadsheet into an existing table. Of course, you would have to know how to import the Excel spreadsheet first—and that's another lesson in and of itself.

There are several rules that you must follow when using an append query:

- The appended data must meet the data validation and referential integrity rules of the table it is being added to.

- The appended data must have its own unique primary-key values. If the primary-key field in the table to which the data is being added is an AutoNumber field, do not append that field—Access will generate new numbers for the new records.

- The type of data in the records you're adding must match the type of data in the table to which you're adding them.

In this lesson you will create an append query to add a new group of tours to the tblCustomerTours table.

1 If necessary, open the Lesson 6 database.

Now let's create a new query.

2 In the Database window, click the Queries icon in the Objects bar and click the New button.

The New Query dialog box appears.

3 Select Design View and click OK.

The query design window and Show Table dialog box both appear. Let's select the tables and/or queries you want to use in the append query.

4 Click the tblCaribbeanTours table, click Add, and then click Close.

Now you need to convert the select query to an append query. Here's how:

5 Select Query → Append Query from the menu.

The Append dialog box appears, as shown in Figure 6-31. You have to tell the append query where you want the results of the query to be added.

6 Select tblCustomerTours from the Table Name list and click OK.

The append query will add the results of its query to the tblCustomerTours table. Notice that an Append To row appears in the design grid, as shown in Figure 6-32. Now you have to specify the fields you want to append.

7 Double-click the CustomerID, Employee, and TourID fields in the tblCaribbeanTours field list.

Since the field names are the same in both tables, Access automatically fills in the Append To row with the names of the fields you're appending records to. If some of the fields you're appending have a different field name, you will have to specify to which field they should be added from the Append To row.

8 Double-click the No Tickets field in the tblCaribbeanTours field list.

Since there isn't a field named No Tickets in the tblCustomerTours table, Access doesn't automatically fill in the Append To row. You will have to select the name of the field you want to append to.

9 Click the Append To row in the No Tickets field, click the list arrow, and select Number of Tickets.

This will append the fields from the No Tickets field in the tblCaribbeanTours table to the Number of Tickets field in the tblCustomerTours table. Move on to the next step and finish adding the remaining fields that you want to append.

10 Double-click the Date, First Class, Smoker, Ship Via, and Cost fields in the tblCaribbeanTours field list.

⸗ NOTE ⸗ *As with any action query, you should always preview the results in Datasheet view first. Click the View button on the toolbar to display the results of the Append query in Datasheet view.*

11 Click the View button on the toolbar to preview the results of the append query in Datasheet view.

The append query displays the records it will add or append to the tblCustomerTours table.

12 Click the View button on the toolbar to return to Design view and click the Run button on the toolbar.

Access asks you to confirm the addition of the records to the tblCustomerTours table.

13 Click Yes.

Access adds the records from the tblCaribbeanTours table to the tblCustomerTours table.

14 Close the query without saving your changes and open the qryToursByName query.

Notice the new tblCaribbeanTours records that have been added by the append query.

15 Close the qryToursByName query.

QUICK REFERENCE

TO CREATE AN APPEND QUERY:

1. CREATE A NEW QUERY, SELECT DESIGN VIEW AND CLICK OK. CLICK THE TABLES AND/OR QUERIES YOU WANT TO USE IN THE APPEND QUERY, CLICK ADD, CLOSE.

2. CLICK THE QUERY TYPE BUTTON LIST ARROW ON THE TOOLBAR AND SELECT APPEND QUERY.

   OR...

   SELECT QUERY → APPEND QUERY FROM THE MENU.

3. SELECT THE TABLE TO WHICH YOU WANT TO ADD THE RESULTS OF THE QUERY.

4. IF YOU SELECT AN EXISTING TABLE, CLICK ONE OF THE FOLLOWING OPTIONS:

   CURRENT DATABASE: IF THE TABLE IS IN THE CURRENTLY OPEN DATABASE.

   ANOTHER DATABASE: TYPE THE NAME OF THE OTHER DATABASE (INCLUDING THE PATH, IF NECESSARY).

5. CLICK OK.

6. ADD THE FIELDS YOU WANT TO APPEND AND IDENTIFY A MATCHING FIELD IF ACCESS DOESN'T SUPPLY ONE.

7. CLICK THE VIEW BUTTON ON THE TOOLBAR TO VIEW THE RESULTS OF THE QUERY OR THE RUN BUTTON ON THE TOOLBAR AND CLICK YES TO CONFIRM THE ADDITION.

Figure 6-33. Type the name of the table you're creating in the Make Table dialog box.

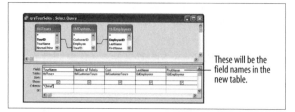

These will be the field names in the new table.

Figure 6-34. The make-table query will create a table using the tables, fields, and criteria you specify.

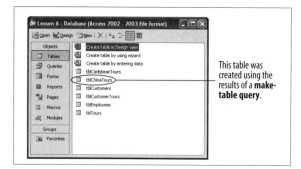

This table was created using the results of a **make-table query**.

Figure 6-35. The make-table query uses its results to create a new table.

Like all queries, a *make-table query* asks a question of the information in one or more tables and then retrieves results. Instead of displaying the results, however, a make-table query creates a new table with the results of the query. Make-table queries are useful for:

- Exporting a table to another database or application.
- Creating a backup copy of a table.
- Creating an archive table that stores old records.
- Creating a table that includes information or fields from more than one table.

In this lesson you will create a make-table query to create a table with information about all China tour records.

1 Click the qryTourSales query and then click the Design button.

The query opens in Design view. First you need to add the fields that you want to include in your new table.

2 Double-click the TourName field in the tblTours field list, the Number of Tickets, Date, and Cost fields in the tblCustomerTours field list, and the LastName and FirstName fields in the tblEmployees field list.

The make-table query will create a table with these fields, as shown in Figure 6-34. Next you need to specify any limiting criteria.

3 Click the TourName column's Criteria row and type China.

Access will add the "quotation marks" around the text string "China" for you. The make-table query will only include China tours when it creates the new table.

Here's how to change the query type to a make-table query:

4 Click the Query Type button list arrow and select Make-Table Query from the list.

Access displays the Make Table dialog box, as shown in Figure 6-33. Here you need to tell Access the name of the new table.

5 Type tblChinaTours in the Table Name box and click OK.

You're ready to have the make-table query create the new table. Preview the results of the query first.

⁞ NOTE ⁞ *As with any action query you should always preview the results in Datasheet view first. Click the View button on the toolbar to display the results of the make-table query in Datasheet view.*

6 Click the View button on the toolbar to preview the results of the make-table query in Datasheet view.

The make-table query displays the records it will use to create the new tblChinaTours table.

7 Click the View button on the toolbar to return to Design view and click the Run button on the toolbar.

Access asks you to confirm the creation of the tblChinaTours table.

8 Click Yes.

Access creates the new tblChinaTours table based on the results of the make-table query, as shown in Figure 6-35. Now let's open the new table.

9 Close the query without saving your changes, click the Tables icon in the Objects bar, and double-click the tblChinaTours table.

Verify the results of the make-table query, then...

10 Close the tblChinaTours table.

QUICK REFERENCE

TO CREATE A MAKE-TABLE QUERY:

1. IN DESIGN VIEW, CREATE A SELECT QUERY; INCLUDING ANY TABLES, FIELDS, CALCULATED FIELDS, AND CRITERIA.

2. CLICK THE QUERY TYPE BUTTON LIST ARROW ON THE TOOLBAR AND SELECT MAKE-TABLE QUERY.

   OR...

   SELECT QUERY → MAKE-TABLE QUERY FROM THE MENU.

3. TYPE THE NAME OF THE TABLE YOU WANT TO CREATE, OR CLICK THE DROP-DOWN LIST AND SELECT A TABLE FROM THE LIST IF YOU WANT TO REPLACE THE EXISTING ONE.

4. IF YOU SELECT AN EXISTING TABLE, CLICK ONE OF THE FOLLOWING OPTIONS:

   CURRENT DATABASE: IF THE TABLE IS IN THE CURRENTLY OPEN DATABASE.

   ANOTHER DATABASE: AND TYPE THE NAME OF THE OTHER DATABASE (INCLUDING THE PATH, IF NECESSARY).

5. CLICK OK.

6. CLICK THE VIEW BUTTON ON THE TOOLBAR TO VIEW THE RESULTS OF THE QUERY OR THE RUN BUTTON ON THE TOOLBAR AND CLICK YES TO CONFIRM THE CREATION.

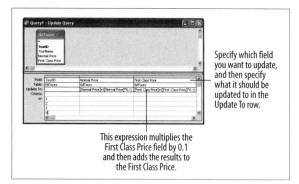

Specify which field you want to update, and then specify what it should be updated to in the Update To row.

This expression multiplies the First Class Price field by 0.1 and then adds the results to the First Class Price.

Figure 6-36. An update query.

Figure 6-37. Access asks you to confirm the record update.

TourID	TourName	Normal Price	First Class Pric
1	Europe 10 Days	$1,925.00	$2,145.00
2	Europe 15 Days	$2,695.00	$2,854.50
3	Europe 21 Days	$3,245.00	$3,465.00
4	Yucatan	$675.00	$795.00
5	China	$3,150.00	$3,295.00
6	Russia and the Baltics	$2,795.00	$2,995.00
7	Western Canada	$995.00	$1,195.00
8	Historical USA	$1,450.00	$1,650.00
9	British Isles	$1,925.00	$2,145.00
10	African Safari	$1,995.00	$2,295.00
11	Caribbean Cruise	$675.00	$795.00
(AutoNumber)		$0.00	$0.00

Figure 6-38. The update query has updated the selected records and raised their price fields by 10 percent.

You can use an *update query* to change a pile of records at the same time. For example, you could create an update query to lower prices by eight percent or to change the sales representative for all your clients in Oregon from "Mr. Potter" to "George Bailey." Just like other action queries, you create an update query by first creating a select query and then converting the select query to an update query.

In this lesson you will create an update query to raise the prices of all trips to Europe by 10 percent.

1 From the Database window, click the Queries icon in the Objects bar and click the New button.

The New Query dialog box appears.

2 Select Design View and click OK.

The query design window and Show Table dialog box both appear. Here you have to select the tables and/or queries you want to use in the update query.

3 Double-click the tblTours table and click Close.

Now you need to convert the select query to an update query. Here's how:

4 Click the Query Type button list arrow and select Update Query from the list.

Access converts the select query to an update query. Notice an Update To row appears in the design grid. Now you have to specify the fields you want to update.

5 Double-click the TourID, Normal Price, and First Class Price fields in the tblTours field list.

The next step is a little bit tricky—you have to tell Access which fields to update and how to update them. You want to raise the price of both the Normal Price and First Class Price fields by 10 percent—you will have to write an expression (or formula) in the Update To rows of both fields to make this little bit of magic happen.

6 Click the Normal Price column's Update To row and type [Normal Price]+([Normal Price]*.1).

So what does this confusing expression actually mean? Let's assume the Normal Price for a record is $100. The expression would then look something like this: [$100] + ([$100] * .1).

Access first calculates anything it sees in parentheses, so it multiples $100 × 0.1 (or 10%) and comes up with $10. Access then adds this $10 to the Normal Price (as in $10 + $100) and comes up with $110. Make a little more sense? Hope so—because you have to do the same thing to the First Class Price field.

7 Click the First Class Price column's Update To row and type:

[First Class Price]+([First Class Price]*.1).

Next you need to specify any limiting criteria. You want to raise prices for only those tours that are in Europe. Sadly, the only way to determine this is by looking at the values in the tblTours table. Here are all the European TourIDs: 1, 2, 3, and 9. You will have to create an OR statement in your query to make sure you get them all.

8 Click the TourID field's Criteria row and type 1.

This will select the record whose TourID is "1," but what about the rest?

9 Press the ↓ (down arrow key) to select the TourID field's second Criteria row (the or row) and type 2.

This will select the records whose TourID is "2." Go to the next step and finish adding the rest of the OR criteria.

10 Press the ↓ (down arrow key) to select the TourID field's third Criteria row, type 3, press the ↓ (down arrow key) to select the TourID field's fourth Criteria row and type 9.

Compare your query to the one in Figure 6-36. Look the same? Let's run the update query.

11 Click the Run button on the toolbar.

Access asks about the updating the selected records, as shown in Figure 6-37.

12 Click Yes.

Access updates the selected records by raising both their Normal Price and First Class Price fields by 10 percent. Let's open the new table.

13 Close the query without saving your changes, click the Tables icon in the Objects bar, and double-click the tblTours table.

Compare your table with Figure 6-38. Notice that the prices of four European tours have been increased by ten percent.

14 Close the tblTours table and close the database.

QUICK REFERENCE

TO CREATE AN UPDATE QUERY:

1. CREATE A NEW QUERY IN DESIGN VIEW, THEN SELECT THE TABLES AND/OR QUERIES YOU WANT TO USE IN THE UPDATE QUERY.

2. CLICK THE QUERY TYPE BUTTON LIST ARROW ON THE TOOLBAR AND SELECT UPDATE QUERY.

   OR...

   SELECT QUERY → UPDATE QUERY FROM THE MENU.

3. DOUBLE-CLICK THE FIELDS THAT YOU WANT TO APPEAR IN THE QUERY OR CLICK AND DRAG THE FIELDS ONTO THE DESIGN GRID.

4. ENTER AN EXPRESSION TO UPDATE THE SELECTED FIELD.

5. ENTER ANY CRITERIA, IF NEEDED, TO SELECT WHICH RECORDS SHOULD BE UPDATED.

6. CLICK THE VIEW BUTTON TO VIEW THE RESULTS OF THE UPDATE QUERY.

7. IF YOU'RE SATISFIED THAT THE APPROPRIATE RECORDS WILL BE UPDATED, CLICK THE RUN BUTTON ON THE TOOLBAR AND CLICK YES TO CONFIRM THE UPDATE.

Lesson Summary

A Quick Review

To Create a Query in Design View: Click the Queries icon in the Objects bar, then double-click Create query in Design view. Select the table or query you want to use and click Add. Repeat as necessary for additional tables or queries that you want to add to the query and click Close when you're finished. Double-click the fields that you want to appear in the query or click and drag the fields onto the design grid. In the design grid, enter any desired search criteria for the field in the Criteria row and/or click the Sort box list arrow for the field and select a sort order. Click the Save button on the toolbar, click Yes to save the query, enter a query name, and click OK.

Understanding the Different Types of Queries

The Types of Queries Are:

- Select queries
- Parameter queries
- Crosstab queries
- Make-table queries
- Append queries
- Delete queries
- Update queries
- Union queries

Creating a Multiple-Table Query

To Create a Multiple-Table Query in Design View: Click the Queries icon in the Objects bar, then double-click Create query in Design view. Select the table or query you want to use and click Add. Repeat as necessary for additional tables or queries that you want to add to the query and click Close when you're finished. If Access doesn't automatically join the tables, click the related field in the first table and drag it to the related field in the second table. Repeat as necessary to connect all the tables. Double-click the fields that you want to appear in the query or click and drag the fields onto the design grid. In the design grid, enter any desired search criteria for the field in the Criteria row and/or click the Sort box list arrow for the field and select a sort order. Click the Save button on the toolbar, click Yes to save the query, enter a query name, and click OK.

Creating a Calculated Field

To Create an Expression or Calculation in a Query: Display the query in Design view. Click the Field row of a blank column in the design grid, enter the field name for the calculated field followed by a : (colon), then enter the expression you want Access to calculate, using the proper syntax (or you can use the Expression Builder to help you create this expression).

Working with Expressions and the Expression Builder

To Create an Expression with the Expression Builder: Display the query in Design view and click the Field row of a blank column in the design grid. Click the Build button on the toolbar, double-click the field you want to use in the calculation, click the button that corresponds to the calculation you want, and then click or type any other fields or values you want to use. Click OK when you're finished.

Using an IIF Function

To Create an IIF (IF...THEN) Function: Display the query in Design view. Click the Field row of a blank column in the design grid, enter the field name followed by a : (colon) and type the expression using the syntax IIf(«expr», «truepart», «falsepart») (or you can use the Expression Builder to help you create the IIf expression).

Summarizing Groups of Records

To Calculate or Summarize a Group of Records: Display the query in Design view and, if necessary, click the Totals button on the toolbar. Move the field that you want to group data by onto the design grid and make sure Group By appears in that field's Total row. Move the field that you want to perform calculations on onto the design grid. Choose the type of calculation that you want to perform by clicking the field's Total row, clicking the list arrow, and selecting a calculation from the list.

Display Top or Bottom Values

To View Top or Bottom Values: Display the query in Design view, click the appropriate Sort field, and select either Ascending (displays bottom values) or Descending (displays top values). Select an option from the Top Values list on the toolbar.

Parameter Queries

To Create a Parameter Query: Display the query in Design view, click the Criteria row for the field you want to use for your parameter criteria and enter the text of the prompt, surrounded by square brackets [ ].

Finding Duplicate Records

To Use the Find Duplicates Query Wizard: In the Database window, click the Queries icon in the Objects bar and click the New button. Select Find Duplicates Query Wizard and click OK, then select the table or query you want to search and click Next. Double-click the field(s) that may contain the duplicate values and click Next. Double-click any additional fields that you want to appear in the query results, click Next, and then click Finish.

Finding Unmatched Records

To Use the Find Unmatched Query Wizard: From the Database window, click the Queries icon in the Objects bar and click the New button. Select Find Unmatched Query Wizard and click OK, select the table whose values you want to display and click Next. Select the table that contains the related records, click Next, specify the related fields that join the two tables, then click the [<=>] button to join the two tables and click Next. Double-click any additional fields that you want to appear in the query results, click Next, and then click Finish.

Crosstab Queries

To Create a Crosstab Query: In the Database window, click the Queries icon in the Objects bar and click the New button, then select Crosstab Query Wizard and click OK. Select the table or query you want to use in the crosstab query and click Next. Select the field you want to use as the row heading, click Next, select the field you want to use as the column heading, and click Next. Select the field you want to summarize, the type of calculation you want to use to summarize the field, click Next, type a name for the crosstab query, and click Finish.

Delete Queries

To Create a Delete Query: In the Database window, click the Queries icon in the Objects bar and click the New

button. Select Design view and click OK. Add the appropriate tables and/or queries and click Close, then connect any unrelated tables. Click the Query Type button list arrow on the toolbar and select Delete Query or select Query → Delete Query from the menu. Click the View button to view the results of the delete query. If you're satisfied that the appropriate records will be deleted, click the Run button on the toolbar and click Yes to confirm the deletion.

Append Queries

To Create an Append Query: Create a new query, select Design view, and click OK. Click the tables and/or queries you want to use in the append query, click Add, and then click Close when you're finished. Click the Query Type button list arrow on the toolbar and select Append Query or select Query → Append Query from the menu. Select the table to which you want to add the results of the query. If you select an existing table, click one of the following options: Current Database (if the table is in the currently open database) or Another Database (and type the name of the other database, including the path, if necessary). Click OK, then add the fields you want to append and identify a matching field if Access doesn't supply one. Click OK and click the View button on the toolbar to view the results of the query or the Run button on the toolbar to append the records.

Make-Table Queries

To Create a Make-Table Query: In Design view, create a select query; including any tables, fields, calculated fields, and criteria. Click the Query Type button list arrow on the toolbar and select Make-Table Query or select Query → Make-Table Query from the menu. Type the name of the table you want to create, or click the drop-down list and select a table from the list if you want to replace the existing one. If you select an existing table, click one of the following options: Current Database (if the table is in the currently open database) or Another Database (and type the name of the other database, including the path, if necessary). Click OK. Click the View button on the toolbar to view the results of the query or the Run button on the toolbar to create the new table.

Update Queries

To Create an Update Query: Create a new query in Design view, then select the tables and/or queries you want to use in the update query. Click the Query Type button list arrow on the toolbar and select Update Query or select Query → Update Query from the menu. Double-click the fields that you want to appear in the query or click and drag the fields onto the design grid. Enter an expression to update the selected field and enter any criteria, if needed, to select which records should be updated. Click the View button to view the results of the update query. If you're satisfied that the appropriate records will be updated, click the Run button on the toolbar to update the records.

Quiz

1. Which of the following criterion is NOT written using the proper syntax?
   A. "Harris"
   B. Between 1/1/2000 and 12/31/2000
   C. NO VALUE
   D. 500

2. Which of the following types of queries are action queries? (Select all that apply.)
   A. Parameter queries.
   B. Append queries.
   C. Update queries.
   D. Crosstab queries.

3. Which of the following expressions is NOT written in the correct syntax?
   A. [Order Total]*[Tax Rate]
   B. "Order Total"*0.1
   C. [tblCustomerTours]![Cost]*[tblEmployees]![Commission]
   D. 100+10

4. If you are having trouble remembering how to write expressions using the correct syntax, you can use the Expression Builder to help you create the expression. (True or False?)

5. Rebate: IIF([Age]65,"Senior","Adult") This expression is an example of:
   A. Something I learned back in high school algebra and thought I would never see again.
   B. A financial expression.
   C. Something that belongs in a Microsoft Excel book.
   D. A conditional expression.

6. A query prompts a user for a date and then displays only records that contain the specified date. Which type of query is this?
   A. A parameter query.
   B. A crosstab query.
   C. An action query.
   D. An update query.

7. You must create a report if you want to calculate totals for a group of records, as queries can't perform this task. (True or False?)

8. A query summarizes information in a grid, organized by regions and months. Which type of query is this?
   A. A parameter query.
   B. A crosstab query.
   C. An action query.
   D. An update query.

9. Your company finally agreed to buy you a nifty 3COM Palm palmtop. Now you want to extract your clients from the company's database and put them into a separate table that you can export to your Palm. Which type of query could help you accomplish this task?
   A. A parameter query.
   B. A crosstab query.
   C. An update query.
   D. A make-table query.

10. If you are creating a crosstab query, what must the table you are querying contain?

    A. At least one text field.

    B. At least one number field.

    C. More than 100 records.

    D. Lots of confusing information.

11. How can you add a table to the query design window?

    A. Select Edit → Add Table from the menu.

    B. Click the Show Table button on the toolbar.

    C. Select the table from the Table list on the toolbar.

    D. Select Tools → Add Table from the menu.

12. You want a query to calculate the total sales for your employees. How can you do this from the query design window?

    A. Click the Totals button on the toolbar. In the Total row select "Group By" under the Employee field and "Sum" under the Sales field.

    B. Click in the Sales field and click the AutoSum button on the toolbar.

    C. You need to export this information to Microsoft Excel and calculate it there.

    D. Click in the Sales field and select Tools → Auto-Sum from the menu.

Homework

1. Open the Homework database.

2. Using the Customers and Insurance Claims tables, create a multi-table query that counts the total number of claims, grouped by the State field. **Hint:** Use the Count function on any field in the Insurance Claims table.

3. Sort the results of the query alphabetically by date.

4. Add criteria to the query that excludes records from the state of Wisconsin (WI).

5. Change the select query to a delete query and delete all records from the state of Wisconsin (WI).

6. Change the delete query back into a select query. Remove the current criteria and add parameter criteria that ask for the beginning and ending date.

7. Create a concatenated field that combines the FirstName and LastName fields.

8. Save the query as "Homework Query."

9. Close the query and the Homework database.

CHAPTER 7
WORKING WITH FORMS

CHAPTER OBJECTIVES:

Create and modify a form, Lessons 7.1—7.2

Add, delete, move, and size controls, Lessons 7.3—7.4

Change a form's tab order, Lesson 7.5

Work with control properties and settings, Lessons 7.6—7.7

Work with form properties and settings, Lessons 7.8—7.9

Work with and modify controls, Lessons 7.10—7.14

Use the Control Wizard to create interactive forms, Lesson 7.15

Create/use subforms to display information from a one-to-many relationship, Lessons 7.16—7.17

CHAPTER TASK: CREATE AND WORK WITH SEVERAL TYPES OF FORMS

Prerequisites

- **How to use menus, toolbars, dialog boxes, and shortcut keystrokes.**
- **How to open and modify database objects.**
- **How to add and edit database records.**

A form created in Access is similar to the ordinary paper forms that you fill out with a pen or pencil—only you don't have to worry about trying to read poor penmanship. In Access, forms provide an easy way to enter and view data in a table. Here are just a few examples of how forms make working with data easier.

- **Easier to View and Use:** Instead of scrolling back and forth in a table's datasheet, a form lets you focus on one record at a time.

- **See Data Any Way You Want:** You can design forms to present information any way you like.

- **Combine Data from Linked Tables:** One form can display data from several related tables or queries—and your users will never know that they are working with two sources!

And that's just for starters. No doubt about it—forms make your database easier to use. Just like a Windows dialog box (which is really what a form is), Access forms can include fill-in-the-blank fields, check boxes, drop-down lists, and more.

This chapter explains everything you have ever wanted to know about forms—and maybe a few things you didn't want to know.

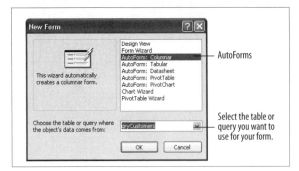

Figure 7-1. Selecting an AutoForm from the New Form dialog box.

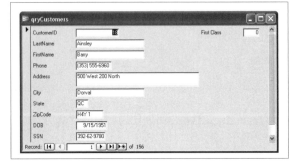

Figure 7-2. A Columnar form created by the AutoForm Wizard.

The fastest and easiest way to create a form in Access is with one of the AutoForm Wizards. The AutoForm Wizard automatically creates a form by arranging all the fields from a table or query.

The AutoForm Wizards are fast and easy to use, but limited—there are only five AutoForm Wizards, and each can create only one type of form, as shown in Table 7-1. Of course, you can always modify a form created by an AutoForm Wizard.

In this lesson you will learn how to create a form using an AutoForm Wizard.

1 Open the Lesson 7 database.

First you need to go to the Forms icon in the Objects bar.

2 Click the Forms icon in the Objects bar, then click the New button.

The New Form dialog box appears, as shown in Figure 7-1. You create a form with the AutoForm Wizard by selecting one of the five AutoForm Wizards…

3 Select AutoForm: Columnar from the list.

… and the table or query you want to use in your form.

4 Click the Choose the table or query where the object's data comes from: ☑ arrow and select qryCustomers from the list.

That's all the information the AutoForm Wizard needs to create your form.

5 Click OK to create the columnar form.

Access takes all the fields in the qryCustomers query, arranges them, and creates a form similar to the one shown in Figure 7-2.

6 Click the Close button to close the form. Click No to saving changes.

AutoForm Wizards forms aren't really very pretty to look at, but they can give you a good start at creating the form you really want since it's a lot easier to modify an existing form than it is to create one from scratch.

Table 7-1. Available Form Layouts

Form Type	Form Layout	Description
Columnar		Displays only one record at a time. Data for each record is displayed vertically. Technically, Columnar form's Default View property is set to Single.

Table 7-1. Available Form Layouts (Continued)

Form Type	Form Layout	Description
Tabular		Displays several records at once. Data for the records is displayed horizontally. Technically, Tabular form's Default View property is set to Continuous.
Datasheet		Displays several records at once in Datasheet View. Technically, Datasheet form's Default View property is set to Datasheet.
PivotTable		Dynamically analyzes information and summarizes it into a datasheet-like table.
PivotChart		Dynamically analyzes information and summarizes it into a chart.

QUICK REFERENCE

TO CREATE A FORM WITH AUTOFORM:

1. FROM THE DATABASE WINDOW, CLICK THE FORMS ICON IN THE OBJECTS BAR AND CLICK THE NEW BUTTON.

2. SELECT ONE OF THE FOLLOWING:

   AUTOFORM: COLUMNAR

   AUTOFORM: TABULAR

   AUTOFORM: DATASHEET

   AUTOFORM: PIVOTTABLE

   AUTOFORM: PIVOTCHART

3. CLICK THE TABLE OR QUERY YOU WANT TO USE FOR THE FORM FROM THE DROP-DOWN LIST.

4. CLICK OK.

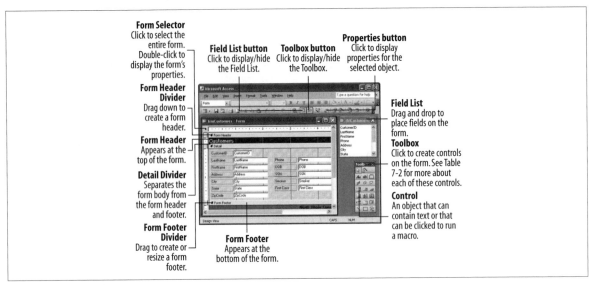

Figure 7-3. A form in Design view.

After you create a form, you may decide to modify it to add additional features or make it easier to use. For example, you might want to add or delete a field or change the location of a field on the form. You modify a form in Design view, which you can get to in two different ways:

- **From the database window:** Click the Forms icon to list the forms in the database. Click on the form you want to modify and click the Design button.

- **From a form window:** Click the View button on the toolbar or select View → Design View from the menu.

This lesson will introduce you to form Design view.

1 From the Database window, click the Forms icon in the Objects bar if it isn't already selected, then select the frmCustomers form and click the Design button.

The frmCustomers form appears in Design view, as shown in Figure 7-3.

Don't let Design view scare you. It looks more complicated than it really is. In some ways, form Design view is similar to many Paint programs. Think of the form as your canvas and the Toolbox and Field List as the paintbrushes you use to add fields, text boxes, and buttons to the form.

Any graphic object that appears on forms and reports is called a *control*. A text box used to enter and display information, a text label, and a button you click to print a report would all be examples of controls. You add controls to a form by clicking the control you want to use and then by clicking and dragging it on the form to draw the control. Table 7-2 shows and describes Toolbox buttons and controls.

Table 7-2. Toolbox Buttons and Controls

Toolbox Button	Description
	Click this button and then click the control you want to select. To select multiple controls, click this button and hold down the Shift key as you click each control, or drag a rectangle around all controls you want to select.
	Click to use Control Wizards when you add controls to your form.
	Creates a static text label that is the same for every record, such as a heading. Most controls already have a text label attached.
	Creates a text box that displays information from a table and query. You can also use text boxes to enter text.
	Creates a box around a group of option buttons so that the user is only allowed to make one selection from the group box.
	Creates a toggle button that allows you to display and enter data from a Yes/No field.
	Creates an option button (or radio button) that allows the user to make a single selection from two or more choices. Option Buttons are normally used with a Group Box control.
	Creates a box that is checked or unchecked. Use to enter data from a Yes/No field.
	Creates a drop-down box that lets the user enter text or select an item from a list of options.
	Creates a box that lets the user select an item from a list of options.
	Creates a button that runs a macro or Visual Basic function.
	Displays a picture or graphic file that you specify.
	Inserts an OLE object that is not bound to a field in the current database. Use an Unbound Object Frame to display information from an external source or program, such as a spreadsheet, graphic, or other file.
	Inserts an OLE object that is bound to a field in the database. Use Bound Object Frames to display pictures or other OLE information in the database. Normally used with OLE Object fields.
	Inserts a page break.
	Enables you to create tabs (like the ones found in some dialog boxes) to include more than one page of controls on the form.
	Inserts another form within the main form. Use when you want to show data from a one-to-many relationship.
	Enables you to draw a line.
	Enables you to draw a rectangle.
	Click to display other OLE objects.

QUICK REFERENCE

TO MODIFY A FORM:

1. FROM THE DATABASE WINDOW, CLICK THE FORMS ICON IN THE OBJECTS BAR.

2. CLICK THE FORM YOU WANT TO MODIFY AND CLICK THE DESIGN BUTTON.

OR...

OPEN THE FORM AND CLICK THE VIEW BUTTON ON THE TOOLBAR.

Adding and Deleting Fields

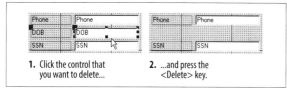

1. Click the control that you want to delete...

2. ...and press the <Delete> key.

Figure 7-4. Deleting a control is a quick and easy process.

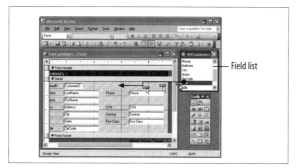

Field list

Figure 7-5. Add a field to a form by clicking and dragging it from the Field List onto the form.

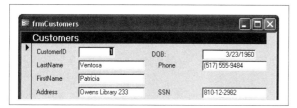

Figure 7-6. The modified form.

Once you have created a form, you can delete unnecessary fields or add more fields to display additional information. You add fields to a form by dragging the fields from the Field List onto the form. The *Field List* lists all the fields from the table or query you used to create the form.

In this lesson you will modify an existing form by adding and deleting fields.

1 Make sure you have the frmCustomers **form open in Design view.**

First you click the control you want to delete.

2 Click the DOB **text box to select it.**

Handles appear around the control, indicating that it is selected.

≈ NOTE ≈ *Selecting a label will select only the label. Selecting a text box will select both the text box and the corresponding label.*

3 Press the Delete **key to delete the DOB text box.**

Poof! The DOB text box disappears without any fuss, as shown in Figure 7-4.

So much for deleting fields. Here's how to add a field:

4 If the Field List isn't displayed, click the 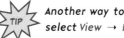 Field List **button on the toolbar.**

TIP *Another way to display the Field List is to select* View → Field List *from the menu.*

The Field List displays all the fields from the table or query you used to create the form—although you will usually have to scroll down the Field List to find the field that you want. Once the Field List is displayed you can click and drag the field you want to add from the Field List to where you want the field to appear on your form.

Move on to the next step and add the DOB field you had previously deleted from the form.

5 Scroll down the Field List **until you find the** DOB **field. Click and drag the** DOB **field just above the Phone field, as shown in Figure 7-5, then release the mouse button.**

The DOB field appears above the Phone field. Don't worry if the DOB field isn't positioned perfectly—you'll learn how to move controls in the next lesson.

See how your form looks in Form View.

6 Click the View button **on the toolbar to display the form in Form View.**

Compare your form with the one in Figure 7-6.

7 Select File → Save As **from the menu. Save the form as** frmFirstForm.

QUICK REFERENCE

TO ADD A FIELD TO A FORM:

1. DISPLAY THE FORM IN DESIGN VIEW AND CLICK THE FIELD LIST BUTTON ON THE TOOLBAR, IF NECESSARY.

2. FIND THE FIELD YOU WANT TO ADD TO THE FORM IN THE FIELD LIST, THEN CLICK AND DRAG THE FIELD TO THE DESIRED LOCATION ON THE FORM.

TO DELETE A FIELD OR CONTROL:

1. CLICK THE FIELD OR CONTROL TO SELECT IT.

2. PRESS DELETE.

Moving and Sizing Controls

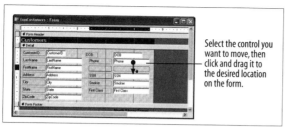

Figure 7-7. To move a control, position the mouse over a border of the control until the pointer changes to a hand cursor, and then drag and drop the control to a new location on the form.

Figure 7-8. Most controls have a corresponding label.

It's easy to change the location and size of a control on a form. Moving a control allows you to change the order of information appearing on the form. When you size a control, you increase or decrease the amount of information the control can display. Once you have selected a control on a form, *sizing handles* appear around the edges of the control. Now you can drag its sizing handles to adjust the size of the control or move the control to a new location on the form.

This lesson will give you some experience moving and sizing the controls on the form you created in the previous lesson.

1 Make sure that you have the frmFirstForm form open in Design View.

You need to select a control before you can move or size it.

2 Click the Phone text box to select it.

Sizing handles appear around the selected Phone field. Here's how to move a control:

3 Position the pointer on any border of the Phone text box (but not over a sizing handle) until it changes to a 🖐.

When the mouse pointer changes to a 🖐, it means that you can drag and drop the control to a location.

> ⋛ NOTE ⋛   *It takes a good deal of precision to position the pointer over the tiny border of a control. Move the pointer very slowly and wait until it turns into a 🖐 before you try to move the control.*

4 Click and hold down the mouse button while the 🖐 pointer is still over the border of the Phone text box. Drag the field directly to the right of the FirstName text box and directly above the SSN text box, as shown in Figure 7-7, then release the mouse button.

By simply dragging and dropping with the mouse, you can move any object on a form or report—any shapes, lines, pictures, or text boxes.

Sometimes, you may want to move the object just a smidgen. You can use the keyboard to move or nudge controls with greater precision. To move the control, simply hold down the Ctrl key as you press any of the arrow keys on the keyboard.

5 With the Phone field still selected, hold down the Ctrl key and press the ← (left arrow) key.

The Phone field moves to the left a smidgen. Go to the next step and try moving the DOB field.

6 Follow the procedure you learned in Step 5 and move the DOB text box directly to the right of the Last-Name text box and directly above the Phone text box.

Don't worry if the DOB field isn't the same size or aligned with the other controls—we'll fix that in a minute.

Notice that the DOB text box moves with its label control. You can move labels and controls independently of one anther by dragging them by their upper left sizing handles.

7 Position the pointer over the upper left sizing handle of the DOB label until it changes to a 🖐.

When the mouse pointer changes to a 🖐, it means that you can drag and drop the text box or label independently of one another.

> ⋛ NOTE ⋛   *Most controls have a corresponding label, as shown in Figure 7-8. Make sure that you position the mouse over the DOB label and not the DOB text box.*

8 Click and hold down the mouse button while the 🖑 pointer is still over the upper left sizing handle of the DOB label. Drag the DOB label so that the DOB label is left-aligned with the Phone label below it.

Enough about moving controls and labels—here's how to change their size.

When you select a control, *sizing handles* appear around its edge. You can use these sizing handles to change the size and proportions of the selected control. Move on to the next step to see how we can change the size of the selected DOB label.

9 With the DOB label still selected, position the pointer over the middle-right sizing handle until it changes to a ↔. Click and hold down the mouse but-

ton and drag to the right until the label is the same width as the other labels on the form, then release the mouse button.

As you drag a control's sizing handle, a dotted outline appears to help you resize it.

10 Click the DOB text box. Follow the procedure you learned in Step 9 and resize the DOB text box so that it is the same width as the other text boxes in the form.

That's all there is to moving and sizing controls on a form.

11 Click the Save button on the Form Design toolbar to save your changes.

QUICK REFERENCE

TO RESIZE A CONTROL:

1. CLICK THE CONTROL TO SELECT IT.

2. CLICK ONE OF THE CONTROL'S SIZING HANDLES AND DRAG UNTIL THE CONTROL REACHES THE DESIRED SIZE.

TO MOVE A CONTROL:

- CLICK AND DRAG THE CONTROL TO THE DESIRED LOCATION. RELEASE THE MOUSE BUTTON TO DROP THE CONTROL.

TO MOVE A TEXT BOX OR TEXT LABEL INDEPENDENTLY OF EACH OTHER:

- POSITION THE POINTER OVER THE UPPER LEFT SIZING HANDLE OF THE CONTROL UNTIL IT CHANGES TO A HAND CURSOR, THEN CLICK AND DRAG THE CONTROL.

Figure 7-9. The tab order determines the order by which you advance from one field to the next when you press Tab.

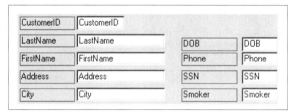

Figure 7-10. Even when you reposition fields on a form, the tab order remains the same.

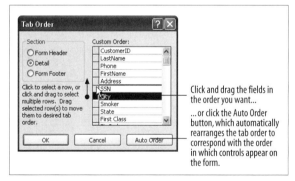

Click and drag the fields in the order you want...

...or click the Auto Order button, which automatically rearranges the tab order to correspond with the order in which controls appear on the form.

Figure 7-11. Changing the tab order.

If you add, remove, or move fields on a form, you'll want to change the form's *tab order*. A form's tab order determines the order in which you advance from one field to the next when you press the Tab key. When a form is first created, the order of the fields determines the initial tab order. Even when you reposition the fields on a form, the form's tab order remains the same. For example, the tab order shown in Figure 7-9 is from when the form was originally created. Because you have rearranged several controls, the tab order no longer reflects the order in which the fields appear on the form, as shown in Figure 7-10. This isn't really a big problem, since it's easy to change the tab order.

To change the tab order for a form select View → Tab Order from the menu. The Tab Order dialog box will appear, as shown in Figure 7-9. From here all you have to do is click and drag the field in the order you want. Or you can click the Auto Order button, which automatically rearranges the tab order to correspond with the order in which controls appear on the form.

1 Make sure that you have the frmFirstForm form open.

First let's see the current tab order of the frmFirstForm form.

2 Switch to Form view by clicking the View button on the Form Design toolbar.

Go to the next step and see what happens when you try tabbing through the fields on the form.

3 Press the Tab key several times.

When you press the Tab key, the cursor jumps from the CustomerID field to the LastName field to the... Phone field? The tab order for the frmFirstForm form was determined when the form was created. You may have moved the Phone name field in the previous lesson, but its position in the tab order hasn't changed.

You can view and change the tab order by opening the Tab Order dialog box. First you need to be in Design view.

4 Click the View button on the Form Design toolbar to switch to Design view.

Here's how to display the Tab Order dialog box.

5 Select View → Tab Order from the menu.

The Tab Order dialog box appears, as shown in Figure 7-9. The order of the fields in the list is the order in which you will advance from one field to the next when you press the Tab key. There are a couple of ways to change the tab order. The fast and easy way is to click the Auto Order button, which automatically rearranges the tab order to correspond with the order in which controls appear on the form.

⸱ NOTE ⸱   *The initial tab order of a form and the Auto Order option both create a tab order from left to right, top to bottom.*

6 Click the Auto Order button.

Access looks at the order in which fields appear on the form and adjusts the tab order accordingly.

Sometimes the tab order may not be intuitive for data entry and you may want to manually change it. For example, you may want to modify the tab order so that the address, city, state, and Zip Code fields are together. Here's how to manually change a field's position in the tab order.

7 Click the ▢ City row selector in the Custom Order list.

Now that you have selected the City row you can change its order by dragging it to a new location in the list.

8 Drag the City row until it is below the Address row, as shown in Figure 7-11, then release the mouse button.

Move on to the next step and finish arranging the fields in the tab order.

9 Drag the State row below the City row and drag the ZipCode row below the State row.

You're finished changing the tab order for the frm-FirstForm form.

10 Click OK to close the Tab Order dialog box.

Let's test the new tab order.

11 Switch to Form View by clicking the View button on the Form Design toolbar. Press the Tab key several times and notice the order in which the cursor moves from field to field.

You've finished this lesson so…

12 Save your changes and then close the frmFirst-Form form.

QUICK REFERENCE

TO CHANGE A FORM'S TAB ORDER:

1. DISPLAY THE FORM IN DESIGN VIEW.

2. SELECT VIEW → TAB ORDER FROM THE MENU.

3. CLICK THE ROW SELECTOR FOR THE CONTROL YOU WANT TO MOVE.

4. CLICK AND DRAG THE ROW SELECTOR TO THE DESIRED LOCATION.

5. REPEAT STEPS 3 AND 4 TO CHANGE THE ORDER OF ADDITIONAL CONTROLS.

TO AUTOMATICALLY CHANGE THE TAB ORDER:

1. DISPLAY THE FORM IN DESIGN VIEW.

2. SELECT VIEW → TAB ORDER FROM THE MENU.

3. CLICK THE AUTO ORDER BUTTON TO AUTOMATICALLY REORDER THE FORM CONTROLS, BASED ON THEIR POSITION IN THE FORM.

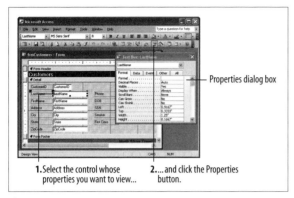

1. Select the control whose properties you want to view...

2. ...and click the Properties button.

Figure 7-12. Here the Properties dialog box displays the properties for the LastName text box control.

Every control on a form—every text box, every label, and every check box—has a set of properties that you can modify. A *property* is an attribute that defines an object's appearance, behavior, or characteristics. For example, the properties of a house would be its color, square footage, and shape. A property for a field on a form might be the number of decimal places displayed or the default value for the field. Because you can almost always change an object's properties, you can think of them as the object's settings.

Different types of controls have different properties. For example, label controls have a *Caption* property that determines the text that is displayed in the label, while text box controls have a *Control Source* property that determines which field is displayed in the control. Most controls have several dozen different properties or settings. Fortunately, Access organizes these properties into different categories, as shown in Table 7-3.

There are several ways to view the properties for any object:

- Right-click the control and select Properties from the shortcut menu.
- Select the control and click the Properties button on the toolbar.
- Select the control and select View → Properties from the menu.

This lesson explains how to view and change a control's properties.

1 Open the frmCustomers form in Design view.

Here's one way to view the properties for a control:

2 Select the LastName text box control and display its properties by clicking the Properties button on the Form Design toolbar.

> **TIP**
> Other ways to view a control's properties are to right-click the control and select *Properties* from the shortcut menu, or select the control and select View → *Properties* from the menu.

The Properties dialog box appears and displays the properties for the LastName text box control, as shown in Figure 7-12. To change a property, simply find and click the appropriate property box and make the changes. Some property boxes will display one of the following buttons when clicked:

- ☑ Click to display a list of options to change the settings for the selected property.
- ⋯ Click to invoke a Wizard or display a dialog box that you can use to change the settings for the selected property.

Move on to the next step and we'll try changing one of the LastName text box control's properties.

3 Click the Format tab, if necessary, then find and click in the Back Style box and select Transparent from the menu.

> ⁝ NOTE ⁝
> Most controls have dozens and dozens of properties. You will often have to click the appropriate tab and then do some scrolling to find the property box that you're looking for.

The back of the LastName text box control becomes transparent and displays the gray background of the underlying form. The transparent Back Style property of the LastName text box control looks out of place, so let's change it back.

4 Click in the Back Style box and change the property of the LastName text box control back to Normal.

Once the Properties dialog box is open, you can simply click any control to display its properties.

5 Click the LastName label (NOT the LastName text box).

The Properties dialog box now displays the properties for the LastName label. You can tell which control's properties are being displayed by looking at the Title bar of the Properties dialog box.

6 Click on the Close button to close the Properties dialog box.

Table 7-3. Tabs in the Properties Dialog Box

Tab	Description
Format	Properties that determine the object's appearance, such as color, text formatting, line and border color/thickness, and special effects. The purpose of many Formatting properties should be pretty obvious—for example, Font Size determines the font size of the control.
Data	Properties that determine where a control get its data, its default value (if any), and data validation rules for the control.
Event	Actions to which you can assign a macro or Visual Basic procedure. For example, clicking a button or entering information in a particular field could trigger a macro to run.
Other	Miscellaneous but important properties, such as the name of the control, if tabbing to the control is allowed, and if a message should appear in the Status bar when the control is selected.
All	Displays all the properties for the control.

QUICK REFERENCE

TO DISPLAY THE PROPERTIES FOR ANY CONTROL:

1. DISPLAY THE FORM IN DESIGN VIEW.

2. SELECT THE CONTROL AND CLICK THE PROPERTIES BUTTON ON THE TOOLBAR.

  OR...

RIGHT-CLICK THE CONTROL AND SELECT PROPERTIES FROM THE SHORTCUT MENU.

OR...

SELECT THE CONTROL AND SELECT VIEW → PROPERTIES FROM THE MENU.

Every control on a form or report has dozens of different control properties or settings—so how do you keep them all straight? Table 7-4 shows you how—this lesson is really a cheat sheet that you can use whenever you're not sure what exactly a particular control property is or does. The most important properties are marked with a *.

Table 7-4. Common Form and Report Control Properties

Property	Tab	Description
Caption*	Format	Displays a descriptive caption for a form or text label.
Format *	Format	Customizes the way numbers, dates, times, and text are displayed and printed.
Decimal Places *	Format	Determines the number of decimal places displayed.
Visible *	Format	Shows or hides a control. Useful if you want to use information on the form without it being visible. For example, you could use the value in a hidden control as the criteria for a query.
Display When	Format	Determines whether a section or control always appears or only appears when it is displayed on screen or printed.
Scroll Bars	Format	Determines whether scroll bars appear in the control.
Left *	Format	Determines the horizontal position of the control.
Top *	Format	Determines the vertical position of the control.
Width *	Format	Determines the width of a control.
Height *	Format	Determines the height of a control.
Back Style	Format	Determines whether a control is transparent or not.
Back Color	Format	Determines the color of a control. Click the ⟦…⟧ button to select a color from a palette.
Special Effect	Format	Applies a 3-D effect to a control.
Border Style	Format	Determines the line style of a control's border—select from transparent lines, solid lines, dashed lines, etc.
Border Color	Format	Determines the color of a control's border. Click the ⟦…⟧ button to select a color from a palette.
Border Width	Format	Determines the width of a control's border (in points).
Fore Color	Format	Determines the color of text in a control or the fill color of an object. Click the ⟦…⟧ button to select a color from a palette.
Font Name	Format	Determines the font used in a control (such as Arial or Times New Roman).
Font Weight	Format	Determines the thickness (boldface) of text in a control.
Font Italic	Format	Determines whether the text in a control appears in italics.
Font Underline	Format	Determines whether the text in a control is underlined.
Text Align	Format	Determines how text should be aligned in a control.
Control Source *	Data	Determines the data that appears in the control.
Input Mask *	Data	Limits the amount and type of information that can be entered in a field, such as (___) ___ -_____ for a phone number. Click the ⟦…⟧ button to create an input mask using the Input Mask Wizard.
Default Value *	Data	Specifies a value that is automatically entered in this field for new records.
Validation Rule *	Data	Allows you to enter an expression that is evaluated when data in the field is added or changed.

Table 7-4. Common Form and Report Control Properties (Continued)

Property	Tab	Description
Validation Text *	Data	Allows you to enter a message that is displayed when data doesn't meet the Validation Rule property.
Locked *	Data	Determines whether changes can be made to a field's data.
Event Tab	Event	Allows you to assign a macro or Visual Basic procedure to a specific event, such as when you click or update a control.
Name *	Other	Specifies the name of the control that identifies it in expressions, macros, and Visual Basic procedures.
Status Bar Text	Other	Specifies a message to display in the Status bar when the control is selected.
Enter Key Behavior	Other	Determines if pressing the Enter key adds a new line of text in a control or if it moves to the next field.
Allow AutoCorrect	Other	Determines if AutoCorrect (i.e., "teh" → "the") is used in a control.
AutoTab	Other	Used with the Input Mask property. Determines whether an automatic tab to the next field occurs when the last character permitted by a text box control's input mask is entered.
Tab Stop	Other	Determines whether users are able to tab to the control.
Tab Index	Other	Determines the tab order.
Shortcut Menu Bar	Other	Specifies a user-created shortcut menu that appears when the control is right-clicked.
ControlTip Message	Other	Specifies a brief message that appears when a user points at the control for a couple of seconds.
Help Context Id	Other	Specifies an identifier number for a user-created Help file that appears when the user selects the control and presses F1.
Tag	Other	Specifies extra, user-defined information that is stored in the object.

Working with Form Properties

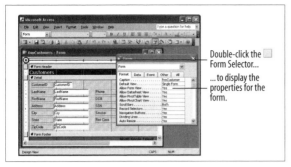

Figure 7-13. The Form Selector is the key to selecting a form and displaying its properties.

In the previous few lessons, you've been learning how to view and change the properties for form controls. In this lesson you will learn how to view and change the properties and settings of the form itself. That's right—just like controls, forms also have their own set of properties that you can view and manipulate. So why would you want to change a form's properties? Modifying a form's properties can be especially important if you are creating a database that will be used by novice users. For example, by modifying a form's properties you can:

- Allow users to edit exiting records in a table or query—but not add any additional records.
- Display one record at a time on each form or display many records at once.
- Determine the size and location of the form.

To view the properties for a form or report, simply double-click the ☐ Form Selector, as shown in Figure 7-13. In this lesson you will learn how to work with a form's properties.

1 Open the frmCustomers form in Form view.

In its current state, the frmCustomers form displays one record at a time and has a rather confusing caption in the title bar: "frmCustomers." These are form properties that you can change. You must be in Design view in order to view and change a form's properties.

2 Click the View button on the toolbar to switch to Design view.

To view the properties for a form, double-click the ☐ Form Selector, as shown in Figure 7-13. Move on to the next step and try it!

3 Double-click the ☐ Form Selector.

Microsoft Access displays the properties for the form. First, let's give the "frmCustomers" title bar a more descriptive name.

4 Click the Format tab, if necessary, click in the Caption box, and replace its text with Customers.

One of the most important form properties is the *Default View* property, which determines how many records a form can display at once. Let's take a closer look at this property…

5 Click the Format tab, click the Default View box, and click the ⬇ down arrow.

You have five options. They are:

- **Single Form:** Displays one record at a time on a form.
- **Continuous Forms:** Displays multiple records on a form. The main difference between Datasheet and Continuous Forms is that a continuous form can be customized.
- **Datasheet:** Displays multiple records in a table, using one line per record. Tables and queries display information in datasheets.
- **PivotTable:** Dynamically analyzes information and summarizes it into a datasheet-like table.
- **PivotChart:** Dynamically analyzes information and summarizes it into a chart.

6 Select Datasheet from the list.

That's enough changes for now.

7 Close the Properties dialog box.

Let's see how the form looks with its new properties.

8 Click the View button on the toolbar to display the form.

Access now displays the frmCustomers form in Datasheet view, and it has a new caption in the title bar.

9 Click the Close button to close the frmCustomers form without saving any changes.

You're probably wondering how you are going to get a handle on all these form properties. Don't worry—you will probably never touch 95 percent of them. And when you actually do have to roll up your sleeves and tackle form properties, you'll find the cheat sheet in the next lesson invaluable.

QUICK REFERENCE

TO VIEW AND CHANGE FORM PROPERTIES:

1. DISPLAY THE FORM IN DESIGN VIEW.

2. DOUBLE-CLICK THE FORM SELECTOR.

3. CLICK THE APPROPRIATE PROPERTY TAB AND PROPERTY BOX AND MAKE THE DESIRED CHANGES.

If you thought controls had lots of properties, wait until you see how many properties forms and reports have! Table 7-5 is another "cheat sheet" that lists the various form properties. Some of the most important properties are marked with a *.

Table 7-5. Important Form Properties

Property	Tab	Description
Caption *	Format	Displays a descriptive caption in the form's title bar.
Default View *	Format	Determines the view the form is in when opened.
		Single Form: Displays one record at a time.
		Continuous Forms: Displays multiple records in a form.
		Datasheet: Displays multiple records in a Datasheet.
		PivotTable: Dynamically analyzes data, summarizes into a table.
		PivotChart: Dynamically analyzes data, summarizes into a chart.
Allow Form View Allow Datasheet View Allow PivotTable View Allow PivotChart View	Format	Determines if users can switch to this view.
Scroll Bars *	Format	Determines whether scroll bars appear on the form.
Record Selectors *	Format	Determines whether a form contains a record selector.
Navigation Buttons *	Format	Determines whether a form has navigation buttons.
Dividing Lines	Format	Determines if lines appear between records in continuous forms.
Auto Resize	Format	Resizes the form automatically to display a complete record.
Border Style *	Format	Determines the type of window the form appears in: None, Thin, Sizable, or Dialog.
Control Box	Format	Determines if a control menu appears in the form.
Min Max Buttons	Format	Determines if minimize and/or maximize buttons appear in the form.
Close Button	Format	Determines if a close button appears on the form.
Width *	Format	Determines the width of the form.
Height *	Format	Determines the height of the form.
Picture	Format	Adds a graphic or picture for the form or report background. Click the Build button to browse for the folder and file.
Picture Type	Format	Determines if the picture is embedded or linked.
Picture Size Mode	Format	Determines how the contents of a picture frame are displayed: Clip, Stretch, or Zoom.
Picture Alignment	Format	Determines the alignment of a picture within a frame.
Picture Tiling	Format	Determines whether a picture is tiled within a frame.
Grid X	Format	Determines the number of subdivisions (horizontal) in a grid.
Grid Y	Format	Determines the number of subdivisions (vertical) in a grid.
Layout for Print	Format	Determines whether the form uses printer fonts.
Palette Source	Format	Specifies the path and file name for the graphic file used as a palette.
Record Source *	Data	Specifies the table or query whose data will be used in the form.
Filter	Data	Specifies a filter that is loaded automatically with the Form/Report.

Table 7-5. Important Form Properties (Continued)

Property	Tab	Description
Order By	Data	Specifies a sort order that is loaded automatically with the Form/Report.
Allow Filters	Data	Determines whether filters may be applied to the form.
Allow Edits ✳	Data	Determines whether records can be modified in the form.
Allow Deletions ✳	Data	Determines whether records can be deleted in the form.
Allow Additions ✳	Data	Determines whether records can be added in the form.
Data Entry ✳	Data	Allows you to select "Yes" if you only want to use the form to add new records.
Event Tab	Event	Allows you to assign a macro or Visual Basic procedure to a specific event, such as when you click or update a control.
Pop Up	Other	Determines whether the form appears in a pop-up window that remains on top of all other windows.
Modal	Other	Determines whether the form keeps the focus (you can't switch to any other windows or forms) until it is closed.
Cycle	Other	Determines how the tab key should cycle.
Menu Bar	Other	Allows you to select a custom menu bar that you created that should appear when the form is active.
Toolbar	Other	Allows you to select a custom toolbar that you created that should appear when the form is active.
Shortcut Menu	Other	Determines if right mouse button shortcut menus are permitted in the form.
Shortcut Menu Bar	Other	Specifies a user-created shortcut menu that appears when a user clicks the right-mouse button.
Fast Laser Printing	Other	Print the form using optimized laser-printer formatting.
Help File	Other	Specifies the name of the custom Help file for the form.
Help Context Id	Other	Specifies an identifier number for a user-created Help file that appears when the user selects the control and presses F1.
Tag	Other	Specifies extra user-defined information that is stored in the form.
Has Module	Other	Specifies if the form has Visual Basic code behind it.

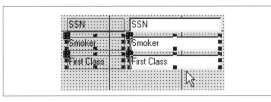

Figure 7-14. One way of selecting multiple controls is by pressing and holding down the Shift key as you click each control that you want to select.

Figure 7-15. Another way to select multiple controls is by drawing a box around the controls that you want to select.

The advantage of selecting multiple controls in a form or report is that you can edit, delete, move, format, or resize a whole bunch of controls at once, instead of having to edit each control individually. In this lesson you will learn how to select multiple controls on a form.

1 Open the frmCustomers **form in Design view.**

To delete a control you have to select it and press the Delete key. Sometimes you will want to delete several controls; instead of selecting and deleting each individual control, you can select and delete several controls at the same time. There are several ways you can select more than one control:

- Press and hold down the Shift key as you click each control that you want to select.

- If necessary, click the ![button] Select Objects button on the Toolbox toolbar. Then use the arrow pointer (![arrow]) to draw a box around the controls that you want to select, as shown in Figure 7-14. The disadvantage of this method is it's not as selective as using the Shift + click method.

- If the controls you want to select are aligned along a horizontal line, click to the left of the objects in the vertical ruler to select every control to the right of the ruler.

2 Hold down the Shift **key as you click the** Smoker **and** First Class **text boxes as shown in Figure 7-15.**

Handles appear around the controls, indicating that they are selected.

3 Press the Delete **key to delete the selected controls.**

The Smoker and First Class text box controls are both deleted.

QUICK REFERENCE

TO SELECT MULTIPLE CONTROLS:

- PRESS AND HOLD DOWN THE SHIFT KEY AS YOU CLICK EACH CONTROL THAT YOU WANT TO SELECT.

OR...

- USE THE ARROW POINTER (![arrow]) TO DRAW A BOX AROUND THE CONTROL THAT YOU WANT TO SELECT.

OR...

- IF THE CONTROLS ARE ALIGNED ALONG A HORIZONTAL OR VERTICAL LINE, CLICK THE HORIZONTAL OR VERTICAL RULER ABOVE OR TO THE LEFT OF THE CONTROLS.

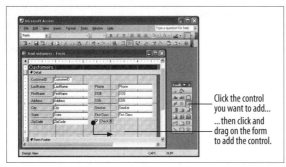

Click the control you want to add...

...then click and drag on the form to add the control.

Figure 7-16. Add a control to a form by clicking the control on the Toolbox and then clicking and dragging on the form.

In this lesson you will learn how to add a control by clicking and dragging and by copying and pasting.

1 Click the Check Box button on the Toolbox.

⋛ NOTE ⋛ *If the Toolbox isn't displayed, click the* ⚒ *Toolbox button on the Form Design toolbar.*

The mouse pointer changes to a ⁺☑ indicating that you can click and drag a check box control on the form.

2 Place the ⁺☑ pointer below the SSN text box. Click and drag the ⁺☑ pointer down and to the right and release the mouse button, as shown in Figure 7-16.

Congratulations! You've just added a check box control to your form.

If your form already has a control that's similar to the one you want to add, it's often easier to add the new control by copying and pasting the similar control than it is to add a control using the Toolbox. Once you have pasted the control, you can easily modify its properties, such as its text label data source. Here's how to copy a control.

3 Select the check box control you just added and click the Copy button on the Form Design toolbar.

Access copies the selected check box control to the Windows Clipboard. You can also cut controls on a form by selecting them and clicking the Cut button on the Form Design toolbar or by pressing Ctrl + X. Now let's paste the copied control.

4 Click the 🖺 Paste button on the Form Design toolbar.

Access pastes the copied check box onto the form as a new check box with its own name and label. We'll modify the two new check box controls in the next lesson.

Changing a Control's Data Source

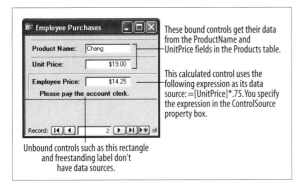

Figure 7-17. Examples of bound, unbound, and calculated controls.

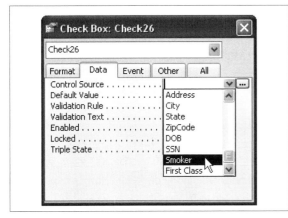

Figure 7-18. Setting the Control Source property.

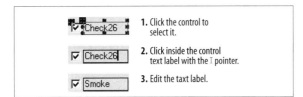

Figure 7-19. The steps in modifying a control's text label.

There are three types of controls that you can add to your forms, as illustrated in Figure 7-17. They are:

- **Bound Controls:** Bound controls are bound or connected to an underlying field in a table or query. You use bound controls to display, enter, and update field values in your database. The fields that you can add to a form using the Field List are all examples of bound controls.

- **Unbound Controls:** Unbound controls are not bound or connected to an underlying field in a table or query. You use unbound controls to display information. Labels, text boxes, and buttons can all be inserted on a

form as unbound controls. The two check boxes you added to the form in the previous lessons are both examples of unbound controls because they aren't connected to an underlying field in a table or query.

- **Calculated Controls:** Calculated controls are based on an expression and are used to calculate values in a form, such as arithmetic problems. Technically, calculated controls are unbound controls because they do not update any table fields.

A control's *Control Source property* determines what is displayed in a control—here's how:

- A bound control's Control Source property contains the name of the underlying database field to which it is bound.

- An unbound control's Control Source property does not contain the name of an underlying database field.

- A calculated control's Control Source property contains an expression that calculates the values displayed in the control.

This lesson explains how you can change a control's Control Source property.

1 Select the first check box control you added in the previous lesson, and display its properties by clicking the Properties button on the Form Design toolbar.

The Properties dialog box appears. You can find the Control Source property on the Data Tab.

2 Click the Data tab.

The Data tab appears, as shown in Figure 7-18. You can determine what is displayed in the control by setting the Control Source property. You can bind the control to a field in the form's underlying query or table by clicking the ⊻ button, or you can type text or an expression directly into the Control Source box. We want to bind the selected check box to the Smoker field.

3 Click in the Control Source box, click the ⊻ button, and select Smoker from the list, as shown in Figure 7-18.

The check box is now bound to the Smoker field in the tblCustomers table. Next let's bind the other check box control you added to the First Class field.

4 With the Properties dialog box still open, click the second check box control you added in the previous lesson.

The Properties dialog box is updated and displays the settings for the selected check box control.

5 Click in the Control Source box, click the button, and select First Class from the list.

You're done specifying the data sources for the two check boxes so you can close the Properties dialog box.

6 Click the Close button to close the Properties dialog box.

Before we're finished, we have to give the two check boxes more meaningful text labels. Here's how:

7 Position the pointer over the first check box text label, until it changes into a ⌶, and then click inside the text label, as illustrated in Figure 7-19.

Now you can edit the check box text label.

8 Replace the text label text with Smoker.

Now move on to the next step and change the text label for the second check box.

9 Following the same procedures as Steps 7–8, rename the second check box text label First Class.

That's it! You're done binding the check boxes to two underlying database fields.

10 Click on the Close button to close the frmCustomers form and click Yes to save your changes.

QUICK REFERENCE

TO CHANGE A CONTROL'S DATA SOURCE:

1. DISPLAY THE FORM IN DESIGN VIEW.

2. SELECT THE CONTROL AND CLICK THE PROPERTIES BUTTON ON THE TOOLBAR.

   OR...

   RIGHT-CLICK THE CONTROL AND SELECT PROPERTIES FROM THE SHORTCUT MENU.

   OR...

   SELECT THE CONTROL AND SELECT VIEW → PROPERTIES FROM THE MENU.

3. CLICK THE DATA TAB.

4. CLICK THE CONTROL SOURCE BOX, CLICK THE ARROW, AND SELECT THE FIELD THAT YOU WANT TO BIND THE CONTROL TO.

   OR...

   CLICK THE CONTROL SOURCE BOX AND ENTER AN EXPRESSION.

5. CLOSE THE PROPERTIES DIALOG BOX.

Creating a Calculated Control

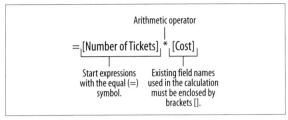

Figure 7-20. To enter database fields in an expression, type the field name in brackets.

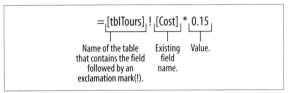

Figure 7-21. If a database field name exists in more than one table, you will need to enter the name of the table that contains the field in brackets, followed by an exclamation mark (!).

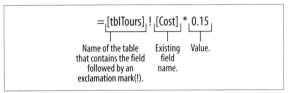

Figure 7-22. You create a calculated field by entering an expression in the Control Source box.

A *calculated control* is an unbound control that displays totals and other arithmetic computations on a form. You create calculated controls by entering an *expression* (or formula) to perform the calculation in the control's Control Source property.

In forms, expressions start with the equal sign (=), which tells Access that you want to perform a calculation. After the equal sign, you must specify two more types of information: the values you want to calculate and the arithmetic operator(s) or function name(s) you want to use to calculate the values. Expressions can contain explicit val-

ues, such as the numbers "4" or "5" or can reference the values contained in database fields. For example, the formula =[Cost]*[Commission] would multiply the values in the Cost and Commissions fields. To enter fields in an expression, type the field name in brackets ([Order Total]), as shown in Figure 7-20. If a field name exists in more than one table, you will need to enter the name of the table that contains the field in brackets ([Customer Tours]) followed by an exclamation mark (!) and then the field, such as [Order Total], as shown in Figure 7-21.

1 Open the frmTours **form in Design view.**

You want the Total text box to be a calculated control that finds the total cost of each tour by multiplying the Number of Tickets field by the Cost field.

2 Select the Total **text box, click the** Properties **button on the Form Design toolbar, and click the** Data **tab.**

You need to enter the expression in the Control Source box.

3 Click in the Control Source **box and type the expression** =[Number of Tickets]*[Cost] **as shown in Figure 7-22.**

Let's see how our new calculated control works.

4 Close the Properties dialog box and click the View button **on the Form Design toolbar to switch to Form view.**

The Total field displays the results of the expression you entered in Step 3.

5 Click the Close button **to close the** frmTours **form. Click** Yes **to save.**

Although you worked on a form in this lesson, you can also use expressions to create calculated controls and fields in queries and reports.

QUICK REFERENCE

TO CREATE A CALCULATED CONTROL:

1. DISPLAY THE FORM IN DESIGN VIEW.

2. SELECT THE CONTROL AND CLICK THE PROPERTIES BUTTON ON THE TOOLBAR.

3. CLICK THE DATA TAB AND CLICK IN THE CONTROL SOURCE BOX.

4. TYPE THE EXPRESSION, USING PROPER ACCESS SYNTAX.

   OR...

   CLICK THE BUILD BUTTON AND USE THE EXPRESSION BUILDER TO CREATE THE EXPRESSION.

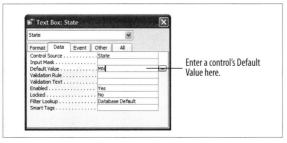

Figure 7-23. Setting the Default Value property for a control.

Enter a control's Default Value here.

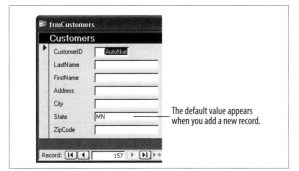

Figure 7-24. The default value will appear in the control when you add a new record with the form.

The default value appears when you add a new record.

You can enter a *default value* to specify a value that is automatically entered in a field when a new record is created. For example, if most of your clients are from Texas, you could set the default value for the State field to "TX." When users add a record using a form, they can either accept the "TX" default value for the State field or enter their own value.

1 Open the frmCustomers form in Design view.

Since the majority of your customers are from Minnesota, you decide to add "MN" as the default value for the State field.

2 Click the State field, display its properties by clicking the Properties button on the Form Design toolbar, and click the Data tab.

Now you can add a default value to the State field.

3 Click the Default Value box and type MN, as shown in Figure 7-23.

Let's see how the new default-value property works.

4 Click the Close button to close the Properties dialog box and click the View button on the Form Design toolbar to switch to Form view.

You will need to add a new record in order to see any default values.

5 Click the New Record button on the Record Navigation bar.

Access adds a new blank record to the form. Notice that the State field already contains the "MN" default value, as shown in Figure 7-24. If the customer is from another state, you can simply replace the default value with your own data.

6 Click the Close button to close the frmCustomers form and click Yes to save your changes.

One more important note about form control properties: Control properties in a form are *inherited*, or passed down, from the original properties in the underlying table or query. For example, if you set the Default Value property for a *table's* State field to "TX," the "TX" Default Value property will be passed on to a related State control on a form by default.

QUICK REFERENCE

TO SET A CONTROL'S DEFAULT VALUE:

1. DISPLAY THE FORM IN DESIGN VIEW.

2. DISPLAY THE PROPERTIES FOR THE DESIRED CONTROL.

3. CLICK THE DATA TAB.

4. CLICK THE DEFAULT VALUE BOX AND TYPE THE DEFAULT VALUE YOU WANT TO APPEAR FOR NEW RECORDS.

5. CLOSE THE PROPERTIES DIALOG BOX.

Figure 7-25. You can turn the Control Wizard on or off by toggling the Control Wizards button on the Toolbox.

Figure 7-26. The Combo Box Wizard.

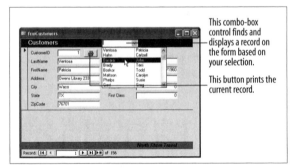

Figure 7-27. Two interactive controls added to a form using the Control Wizard.

The *Control Wizard* (no relation to Merlin) helps you add powerful, interactive controls to your form, as shown in Figure 7-27. Some examples include:

- List and combo box controls that can look up values in a table and then display the corresponding record on a form.
- Buttons that can open, print, or close tables, forms, queries, pages, and reports.
- Subforms, subreports, and charts that display related data from different tables.

When you add a control using the Control Wizard, you are asked a series of questions about what you want the control to do. The Control Wizard then creates the control, making the appropriate property settings and even adding several lines of Visual Basic code to the control for you.

1 Open the frmCustomers **form in Design view.**

To use the Control Wizard, simply make sure that the Control Wizards button on the Toolbox is shaded orange, as shown in Figure 7-25, and then add the control. The Control Wizard will appear anytime you try to create a list box, combo box, option group, button, chart, subreport, or subform.

2 Make sure the 🔨 Control Wizards button **on the Toolbox is pressed in.**

The Control Wizard is so incredibly cool and useful that you are strongly recommended to always keep it on.

⸪ NOTE ⸪   *If the Toolbox isn't displayed, click the Toolbox button on the Form Design toolbar.*

First let's add a combo box control to the form.

3 Click the Combo Box button **on the Toolbox.**

The mouse pointer changes to a 📇 indicating that you can click and drag a combo box control on the form.

4 Place the 📇 pointer in the form header, about one inch to the right of the "Customers" label. Click and drag the 📇 pointer to the right about an inch and release the mouse button.

Because the Control Wizard is on, the Combo Box Wizard dialog box appears, as shown in Figure 7-26. Each type of control will have its own Control Wizard and its own set of options. For this exercise, you want to select the third option.

5 Select the Find a record on my form based on the value I selected in my combo box **option and click Next.**

Next the Control Wizard asks which values you want to add to your combo box control

6 Click the ▶ button **three times to add the** Custo-merID, LastName **and** FirstName **fields to the combo box and click** Next.

Next the Control Wizard asks how wide you want the columns in your combo box control and if you want to hide the key column. Everything looks okay here, so…

7 Click Next.

Finally, you are asked to give your combo box a name. You can accept the default name provided by the Control Wizard or you can provide your own name.

8 Type Lookup Name **and click** Finish.

Poof! The Control Wizard adds the combo box. Next let's add a command button that will print the current record when clicked.

9 Click the ◢ Command Button button **on the Toolbox and add a button to the right of the** Custom-erID **text box by clicking and dragging.**

Because the Control Wizard is on, the Command Button Wizard appears. Command Buttons have lots of options that you can choose from, broken down by categories.

10 Select Record Operations **from the Categories list and select** Print Record **from the Actions list.**

This will make the command button print the current record when clicked.

11 Click Next.

Here you can specify the text or picture that will appear in the button.

12 Click Finish.

Access adds the command button to the form.

13 Click the View button **on the Form Design toolbar.**

Let's see how our new controls work.

14 Select a name from the new Lookup Name combo box.

Access finds and displays the record that you select from the combo box.

15 Click the Close button **to close the** frmCus-tomers **form and** Yes **to save.**

Try experimenting and adding controls to your forms using the Control Wizard. You'll be amazed at how much you can accomplish without knowing any programming!

QUICK REFERENCE

TO CREATE A LIST BOX OR COMBO BOX:

1. DISPLAY THE FORM IN DESIGN VIEW.

2. CLICK THE TOOLBOX BUTTON ON THE TOOLBAR, IF NECESSARY, AND MAKE SURE THE CONTROL WIZARDS BUTTON ON THE TOOLBOX IS SELECTED.

3. CLICK THE COMBO BOX OR LIST BOX BUTTON ON THE TOOLBOX.

4. IN THE FORM WINDOW, CLICK AND DRAG WHERE YOU WANT THE CONTROL TO APPEAR.

5. SPECIFY WHETHER YOU WANT THE CONTROL TO GET ITS VALUES FROM A TABLE OR QUERY, OR IF YOU WANT THE CONTROL TO FIND A RECORD ON THE FORM.

6. SELECT THE TABLE THAT CONTAINS THE FIELDS YOU WANT TO INCLUDE IN THE LIST AND CLICK NEXT.

7. SELECT THE FIELDS YOU WANT TO APPEAR IN YOUR LIST AND CLICK NEXT.

8. ADJUST THE COLUMN WIDTHS, IF NECESSARY, AND CLICK NEXT.

9. IF NECESSARY, SPECIFY WHICH COLUMN CONTAINS THE VALUE THAT WILL BE STORED AND CLICK NEXT.

10. SPECIFY WHETHER ACCESS SHOULD MERELY DISPLAY THE VALUE OR DISPLAY IT IN A FIELD.

11. ENTER A LABEL AND CLICK FINISH.

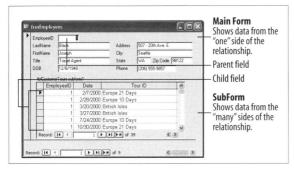

Figure 7-28. Subforms are great for working with data in multiple tables with one-to-many relationships. Here the subform displays all the tours made by each employee.

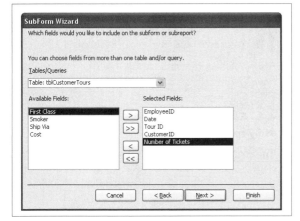

Figure 7-29. Select the table or query and fields that you want to include on your subform.

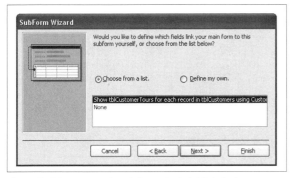

Figure 7-30. You need to define which fields link the main form and subform.

A *subform* is a form within a form. The primary form is called the *main form*, and the form within the form is called the *subform*, as shown in Figure 7-28. Subforms are especially useful when you want to show data from tables or queries with a one-to-many relationship. For

example, a Customer form might have a subform that displays each customer's Orders. Subforms are a great way to display information from a one-to-many table relationship.

The main form and subform are linked so that the subform displays only records that are related to the current record in the main form. For example, when the main form displays a particular customer, the subform displays only orders for that customer.

1 Open the frmEmployees form in Design view.

Usually you will want to have the Control Wizard assist you when you add a subform.

2 Make sure the ⚙ Control Wizards button on the Toolbox is pressed in.

The Control Wizard is on whenever its button is depressed.

⁝ NOTE ⁝ *If the Toolbox isn't displayed, click the* 🔧 *Toolbox button on the Form Design toolbar.*

Before you add a subform, make sure that you have enough room for it on the main form.

3 Resize the main-form window as needed, so that you have enough room to add the subform.

You're ready to add the subform! Here's how:

4 Click the ▦ Subform/Subreport button on the Toolbox.

The mouse pointer changes to a ⁺▦ indicating that you can click and drag the subform onto the main form.

5 Place the ⁺▦ pointer just below the DOB field. Click and drag the ⁺▦ pointer down and to the right, until the subform covers most of the bottom half of the main form.

The Subform Wizard appears and asks if you want to use an existing form for your subform or if you want to build a new form, using tables or queries. In this exercise we will have the Wizard build us a new form using tables and queries as our subform.

6 Click Next.

The next step of the Wizard appears. Here you have to select the table or query and fields that you want to display in your subform, as shown in Figure 7-29. We want our subform to display the tours that each employee has sold, so we will select the qryCustomer-Tours query as the source for our subform.

7 Select Query: qryCustomerTours from the Tables/Queries combo box.

Now you need to select the fields you want to appear in the subform. You *must* select the related field used to join the main form and subform. This related field must appear on both the main form (where it is called the *parent field*) and on the subform (where it is called the *child field*). In this exercise we will use the EmployeeID field to link the two forms.

⋛ NOTE ⋛   *It's very important that the underlying tables or queries of the main form and subform have a related field and that the related field appears somewhere on both forms. See Lesson 5.2 in Chapter 5 if you're having trouble understanding this concept.*

8 Select the EmployeeID field and click the ▶ button to add the field to the Selected Fields list.

Now that you've added the most important field that will link the two forms, you can add the remaining fields that you want to appear on the subform.

9 Add the Date, TourID, CustomerID, and Number of Tickets fields to the Selected Fields list.

If you're this far, you should be a pro at adding and removing fields using the Wizard. Just make sure that you add the fields in the order specified in Steps 8 and 9.

10 Click Next.

The next step in the Wizard, as shown in Figure 7-30, is to define the fields that link the main form and the subform. The Subform Wizard is often smart enough to recognize the field and use it to link the two forms—as it is in this exercise. If not, you will have to click the Define my own option and select the two related fields.

11 Click Next and then click Finish.

Access creates the subform and adds it to the main form.

12 Save your changes to the frmEmployees form and display it in Form view.

The frmEmployees form displays information on each employee and the new subform displays the tours that employee booked.

Subforms created with the Subform Wizard are usually a little rough around the edges and will require a little clean-up work on your part. We'll learn how to modify and work with a subform in the next lesson.

QUICK REFERENCE

TO CREATE A SUBFORM:

1. DISPLAY THE FORM IN DESIGN VIEW.

2. CLICK THE *TOOLBOX BUTTON* ON THE TOOLBAR, IF NECESSARY.

3. MAKE SURE THE *CONTROL WIZARDS BUTTON* ON THE TOOLBOX IS SELECTED.

4. RESIZE THE FORM IF NECESSARY.

5. CLICK THE *SUBFORM/SUBREPORT BUTTON* ON THE TOOLBOX.

6. IN THE FORM WINDOW, CLICK AND DRAG WHERE YOU WANT THE SUBFORM TO APPEAR.

7. CLICK *NEXT*.

8. SPECIFY THE TABLE OR QUERY YOU WANT TO USE FOR THE SUBFORM AND SELECT THE FIELDS YOU WANT TO APPEAR IN THE SUBFORM.

9. CLICK *NEXT*.

10. IF NECESSARY, SPECIFY THE PARENT AND CHILD FIELDS THAT LINK THE MAIN FORM AND SUBFORM.

11. CLICK *FINISH*.

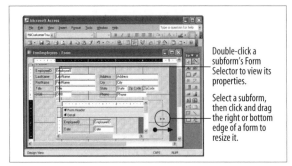

Double-click a subform's Form Selector to view its properties.

Select a subform, then click and drag the right or bottom edge of a form to resize it.

Figure 7-31. Modifying a subform in Design view.

Subforms rarely come out the way you want them to the first time: They may be too small or too large and must be resized so that the main form and subform fit together nicely. If you're using an existing form as a subform, you may need to change the subform layout. Subforms can be displayed using one of three different formats:

- **Single Form:** Displays one record at time on a form.
- **Continuous Forms:** Displays multiple records on a form. The main difference between datasheets and continuous forms is that you can design and customize continuous forms.
- **Datasheet:** Displays multiple records in a table, using one line per record. Tables and queries display their data in Datasheet layout.
- **PivotTable:** Dynamically analyzes information and summarizes it into a datasheet-like table.
- **PivotChart:** Dynamically analyzes information and summarizes it into a chart.

1 Make sure that you have the frmEmployees form you modified in the previous lesson open in Form view.

When you add records on a main form or subform, Access stores the appropriate data in each table. Usually you won't even realize that you are working with several tables!

Let's see how the new subform works.

2 Click the ▶ Next Record button **on the main form's Record Navigation bar.**

Notice that the subform displays tours booked by the current employee.

Also, notice that the main form and sub form each have their own set of navigation buttons that you can use to add and move between records. Try adding a new record to the subform.

3 Click the ▶✳ New Record button **on the Record Navigation bar.**

The record indicator jumps to the blank row at the end of the subform datasheet and the blinking insertion point (|) appears in the EmployeeID field. Notice that Access has automatically filled in the EmployeeID field with the main form's EmployeeID.

⸭ NOTE ⸭ *If you have set referential integrity between two or more related fields in a subform's underlying table or query, you will have to obey those referential integrity rules in order to add or edit a record in the subform. For example, you can't enter a number in the TourID field unless that number exists in the qryCustomerTours query.*

4 Enter a new record in the subform using the following information:

EmployeeID	Date	TourID	CustomerID	Number of Tickets
(Current)	9/2/01	China	Ali	2

It's easy to switch between the main form and subform: simply click a field or control in the form you want to move to or press Ctrl + Shift + Tab.

5 Click any field in the main form to move to the main form.

Here's how to modify a subform:

6 Switch to Design view.

First get rid of that annoying subform label.

7 Select the label for the subform and press Delete.

Here's how to change the layout of a subform:

8 Double-click the subform's ☐ Form Selector in the upper left corner of the subform.

The Properties dialog box appears.

9 Click the Format tab, click in the Default View box, click the ✔ button and select Continuous Forms. Close the Properties dialog box.

Now you need to resize the subform control and the main form.

10 Click the subform to select it, then click and drag the right edge of the subform to eliminate the wasted, empty space, as shown in Figure 7-31.

Let's see how our form looks.

11 Display the frmEmployees form in Form view.

The subform is displayed in continuous form layout instead of Datasheet layout.

12 Save your changes to the form and close the Lesson 7 database.

Whew! We just covered a lot of ground in this chapter. Try moving on to the Chapter Review to see how much you remember.

QUICK REFERENCE

TO MODIFY A SUBFORM:

1. CLICK ANYWHERE IN THE SUBFORM.

2. EDIT THE SUBFORM AS NEEDED.

TO DISPLAY A SUBFORM'S PROPERTIES:

• DOUBLE-CLICK THE SUBFORM'S FORM SELECTOR.

Chapter Seven Review

Lesson Summary

Creating a Form with AutoForm

To Create a Form with AutoForm: From the Database window, click the Forms icon in the Objects bar and click the New button. Select the type of form you want to create: Columnar, Tabular, Datasheet, PivotTable, or Pivot-Chart. Click the table or query you want to use for the form from the drop-down list and Click OK.

Modifying a Form

To Modify a Form: From the Database window, click the Forms icon in the Objects bar, click the form you want to modify and click Design, or open the form and click the View button on the toolbar.

Adding and Deleting Fields

To Add a Field to a Form: Display the form in Design View and click the Field List button on the toolbar if necessary, find the field you want to add to the form in the Field List, then click and drag the field to the desired location on the form.

To Delete a Field or Control: Click the field or control to select it and then press Delete.

Moving and Sizing Controls

To Resize a Control: Click the control to select it, grab one of its sizing handles, drag and then release the mouse button when the control reaches the desired size. Hold down the Shift key while dragging to maintain the control's proportions while resizing it.

To Move a Control: Click the control and hold down the mouse button, drag the control to a new location and then release the mouse button to drop the control.

To Move a Text Box or Text Label Independently of Each Other: Position the pointer over the upper left sizing handle of the control until it changes to the hand icon, then click and drag the control.

Changing the Tab Order

To Change a Form's Tab Order: Display the form in Design View and select View → Tab Order from the menu. Click the row selector for the control you want to move and click and drag the row selector to the desired location. Repeat as needed to change the tab order of additional controls.

To Automatically Change the Tab Order: Display the form in Design View and select View → Tab Order from the menu. Click the Auto Order button to automatically reorder the form controls, based on their position in the form.

Working with Control Properties

To Display the Properties for Any Control: Display the form in Design View and do any of the following:

- Select the control and click the Properties button on the toolbar.
- Right-click the control and select Properties from the shortcut menu.
- Select the control and select View → Properties from the menu.

Working with Form Properties

To View and Change Form Properties: Display the form in Design View and double-click the Form Selector. Click the appropriate property tab and property box and make the desired changes.

Working with Multiple Controls

To Select Multiple Controls: Do any of following:

- Press and hold down the Shift key as you click each control that you want to select.
- Use the arrow pointer to draw a box around the control that you want to select.
- If the controls are aligned along a horizontal or vertical line, click the horizontal or vertical ruler above or to the left of the controls.

Adding, Cutting, Copying, and Pasting Controls

To Add a Control: Click the Toolbox button on the toolbar if necessary, click the button on the Toolbox for the type of control you want to add, in the Form window, click and drag the pointer where you want the control to appear.

To Cut a Control: Select the control and:

- Click the Cut button on the toolbar or…

- Press Ctrl + X or…

- Select Edit → Cut from the menu.

To Copy a Control: Select the control and:

- Click the Copy button on the toolbar or…

- Press Ctrl + C or…

- Select Edit → Copy from the menu.

To Paste a Control: Select the control and:

- Click the Paste button on the toolbar or…

- Press Ctrl + V or…

- Select Edit → Paste from the menu.

Changing a Control's Data Source

To Change a Control's Data Source: Display the Form in Design View, select the control and click the Properties button on the toolbar, or right-click the control and select Properties from the shortcut menu, or select the control and select View → Properties from the menu. Click the Data tab, click the Control Source box, and then either click the arrow and select the field that you want to bind the control to or enter an expression. Close the Properties dialog box when you're finished.

Creating a Calculated Control

To Create a Calculated Control: Display the form in Design View, select the control and click the Properties button on the toolbar. Click the Data tab and click in the Control Source box, type the expression or use the Expression Builder to create the expression, and then close the Properties dialog box.

Changing a Control's Default Value

To Set a Control's Default Value: Display the form in Design View, display the properties for the desired control, and click the Data tab. Click the Default Value box and type the default value you want to appear for new records. Close the Properties dialog box when you're finished.

Using the Control Wizard

To Create a List Box or Combo Box: Display the form in Design View, click the Toolbox button on the toolbar if necessary and make sure the Control Wizards button on the Toolbox is selected. Click the Combo Box or List Box button on the Toolbox. In the form window, click and drag where you want the control to appear. Specify whether you want the control to get its values from—a table or query, or if you want the control to find a record on the form. Select the table that contains the fields you want to include in the list, click Next, select the fields you want to appear in your list and click Next. Adjust the column widths if necessary, click Next. If necessary, specify which column contains the value that will be stored and click Next. Specify whether Access should merely display the value or display it in a field. Enter a label and click Finish.

Creating a Subform

To Create a Subform: Display the form in Design View, click the Toolbox button on the toolbar if necessary and make sure the Control Wizards button on the Toolbox is selected. Resize the form if necessary, then click the Subform/Subreport button on the Toolbox and click and drag where you want the subform to appear in the form. Click Next and specify the table or query you want to use for the subform and select the fields you want to appear in the subform. Click Next, specify the parent and child fields that link the main form and subform if necessary, and click Finish.

Modifying and Working with Subforms

To Modify a Subform: Click anywhere in the subform and edit the subform as needed.

To Display a Subform's Properties: Double-click the subform's Form Selector.

Quiz

1. Which of the following statements about the Auto-Form Wizard is NOT true?

   A. The AutoForm Wizard is the fastest and easiest way to create a form in Microsoft Access.

   B. The AutoForm Wizard can only create five types of forms: Datasheet, Columnar, Tabular, PivotTable, or PivotChart.

   C. Forms created with the AutoForm Wizard usually come out looking sharp and professional and don't require any further clean-up work.

   D. The AutoForm Wizard can only create forms based on a single table or query.

2. Which of the following statements is NOT true?

   A. The Field List displays all the fields from a form's underlying table or query.

   B. Click the Field List button on the Toolbar to display the Field List.

   C. You can add fields to a form by dragging them from the Field List onto the form.

   D. The Field List displays all the fields from every table in a database.

3. Controls and their corresponding text labels cannot be moved independently of one another. (True or False?)

4. If you move a control on a form, the *Tab Order*, in which you advance from one field to the next when you press the Tab key, is automatically updated. (True or False?)

5. A form that has a Datasheet Default View property would display one record at a time in the form. (True or False?)

6. A calculated field... (Select all that apply.)

   A. ...is a bound control.

   B. ...is a control that contains an expression.

   C. ...can perform calculations on fields values, such as =[Cost]*[Commission].

   D. ...can perform calculations on explicit values, such as =2+4.

7. Which of the following set(s) of tables would benefit from a subform? (Select all that apply.)

   A. A Customer table and the Customer Orders table.

   B. A Customer table and Products table.

   C. A Customer table and Foreign Currency table.

   D. A Customer table and a Customer Contacts table.

8. When you add a subform to a main form, Access always recognizes how the two forms are related (True or False?)

Homework

1. Open the Homework database.

2. Use AutoForm to create and save a columnar form named "Customers," using the Customers table as the underlying data source.

3. Add a text box control with today's date in the bottom-right corner of the Customers form.**Hint:** You will need to change the text box control's data source to the expression =Today( ).

4. Rearrange the control fields on the form, so that the LastName and FirstName fields appear before the SSN field.

5. Change the Customer form's tab order to reflect the new field order.

6. Delete the DOB field control from the form.

7. Resize the Customers form as necessary, then use the SubForm Wizard to create a subform based on the Insurance Claims table.

8. Modify the Insurance Claims subform so that its Default View property is Single Form View.

9. Save your changes to the main form and the subform. Then close the form and the Homework database.

Quiz Answers

1. C. The AutoForm Wizard can create forms in record time, but they aren't usually well-organized or professional looking.

2. D. The Field List only displays fields from a form's underlying table or query.

3. False. You can click and drag the upper left sizing handle to move a label or control independently of one another.

4. False. If you add or move a control on a form, you would have to change the form's tab order yourself—Microsoft Access won't do it for you.

5. False. A form whose Default View property was set to Datasheet would display multiple records. A form whose Default View property was set to Single Form would display one record on the form at a time.

6. B, C, and D. All of these statements are true.

7. A and D. Because subforms are great at displaying information from one-to-many relationships, both of these tables would benefit from being displayed in a subform.

8. False. If you include the field that links the two tables, Access will automatically recognize it, if you have already joined the two tables. If the tables aren't related, you may have to manually join the tables by connecting their related fields.

WORKING WITH REPORTS

CHAPTER OBJECTIVES:

Create and modify a report, Lessons 8.1—8.2

Add and delete fields, Lesson 8.3

Move and size controls, Lesson 8.4

Adjust page margins and orientation, Lesson 8.5

Add page numbers and dates, Lesson 8.6

Work with report sections, Lessons 8.7, 8.10

Use reports to group and sort records, Lesson 8.8

Create calculated controls, Lesson 8.9

Add a chart to a report, Lesson 8.11

CHAPTER TASK: CREATE AND MODIFY A VARIETY OF REPORTS

Prerequisites

- **How to use menus, toolbars, dialog boxes, and shortcut keystrokes.**
- **How to open and modify database objects.**
- **How to add and edit database records.**

It's easy to print a simple list of records in a table or query—just click the Print button on the toolbar. But if you want your printed hard copies to look professional and include calculations, graphics, or a customized header or footer, you'll need to create a report. Reports present information from tables and queries in a format that looks great when printed.

Reports can also summarize and analyze the information in your database. For example, a report might tell you which of your employees had used the most sick days for the past year. Here are just a few examples of how reports work well for presenting information:

- **Formatting Options:** Change the type, size, and color of the fonts used in a report or add lines, boxes, and graphics.

- **Sorting and Grouping Options:** Reports are great for summarizing and organizing information. For example, you could create a report to total sales by day, week, or month.

- **Combine Data from Linked Tables:** One report can display data from several related tables or queries.

This chapter explains all the ins and outs of creating and working with reports.

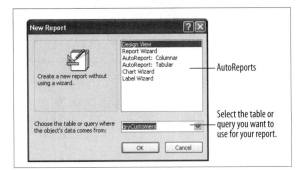

Figure 8-1. The New Report dialog box.

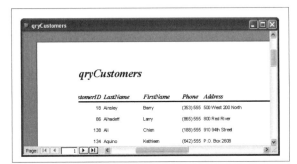

Figure 8-2. A Tabular report created by the AutoReport Wizard.

The fastest and easiest way to create a simple report in Access is with the AutoReport Wizard. The AutoReport Wizard can automatically create a report by arranging all the fields from a table or query into a neatly formatted report, as shown in Table 8-1.

The AutoReport Wizard is easy to use, but limited—it only works with one table or query and there are only two types of reports that it can create. Of course, you can always modify a report created by using the AutoReport Wizard.

In this lesson you will learn how to create a report using an AutoReport Wizard.

1 Open the **Lesson 8** database.

In the Database window, you need to select the Reports icon in the Objects bar.

2 Click the **Reports** icon in the Objects bar, then click the **New** button.

The New Report dialog box appears, as shown in Figure 8-1. You can create a report with the AutoReport Wizard by selecting one of the two AutoReport Wizards...

3 Select **AutoReport: Tabular** from the list.

... and the table or query you want to use for your report.

4 Click the **Choose** the table or query where the object's data comes from: **list arrow and select qryCustomers from the list.**

That's all the information the AutoReport Wizard needs to create your report.

5 Click **OK** to create the tabular report.

Access takes all the fields in the qryCustomers query, arranges them, and creates a report similar to the one shown in Figure 8-2. Yuck! Ugly-looking report, isn't it?

6 Close the report without saving your changes.

The reports created by the AutoForm Wizards aren't very pretty to look at, but they're fast and easy to create. If you want to have more control over what appears on your report, use the Report Wizard. Either way you will probably want to do some clean-up work, such as renaming the report's column headings and moving/resizing its controls.

Table 8-1. Available AutoReport Layouts

Report Layout	Description
Customers LastName — Ainsley FirstName — Barry Phone — (353) 555-6960 Address — 500 West 200 North City — Dorval	Displays each record's data vertically. Each field of each record appears on a single line by itself.
Customers **Last Name** **First Name** **Phone** Ainsley — Barry — (353) 555-6960 Alhadeff — Larry — (865) 555-8921 Ali — Chien — (188) 555-6869 Aquino — Kathleen — (642) 555-3297	Displays each record's data horizontally. Each field appears in a column.

QUICK REFERENCE

TO CREATE A REPORT WITH AUTOREPORT:

1. IN THE DATABASE WINDOW, CLICK THE REPORTS ICON IN THE OBJECTS BAR AND CLICK THE NEW BUTTON.

2. SELECT ONE OF THE FOLLOWING:

    AUTOREPORT: COLUMNAR

    AUTOREPORT: TABULAR

3. SELECT THE TABLE OR QUERY YOU WANT TO USE FOR THE REPORT FROM THE DROP-DOWN LIST.

4. CLICK OK.

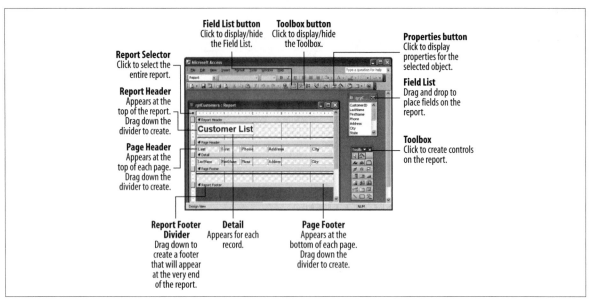

Figure 8-3. A report in Design view.

After you create a report (from scratch, using the Report Wizard, or using the AutoReport Wizard), you may decide to modify it to make it easier to read and understand. For example, you might want to add or delete a field, change a column heading, or change the locations of the fields in the report. You modify a report in Design view, which you can get to from:

- **The database window:** Click the Reports icon in the Objects bar to list the reports in the database. Click on the report you want to modify and click the Design button.

- **Any report window:** Click the View button on the toolbar or select View → Design View from the menu.

This lesson will introduce you to report Design view.

1 In the Database window, click the Reports icon in the Objects bar if it isn't already selected, then select the rptCustomers report and click the Design button.

The rptCustomers report appears in Design view, as shown in Figure 8-3.

If you have already worked with forms in Design view, you should be in familiar territory—Design view is remarkably similar for both forms and reports. Just as it is with forms, report Design view is similar to many Paint programs: Think of the report as your canvas and the Toolbox and Field List as the paintbrushes you use to add fields, headings, and lines to the report.

Any object that appears on a report is called a *control*. A text box used to display record information (usually fields from a table or query) or a column heading are both examples of controls. You add controls to a report by clicking the control you want to use and then dragging it onto the report. See Table 8-2 for Toolbox buttons and controls.

Table 8-2. Toolbox Buttons and Controls

Toolbox Button	Description
	Click this button and then click the control you want to select. To select multiple controls, click this button and hold down the Shift key as you click each control, or drag a rectangle shape around all the controls you want to select.
	Click to use Control Wizards when you add controls to your report.
	Creates a text label that appears the same for every record, such as a heading. Most controls already include a text label.
	Creates a text box that displays information from tables and queries in a report.
	Creates a box around a group of option buttons so that the user is only allowed to make one selection from the group box. Normally used in forms, not reports.
	Creates a toggle button. Normally used in forms, not reports.
	Creates an option button (or radio button) that displays data from two or more options. Normally used in forms, not reports.
	Creates a box that is empty or contains a checkmark. Use to display data from a Yes/No field.
	Creates a combo box. Normally used in forms, not reports.
	Creates a list box. Normally used in forms, not reports.
	Creates a button that runs a macro or Visual Basic function. Normally used in forms, not reports.
	Displays a picture by using a graphic file that you specify.
	Inserts an OLE object that is not bound to a field in the current database. Use an Unbound Object Frame to display information from an external source or program, such as a spreadsheet, graphic, or other file.
	Inserts an OLE object that is bound to a field in the database. Use Bound Object Frames to display pictures or other OLE information in the database.
	Inserts a page break.
	Creates a tab control. Normally used in forms, not reports.
	Inserts another report within the main report. Use when you want to show data from a one-to-many relationship.
	Enables you to draw a line in the report.
	Enables you to draw a rectangle in the report.
	Click to display other toolboxes and OLE objects.

QUICK REFERENCE

TO MODIFY A REPORT:

1. IN THE DATABASE WINDOW, CLICK THE REPORTS ICON IN THE OBJECTS BAR.

2. CLICK THE REPORT YOU WANT TO MODIFY AND CLICK THE DESIGN BUTTON.

OR...

OPEN THE REPORT AND CLICK THE VIEW BUTTON ON THE TOOLBAR.

Figure 8-4. Add a field to a report by clicking and dragging it from the Field List onto the report.

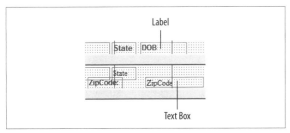

Figure 8-5. Adding a field or control to a report often produces unwanted results: Here the ZipCode field is the wrong size and creates an unneeded text label.

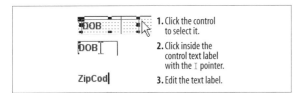

Figure 8-6. The steps in modifying a text label.

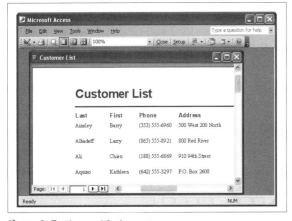

Figure 8-7. The modified report.

Once you have created a report, you can delete a field that you don't need or make a report more comprehensive by adding more fields to display additional information.

In this lesson you will modify an existing report by adding and deleting fields.

1 Make sure you have the rptCustomers report open in Design view. Maximize the report window.

First, click the control you want to delete.

2 Click the DOB text box (in the Detail section) to select it.

Handles appear around the control, indicating that the control is selected.

3 Press the Delete key to delete the DOB text box.

The DOB text box disappears from the report screen.

Unfortunately, adding fields to a report isn't quite as easy…

4 If the Field List isn't displayed, click the Field List button on the toolbar.

The Field List displays all the fields from the table or query you used to create the report—though you will often have to scroll down the Field List to find the field that you want. Once the Field List is displayed, you can click and drag the field you want to add from the Field List onto the report, as shown in Figure 8-4.

5 Scroll down the Field List until you find the ZipCode field. Click and drag the ZipCode field to the right of the State field, then release the mouse button.

The ZipCode field appears on the report with less than desirable results, as shown in Figure 8-5. An annoyance with adding controls to a report is that you almost always have to do some clean-up work afterwards. For example, the ZipCode field has an unneeded text label and isn't positioned correctly. Don't worry about the positioning for now—you'll learn how to move controls in the next lesson. We can fix some of the other problems, however, starting with getting rid of the unneeded text label.

6 Click the unneeded ZipCode text label (NOT the actual ZipCode text box!) and press Delete.

Before we're finished, we have to give the ZipCode field a more meaningful text heading. Here's how:

7 Click the DOB text label to select it.

8 Position the pointer over the DOB text label until it changes into a ⊺ , and then click inside the text label.

Now you can edit the text label, as shown in Figure 8-6.

9 Replace the text label text with Zip Code.

Let's see how the modified report looks.

10 Click the View button on the toolbar to display the report in Print Preview.

Compare your report with the one in Figure 8-7.

11 Close Print Preview and click Yes to save your changes.

QUICK REFERENCE

TO ADD A FIELD TO A REPORT:

1. DISPLAY THE REPORT IN DESIGN VIEW AND CLICK THE FIELD LIST BUTTON ON THE TOOLBAR, IF NECESSARY.

2. FIND THE FIELD YOU WANT TO ADD TO THE REPORT IN THE FIELD LIST, THEN CLICK AND DRAG THE FIELD TO THE DESIRED LOCATION ON THE REPORT.

TO DELETE A FIELD OR CONTROL:

1. CLICK THE FIELD OR CONTROL TO SELECT IT.

2. PRESS DELETE.

Moving and Sizing Controls

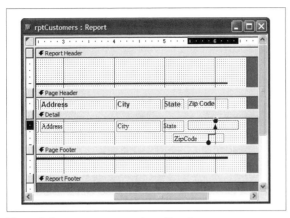

Figure 8-8. To move a control, position the mouse over a border of the control until the pointer changes to a hand cursor, and then drag and drop the control to a new location on the report.

It's easy to change the location and size of a control on a report—and it's something you will usually have to do whenever you add a control, since Access rarely places things exactly right in the first place. When you *size* a control, you increase or decrease the amount of information the control can display. When you select a control on a report, *sizing handles* appear around the edges of the control. Once you have selected a control, you can drag its sizing handles to adjust the size of the control or move the control to a new location on the report.

This lesson will give you some experience moving and sizing the control you created in the previous lesson.

1 If necessary, open the Lesson 8 database and click the Reports icon.

Now we need to open the rptCustomers report in Design view.

2 Click the rptCustomers report and then click the Design button.

You need to select a control before you can move or size it.

3 Click the ZipCode text box to select it.

Sizing handles appear around the selected ZipCode field. Here's how to move a control:

4 Position the pointer over any border of the Zip-Code text box (but not over a sizing handle) until it changes to a 🖐.

When the mouse pointer changes to a 🖐, it means that you can drag and drop the control to a new location.

≷ NOTE ≷   *It takes a good deal of precision to position the pointer over the tiny border of a field. Move the pointer very slowly and wait until you see it turn into a 🖐 before you try to move the control.*

5 Click and hold down the mouse button while the 🖐 pointer is still over the border of the ZipCode text box. Drag the field directly to the right of the State text box, as shown in Figure 8-8, then release the mouse button.

By simply dragging and dropping with the mouse, you can move any object on a report—any shapes, lines, pictures, or text boxes.

Sometimes, after moving an object, you'll find you want to move the object just a smidgen. You can use the keyboard to move or nudge controls with greater precision. Simply hold down the Ctrl key as you press any of the arrow keys on the keyboard.

6 With the ZipCode text box still selected, hold down the Ctrl key and press the ← (left arrow) key.

The ZipCode text box moves to the left a smidgen.

7 Make sure the ZipCode text box is still selected. Position the pointer over the middle-right sizing handle until it changes to a ↔. Click and hold down the mouse button and drag to the left until the label is about two-thirds of its original size, then release the mouse button.

As you drag a control's sizing handle, a dotted outline appears to help you resize it. That's all there is to moving and sizing controls on a report.

8 Click the Save button on the toolbar to save your changes.

QUICK REFERENCE

TO RESIZE A CONTROL:

- CLICK THE CONTROL TO SELECT IT, CLICK AND DRAG ONE OF ITS SIZING HANDLES, AND RELEASE THE MOUSE BUTTON WHEN THE CONTROL REACHES THE DESIRED SIZE.

- HOLD DOWN THE SHIFT KEY WHILE DRAGGING TO MAINTAIN THE CONTROL'S PROPORTIONS WHILE RESIZING IT.

TO MOVE A CONTROL:

- CLICK THE CONTROL AND HOLD DOWN THE MOUSE BUTTON, DRAG THE CONTROL TO A NEW LOCATION, THEN RELEASE THE MOUSE BUTTON TO DROP THE CONTROL.

TO COPY A CONTROL USING DRAG AND DROP:

- FOLLOW THE SAME PROCEDURES AS MOVING A CONTROL, ONLY HOLD DOWN THE CTRL KEY WHILE YOU DRAG THE CONTROL.

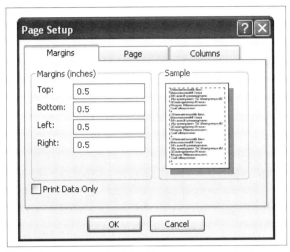

Figure 8-9. The Margins tab of the Page Setup dialog box.

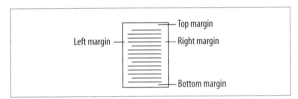

Figure 8-10. Margins on a page.

Figure 8-11. The Page tab of the Page Setup dialog box.

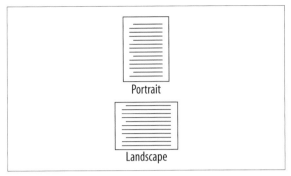

Figure 8-12. Comparison of portrait and landscape page orientations.

You're probably already aware that *margins* are the empty space between the text and the left, right, top, and bottom edges of a printed page. The default margins for a report are one inch at the top, bottom, left, and right. There are many reasons to change a report's margins: To make room for more data, to add some extra space if you're binding a document, or to leave a blank space to write in notes. If you don't already know how to adjust a page's margins, you will after this lesson.

This lesson also explains how to change the page orientation. Everything you print uses one of two different types of paper orientations: *portrait* and *landscape*. In Portrait orientation, the paper is taller than it is wide—like a painting of a person's portrait. In Landscape orientation, the paper is wider than it is tall—like a painting of a landscape.

1 Make sure that you have the rptCustomers report open in Design view.

Here's how to modify the page setup for a report:

2 Click File → Page Setup from the menu and click the Margins tab if it is not already selected.

⁚ NOTE ⁚ *The default margins are one inch at the top, bottom, left, and right.*

The Margins tab of the Page Setup dialog box appears, as shown in Figure 8-9. Here you can view and adjust the margin sizes (see Figure 8-10) for the current worksheet. Notice that there are margin settings in the Top, Bottom, Left, and Right boxes.

3 Click the Top Margin box and type .5.

This will change the size of the top margin from 1.0″ to 0.5″.

4 Repeat Step 2 and change the Bottom, Left, and Right margins to 0.5 inches.

Do you think you have a handle on changing a report's margins? Good, because without further ado, we'll move on to page orientation.

5 Click the Page tab.

The Page tab appears, as shown in Figure 8-11.

6 In the Orientation area, click the Landscape option.

This will change the worksheet's orientation to Landscape (see Figure 8-12) when it is printed.

7 Click OK.

The Page Setup dialog box closes, and the report's margins and page orientation settings are changed.

When you change a report's margins, you will usually want to resize the report itself—here's how:

8 If necessary, scroll to the right edge of the report. Click and drag the right edge of the report to the right to the 7.5 inch mark on the ruler.

Let's see how the newly formatted report looks.

9 Click the View button on the toolbar.

The report is previewed on the screen—and it's easy to see the new landscape orientation. You can reduce or enlarge the display by clicking the area of the report you want to magnify with the 🔍 pointer.

10 Move the 🔍 pointer over an area of the report and click the mouse button. Click the mouse button again when you have finished looking at the enlarged area.

Once again, Access displays the entire report. Now let's close Print Preview.

11 Click Close and click the Save button to save your changes.

QUICK REFERENCE

TO ADJUST MARGINS:

1. SELECT FILE → PAGE SETUP FROM THE MENU AND CLICK THE MARGINS TAB.

2. ADJUST THE APPROPRIATE MARGINS.

TO CHANGE A PAGE'S ORIENTATION:

1. SELECT FILE → PAGE SETUP FROM THE MENU, AND CLICK THE PAGE TAB.

2. IN THE ORIENTATION SECTION, SELECT EITHER THE PORTRAIT OR LANDSCAPE OPTION.

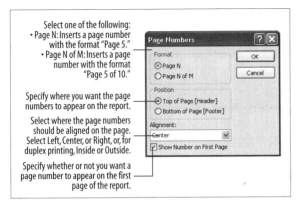

Select one of the following:
- Page N: Inserts a page number with the format "Page 5."
- Page N of M: Inserts a page number with the format "Page 5 of 10."

Specify where you want the page numbers to appear on the report.

Select where the page numbers should be aligned on the page. Select Left, Center, or Right, or, for duplex printing, Inside or Outside.

Specify whether or not you want a page number to appear on the first page of the report.

Figure 8-13. The Page Numbers dialog box.

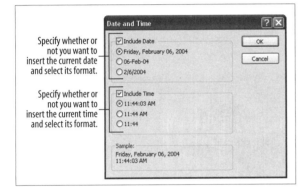

Specify whether or not you want to insert the current date and select its format.

Specify whether or not you want to insert the current time and select its format.

Figure 8-14. The Date and Time dialog box.

Reports that are several pages long often have information such as the page number or the date located at the top (header) or bottom (footer) of every page. In this fast and easy lesson you will learn how to use the Page Number command and Date and Time command to add page numbers and/or the current date to your report.

1 Make sure that you have the rptCustomers report open in Design view.

Here's how to add page numbering to a report:

2 Select Insert → Page Numbers from the menu.

The Page Numbers dialog box appears, as shown in Figure 8-13. The Page Numbers dialog box gives you several choices for how the page numbers can be formatted:

- **Page N:** Prints only the page number (for example, "Page 5.")
- **Page N of M:** Prints the page number and the total number of pages (for example, "Page 5 of 15.")

3 Select the Page N of M option.

Next you need to specify where on the page you want the page number to appear—at the top or bottom of the page—and how you want the page numbers aligned.

4 Select the Bottom of Page [Footer] option and select Right from the Alignment list.

That's all there is to adding page numbers to a report.

5 Click OK to close the Page Numbers dialog box.

The Page Numbers dialog box closes, and Access adds a text box with a page number expression (="Page " & [Page] & " of " & [Pages]) to the Page Footer.

Here's how to add the date and time to your reports:

6 Select Insert → Date and Time from the menu.

The Date and Time dialog box appears, as shown in Figure 8-14. You can specify to add the date, time, or both to your reports. For this exercise, you only want the current date to appear on your report.

7 Click the Include Time check box to remove its check mark.

Just like the Page Number dialog box, the Date and Time dialog box gives you several choices for how the date and/or time can be formatted. The currently selected date format (the first option) will work fine here so you can close the Date and Time dialog box.

8 Click OK to close the Date and Time dialog box.

The Date and Time dialog box closes and Access adds a text box with a date number expression [=Date( )] to the Report Header.

Microsoft Access isn't particularly bright and may place the date, time, or page numbers on top of an existing control, as has happened here. To correct the problem you will have to move the new control to a different location on the report.

9 Click and drag the Date control [=(Date( )] to the far right side of the report header.

Let's see how our modified report looks.

10 Click the View button on the toolbar.

The report is previewed on the screen, and you can see the date and the page numbering. Now let's save this report and close it.

11 Click Close, click the Save button, and then close the rptCustomers report.

QUICK REFERENCE

TO ADD PAGE NUMBERS:

1. DISPLAY THE REPORT IN DESIGN VIEW.

2. SELECT INSERT → PAGE NUMBERS FROM THE MENU.

3. SELECT THE PAGE-NUMBER FORMAT, POSITION, AND ALIGNMENT OPTIONS.

4. CLICK OK.

TO INSERT THE DATE AND/OR TIME:

1. DISPLAY THE REPORT IN DESIGN VIEW.

2. SELECT INSERT → DATE AND TIME FROM THE MENU. CHECK OR UNCHECK THE INCLUDE DATE BOX AND SELECT A FORMATTING OPTION.

3. CHECK OR UNCHECK THE INCLUDE TIME BOX AND SELECT A FORMATTING OPTION.

4. CLICK OK.

Understanding Report Sections

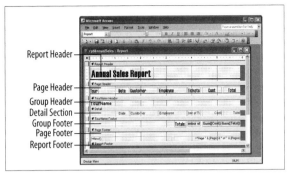

Figure 8-15. A report's sections displayed in Design view.

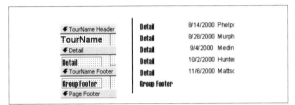

Figure 8-16. Notice how the placement of the "Detail" and "Group Footer" text labels in different report sections affects how and where they appear in the report.

As if reports weren't confusing enough as a whole, Access breaks them up into separate parts called *sections*. Each section has its own specific purpose and always prints in the same order on a report. Take a look at Table 8-3 to familiarize yourself with these sections. If you've ever used a word-processing program to create a report for school or work, you're familiar with the section concept—you can add headers and footers to your documents that contain such information as the report name or page number.

1 Double-click the rptAnnualSales report to open it in Print Preview.

A report's sections aren't as easy to see in Print Preview, but they're still there. Let's examine this report, from top to bottom…

- First notice the "Annual Sales Report" title. In this report the title appears in the *Report Header section*, so it will appear at the top of the first page of the report.

- Next take a look at the column headings ("Tour," "Date," etc.). These column headings are in the *Page Header section* and will appear on top of each page.

- Next come the tour names, which appear in the *Group Header section*. You use group header and group footer sections to group related records together. Reports may have more than one group section to create subgroups.

- Here's what the report's all about: the *Detail section*. The Detail section contains the actual records shown in the report.

- After the Detail section come the report's *footer sections*. You don't need a guided tour of the report's footer sections, as they are really just the same as the report's header sections, only in reverse.

It's difficult to see and appreciate report sections in Print Preview, so let's move on to the next step and we'll get a "behind the scenes look" at the report.

2 Click the View button on the toolbar to switch to Design view.

Access displays the rptAnnualSales report in Design view, as shown in Figure 8-15. Now it's easy to see the report sections—what a difference a change in perspective makes! To better illustrate how information is displayed in report sections, we will add a couple of identifying text boxes to the report.

3 Click the *Aa* Label button on the Toolbox.

The pointer changes to the ^{+}A label tool. Click and drag where you want the label.

4 Position the ^{+}A pointer in the far-left side of the Detail section (to the left of the Date field). Click and drag the text label and type Detail.

Since you added the text label to the report's Detail section, it will appear with each record. Move on to the next step and we'll add an identifying text label to another report section. It's often easier to copy an existing control and then modify it than it is to create a new control from scratch. Here's how to do it:

5 Select the Detail label, click the Copy button on the toolbar, click the TourName Footer section line and click the Paste button on the toolbar.

Access pastes the Detail label in the report's Tour-Name Group Footer.

6 Change the copied label's text to Group Footer.

Let's see where these text labels will appear on the report.

7 Click the View button to switch to Print Preview.

Access displays the report in Print Preview, as shown in Figure 8-16.

8 Scroll down the report and notice where the Detail and Group Footer labels appear. Close the report without saving your changes when you finish.

Table 8-3. Report Sections

Resolution	Description
Report Header	Contains text that appears at the top of the first page of a report, such as the name of the report.
Page Header	Contains text that appears at the top of each page of a report, such as the report's column headings.
Group Header	Used to place text, such as a group name, at the beginning of each group of records.
Detail	Contains text and the actual fields that are displayed for each record. This would be equivalent to the main body in a word-processing document.
Group Footer	Used to place text and numeric summaries, such as totals or averages, at the end of each group of records.
Page Footer	Contains text that appears at the bottom of each page of a report, such as page numbers.
Report Footer	Contains text that appears at the end of the last page of a report. Often also contains numeric summaries for the report, such as a grand total.

QUICK REFERENCE

TO RESIZE A REPORT SECTION:

1. DISPLAY THE REPORT IN DESIGN VIEW.
2. CLICK AND DRAG THE SECTION LINE UP OR DOWN.

UNDERSTANDING REPORT SECTIONS:

• BE FAMILIAR WITH THE VARIOUS REPORT SECTIONS DESCRIBED IN TABLE 8-3.

Sales by Date

Date	Employee	Tour
1/10/00	Black, Joseph	Yucata
3/27/00	Black, Joseph	British I
6/5/00	Black, Joseph	Historic
2/14/00	Burr, Aaron	China
2/28/00	Burr, Aaron	British I
2/28/00	Burr, Aaron	Europe
4/24/00	Burr, Aaron	China
4/24/00	Burr, Aaron	Historic
6/12/00	Burr, Aaron	Historic

This report isn't grouped by fields; information runs together, making the report difficult to read.

Sales by Date
January

Employee	Tou
Norton, LeAnn	Russ
Black, Joseph	Yuca
Wyatt, Maria	Euro
Wyatt, Maria	Wes

February

Employee	Tou
Fuentes, Bern	Wes
Fuentes, Bern	Wes
Burr, Aaron	Euro

This report is grouped by the Date fields; information is grouped and organized by the month.

Figure 8-17. Grouping records by a specific field makes them easier to read. Compare the report that is grouped by date with the report that isn't.

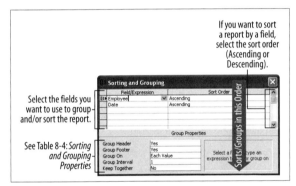

Figure 8-18. The Sorting and Grouping dialog box. You can learn more about its details in Table 8-4.

Organizing records into logical groups often makes them easier to read and understand. For example, the second report in Figure 8-17 is grouped by the date field, so that you can quickly see how many sales occurred in a particular month. If you create a report using the Report Wizard (the preferred method), you specify which fields you want to use to group and/or sort your report by. If you're modifying an existing report or creating a report from scratch, you can use the Sorting and Grouping dialog box to create your groups. More importantly, if you use a Wizard to create a report for you, you can use the Sorting and Grouping dialog box to change the grouping and sorting options for the report.

1 If necessary, open the Lesson 8 database.

Now let's open the rptEmployeeSales report in Design view.

2 Click the rptEmployeeSales report and then click the Design button.

In its current state, the rptEmployeeSales report has Report Header, Page Header, Page Footer, and Report Footer sections, but it doesn't have any grouping sections. To add a Group Section to a report you need to summon the Sorting and Grouping dialog box.

3 Click the  Sorting and Grouping button on the toolbar.

> **TIP** *Another way to sort and group is to select* View → Sorting and Grouping *from the menu.*

Access displays the Sorting and Grouping dialog box, which displays any fields that are currently being used for sorting or grouping your report, as shown in Figure 8-18. To add a section to group and/or sort by, select a blank row and select a field from the Field/Expression drop-down list. In this exercise you will use the Employee field to group and sort the report.

4 Click inside the first blank Field/Expression row, click the list arrow, and select Employee from the list.

You can also specify the order in which Access sorts the records by selecting the order you want to sort by (Ascending or Descending) from the Sort Order list. Since you want to sort the Employee field in Ascending order, you can leave the Sort Order alone.

To make a Group Header or Group Footer, use the Group Properties settings at the bottom of the dialog box. (See Table 8-4 for Sorting and Grouping Properties.) You want to add a Group Header for the Employee field—here's how to add one:

5 With the Employee field still selected, click the Group Header box in the Group Properties section and select Yes from the drop-down list.

Access adds an Employee Group Header to the report.

The order of the fields in the Sorting and Grouping dialog box is *very important*. The field in the first row is the first sorting/grouping level, the second row is the second sorting/grouping level, and so on. You want to group and sort your report by the Employee field, *then* by the Date field, so you need to rearrange the field order.

6 Click the Employee row selector, drag it above the Date row, and release the mouse button. Close the Sorting and Grouping dialog box.

Now that you have created the Group Header, you need to specify what you want to appear in it—usually the field that the Group Header is based on. In this report you will want to move the Employee text box control field from the Detail section to the Employee Group Header section.

7 Cut the Employee field from the Detail section and paste it in the Employee Header section.

Let's see how the modified report looks.

8 Click the View button to switch to Print Preview.

Access groups and sorts the report by the Employee field.

9 Click Close to exit Print Preview.

Table 8-4. Sorting and Grouping Properties

Group Property	Description
Group Header	Specify whether you want the report to contain a header section for this group.
Group Footer	Specify whether you want the report to contain a footer section for this group.
Group On	Allows you to choose the size of the group. For example, if you're using a date field to group a section, you can group each value by day, week, month, or year.
Group Interval	Allows you to choose the size of the interval from a drop-down list. You must have chosen an option other than Each Value from the Group On list.
Keep Together	No: Prints the group without keeping the group header, detail section, and group footer on the same page.
	Whole Page: Prints the group header, detail section, and group footer on the same page.
	With First Detail: Prints the group header on a page only if it can also print the first detail record.

QUICK REFERENCE

TO GROUP RECORDS:

1. DISPLAY THE REPORT IN DESIGN VIEW.

2. CLICK THE SORTING AND GROUPING BUTTON ON THE TOOLBAR.

3. CLICK THE FIELD/EXPRESSION CELL, CLICK THE LIST ARROW, AND SELECT A FIELD FOR GROUPING RECORDS.

4. CLICK THE CORRESPONDING SORT ORDER CELL, CLICK THE LIST ARROW, AND SELECT THE DESIRED SORT ORDER.

5. SELECT ANY GROUP PROPERTIES YOU WANT TO USE IN THE GROUP PROPERTIES AREA.

6. REPEAT STEPS 3-5 FOR EACH FIELD/EXPRESSION YOU WANT TO USE TO GROUP AND SORT YOUR DATA.

7. CLOSE THE SORTING AND GROUPING DIALOG BOX WHEN YOU'RE FINISHED.

Creating Calculated Controls

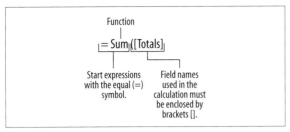

Figure 8-19. Example of a calculated control used to total the Totals field.

Figure 8-20. Calculated controls usually appear in the footer sections of a report.

Footers are most often used to summarize report information. For example, a Group Footer could total the number of harassing phone calls each telemarketer made and the Report Footer could calculate the number of harassing phone calls made by all telemarketers.

If you create a report using the Report Wizard (the preferred method), you will specify which fields you want to summarize and the calculation you want to use to summarize them. Of course, you can always add your *calculated control* or calculated field to summarize information on an existing report. Figure 8-19 shows an example of a calculated control. A calculated control displays totals and other arithmetic computations on a form or report. Table 8-5 describes the functions you will use most often to summarize your reports.

1 Make sure you have the modified rptEmployee-Sales report you worked on in the previous lesson open in Design view.

The section footer in which you place a calculated control is very important, as each footer section calculates/summarizes records differently:

- **Group Footer:** Calculates all the records in a group.
- **Page Footer:** Calculates all the records on the page.
- **Report Footer:** Calculates all the records in the report.

You want to add a calculated control to the Report Footer that will calculate the total sales for all records. First though, you will need to resize the Report Footer so that there is enough room to add such a control. Here's how to change the size of a section.

2 Click and drag the Report Footer section divider down a half-inch.

Now that you have enough room in the Report Footer you can add the calculated control. There are two ways to add a calculated control to a form or report:

- Click the Text Box control on the Toolbox and click and drag where you want to add the control.
- Copy an existing text box control, select the desired location, and paste the copied text box control.

You can use either method, but the copy and paste method is a little faster and easier because it copies formatting options and gives the new control a consistent look.

3 Select the Total text box control in the Detail section and click the Copy button on the toolbar. Click the Report Footer section divider and click the Paste button on the toolbar.

Access pastes the copied control. Next you have to add an expression to the control.

4 With the new Total text box in the Report Footer still selected, click the Properties button on the toolbar.

The Properties dialog box appears. You need to enter the expression in the Control Source property, which you can find on the Data tab.

5 Click the Data tab, click in the Control Source box, type =SUM([Total]), and close the Properties dialog box.

You're finished adding a calculated control that will total the Total fields on the report.

Next you want to add another footer and calculated control that will total the total sales by employee. First you need to add an Employee Group Footer section to your report.

6 Click the ▥ Sorting and Grouping button **on the toolbar.**

> **TIP** *Another way to sort and group is to select View → Sorting and Grouping from the menu.*

The Sorting and Grouping dialog box appears.

7 Click the Employee **field, click the** Group Footer **box in the** Group Properties **section, click the list arrow, select** Yes **from the list, and then close the Sorting and Grouping dialog box.**

Because the Total text box control you created in Steps 3–5 already contains the SUM expression you need, you can simply copy and paste the control in the Group Footer.

8 Copy the Total **text box control in the** Report Footer **section, click the** Employee Footer **section divider, and paste the control.**

You need to add some meaningful labels to your report. Often, it's useful to add a calculated control that mixes some text with the current value of a field to produce an informative notice for the report.

9 Copy the Total **text box control in the** Employee Footer **section and paste it in the same section. Change the** Data Source **property of the pasted control to** ="Total for " & [Employee].

This expression will display the text "Total for" and the employee's name. Let's finish tidying up the report.

10 Add a Grand Totals: **text label to the Report Footer section, then click and drag the three new calculated fields and one text label so that your report looks like the one in Figure 8-20.**

Let's see how our report looks.

11 Click the View **button to switch to Print Preview. Scroll down and notice the calculated controls. When you're finished, save your changes and close the report.**

Table 8-5. Common Summary Functions

Function	Description	Example
Sum	Totals all the values listed in a field.	Sum([InvoiceTotal])
Maximum	Finds and displays the largest value listed in a field.	Max([InvoiceTotal])
Minimum	Finds and displays the smallest value listed in a field.	Min([InvoiceTotal])
Average	Calculates the average of all the values listed in a field.	Avg([InvoiceTotal])
Count	Counts how many values are listed in a field.	Count([InvoiceTotal])

QUICK REFERENCE

TO CREATE A CALCULATED CONTROL:

1. DISPLAY THE REPORT IN DESIGN VIEW.

2. SELECT THE CONTROL AND CLICK THE PROPERTIES BUTTON ON THE TOOLBAR.

   OR...

   RIGHT-CLICK THE CONTROL AND SELECT PROPERTIES FROM THE SHORTCUT MENU.

   OR...

   SELECT THE CONTROL AND SELECT VIEW → PROPERTIES FROM THE MENU.

3. CLICK THE DATA TAB AND CLICK IN THE CONTROL SOURCE BOX.

4. TYPE THE EXPRESSION IN THE CONTROL SOURCE (SEE TABLE 8-5 FOR SOME EXAMPLES).

   OR...

   CLICK THE BUILD BUTTON AND USE THE EXPRESSION BUILDER TO CREATE THE EXPRESSION, THEN CLICK OK WHEN YOU'RE FINISHED.

5. CLOSE THE PROPERTIES DIALOG BOX.

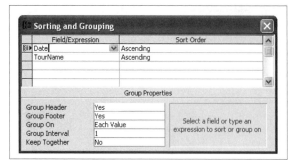

Figure 8-21. The Sorting and Grouping dialog box. You can learn more about its options in Table 8-4.

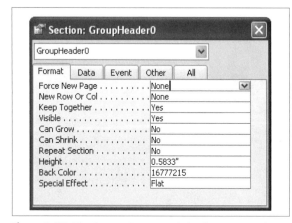

Figure 8-22. The Section Properties dialog box. You can learn more about its options in Table 8-6.

When you want to fine-tune how a group or section works, there are two different places to go:

- **The Sorting and Grouping dialog box:** Contains important sorting and grouping settings, such as if you want your report to display any Group Headers and/or Footers. To display the Group Properties dialog box, click the Sorting and Grouping button on the toolbar.

- **The Section Properties dialog box:** Contains miscellaneous properties for each report section, such as the section's background color. To display the properties or settings for a report section, click the section divider line and then the Properties button on the toolbar, or right-click the section divider line and select Properties from the shortcut menu, or double-click the section divider line.

Some of the settings you might want to adjust might be the Group Interval property (especially for sections grouped by date fields) and the Force New Page property, which tells Access to start a new page before or after each

report section. In this lesson you will learn how to tweak your report section settings.

1 Double-click the rptSalesByMonth report to open it in Print Preview.

In this report Access uses the Date field to group records—Access creates a Date group for each Date value, or day. The report would be meaningful if Access grouped dates by month. Before we can change the report, we need to switch to Design view.

2 Click the View button on the toolbar to switch to Design view.

You can change the grouping interval to specify how records are grouped in a report in the Sorting and Grouping dialog box.

3 Click the [≡] Sorting and Grouping button on the toolbar.

> **TIP**
> Another way to sort and group is to select View → Sorting and Grouping from the menu.

The Sorting and Grouping dialog box appears, as shown in Figure 8-21. The *Group On* property lets you specify how you want to group records. For example, you can use the Group On property to group a Date field by year.

Let's change the Date Group Interval so that the report groups sales on a monthly basis.

4 Click the Date field, click in the Group On box in the Group Properties section, select Month from the list, and then close the dialog box.

You won't be able to see any of the grouping changes until you display the report in Print Preview—and we'll do that in a minute. Every report section has its own set of properties or settings that you can view and change. You can view the properties for a report section by double-clicking the section's divider line.

5 Double-click the Date Header section divider line.

Access displays the properties for the Date Header section, as shown in Figure 8-22. Table 8-6 describes these options in more detail.

6 Click the Format tab.

We want to change the background color of the section. Here's how to do it.

7 Click the Back Color box, click the ⊡ button, select a gray color and click OK, then close Section Properties dialog box.

Let's see how the modified report looks.

8 Click the View button on the toolbar to display the report in Print Preview. Scroll through the report's pages and notice how the Date Section is now grouped by month.

9 Click Close, save your changes, and close the report.

Table 8-6. Important Section Properties

Property	Description
Force New Page	Allows you to tell Access to start a new page before or after this section whenever the group changes.
New Row Or Col	Works the same as the Force New Page property when you're printing a report in columns.
Keep Together	Used to specify whether you want to allow Access to put breaks when they occur naturally (No) or forces Access to keep the entire section on one page when possible (Yes).
Visible	Used to specify if you want to see the section (Yes) or not (No). Hiding a report's Detail Section is useful when you want to create a summary report that uses a Group Footer to total database information without displaying the individual records.
Can Grow	Used to specify whether the section can grow larger to accommodate more data in the last field in the section (the field control Can Grow property must also be set to Yes).
Can Shrink	Enables the section to grow smaller if the extra space is not needed. (Used in conjunction with the Can Shrink property for a field control.)
Repeat Section	When a group is split across several pages, use the Repeat Sections property to specify whether or not Access should repeat the heading on the new page.
Height	Access automatically sets this property as you drag the section divider up or down on the screen. You can specify an exact size (for example, if you want the section to be precisely three inches tall) by entering it here.
Back Color	Used to specify the color of the section. Click the ⊡ button to select the color.
Special Effect	Adjusts the visual effects for the section. Your choices are limited to Flat (the default setting), Raised, or Sunken.

QUICK REFERENCE

TO MODIFY A REPORT'S SECTION AND GROUPING OPTIONS:

1. DISPLAY THE REPORT IN DESIGN VIEW.

2. CLICK THE SORTING AND GROUPING BUTTON ON THE TOOLBAR.

TO MODIFY A SECTION'S PROPERTIES:

1. DISPLAY THE REPORT IN DESIGN VIEW.

2. DOUBLE-CLICK THE SECTION LINE FOR THE SECTION WHOSE PROPERTIES YOU WANT TO VIEW/MODIFY.

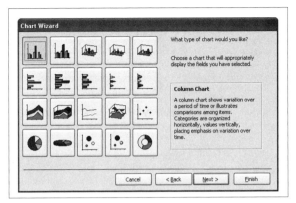

Figure 8-23. Selecting a chart type in the Chart Wizard.

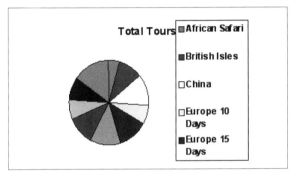

Figure 8-24. A pie chart that plots tours.

You already know what a chart is—charts illustrate data, relationships, or trends graphically. Like the saying "a picture is worth a thousand words," charts are often better at presenting information than hard-to-read numbers in a datasheet. Microsoft Access comes with a great built-in program for creating charts called Microsoft Graph. You can insert charts and graphs on forms and reports, and this lesson will show you how.

1 In the Database window, click the Reports icon in the Objects bar and click the New button.

The New Report dialog box appears.

2 Select Chart Wizard from the list, select qryCustomerTours from the drop-down list, and click OK.

The first screen of the Chart Wizard appears. Here you have to tell the Wizard which fields you want to display on the chart.

3 Double-click the TourName field in the Available Fields list.

The TourName field appears in the "Fields for Chart" list.

4 Click Next.

The Chart Wizard asks what type of chart you want to use to display your data, as shown in Figure 8-23. Table 8-7 shows the more common charts and gives an explanation on how and when they are used.

5 Select the Pie Chart and click Next.

Next the Chart Wizard asks how you want to lay out the data in your chart. You do this by dragging and dropping the data fields to the appropriate areas on the chart. Since we chose a simple pie chart, everything is already correctly laid out for us.

6 Click Next.

You can specify a chart title if you're not thrilled with Microsoft Access's imaginative suggestions. You can also specify whether or not you want to include a legend with your chart.

7 Click in the What title would you like for your chart? box and type Total Tours. Click Finish to create the pie chart.

Access creates the pie chart, as shown in Figure 8-24.

⸸ NOTE ⸸ *The Microsoft Graph program seems to have some bugs, so the legend of your chart may be missing some items.*

8 Exit Microsoft Access without saving any changes.

Table 8-7. Types of Charts and Graphs

Chart or Graph Type	Description
	Column charts are used when you want to compare different values vertically side by side. Each value is represented in the chart by a vertical bar. If there are several values in an item, each value is represented by a different color.
	Bar charts are just like column charts, except they display information in horizontal bars rather than vertical columns.
	Line charts are used to illustrate trends. Each value is plotted as a point on the chart and is connected to other values by a line. Multiple items are plotted using different lines.
	Area charts are the same as line charts, except the area beneath the line is filled with color.
	Pie charts are useful for showing values as a percentage of a whole. The values for each item are represented by different colors.
	Scatter charts are used to plot clusters of values using single points. Multiple items can be plotted by using different colored points or different point symbols.
	Combination charts combine two different types of charts together (for example, a combination chart might contain both a column chart and a line chart).

QUICK REFERENCE

TO INSERT A CHART INTO A REPORT:

1. DISPLAY THE REPORT IN DESIGN VIEW.

2. SELECT INSERT → CHART FROM THE MENU, AND THEN DRAG AND DROP A CHART ONTO THE REPORT, WHICH OPENS THE CHART WIZARD.

3. SELECT THE TABLE OR QUERY YOU WANT TO CHART FROM THE LIST, AND CLICK NEXT TO CONTINUE.

4. DOUBLE-CLICK EACH FIELD YOU WANT TO ADD TO THE CHART AND CLICK NEXT TO CONTINUE.

5. CLICK THE CHART TYPE YOU WANT AND CLICK NEXT TO CONTINUE.

6. MAKE ANY LAYOUT MODIFICATIONS TO THE CHART AND CLICK NEXT TO CONTINUE.

7. ENTER A CHART NAME AND CLICK FINISH.

Lesson Summary

Creating a Report with AutoReport

To Create a Report with AutoReport: In the Database window, click the Reports icon in the Objects bar, click the New button, and select either AutoReport: Columnar or AutoReport: Tabular. Click the table or query you want to use for the report from the drop-down list and Click OK.

Modifying a Report

To Modify a Report: In the Database window, click the Reports icon in the Objects bar, click the report you want to modify and click the Design button, or open the form and click the View button on the toolbar.

Adding and Deleting Fields

To Add a Field to a Report: Display the report in Design view and click the Field List button on the toolbar, if necessary. Find the field you want to add to the report in the Field List, then click and drag the field to the desired location on the report.

To Delete a Field or Control: Click the field or control to select it and press Delete.

Moving and Sizing Controls

To Resize a Control: Click the control to select it, click and drag one of its sizing handles, and release the mouse button when the control reaches the desired size. Hold down the Shift key while dragging to maintain the control's proportions while resizing it.

To Move a Control: Click the control and hold down the mouse button, drag the control to a new location, then release the mouse button to drop the control.

To Move a Text Box or Text Label Independently of Each Other: Position the pointer over the upper left sizing handle of the control until it changes to a hand, then click and drag the control.

To Copy a Control Using Drag and Drop: Follow the same procedures as moving a control, only hold down the Ctrl key while you drag the control.

Adjusting Page Margins and Orientation

To Adjust Margins: Select File → Page Setup from the menu and click the Margins tab, adjust the appropriate margins.

To Change a Page's Orientation: Select File → Page Setup from the menu, and click the Page tab. In the Orientation section, select either the Portrait or Landscape option.

Adding Page Numbers and Dates

To Add Page Numbers: Display the report in Design view, select Insert → Page Numbers from the menu, select the page-number format, position, and alignment options, and click OK.

To Insert the Date and/or Time: Display the report in Design view, select Insert → Date and Time from the menu, check or uncheck the Include Date box and select a formatting option. Check or uncheck the Include Time box, select a formatting option, and click OK.

Understanding Report Sections

To Resize a Report Section: Display the report in Design view, then click and drag the section line up or down.

Grouping and Sorting Records

To Group Records: Display the report in Design view and click the Sorting and Grouping button on the toolbar. Click the Field/Expression cell, click the list arrow, and select a field for grouping records. Click the corresponding Sort Order cell, click the list arrow, select the desired sort order, and select any Group Properties you want to use in the Group Properties area. Repeat these steps for each Field/Expression you want to use to group and sort your data. Close the Sorting and Grouping dialog box when you're finished.

Creating Calculated Controls

To Create a Calculated Control: Display the form in Design view, select the control, and click the Properties button on the toolbar. Click the Data tab, click in the Control Source box, type the expression, and then close the Properties dialog box.

Working with Section Properties

To Modify a Report's Section and Grouping Options: Display the report in Design view, and then click the Sorting and Grouping button on the toolbar.

To Modify a Section's Properties: Display the report in Design view, then double-click the section line for the section whose properties you want to view/modify.

Creating Charts with the Chart Wizard

To Insert a Chart into a Report: Display the report in Design view, select Insert → Chart from the menu, and then drag and drop a chart onto the report, which opens the Chart Wizard. Select the table or query you want to chart from the Table or Query list, and click Next to continue. Double-click each field you want to add to the chart and click Next to continue. Click the chart type you want and click Next to continue. Make any layout modifications to the chart and click Next to continue. Enter a chart name and then click Finish.

Quiz

1. Which of the following statements about the AutoReport Wizard is NOT true?

    A. The AutoReport Wizard is the fastest and easiest way to create a report in Microsoft Access.

    B. The AutoReport Wizard can only create two types of reports: Columnar and Tabular.

    C. Reports created with the AutoReport Wizard usually come out looking sharp and professional and don't require further clean-up work.

    D. The AutoReport Wizard can only create reports based on a single table or query .

2. Which of the following statements is NOT true?

    A. The Field List displays all the fields from a report's underlying table or query.

    B. Click the Field List button on the Toolbar to display the Field List.

    C. You can add fields to a report by dragging them from the Field List onto the report.

    D. The Field List displays all the fields from every table in a database.

3. Controls and their corresponding text labels cannot be moved independently of one another. (True or False?)

4. Which of the following statements is NOT true?

    A. You can move a control to a different location on a report by clicking, dragging, and dropping the control.

    B. To add a page number to a report, select View → Header/Footer from the menu and click the Page Number button on the Header/Footer toolbar.

    C. You can resize a report by clicking and dragging the right edge of the report.

    D. You can resize a control by clicking the control to select it, grabbing one of its sizing handles, and dragging and releasing the mouse button when the control reaches the desired size.

5. You want a report to group and total sales by month. Where would you place a calculated control containing the following expression =SUM([Sales]) to calculate the totals for each month?

    A. In the Month Group Footer section.

    B. In the Page Footer section.

    C. In the Report Footer section.

    D. In the Summary section.

6. Which of the following is NOT a report section?

    A. Report Header section.

    B. Page Header section.

    C. Summary section.

    D. Detail section.

7. The only way to sort a report's records is to base the report on a query, which actually does the work of sorting the records. (True or False?)

8. Which of the following expressions is incorrect?

    A. =Total for: [Employee].

    B. =[InvoiceDate]+30.

    C. =[LastName]&" "&[FirstName].

    D. =[Units]*[UnitPrice].

9. You want to track the progress of the stock market on a daily basis. Which type of chart should you use?

    A. Line chart.

    B. Column chart.

    C. Row chart.

    D. Pie chart.

10. How do you adjust a page's margins?

    A. Click and drag the edge of the page to where you want the margin set.

    B. Select Format → Page Setup from the menu, click the Margins tab, and adjust the margins.

    C. Select File → Page Setup from the menu, click the Margins tab, and adjust the margins.

    D. Click the Margins button on the Formatting toolbar.

11. How can you view a report's sorting and grouping options?

    A. Select Format → Sorting and Grouping from the menu.

    B. By double-clicking the Report Selector box in the upper left corner of the report.

    C. Select File → Page Setup from the menu and click the Sorting and Grouping tab.

    D. Click the Sorting and Grouping button on the toolbar.

12. What is the procedure for selecting multiple controls on a report?

    A. Press and hold down the Shift key as you click each object that you want to select.

    B. Use the arrow pointer to draw a box around the object that you want to select.

    C. If the controls are aligned along a horizontal or vertical line, click the horizontal or vertical ruler above or to the left of the controls.

    D. All of these.

Homework

1. Start Microsoft Access, if necessary, and then open the Homework database.

2. Use AutoReport to create and save a tabular report named "Customers," using the Customers table as the underlying data source.

3. Delete the DOB field from the report.

4. Change all of the report's margins to a half-inch.

5. Sort the information on the report by DOB.

6. Save your changes and close the Homework database.

Quiz Answers

1. C. The AutoReport Wizard can create reports in record time, but they aren't usually well-organized or professional looking.

2. D. The Field List only displays fields from a report's underlying table or query.

3. False. You can click and drag the upper left sizing handle to move a label or control independently of one another.

4. B. This procedure will let you add page numbers in Microsoft Word, but not in Microsoft Access.

5. A. You would want the calculated control in the Month Group Footer section to total monthly sales.

6. C. Although you can summarize information in a report section, there isn't actually a section called a "Summary section."

7. False. Although you can sort a report using a query, you can also simply click the Sorting and Grouping button on the toolbar and specify the field you want to use to sort the report.

8. A. This expression is missing the quotation marks (") and the ampersand (&) symbol. The corrected expression would be =`"Total for: "&[Employee]`.

9. A. Line charts are used to illustrate trends. If you used the other three chart types to track the stock market, there would be too many data points.

10. C. You adjust a page's margins by selecting File → Page Setup from the menu, clicking the Margins tab, and adjusting the margins.

11. D. Click the Sorting and Grouping button on the toolbar to view a report's sorting and grouping options.

12. D. All of these are procedures for selecting multiple controls on a report.

CHAPTER 9

FORMATTING FORMS AND REPORTS

CHAPTER OBJECTIVES:

Format fonts using the Formatting toolbar, Lesson 9.1

Change text alignment, Lesson 9.2

Use AutoFormat to quickly format forms and reports, Lesson 9.3

Change the color of text, objects, and borders, Lesson 9.4

Apply 3-D effects to the controls on forms and reports, Lesson 9.5

Use the Format Painter to copy control formatting options, Lesson 9.6

Add pictures and lines to forms and reports, Lesson 9.7

Align controls with one another, Lesson 9.8

Format a control by changing its Formatting Properties, Lesson 9.9

CHAPTER TASK: APPLY FORMATTING OPTIONS TO EXISTING FORMS AND REPORTS

Prerequisites

- **How to use menus, toolbars, dialog boxes, and shortcut keystrokes.**
- **How to open and modify forms and reports in Design View.**

Forms and reports created with a Microsoft Access Wizard are informative and functional—but they are rarely well designed. Some of the forms and reports set up by the Form Wizard or Report Wizard are even downright ugly. Don't worry—this chapter will help you fix the design of your forms and reports.

This chapter guides you through the process of creating sharp-looking forms and reports that have colorful fonts, neat-looking borders, even controls with 3-D effects. This chapter explains how to format your forms and reports to make them more visually attractive and easier to read. You will learn how to change the appearance, size, and color of fonts and how to align text inside a control. This chapter also describes how you can add pictures and graphics to your forms and reports.

Formatting Fonts with the Formatting Toolbar

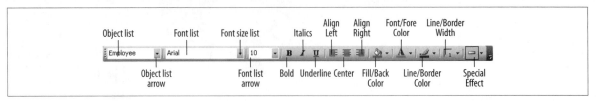

Figure 9-1. The Formatting toolbar.

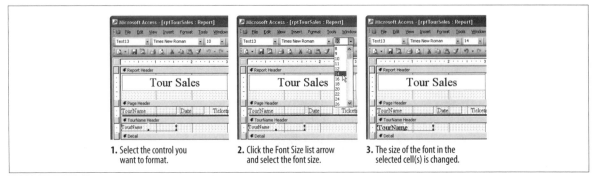

1. Select the control you want to format.

2. Click the Font Size list arrow and select the font size.

3. The size of the font in the selected cell(s) is changed.

Figure 9-2. The steps for changing font size.

You can emphasize text on a form or report by making the text darker and heavier (**bold**), slanted (*italics*), larger, or in a different typeface (or font). Table 9-1 shows examples of common font types and sizes. The Formatting toolbar makes it easy to apply character formatting. The Formatting toolbar includes buttons for applying the most common formatting options.

1 Start Microsoft Access, open the Lesson 9 database, click the Reports icon in the Objects bar, and double-click the rptTourSales report.

Access displays the rptTourSales report in Print Preview. A quick look at this report is all you need to realize that the Report Wizard could use a few remedial graphical design classes. Fortunately, a little moving, resizing, and formatting will fix all of the report's design problems.

2 Click the View button on the Print Preview toolbar to switch to Design view.

In order to format a control, you must first select it. The TourName text box in the TourName Header needs to stand out a little more from the rest of the report.

3 Click the TourName text box control in the TourName Header to select it.

Handles appear around the text box control, indicating that the control is selected. Once you have selected a control, you can format it.

4 Click the Font list arrow on the Formatting toolbar (see Figure 9-1), then scroll to and select Arial from the list of fonts.

The text in the TourName text box control appears in Arial font. Arial and Times New Roman are two of the most commonly used fonts in Windows.

You can also use the Formatting toolbar to change the size of a font. Font sizes are measured in *points* (pt.), which are 1/72 of an inch. The larger the number of points, the larger the font.

5 With the TourName text box still selected, click the Font Size list arrow (▼) on the Formatting toolbar and select 14, as shown in Figure 9-2.

The TourName text box appears in a larger font size (14-point type instead of the previous 11-point type). Wow! That font formatting really makes the title stand out from the rest of the report, doesn't it?

⸴ NOTE ⸴ *When you change a control's font size, you will often have to resize the control so that it can properly display its contents.*

All the column-heading labels in the Page Header section need to be emphasized as well. You *could* select and format each label individually, but it's much faster to select and format all of them at the same time. If the controls you want to format are arranged along a horizontal line, you can click to the left of the controls, in the vertical ruler, to select all of them.

6 Select all the labels in the Page Header section by clicking in the vertical ruler to the left of the TourName label.

Access selects everything to the right of where you clicked the mouse. Let's apply boldface formatting to the selected text labels.

7 Click the Bold button on the Formatting toolbar.

The selected controls appear in bold.

8 Click the Save button to save your changes to the report.

Table 9-1. Examples of Common Font Types and Sizes

Common Font Types	Common Font Sizes
Courier	8 point
Garamond	10 point
Helvetica	12 point
Times New Roman	14 point

QUICK REFERENCE

TO CHANGE FONT SIZE:

• SELECT THE CONTROL AND SELECT THE PT. SIZE FROM THE `10` FONT SIZE LIST ON THE FORMATTING TOOLBAR.

TO CHANGE FONT TYPE:

• SELECT THE CONTROL AND SELECT THE FONT FROM THE `Times New Roman` FONT LIST ON THE FORMATTING TOOLBAR.

TO FORMAT TEXT WITH BOLD, ITALICS, OR UNDERLINING:

• SELECT THE CONTROL AND CLICK THE BOLD, ITALIC, OR UNDERLINE BUTTON ON THE FORMATTING TOOLBAR.

Changing Text Alignment

Figure 9-3. Examples of different alignment options.

Figure 9-4. The alignment buttons on the toolbar only affect how text is aligned inside a control. You have to manually align a control to the left, center, or right of a form or report by clicking and dragging.

This lesson explains how to align a control's text to the left, center, or right. Figure 9-3 gives a better idea of what the various alignments look like. Alignment only affects what's inside of a control: If you apply center formatting to a text box, Access will center the text inside the text box—it won't center the text box control on the form or report, as shown in Figure 9-4. If you want to align a control to the left, center, or right of a form or report, you'll have to do it the old-fashioned way—by clicking and dragging the control.

1 Make sure that the rptTourSales report is open in Design view.

Again, you first need to select the control you want to format.

2 Select the Date text label in the Page Header and click the Center button on the Formatting toolbar.

Access centers the text inside the Date text label. Easy, isn't it? Let's try aligning one more control.

3 Click the TourName text label in the Page Header and click the Align Right button on the Formatting toolbar.

Access right-aligns the text inside the TourName text label.

4 Click the Save button to save your changes to the report.

Table 9-2 shows the alignment formatting buttons on the formatting toolbar.

> **QUICK REFERENCE**
>
> **TO CHANGE TEXT ALIGNMENT:**
> • SELECT THE CONTROL AND CLICK THE ALIGN LEFT, CENTER, OR ALIGN RIGHT BUTTON ON THE FORMATTING TOOLBAR.

Table 9-2. Alignment Formatting Buttons on the Formatting Toolbar

Button Name	Example	Formatting
	Left	Aligns text to the left side of the control.
	Center	Centers text in a control.
	Right	Aligns text to the right side of the control.

Using AutoFormat

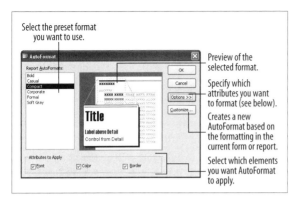

Figure 9-5. The AutoFormat dialog box.

You've just finished creating a report using the Report Wizard when you suddenly realize that you hate how it looks! Don't worry—you can apply a new design to your forms and templates at any time with the AutoFormat command. AutoFormat is a built-in collection of formats such as font sizes, patterns, and alignments you can quickly apply to a form or report. AutoFormat is a great feature if you want your forms and reports to look sharp and professional but don't have the time to format them yourself.

1 Make sure the rptTourSales report is open in Design view.

Here's how to format a report using AutoFormat:

2 Click the AutoFormat button on the Report Design toolbar.

The AutoFormat dialog box appears, as shown in Figure 9-5. The present formats are listed in the Auto-Format list. Yep, they're the same choices as you get in the Report or Form Wizard. You can see what a format looks like by selecting it and looking at the sample area in the dialog box.

3 Click the Options button.

The AutoFormat dialog box expands to show three check boxes. You can control the type of formatting that is applied by checking or unchecking any of the boxes. If you want AutoFormat to skip one of the formatting categories, simply uncheck the appropriate box.

4 Select the Compact option from the Report Auto-Formats list and click OK.

The dialog box closes, and the report is formatted with the Compact formatting option.

5 Click the Save button to save your changes and then click the Close button to close the rptTourSales report.

QUICK REFERENCE

TO FORMAT A FORM OR REPORT WITH AUTOFORMAT:

1. DISPLAY THE FORM OR REPORT YOU WANT TO FORMAT IN DESIGN VIEW.

2. CLICK THE AUTOFORMAT BUTTON ON THE REPORT DESIGN TOOLBAR.

3. SELECT ONE OF THE AUTOFORMATS FROM THE LIST AND CLICK OK.

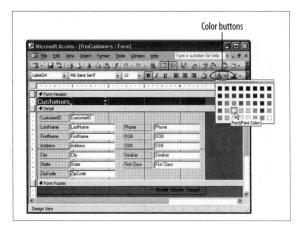

Color buttons

Figure 9-6. Use the color buttons to apply color to the text, background, and border of a control.

In this day of color, laser, and inkjet printers, and high-resolution 21-inch monitors, choosing an appropriate color for your report or form is an important formatting decision. If used tastefully, colors can make your forms and reports look more visually attractive. You can add color to lines, text, rectangles—even to the background of your headers and footers!

In this lesson, you will learn how to use the color buttons on the Formatting toolbar to apply color to your reports and forms.

1 Click the Forms icon in the Objects bar and open the frmCustomers form in Design view.

There are three color buttons on the Formatting toolbar—each color button applies color to a different element. It can be a little confusing to figure out which color button to use at first, so you'll want to refer to Table 9-3 until you get the hang of it.

2 Click the Customers text label in the Form Header, click the Font/Fore Color button list arrow on the Formatting toolbar, and select a yellow color, as shown in Figure 9-6.

You can also apply color to the sections of a report or form.

3 Click the Form Header section divider, click the Fill/Back Color button list arrow on the Formatting toolbar, and select a dark blue color.

Table 9-3. Color Buttons on the Formatting Toolbar

Color Button	Description
	Applies color to the background of the selected control(s).
	Applies color to the text in the selected control(s).
	Applies a color or transparency to the line or border of the selected control(s).

QUICK REFERENCE

TO CHANGE A CONTROL'S COLORS:

SELECT THE CONTROL AND CLICK ONE OF THE FOLLOWING FORMATTING TOOLBAR BUTTONS:

- FILL/BACK COLOR
- FONT/FORE COLOR
- LINE/BORDER COLOR

Applying Special Effects

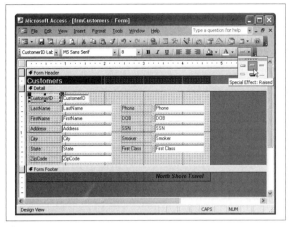

Figure 9-7. Applying a special effect to a control.

You can apply special-effect formatting to the controls in your forms and reports to give them a polished, high-tech appearance. For example, you can give a form a three-dimensional look by applying a sunken or raised effect to its controls. Applying special-effect formatting is pretty straightforward: Simply select the controls you want to format and then select one of the six special-effect options (listed in Table 9-4) from the Special Effect button list.

1 Make sure the frmCustomers form is open in Design view.

Normally, you will want to apply special-effect formatting to *both* a control and its corresponding text label, so you will have to select both controls using one of the multiple-selection techniques you've (hopefully) learned.

2 Click the CustomerID text box control to select it, then hold down the Shift key as you click the CustomerID text label.

You're ready to apply a special effect to both controls.

3 Click the  Special Effect button list arrow on the Formatting toolbar and select Special Effect: Raised, as shown in Figure 9-7.

QUICK REFERENCE

TO APPLY A SPECIAL EFFECT TO A CONTROL:

• SELECT THE CONTROL, CLICK THE **SPECIAL EFFECT** BUTTON LIST ARROW, AND SELECT THE DESIRED SPECIAL EFFECT.

Table 9-4. Available Special-Effect Options

Special Effect	Example	Special Effect	Example
Flat	Date: 5/1/1992	Raised	Date: 5/1/1992
Sunken	Date: 5/1/1992	Etched	Date: 5/1/1992
Shadowed	Date: 5/1/1992	Chiseled	Date: 5/1/1992

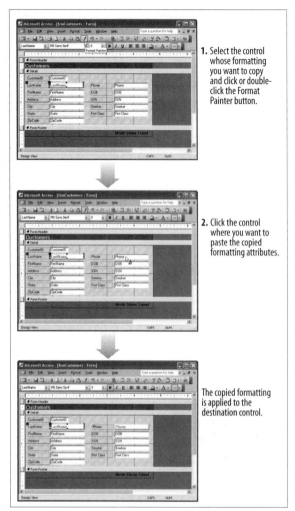

1. Select the control whose formatting you want to copy and click or double-click the Format Painter button.

2. Click the control where you want to paste the copied formatting attributes.

The copied formatting is applied to the destination control.

Figure 9-8. Use the Format Painter to copy formatting from one control to another.

If you find yourself applying exactly the same formatting to several controls repeatedly, the Format Painter is the tool for you. The Format Painter allows you to copy the formatting attributes from one control and then apply them to another. Sound confusing? It won't once you have finished this lesson.

1 Make sure the frmCustomers form is open in Design view.

First you need to select the control whose formatting attributes you want to copy or else format a control so that you can copy its formatting—and that's what we'll do in the next steps.

2 Click the LastName text box control to select it.

We want to format this control so that we can copy its formatting attributes and paste them to other controls on the form.

3 Click the Font/Fore Color button list arrow on the Formatting toolbar and select a red color, then click the Bold button on the Formatting toolbar, and finally click the Special Effect button list arrow on the Formatting toolbar and select the Raised effect.

The control is now formatted with bold red text and a raised effect.

It took some work to apply that formatting, didn't it? Now imagine you want to format all the controls on the form with the same formatting options. Instead of doing all that formatting, you can use the Format Painter tool to copy the formatting from the Last-Name text box control and paste or apply the copied formatting to the other controls on the form. First, you need to select the control with the formatting you want to copy and then do one of the following:

• **Single-click the Format Painter button:** Copy and apply the formatting to a single control.

• **Double-click the Format Painter button:** Copy and apply the formatting to multiple controls. Click the Format Painter button when you're finished pasting the formatting.

Since we want to paste the LastName text box control's formatting to several controls, we'll double-click the Format Painter button.

4 With the LastName text box control still selected, double-click the Format Painter button on the toolbar, as shown in Figure 9-8.

Notice that the pointer changes to a ⬚. Next, you need to paste, or apply the copied formatting.

5 Click the Phone text box control with the Format Painter (⬚).

The Format Painter applies the copied formatting to the Phone text box control, saving you some time and work from manually formatting the control. Since we double-clicked the Format Painter, the pointer remains a ⬚ so that we can paste the copied formatting to multiple controls.

6 Click the FirstName text box control with the Format Painter ().

When you're finished with the Format Painter, click the Format Painter button to switch the pointer back to an ordinary selection arrow.

7 Click the Format Painter button on the Formatting toolbar to stop pasting formatting attributes.

You're finished with this lesson so…

8 Click the Close button to close the frmCustomers form and click No to close without saving your changes.

QUICK REFERENCE

TO COPY FORMATTING WITH THE FORMAT PAINTER:

1. SELECT THE CONTROL WITH THE FORMATTING OPTIONS YOU WANT TO COPY.

2. CLICK THE FORMAT PAINTER BUTTON ON THE TOOLBAR.

3. SELECT THE CONTROL WHERE YOU WANT TO APPLY THE COPIED FORMATTING.

TO COPY SELECTED FORMATTING TO SEVERAL LOCATIONS:

1. SELECT THE CONTROL WITH THE FORMATTING OPTIONS YOU WANT TO COPY.

2. DOUBLE-CLICK THE FORMAT PAINTER BUTTON.

3. SELECT THE CONTROLS WHERE YOU WANT TO APPLY THE COPIED FORMATTING.

4. CLICK THE FORMAT PAINTER BUTTON WHEN YOU'RE FINISHED.

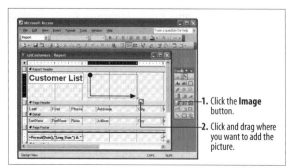

Figure 9-9. Inserting a picture into a report.

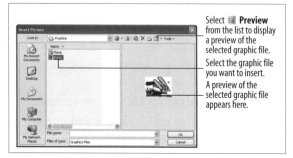

Figure 9-10. The Insert Picture dialog box.

Pictures, graphics, and illustrations can make your reports more professional looking. This lesson explains how to insert clip art and graphics in your reports. You can insert graphics and pictures created with graphics programs such as Microsoft Paint (which comes with Windows), scanned pictures, or graphics from a clip-art library.

1 Make sure that you have the rptCustomers report open in Design view.

Here's how to insert a picture or graphic onto a report (this works for forms too!):

2 Click the 🖼 Image button on the Toolbox.

The pointer changes to a ⁺🖼 . You use this pointer to determine where you want to place the image.

3 Click and drag the ⁺🖼 pointer in the Report Header section down and to the right about an inch and a half, as shown in Figure 9-9.

As soon as you finish clicking and dragging, the Insert Picture dialog box appears, as shown in Figure 9-10. You need to specify the name and location of the graphic file you want to insert.

4 Browse to your Practice folder.

All the graphic files located in your Practice folder appear in the file window.

5 Select the Plane file.

You can display a preview of the graphic in the right side of the Insert Picture dialog box by clicking the ▦ ▾ list and selecting Preview.

6 Click OK to insert the Plane graphic.

Access inserts the plane picture on the report.

Reports with lots of information can sometimes be difficult to read. You can add vertical and/or horizontal lines to make your reports more organized.

7 Click the ╲ Line button on the Toolbox.

The pointer changes to a ⁺╲ line-draw tool. Unless you actually want to draw a diagonal line, hold down the Shift key as you click and drag to draw a straight line.

8 Position the ⁺╲ pointer in the far left side of the top of the Detail section (just above the LastName text box). Hold down the Shift key, then click the mouse and drag the ⁺╲ pointer to the far right edge of the report.

More than likely your screen will not be wide enough to display the entire report—don't worry, simply drag the ⁺╲ pointer *past* the right edge of the screen to automatically scroll to the right.

TIP

If you want to add a control, such as a line, that is larger than the current screen width, simply click and drag the pointer past the edge of the screen.

Let's see how our report looks.

9 Click the View button to view the report in Print Preview.

Notice that the line you added appears not once but under *every record!* That's because you added the line to the report's Detail section, which prints for every record in the report.

10 Click the Close button to close the report and click Yes to save.

You can also use this technique to add pictures to your forms. Table 9-5 lists some of the types of graphic formats that you can use in Access.

Table 9-5. Common Graphic File Formats

Format	File Size	Description
BMP	Large	Also known as a bitmap, this is a generic graphics format used by Paintbrush and many other programs.
CGM	Small	Clip-art pictures often come in Computer Graphics Metafile format.
GIF	Small	Picture file format commonly used on the Internet.
JPG	Small	Digital photographs are usually saved as JPEG files. Because of their small size, JPEG files are also commonly used on the Internet.
WMF	Small	Another file format used for clip-art pictures
TIF	Large	A file format used by scanners, fax programs, and some drawing programs.

QUICK REFERENCE

TO INSERT A GRAPHIC:

1. CLICK THE IMAGE BUTTON ON THE TOOLBOX.

2. MOVE THE ⊞ POINTER ONTO THE FORM OR REPORT, THEN CLICK AND DRAG TO DRAW A RECTANGLE PLACEHOLDER FOR THE GRAPHIC.

3. SELECT THE GRAPHIC FILE YOU WANT TO INSERT AND CLICK OK.

TO DRAW A LINE:

1. CLICK THE LINE BUTTON ON THE TOOLBOX.

2. MOVE THE ⁺╲ POINTER ONTO THE FORM OR REPORT, THEN CLICK AND DRAG TO DRAW THE LINE.

3. HOLD DOWN THE SHIFT KEY AS YOU DRAG TO DRAW A STRAIGHT LINE.

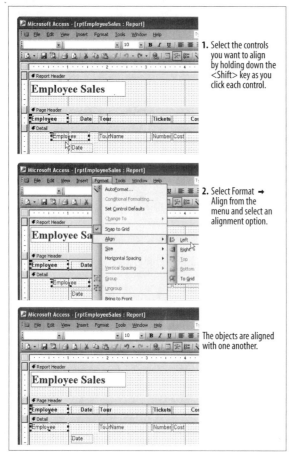

Figure 9-11. The steps for aligning controls with one another.

1. Select the controls you want to align by holding down the <Shift> key as you click each control.

2. Select Format → Align from the menu and select an alignment option.

The objects are aligned with one another.

Forms and reports that have controls scattered randomly about them look terrible. The Align command, located under the Format menu, aligns controls relative to one another. You can align controls so that they are lined up with one another or spaced equally apart from one another. This lesson will give you some practice aligning controls with the Align command.

1 Open the rptEmployeeSales report in Design view.

Someone sure was sloppy when creating this report—its controls are all over the place! You could manually move the controls and align them with one another by using the mouse and eyeballing it, but that would require a lot of time, and (unless you have eyes like a hawk) it would be difficult to align the controls perfectly. Instead, we'll align the controls using the Align command.

First you need to select the controls you want to align with one another. There are three ways to select more than one control:

- Press and hold down the Shift key as you click each control that you want to select.
- Use the arrow pointer (⊾) to draw a box around the controls that you want to select. Point to a location above and to the left of the controls that you want to select, and click and drag the mouse down and to the right until the box surrounds all the controls. When you release the mouse button, all the controls in the box will be selected. The disadvantage of this method is that it's not as selective as using the Shift + click method.
- If the controls you want to select are aligned along a horizontal line, click to the left of the object in the vertical ruler to select every control to the right of the ruler.

2 Hold down the Shift key as you select the Employee text label and Employee text box control as shown in Figure 9-11.

Now you can align the selected controls with each another. Here's how:

3 Select Format → Align → Left from the menu.

The Employee text box control is left-aligned with the Employee text label.

Next let's try vertically aligning two controls—the procedure is almost the same.

4 Hold down the Shift key as you select the Employee text box control and Date text box control.

Now let's vertically align the controls with each other.

5 Select Format → Align → Top from the menu.

Access vertically aligns the two controls with each other.

You can also quickly adjust the amount of horizontal or vertical space between controls by selecting the controls and then selecting a command from either the Horizontal Spacing or Vertical Spacing submenu under the Format menu.

Move on to the next step and we'll adjust the amount of space between the controls on the report.

6 Hold down the Shift key as you click the vertical ruler to the left of the text labels in the Page Header. Keep holding the Shift key and click the vertical ruler to the left of the fields in the Detail section.

You've selected all the text labels in the Page Header and all the fields in the Detail section. Here's how to adjust the spacing between the selected controls with just a few quick clicks of the mouse.

7 Select Format → Horizontal Spacing → Make Equal from the menu.

Access evenly distributes the selected controls.

8 Click and drag the Page Footer divider up to reduce the amount of empty space in the Detail section.

You're finished!

9 Click the Close button and then Yes to close the form and save your changes.

QUICK REFERENCE

TO SELECT MULTIPLE CONTROLS:

• PRESS AND HOLD DOWN THE SHIFT KEY AS YOU CLICK EACH OBJECT THAT YOU WANT TO SELECT.

OR...

• USE THE ARROW POINTER (⤢) TO DRAW A BOX AROUND THE OBJECTS THAT YOU WANT TO SELECT.

OR...

• IF THE CONTROLS ARE ALIGNED ALONG A HORIZONTAL OR VERTICAL LINE, CLICK THE HORIZONTAL OR VERTICAL RULER ABOVE OR TO THE LEFT OF THE CONTROLS.

TO ALIGN OBJECTS WITH EACH OTHER:

1. FOLLOW THE ABOVE STEPS TO SELECT THE OBJECTS YOU WANT TO ALIGN.

2. SELECT FORMAT → ALIGN AND SELECT AN ALIGNMENT OPTION FROM THE MENU.

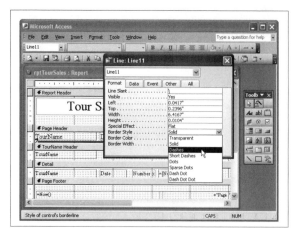

Figure 9-12. Changing a line's Formatting Properties.

The Formatting toolbar is great for quickly applying the most common formatting options to the controls on your forms and reports, but it doesn't offer every formatting option available. To see and/or use every possible formatting option, you need to view the control's *Formatting Properties*. Each type of control has its own set of formatting properties—for example, a line control has a *Border Style* property, which determines if the line should be solid, dashed, or dotted.

To display the Formatting Properties for a control, do one of the following:

- Select the control and click the 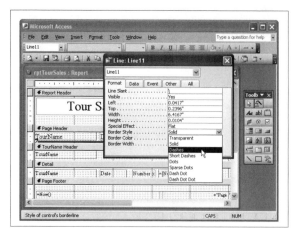 Properties button on the toolbar.
- Right-click the control and select Properties from the shortcut menu.
- Double-click the control.
- Select the control and select View → Properties from the menu.

…and then click the Format tab if necessary. The more common Formatting Properties are listed in Table 9-6.

You might want to review the *Working with Tables and Fields* chapter as well, which contains information on formatting fields.

This lesson will give you some practice working with a control's Formatting Properties.

1 Make sure that you have the rptTourSales report open in Design view.

For this exercise, we'll view and change the Formatting Properties of the dark red line in the report's Page Header.

2 Click the dark red line in the Page Header to select it, then click the Properties button on the toolbar. Click the Format tab if necessary.

The Formatting Properties for the red line appear. There's not much to an ordinary line, so its Formatting Properties are rather limited. One Formatting Property that we can change is the line's Border Style property.

3 Click in the Border Style box, click the arrow, and select Dashes from the list, as shown in Figure 9-12.

The line changes from a solid line to a dashed line. Let's make one more formatting change while the Properties dialog box is still open.

4 With the line still selected and the Properties dialog box still open, click the Border Width list arrow and select 5 pt from the list.

The width of the line changes to three five points.

5 Exit Microsoft Access without saving any of your changes.

Table 9-6. Common Formatting Properties

Property	Description
Format	Customizes the way numbers, dates, times, and text are displayed.
Decimal Places	Determines the number of decimal places displayed (for numeric values).
Visible	Shows or hides a control. Useful if you want to use information on a form without it being visible.
Hide Duplicates	Hides a control on a report when its value is the same as in the preceding record. For example, on a report listing suppliers and their products, each supplier's name can appear once for each group of products, rather than once for each product.

Table 9-6. Common Formatting Properties (Continued)

Property	Description
Can Grow	Determines if a control on a report expands vertically when printed to fit text.
Can Shrink	Determines if a control on a report shrinks vertically when printed to eliminate blank lines.
Left	Determines the horizontal position of a control.
Top	Determines the vertical position of a control.
Width	Determines the width of a control.
Height	Determines the height of a control.
Back Color	Determines the color of a control. Click the button to select a color from a palette.
Special Effect	Applies the specified 3-D effect to the control.
Border Style	Determines the line style of a control's border—select from transparent lines, solid lines, dashed lines, etc.
Border Color	Determines the color of a control's border.
Border Width	Determines the width of a control's border (in points).
Fore Color	Determines the color of text in a control or the fill color of a drawing object.
Font Name	Determines the font used in a control (such as Arial or Times New Roman).
Font Weight	Determines the thickness (boldface) of text in a control.
Font Italic	Determines whether text in a control appears in italics.
Font Underline	Determines whether text in a control is underlined.
Text Align	Determines how text should be aligned in a control.

Lesson Summary

Formatting Fonts with the Formatting Toolbar

To Change Font Size: Select the control and select the pt. size from the Font Size list on the Formatting toolbar.

To Change Font Type: Select the control and select the font from the Font list on the Formatting toolbar.

To Format Text with Bold, Italics, or Underlining: Select the control and click the Bold, Italic, or Underline button on the Formatting toolbar.

Changing Text Alignment

To Change Text Alignment: Select the control and click the Align Left, Center, or Align Right button.

Using AutoFormat

To Format a Form or Report with AutoFormat: Display the form or report you want to format in Design View, click the AutoFormat button on the Report Design toolbar, select one of the AutoFormats from the list, and click OK.

Changing Colors

To Change a Control's Colors: Select the control and click one of the following buttons on the Formatting toolbar:

- Fill/Back Color
- Font/Fore Color
- Line/Border Color

Applying Special Effects

To Apply a Special Effect to a Control: Select the control, click the Special Effect button list arrow, and select the desired special effect.

Using the Format Painter

To Copy Formatting with the Format Painter: Select the control with the formatting options you want to copy, click the Format Painter button on the toolbar, and select the control where you want to apply the copied formatting.

To Copy Selected Formatting to Several Locations: Select the control with the formatting options you want to copy, double-click the Format Painter button, select the controls where you want to apply the copied formatting. Click the Format Painter button when you're finished.

Adding Pictures and Lines

To Insert a Graphic: Click the Image button on the Toolbox, move the image pointer onto the form or report, then click and drag to draw a rectangle placeholder for the graphic. Select the graphic file you want to insert and click OK.

To Draw a Line: Click the Line button on the Toolbox, move the line pointer onto the form or report, then click and drag to draw the line. Hold down the Shift key as you drag to draw a straight line.

Aligning Controls with One Another

To Select Multiple Controls: Do any of the following:

- Press and hold down the Shift key as you click each object that you want to select.
- Use the arrow pointer to draw a box around the objects that you want to select.
- If the controls are aligned along a horizontal or vertical line, click the horizontal or vertical ruler above or to the left of the controls.

To Align Objects with Each Other: Follow the above steps to select the objects you want to align, then select Format → Align and select an alignment option from the menu.

Changing a Control's Formatting Properties

To Format a Control Using the Properties Dialog Box: Display the form in Design View, select the control and click the Properties button on the toolbar, click the Format tab and make the desired formatting changes.

Quiz

1. Fonts are measured in points. The larger the number of points, the smaller the size of the font. (True or False?)

2. You select a control and then click the Align Left button on the Formatting toolbar. What happens?

   A. The control is aligned to the left side of the form or report.

   B. Nothing – the alignment buttons on the Formatting toolbar are used to determine the position of the form or report on the screen.

   C. The text inside the control is aligned to the left side of the control.

   D. Nothing – you must also select the control that you want to use to align the selected control with.

3. AutoFormat automatically applies formatting options as you type. (True or False?)

4. The Fill/Back Color button on the Formatting toolbar applies color to:

   A. The text in the selected control.

   B. The background of the selected control.

   C. The border of the selected control.

   D. All aspects of the control.

5. What does the Special Effect button on the Formatting toolbar do?

   A. It applies a 3-D effect to a selected control.

   B. It lets you select a transitional effect for how a form opens and closes.

   C. It lets you add animation to your forms and reports to make them more entertaining and amusing.

   D. None of the above.

6. Which of the following are reasons why you might want to format a control using the Properties dialog box instead of the Formatting toolbar? (Select all that apply.)

   A. You want to show off your Microsoft Access expertise to do things the hard way.

   B. The Properties dialog box offers every formatting option available for the control—something the Formatting toolbar doesn't have.

   C. The Properties dialog box gives you greater control over how a control is formatted.

   D. You can change the language used in a control using the Properties dialog box. For example, you could select Spanish or French instead of English.

7. You want to insert a graphic of your company's logo on a report. How can you do this? (Select all that apply.)

   A. You can't—Microsoft Access won't let you insert graphic files.

   B. Click the Image button on the Toolbox and drag on the report to draw a placeholder for the graphic.

   C. Select Insert → Picture from the menu.

   D. Select Tools → Insert Picture from the menu.

8. How can you align several controls with each other?

   A. Select the controls by holding down the Shift key as you click each object, then select Format → Align and select an alignment option from the menu.

   B. Select the controls by holding down the Ctrl key as you click each object, then select Format → Align and select an alignment option from the menu.

   C. Select the controls by holding down the Ctrl key as you click each object, then click the appropriate alignment button on the Drawing toolbar.

   D. Select the controls by holding down the Shift key as you click each object, then click the appropriate alignment button on the Drawing toolbar.

Homework

1. Start Microsoft Access, open the Homework database, and open the Test Answers form in Design View.

2. Use AutoFormat to apply the International preset formatting style to the Test Answers form.

3. Change the back color of the Grade text box field to light yellow.

4. Change the font size of the Grade field to 10 pt.

5. Use the Format Painter tool to copy the formatting from the Grade field and apply it to the two remaining fields on the Test Answers form.

6. Resize the controls as necessary to make room for the new font size.

7. Save the changes to the form.

8. Close the Homework database, and exit Microsoft Access.

Quiz Answers

1. False. It's true that fonts are measured in points; however, the larger the number of points, the larger the size of the font.

2. C. The text inside the control is aligned to the left side of the control.

3. False. AutoFormat lets you quickly format a form or report using a set of predefined formatting options.

4. B. The Fill/Back Color button on the Formatting toolbar applies color to the background of a selected control.

5. A. The Special Effect button applies a 3-D effect to a selected control.

6. B and C. The Properties dialog box gives you more control and options over how a control is formatted.

7. B and C. To insert a picture on a form or report, click the Image button on the Toolbox, and drag on the report to draw a placeholder for the graphic, or select Insert → Picture from the menu.

8. A. To align several controls with each other, select the controls by holding down the Shift key as you click each object, then select Format → Align and select an alignment option from the menu.

CHAPTER 10

WORKING WITH MACROS

CHAPTER OBJECTIVES:

Create, edit, and run a macro, Lessons 10.1—10.2

Create a collection of macros in a single group, Lesson 10.3

Assign a macro to a button on a form, Lesson 10.4

Create conditions for a macro, Lesson 10.5

Assign a macro keystroke combination, Lesson 10.6

CHAPTER TASK: CREATE MACROS THAT AUTOMATE DATABASE TASKS

Prerequisites

- **How to use menus, toolbars, dialog boxes, and shortcut keystrokes.**
- **How to open and modify database objects.**

If you find yourself doing the same routine task over and over again, you might want to consider creating a macro to complete the task for you. A *macro* helps you perform routine tasks by automating them. Instead of manually performing a series of time-consuming, repetitive actions, you can record a single macro that does the entire task all at once for you. For example, instead of clicking the Reports icon in the Objects bar in the database window, finding and opening a specific report, printing it, and then closing it, you could create a macro to print the report with the click of a single button.

A macro is a set of one or more actions that perform a particular operation, such as opening a form or printing a report. Macros can help you to automate common tasks. For example, you can run a macro that prints a report when a user clicks a command button.

In a way, you can think of macros as a very simple introduction to programming because you can use them to create automated tasks and somewhat complex procedures. Best of all, you don't have to know a single line of code—Access provides you with everything you need to write a macro.

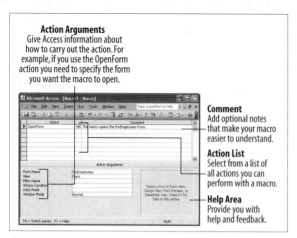

Action Arguments
Give Access information about how to carry out the action. For example, if you use the OpenForm action you need to specify the form you want the macro to open.

Comment
Add optional notes that make your macro easier to understand.

Action List
Select from a list of all actions you can perform with a macro.

Help Area
Provide you with help and feedback.

Figure 10-1. You create macros by entering them directly in Macro Design view.

In some programs, such as Microsoft Excel or Word, you can create macros with a "macro recorder" to record your commands, keystrokes, and mouse clicks. Unfortunately, there isn't a "macro recorder" or Macro Wizard to help you create a macro in Microsoft Access. Instead, you create macros by entering the actions and arguments directly in Macro Design view, shown in Figure 10-1. Don't worry—it's not as difficult as it sounds. Working in Macro Design view really isn't all that different from working in Table Design view—it's where you define and edit your macro objects.

Simple macros that automate a single task, such as opening a form or report, are incredibly simple to create—we'll create such a macro in this lesson. More complicated macros with several steps or procedures may require a little bit of planning. Before you create a complicated macro, think about what you want the macro to do and the individual actions that are required to complete this operation. Practice the steps needed to carry out the operation and write them down as you go—it will make writing the macro a lot easier.

And so, without any further ado, let's create our first macro.

1 Start Microsoft Access, open the Lesson 10 database, click the Macros icon in the Objects bar, and click the New button.

The Macro1: Macro window appears, as shown in Figure 10-1. The Action cell is where you tell Access what you want the macro to do.

2 Click the first blank Action cell, then click the list arrow.

A list of actions appears. An *action*, or command, is the basic building block of a macro—it's an instruction that tells Access what you want the macro to do. There are more than 50 different actions you can choose from. When you start creating your own macros you will almost certainly want to refer to Table 10-3 (found in Lesson 10-6) to help you find the right action.

3 Scroll down and select the OpenForm action.

The *OpenForm* action is added to the first line of the macro window. Most of the time you will have to give Access more information about how to execute each action. For example, here we will have to tell Access which form to open with the OpenForm action. You use *arguments* to supply Microsoft Access with information about how to carry out the action. Each type of action has its own set of arguments, which appear in the Action Arguments panel, located at the bottom of the macro window.

4 Click the Form Name text box in the Action Arguments panel, click the list arrow, and select frmEmployees.

That's the only argument we need to specify for this exercise, but notice that there are additional arguments for the OpenForm action, such as the View argument, which lets you select the view in which to open the form (Form view, Design view, or Print Preview).

If you want, you can type a comment to explain the action in the Comment column. If you've ever had any programming experience, the Comment column is the same as a remark statement.

5 Click the first blank Comment cell and type This macro opens the frmEmployees Form.

Comments are completely optional, but they do make your macros easier to understand, especially if other users will edit them.

6 Click the Save button on the toolbar, save the macro as mcrEmployees and click OK.

You're finished working in the Macro window for now so…

7 Close the Macro window.

Time to test your new macro. The Macros icon in the Objects bar in the Database window should be selected.

8 Double-click the mcrEmployees macro.

Access runs the mcrEmployees macro and opens the frmEmployees form.

9 Close the frmEmployees form.

That's all there is to creating a macro—not nearly as hard as you thought it would be, was it? Even the Microsoft Access developers don't have all the macro actions memorized, so make sure you have Table 10-3 handy so that you know what action to use in your macros.

QUICK REFERENCE

TO CREATE A MACRO:

1. IN THE DATABASE WINDOW, CLICK THE MACROS ICON IN THE OBJECTS BAR AND CLICK THE NEW BUTTON.

2. CLICK THE FIRST BLANK ACTION CELL.

3. CLICK THE LIST ARROW AND SELECT THE ACTION YOU WANT THE MACRO TO PERFORM.

4. SPECIFY ANY REQUIRED ARGUMENTS FOR THE ACTION IN THE ACTION ARGUMENTS AREA.

5. REPEAT STEPS 2-4 FOR EACH ADDITIONAL ACTION YOU WANT THE MACRO TO EXECUTE.

6. CLICK THE SAVE BUTTON ON THE TOOLBAR, GIVE YOUR NEW MACRO A NAME, AND CLICK OK.

7. CLOSE THE MACRO WINDOW.

TO RUN A MACRO:

• CLICK THE MACROS ICON IN THE OBJECTS BAR AND DOUBLE-CLICK THE MACRO YOU WANT TO RUN.

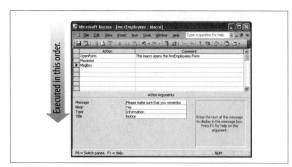

Figure 10-2. The mcrEmployees macro with two additional actions.

Figure 10-3. A message box—the result of the MsgBox action.

Some Microsoft Access tasks require several steps. For example, a particular task might require you to (1) open a form, (2) select a specific record, (3) select a specific field in that record, and then (4) copy the information in that field to the Windows clipboard. Macros can contain as many actions as necessary to automate even the most complicated tasks. Each action appears in its own row and is evaluated and executed in the order in which it appears in the Macro window, from top to bottom.

In this lesson you will edit the macro you created in the previous lesson to change its arguments and add some more steps or actions.

1 Select the mcrEmployees macro and click the Design button.

The mcrEmployees macro opens in Design view. Let's add two more actions to this macro.

2 Click the Action cell just below the OpenForm action, click the list arrow, scroll down the list, and select Maximize.

When you run the macro, the *Maximize* action will maximize the window so that it fills the entire Microsoft Access window. Because the Maximize action is so simple and straightforward, it doesn't have any additional arguments.

Let's add another action to the mcrEmployees macro.

3 Click the Action cell just below the Maximize action, click the list arrow, scroll down, and select MsgBox.

When you run the macro, the *MsgBox* action will display a message box that contains a warning or an informational message. The *Message* argument is the most important argument for the MsgBox action because it determines the text that is displayed in the message box.

4 Click the Message argument box and type Please make sure that you remember to add the employee's phone number!.

There are several other arguments you may want to specify for the MsgBox action, such as the type of icon that is displayed in the message box (None, Critical, Warning?, Warning!, or Information) and the text that is displayed in the title bar of the message box.

5 Click the Type argument box, click the list arrow, and select Information. Click the Title argument box and type Notice.

Your macro should look like the one shown in Figure 10-2. Remember that actions are evaluated and/or executed in the order in which they appear, so the mcrEmployees macro will (1) open the frmEmployees form, (2) maximize the form window, and (3) display the message box.

6 Click the Save button on the toolbar.

That's all the editing we need to do for this lesson.

7 Close the macro window.

Let's test the macro.

8 Double-click the mcrEmployees macro.

Sure enough, the mcrEmployees macro (1) opens the frmEmployees form, (2) maximizes the form window, and (3) displays the message box, as shown in Figure 10-3.

9 Click OK to close the message box, then click the ✕ Close button to close the frmEmployees form.

QUICK REFERENCE

TO MODIFY A MACRO:

- IN THE DATABASE WINDOW, CLICK THE MACROS
  ICON IN THE OBJECTS BAR, SELECT THE MACRO
  YOU WANT TO EDIT, AND CLICK THE DESIGN
  BUTTON.

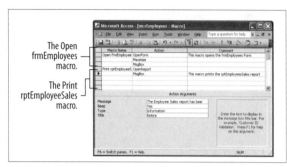

The Open
frmEmployees
macro.

The Print
rptEmployeeSales
macro.

Figure 10-4. Two macros—the Open frmEmployees macro and the Print rptEmployeeSales macro—within a single macro group.

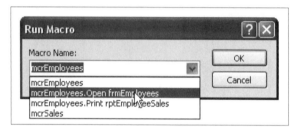

Figure 10-5. The Run Macro dialog box.

If you are creating lots of macros, you might want to consider organizing them into a macro group to help you manage them. A *macro group* stores several related macros together in a single macro object. When you create a macro group, you must give each macro in the macro group its own unique name to identify where each macro starts and ends. You do this by entering the macro names in the *Macro Name column*, which you display by clicking the Macro Names button on the toolbar.

When you combine two or more macros within the same macro group, you must run them separately, by referring to the macro group name, followed by the macro name. For example, mcrEmployees. mcrEmployees frmEmployees refers to the *Open frmEmployees* macro in the *mcrEmployees* macro group.

In this lesson you will learn how to group several related macros together in a macro group.

1 Select the mcrEmployees macro and click the Design button.

In order to work with macro groups, you need to display the Macro Name column.

2 Click the 🔲 Macro Names button on the toolbar.

First you need to give the macro you created in the previous two lessons a name. The cursor is already positioned in the Macro Name cell of the first row.

⟨ NOTE ⟩   *Always enter the macro name in the Macro Name column, next to the Action where the macro starts.*

3 Type Open frmEmployees in the first blank cell in the Macro Name column.

The macro name "Open frmEmployees" identifies the macro you created in the previous two lessons. To create another macro in the same macro group, type its name in the Macro Name column next to the first action of the new macro.

4 Press the ↓ key three times.

The cursor should be positioned in the Macro Name column next to the first blank Action row. This is where you will add another macro to the macro group.

5 Type Print rptEmployeeSales.

"Print rptEmployeeSales" is the name of the new macro we will create.

6 Click the Action cell to the right of the Print rptEmployeeSales macro name, click the list arrow, scroll down, and select OpenReport.

Similar to the OpenForm action, which opens a form, the *OpenReport* action opens a report. Next, you need to specify the arguments for the OpenReport action.

7 Click the Report Name text box in the Action Arguments panel, click the list arrow, and select rptEmployeeSales.

This macro will open the rptEmployeeSales report. Notice Print appears in the View argument box—this will send the rptEmployeeSales report directly to the printer. Let's add a comment to this new macro.

8 Click the blank Comment box in the Print rptEmployeeSales macro row and type This macro prints the rptEmployeeSales report.

You want to add one more action to the Print rptEmployeeSales macro.

9 Click the Action cell just below the OpenReport action, click the list arrow, scroll down, and select MsgBox.

You need to tell Access what you want the message box to say.

10 Click the Message argument box and type The Employee Sales report has been sent to the printer.

Let's specify several additional arguments for the MsgBox action, such as the type of icon that is displayed in the message box.

11 Click the Type argument box, click the list arrow, and select Information. Click the Title argument box and type Notice.

Your macro should look like the one shown in Figure 10-4.

12 Click the Save button on the toolbar and close the macro window.

Let's test our new macro. When you combine several macros within the same macro group you must run

them separately using the Tools command on the Access menu.

⸱ NOTE ⸱   *Don't run a macro group by double-clicking it or selecting it and clicking Run. Doing so will run every macro in the macro group—often with disastrous results!*

13 Select Tools → Macro → Run Macro from the menu.

The Run Macro dialog box appears, as shown in Figure 10-5. Here's where you select the specific macro you want to run.

14 Click the Macro Name list arrow, select mcrEmployees.Open frmEmployees, and click OK.

Access runs the Open frmEmployees macro.

15 Click OK to close the message box and close the frmEmployees form.

If you want, go ahead and repeat Step 13 and run the Print rptEmployeeSales macro. Make sure your computer is connected to a printer, as this macro will send a copy of the rptEmployeeSales report to the printer.

QUICK REFERENCE

TO CREATE A MACRO GROUP:

1. CREATE A NEW MACRO OR EDIT AN EXISTING MACRO.

2. CLICK THE MACRO NAMES BUTTON ON THE TOOLBAR.

3. TYPE THE MACRO NAME IN THE MACRO NAME COLUMN NEXT TO THE ACTION WHERE THE MACRO STARTS.

4. IF NECESSARY, ADD THE MACRO ACTIONS OR EDIT THE EXISTING MACRO ACTIONS.

5. SAVE THE MACRO AND CLOSE THE MACRO WINDOW.

TO RUN A MACRO IN A MACRO GROUP:

1. SELECT TOOLS → MACRO → RUN MACRO FROM THE MENU.

2. CLICK THE MACRO NAME LIST ARROW, SELECT THE MACRO YOU WANT TO RUN, AND CLICK OK.

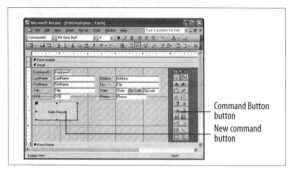

Figure 10-6. Adding a command button to run a macro.

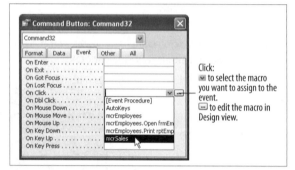

Figure 10-7. Assigning a macro to a command button's "On Click" event.

Running macros from the Database window or menu is a pain in the neck. That's why most database developers assign macros to controls—particularly, buttons—so that when a user clicks the button or control, a macro is activated.

1 Open the frmEmployees form in Design view.

You want to add a command button to the frmEmployees form to open a report that displays the sales for each employee. First you need to add the command button.

2 Click the ![icon] Toolbox button, if necessary, and click the Command Button button on the Toolbox.

The mouse pointer changes to a $+_\square$, indicating that you can click and drag the command button control onto the form.

3 Place the $+_\square$ pointer below the DOB field label and click and drag the $+_\square$ pointer down and to the right to create a command button like the one in Figure 10-6. Click Cancel if the Command Button Wizard appears.

Let's give this button a more meaningful text label.

4 Make sure that the command button is still selected, then click its text label and replace the text with Sales Report. Click anywhere outside of the command button when you're finished.

We're ready to assign a macro to the button—to do this you will need to display the command button's Properties.

5 Select the command button, click the $+_\square$ Properties button on the toolbar, and click the Event tab.

The Event tab lists all the events to which you can assign a macro—most of them you will never use, as you can see in Table 10-1.

6 Click the On Click box, click the list arrow, and select mcrSales, as shown in Figure 10-7. Close the Properties dialog box when you're finished.

Let's see how our new command button works.

7 Click the View button on the toolbar to switch to Form view, then click the new Sales Report button.

Microsoft Access runs the mcrSales macro and displays the Employee Commission Report for the current employee. Let's close the report and save our changes…

8 Close the Employee Commission Report and then click the Save button.

Table 10-1. Event Properties That Can Trigger Macros

Event	Description
Before Update	Macro or function that runs when data in a field or record is changed but before the changes are actually saved to the database. Often used to validate data.
After Update	Macro or function that runs when data in a field or record is changed and is saved to the database.
On Change	Macro or function that runs when the contents of a text box or combo box changes or when you move from one page to another page in a tab control.
On Enter	Macro or function that runs when a control first gets the focus (is selected). The Enter event occurs before the focus moves to a particular control (before the GotFocus event). You can use an Enter macro or event procedure to display instructions when a form or report first opens.
On Exit	Macro or function that runs when a control loses focus (is deselected) on the same form.
On Got Focus	Macro or function that runs when a control gets the focus (is selected).
On Lost Focus	Macro or function that runs when a control loses the focus (is deselected).
On Click	Macro or function that runs when a control is clicked.
On Dbl Click	Macro or function that runs when a control is double-clicked.
On Mouse Down	Macro or function that runs when the user presses the mouse button.
On Mouse Move	Macro or function that runs when the user moves the mouse over a control.
On Mouse Up	Macro or function that runs when the user releases the mouse button.
On Key Down	Macro or function that runs when the user presses a key on the keyboard.
On Key Up	Macro or function that runs when the user releases a key on the keyboard.
On Key Press	Macro or function that runs when the user presses an ANSI key on the keyboard.

QUICK REFERENCE

TO ASSIGN A MACRO TO A CONTROL ON A FORM OR REPORT:

1. OPEN THE FORM OR REPORT IN DESIGN VIEW.

2. CLICK THE CONTROL TO WHICH YOU WANT TO ASSIGN THE MACRO AND CLICK THE PROPERTIES BUTTON ON THE TOOLBAR.

3. CLICK THE EVENT TAB AND CLICK IN THE BOX FOR THE TYPE OF EVENT YOU WANT TO ASSIGN TO THE MACRO.

4. CLICK THE LIST ARROW AND SELECT THE MACRO YOU WANT TO ASSIGN TO THE EVENT.

5. CLOSE THE PROPERTIES DIALOG BOX AND SAVE THE FORM OR REPORT.

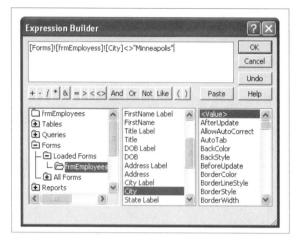

Figure 10-8. The Expression Builder can help you enter conditional expressions in your macros.

Figure 10-9. A conditional expression.

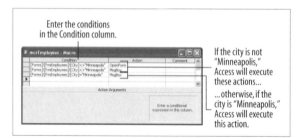

Figure 10-10. The updated mcrSales macro.

A *condition* takes action based on a certain condition. For example, if an employee's weekly sales are more than $2,500, then a condition could calculate a 5-percent commission bonus for the employee; otherwise, it wouldn't calculate a bonus. If you're at all familiar with programming, a condition is similar to an If…Then statement.

You enter conditions in the Condition column in the Macro window. If a condition is true, Access executes the action in that row. If a condition isn't true, Access skips the action in that row and moves to the next row. Conditions often compare values in a specific control on a form or report to a number, date, or constant. For example, the expression in Figure 10-9 evaluates if the value in a City field is not equal to "Minneapolis." Make sure that

you use the proper Microsoft Access syntax when referring to controls in forms or reports.

1 Make sure you have the frmEmployees form from the previous lesson open. Click the View button on the toolbar to switch to Design view.

We want to add a conditional expression to the mcrEmployees macro. If a macro is assigned to a control on a form or report, you can open and edit the macro directly from the form or report without having to access it through the Database window.

2 Select the command button, click the Properties button on the toolbar, click the Event tab, and click the On Click box.

A ⬚ Build button appears in every event property. Click this button to create or modify the macro or Visual Basic procedure assigned to the event.

3 Click the ⬚ Build button.

The mcrSales macro appears in Design view.

4 Click the ⬚ Conditions button on the toolbar.

The Condition column appears. This is where you need to add the conditions you want Access to evaluate before it executes an action. It's often easier if you use the Expression Builder to help you create your macro conditions.

5 Click the first blank cell in the Condition column and click the Build button on the toolbar.

The Expression Builder dialog box appears, as shown in Figure 10-8.

6 Double-click the Forms folder in the bottom-left window, double-click the All Forms folder, then click the frmEmployees folder.

When you select the frmEmployees folder in the left window, the middle window displays all the controls in the selected form.

7 Scroll down the middle window, and find and double-click the City control.

Access adds Forms![frmEmployees]![City] to the expression area. Now you need to specify how you want to evaluate the City field.

8 Click in the Expression box and add "Minneapolis".

Your expression should look similar to the one in Figure 10-9.

9 Click OK.

The Expression Builder dialog box closes. The condition you entered will execute the OpenForm action only if the City field is not equal to "Minneapolis." The condition you entered only affects the first row or action in the macro—the other actions in the macro will execute without being evaluated. If you want to evaluate the other actions, they must each have their own statement in the Condition column. Let's add some more actions to the macro.

10 Copy the first row in the Condition column and paste it in the second and third rows.

Add another action that will execute only if the City is not equal to "Minneapolis."

11 Click the Action cell in the second row, click the list arrow and select MsgBox. Click the Message argument box and type This is the current commission for non-Minneapolis employees.

Next you need to add an action to perform if the City is equal to "Minneapolis."

12 Edit the expression in the third row of the Condition column so it reads [Forms]![frmEmployees]![City]="Minneapolis".

Your macro should look like Figure 10-10. Now you need to specify the action to perform if the condition is true.

13 Click the Action cell next to the condition you edited, click the list arrow, and select MsgBox. Click the Message argument box and type Call Linda Ross for the Minneapolis Commission report.

We're finished modifying the macro.

14 Save your changes and close the Macro Design window. Click the View button on the toolbar to display the form in Form view.

Let's test our conditional macro.

15 Find a record whose City field is NOT "Minneapolis" and click the Sales Report button. Click OK and then close the commission report. Click the Save button and close the frmEmployees form.

QUICK REFERENCE

TO CREATE A CONDITIONAL EXPRESSION IN A MACRO:

1. CREATE A NEW MACRO OR EDIT AN EXISTING MACRO.

2. IN DESIGN VIEW, CLICK THE CONDITIONS BUTTON ON THE TOOLBAR.

3. CLICK THE CONDITION CELL NEXT TO THE ACTION YOU WANT TO EVALUATE.

4. ENTER THE CONDITIONAL EXPRESSION IN THE CONDITION CELL, USING PROPER ACCESS SYNTAX. YOU CAN USE THE EXPRESSION BUILDER TO HELP YOU CREATE THE EXPRESSION BY CLICKING THE BUILD BUTTON ON THE TOOLBAR.

5. REPEAT STEPS 3 AND 4 FOR EACH ACTION YOU WANT TO EVALUATE.

6. SAVE THE MACRO AND CLOSE THE MACRO WINDOW.

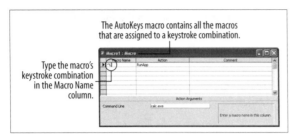

The AutoKeys macro contains all the macros that are assigned to a keystroke combination.

Type the macro's keystroke combination in the Macro Name column.

Figure 10-11. The AutoKeys macro, which is used to assign a keystroke combination to a macro.

Sometimes, instead of assigning a macro to a command button, you may want to assign it to a specific keystroke combination, such as Ctrl + D. Assigning a keystroke combination to a macro makes it fast and easy to access—you can execute the macro at any time by pressing its assigned keystroke combination.

Assigning a keystroke combination to macro can be a somewhat complicated process. There are two things you need to know about assigning a macro to a keystroke combination:

- You must create a special macro group, named *AutoKeys*, which contains all your keystroke-combination macros.

- You type the keystroke combination to which you want to assign the macro in the Macro Name column of the AutoKeys macro window. Enter the keystroke combinations using the examples in Table 10-2. For example, to assign a macro to the keystroke combination Ctrl + D, you would name the macro ^D.

In this lesson you will learn how to create an AutoKeys macro to assign a macro to a keystroke combination.

1 In the Database window, click the Macros icon in the Objects bar and then click the New button.

The Macro window appears. You need to make sure the Macro Name column is displayed in order to tell Access which keystroke combination you want to assign to the macro.

2 Click the 🔲 Macro Names button on the toolbar, if necessary.

Now you need to type the keystroke combination to which you want to assign the macro. Table 10-2 shows the key combinations you can use to make key assignments in an AutoKeys macro group. We want to

assign a macro to the keystroke combination Ctrl + L. Here's what you need to enter:

3 Type ^L in the first blank Macro Name cell, as shown in Figure 10-11.

The name ^L refers to Ctrl + L. The ^ (caret) signifies the Ctrl key and the "L" signifies the "L" key.

⸸ NOTE ⸸ *If you assign a macro to a keystroke combination that Microsoft Access is already using (for example, Ctrl + X is the keystroke combination for the Cut command), the macro you assign to this keystroke combination will override the Microsoft Access keystroke combination assignment.*

Now we need to specify what we want the macro to do.

4 Click the first blank Action cell, click the list arrow, and select RunApp from the list.

The *RunApp* action starts another program, such as Microsoft Excel or Word. We want the RunApp action to start the Calculator program. You need to specify the name and location of the program you want to run in the Action Arguments area.

5 Click the Command Line text box and type calc.exe.

Now let's save the macro, making sure that we name it *AutoKeys*.

6 Click the Save button on the toolbar, type AutoKeys, and click OK.

We're ready to test our AutoKeys macro.

7 Press Ctrl + L.

Microsoft Access executes the macro assigned to the Ctrl + L keystroke combination and starts the Calculator application.

8 Close the AutoKeys macro and the Lesson 10 database.

Give yourself a pat on the back if you've gotten through this chapter. You've just learned how to automate your Microsoft Access databases to work more like a full-featured application—instead of a dull, static database.

Table 10-2. The SendKey Syntax

Heading	Heading
Ctrl + Any Key	^ (For example, enter ^E for **Ctrl + E**.)
Shift + Any Key	+ (For example, enter +E for **Shift + E**.)
Alt	% (For example, enter %E for **Alt + E**.)
Enter	{ENTER}
Esc	{ESC}
Tab	{TAB}
Insert, Delete	{INSERT} or {INS}, {DELETE} or {DEL}
Page Down, Page Up	{PGDN}, {PGUP}
Home, End	{HOME}, {END}
Arrow Keys	{UP}, {DOWN}, {LEFT}, {RIGHT}
Caps Lock	{CAPSLOCK}
Function Keys	{F1}, {F2}, {F3}, etc…

QUICK REFERENCE

TO ASSIGN A MACRO TO A KEYSTROKE COMBINATION:

1. CREATE A MACRO GROUP NAMED AUTOKEYS. THIS WILL STORE ALL THE MACROS THAT ARE ASSIGNED TO A KEYSTROKE COMBINATION.

2. CLICK THE MACRO NAMES BUTTON ON THE TOOLBAR.

3. TYPE THE KEYSTROKE COMBINATION IN SENDKEY SYNTAX IN THE MACRO NAME COLUMN NEXT TO THE ACTION WHERE THE MACRO STARTS. SEE TABLE 10-2.

Table 10-3. Macro Actions and Their Descriptions

Action	Description
AddMenu	Adds a menu to a custom menu bar for a form or report. Each menu on the menu bar requires a separate AddMenu action.
ApplyFilter	Applies a filter or query to a table, form, or report.
Beep	Causes the computer to beep.
CancelEvent	Cancels the event that caused the macro to run.
Close	Closes the specified window or the active window if none is specified.
CopyObject	Copies the specified database object to a different Microsoft Access database or to the same database with a new name.
DeleteObject	Deletes the specified object or the object selected in the Database window if no object is specified.
Echo	Hides or shows the results of a macro while it runs.
FindNext	Finds the next record that meets the criteria specified with the most recent FindRecord action or Find dialog box. Use to move successively through records that meet the same criteria.
FindRecord	Finds the first or next record that meets the specified criteria. Records can be found in the active form or datasheet.
GoToControl	Selects the specified field on the active datasheet or form.
GoToPage	Selects the first control on the specified page of the active form.
GoToRecord	Makes the specified record the current record in a table, form, or query. Use to move to the first, last, next, or previous record.
Hourglass	Changes the mouse pointer to an hourglass while the macro runs.
Maximize	Maximizes the active window.
Minimize	Minimizes the active window.
MoveSize	Moves and/or changes the size of the active window.
MsgBox	Displays a message box containing a warning or informational message.
OpenForm	Opens a form in Form view, Design view, Print Preview, or Datasheet view.
OpenModule	Opens the specified Visual Basic module in Design view.
OpenQuery	Opens a query in Datasheet view, Design view, or Print Preview.
OpenReport	Opens a report in Design view or Print Preview or prints the report immediately.
OpenTable	Opens a table in Datasheet view, Design view, or Print Preview.
OutputTo	Exports the specified database object to a Microsoft Excel file (.xls), rich-text file (.rtf), text file (.txt), or HTML file (.htm).
PrintOut	Prints the active database object. You can print datasheets, reports, forms, and modules.
Quit	Quits Microsoft Access.
Rename	Renames the specified object.
RepaintObject	Completes any pending screen updates or pending recalculations of controls on the specified object or on the active object if none is specified.
Requery	Forces a requery of a specific control on the active database object.
Restore	Restores a maximized or minimized window to its previous size.
RunApp	Starts another program, such as Microsoft Excel or Word.
RunCode	Runs a Visual Basic Function procedure.

Table 10-3. Macro Actions and Their Descriptions (Continued)

Action	Description
RunCommand	Runs a command from Microsoft Access's menus—for example, File → Save.
RunMacro	Runs a macro.
RunSQL	Runs the specified SQL statement for an action query.
Save	Saves the specified object or the active object if none is specified.
SelectObject	Selects a specified database object. You can then run an action that applies to that object.
SendKeys	Sends keystrokes to Microsoft Access or another active application. These keystrokes are processed as if you had typed them yourself on the keyboard.
SendObject	Sends the specified database objects as an attachment in an e-mail.
SetMenuItem	Sets the state of menu items (enabled or disabled, checked or unchecked) on custom menus. Works only on custom menus created using menu bar macros.
SetValue	Sets the value for a control, field, or property on a form or report.
SetWarnings	Turns all system messages on or off. This has the same effect as clicking OK or Yes in each message box.
ShowAllRecords	Removes any applied filter from the active table, query, or form.
ShowToolbar	Shows or hides a built-in toolbar or a custom toolbar.
StopAllMacros	Stops all currently running macros.
StopMacro	Stops the currently running macro. Use to stop a macro when a certain condition is met.
TransferDatabase	Imports or exports data to or from the current database from or to another database.
TransferSpread-sheet	Imports data from a spreadsheet file into the current database or exports data from the current database into a spreadsheet file.
TransferText	Imports data from a text file into the current database or exports data from the current database into a text file.

Lesson Summary

Creating and Running a Macro

- **To Create a Macro:** In the database window, click the Macros icon in the Objects bar and click the New button. Click the first blank Action cell, click the list arrow, and select the action you want the macro to perform. Specify any required arguments for the action in the Action Arguments area. Repeat for each additional action you want the macro to execute. Click the Save button on the toolbar, give your new macro a name, and click OK.

- To Run a Macro: Click the Macros icon in the Objects bar and double-click the macro you want to run.

Editing a Macro

- **To Modify a Macro:** In the Database window, click the Macros icon in the Objects bar, select the macro you want to edit, and click the Design button.

Working with Macro Groups

- **To Create a Macro Group:** Create a new macro or edit an existing macro, then click the Macro Names button on the toolbar. Type the macro name in the Macro Name column next to the action where the macro starts. If necessary, add the macro actions or edit the existing macro actions. Save the macro and close the macro window.

- **To Run a Macro in a Macro Group:** Select Tools → Macro → Run Macro from the menu, click the Macro Name list arrow, select the macro you want to run, and click OK.

Assigning a Macro to an Event

- **To Assign a Macro to a Control on a Form or Report:** Open the form or report in Design view, click the control to which you want to assign the macro and click the Properties button on the toolbar. Click the Event tab, click in the box for the type of event you want to assign to the macro, then click the list arrow and select the macro you want to assign to the event. Close the Properties dialog box and save the form or report.

Creating Conditional Expressions

- **To Create a Conditional Expression in a Macro:** Create a new macro or edit an existing macro. In Design view, click the Conditions button on the toolbar and click the Condition cell next to the action you want to evaluate. Enter the conditional expression in the Condition cell, using proper Access syntax. You can use the Expression Builder to help you create the expression by clicking the Build button on the toolbar. Repeat these steps for each action you want to evaluate. Save the macro and close the macro window.

Assigning a Macro to a Keystroke Combination

- **To Assign a Macro to a Keystroke Combination:** Create a macro group named AutoKeys—this will store all the macros that are assigned to a keystroke combination. Click the Macro Names button on the toolbar. Type the keystroke combination in SendKey syntax in the Macro Name column next to the Action where the macro starts.

Quiz

1. The fastest and easiest way to create a macro in Microsoft Access is with the Macro Recorder. (True or False?)

2. A(n) ___, or command, is the basic building block of a macro.
   A. Expression.
   B. Action.
   C. Procedure.
   D. Function.

3. Macros may contain more than one action to perform several steps in sequence. (True or False?)

4. Which of the following statements is NOT true?
   A. You can add an optional comment to a macro action in the Comment column.
   B. You use *arguments* to supply Microsoft Access with information about how to carry out specific actions.
   C. A *macro group* stores several named macros together in a single group.
   D. To run a specific macro in a macro group, double-click the macro, select the specific macro from the list, and click Run.

5. Which of the following columns cannot be found in the Macro Design window?

A. Macro Name column (if the Macro Names button on the toolbar is selected).
B. Action Arguments column.
C. Condition column (if the Conditions button on the toolbar is selected).
D. Action column.

6. You can assign a macro to a button, so that when a user clicks the button or control, a macro is activated. The procedure for doing this is:
   A. (1) Open the form in Design View, (2) select the button and display its properties, (3) click the Event tab and click the On Click box, (4) click the down arrow and select the macro you want to assign to the button.
   B. (1) Open the macro in Design View, (2) select the form and button you want to assign the macro to from the Assign box, (3) click Event box, click the down arrow and select On Click from the list.
   C. (1) Open the form in Design View, (2) select the button, and (3) select the macro from the Macro List on the toolbar.
   D. Too lengthy and complicated to be described in a brief quiz question.

7. Conditions only effect the corresponding Action row in the macro—the other actions in the macro will execute without being evaluated. If you want to evaluate the other actions, they must each have their own statement in the Condition column. (True or False?)

Homework

1. Open the Homework database.

2. Create a macro named "OpenReport" that opens the Insurance Claims by Date report in Print Preview. Try running this macro.

3. Modify the OpenReport macro—add a conditional expression so that the OpenReport action won't execute if the Score field in the Test Answers form equals an "F." **Hint:** Use the Expression Builder if you need help creating the conditional expression.

4. Add another conditional action to the OpenReport macro—one that displays a message box that says "Sorry, you failed!" if the Score field in the Test Answers form equals an "F."

5. Open the Test Answers form in Design View.

6. Add a command button to the form whose On Click event property runs the OpenReport macro.

7. Save the Test Answers form, display it in Form View, and test the command button.

8. Close the Homework database.

Quiz Answers

1. False. Microsoft Excel and Word both have macro recorders you can use to create macros, but with Microsoft Access, you create macros in the Macro Design window.

2. B. An action is the basic building block of a macro.

3. True. Macros can contain multiple actions to automate several steps in a sequence.

4. D. Double-clicking a macro group will run *every* named macro in the group, often with disastrous results.

5. B. This was a trick question. Macro actions do have arguments; however, they can be found in the Action Arguments panel—not in a column.

6. A. The correct procedure for assigning a macro to a button is: (1) Open the form in Design View, (2) select the button and display its properties, (3) click the Event tab and click the On Click box, (4) click the down arrow and select the macro you want to assign to the button.

7. True. Conditions only effect the corresponding Action row in the macro. If you want to evaluate the other actions, they must each have their own statement in the Condition column.

ADVANCED TOPICS

CHAPTER OBJECTIVES:

Import information from an external file, Lesson 11.1

Export information to an external data file, Lesson 11.2

Import objects from another Microsoft Access database, Lesson 11.3

Link tables from an external database, Lesson 11.4

Export information to a Microsoft Excel worksheet, Lesson 11.5

Export records to a Microsoft Word table, Lesson 11.6

Mail merge records to Microsoft Word, Lesson 11.7

Create and work with hyperlink and OLE object fields, Lessons 11.8—11.9

View database object dependencies, Lesson 11.10

CHAPTER TASK: EXPORT AND IMPORT INFORMATION TO AND FROM A MICROSOFT ACCESS DATABASE

Prerequisites

- **How to use menus, toolbars, dialog boxes, and shortcut keystrokes.**
- **How to open and modify database objects.**
- **A basic understanding of Microsoft Excel and Microsoft Word.**

One of the great benefits of working with Windows is that you can share information between different programs. Nowhere is this truer than with Microsoft Access. This chapter explains how you can use Access with other programs. You'll learn how to import and export databases in other file formats. You'll also learn the difference between importing objects from another database versus linking to objects in another database. And you'll learn how to create a Microsoft Excel worksheet based on an Access query, transfer an Access table to Microsoft Word, or use Word with Access to create mail-merge letters.

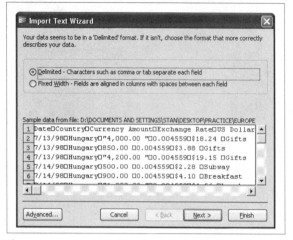

Figure 11-1. Step 1 of the Import Text Wizard: Determine the text file format.

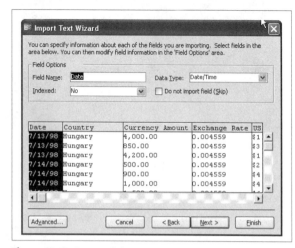

Figure 11-3. Step 4 of the Import Text Wizard: Specify the data type of the imported fields.

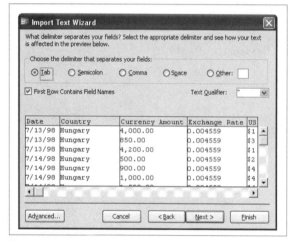

Figure 11-2. Step 2 of the Import Text Wizard: Specify the text delimiter that separates the fields and the field names.

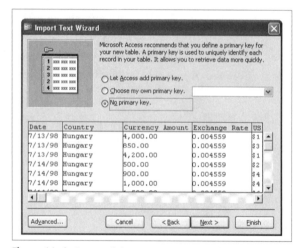

Figure 11-4. Step 5 of the Import Text Wizard: Specify a primary key.

People from different countries speak different languages, so naturally computer programs save files in different formats. Fortunately, just like some people can speak several languages, Access can read and write in other file formats. This lesson shows how to open one of the most common file formats in programs—a tab-delimited text file in Microsoft Access.

1 Start Microsoft Access, if necessary, and open the Lesson 11 database.

Ready? Here's how to import a text file.

2 Select File → Get External Data → Import from the menu.

TIP *Another way to import an external data file is to right-click any empty area of the Database window and select Import from the shortcut menu.*

The Import dialog box appears. Normally, the Import dialog box only displays Microsoft Access databases. To import files created with other programs, you need to select the file type you want from the Files of type list—in your case, text files.

3 Click the Files of type list arrow and select Text Files.

Access displays any text files in the current folder. Next you have to specify the text file that you want to open.

4 Browse to your Practice folder and double-click the Europe Expenses file.

The Import Text Wizard dialog box appears, as shown in Figure 11-1. You must specify how the information is stored in the text file. There are two options:

- **Delimited:** Tabs, colons, semicolons, or other characters separate items in your text file. This is the most common (and default) option.
- **Fixed Width:** All the items in your text file are the same length.

The Europe Expenses is a *tab-delimited* text file—that is, tabs separate its fields—so you don't need to make any changes and can continue on to the next step.

5 Click Next.

The second step of the Import Text Wizard appears, as shown in Figure 11-2. Here you have to specify the delimiter character used to separate the fields in the text file. Surprisingly, Access is usually smart enough to figure out which character is used as the delimiter (usually a tab or comma). What *is* vitally important here is the "First Row Contains Field Names" check box. Hopefully, the data you're importing will include field names in the first row; otherwise, you will have to add the field names to the table yourself later. Luckily, the Europe Expenses text file does include field names in the first row, so we'll need to tell this to Access.

6 Check the First Row Contains Field Names check box.

Quotation marks or *text qualifiers* may surround some text entries and must be removed.

7 Click the Text Qualifier arrow, select " and click Next.

Next Access asks where you want to import the data—to a new table or to an existing table that you select from a drop-down list. We want to store the imported data in a new table, so we don't have to make any changes here.

8 Click Next.

The next step of the Import Text Wizard allows you to specify the data types for the fields in the imported data, as shown in Figure 11-3. For example, you could specify that a particular field is a date or number field. Access is usually quite smart at guessing the data type for most fields, but you might want to double-check each imported field just to be sure. Simply click the field heading that you want to view and make any changes to the data type.

9 Click Next.

Next the Import Wizard asks if you want to add a primary key to the imported data, as shown in Figure 11-4. You can let Access add an AutoNumber primary field to the new table, use one of the imported fields as the primary (providing that it meets the criteria for primary fields), or not use a primary key.

10 Select the No primary key option and click Finish. Click OK to confirm the creation of the new table.

Access imports the text file and stores it in a new table called "Europe Expenses."

Table 11-1 below lists importable and exportable file formats and extensions.

Table 11-1. Importable and Exportable File Formats and Extensions

File Format	Extensions
Microsoft Excel	.xls, .xlt
Lotus 1-2-3	.wk4, .wk3, .fm3, .fmt, .all, .wk1, .wks
Text (both tab- and comma-delimited)	.txt, .csv
Dbase 2, 3, 4	.dbf
Microsoft Access	.mdb

QUICK REFERENCE

TO IMPORT INFORMATION FROM ANOTHER FILE INTO ACCESS:

1. IN THE DATABASE WINDOW, SELECT FILE → GET EXTERNAL DATA → IMPORT FROM THE MENU.

2. SELECT THE TYPE OF FILE YOU WANT TO IMPORT FROM THE FILES OF TYPE LIST.

3. BROWSE TO THE APPROPRIATE DRIVE AND/OR FOLDER AND DOUBLE-CLICK THE FILE YOU WANT TO IMPORT.

4. FOLLOW THE ONSCREEN INSTRUCTIONS OF THE IMPORT TEXT WIZARD TO IMPORT THE DATA.

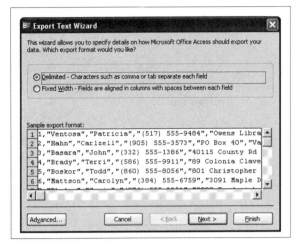

Figure 11-5. Step 1 of the Export Text Wizard: Determine the text file format.

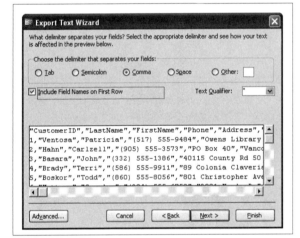

Figure 11-6. Step 2 of the Export Text Wizard: Specify the text delimiter that separates the fields if you want to include the field names in the exported file.

Figure 11-7. The exported text file viewed in the Notepad program.

When you *export* an Access table, you save its information in a different format so that it can be understood and opened by different programs. For example, you might export an Access table to an Excel worksheet.

In this lesson you will learn how to export an Access table to a comma-delimited text file.

1 **Make sure the Database window is displayed and click the** Tables **icon in the Objects bar, if necessary.**

You want to export the tblCustomers table to a comma-delimited text file so that it can be opened by other programs.

2 **Right-click the** tblCustomers **table and select** Export **from the shortcut menu.**

A dialog box appears, and Access asks where you want to export the table. You need to specify a file name and file format.

3 **If necessary, browse to your Practice folder. Type** Customers **in the** File Name **box. Click the** Save as type **list arrow and select** Text Files. **Click the** Export **button when you're finished.**

> **TIP**
> *Another way to export a table is to select the table and select* File → Export *from the menu.*

The Export Text Wizard appears, as shown in Figure 11-5. Here you need to specify how the information is stored in the text file. There are two options:

- **Delimited:** Tabs, colons, semicolons, or other characters separate items in your text file. This is the most common (and default) option.

- **Fixed Width:** All the items in your text file are aligned in columns.

If you're saving to a text file you will almost always want to select the "Delimited" option.

4 **Click** Next.

The second step of the Export Text Wizard appears, as shown in Figure 11-6. Here you have to specify the character you want to use as the delimiter to separate the fields in the text file (usually a tab or comma). What *is* vitally important here is the "Include Field Names on First Row" check box. You will usually want to include field names in the first row—otherwise you may have to add the field names to the data by yourself later.

5 Click the Include Field Names on First Row check box to select it, then click Finish. Click OK to close the confirmation message.

Access exports the tblCustomers table to a comma-delimited text file. If you want, move on to the next couple of steps and we'll see how the exported text file looks. Otherwise, feel free to skip them and move on to the next lesson.

6 Click the Windows Start button and select All Programs → Accessories → Notepad.

Windows starts the Notepad program.

7 Select File → Open from the menu.

The Open dialog box for the Notepad program appears.

8 Browse to your Practice folder and double-click the tblCustomers text file.

The comma-delimited text file appears, as shown in Figure 11-7. It doesn't look pretty, but the information you're looking at is in a format that is very easy for most computer programs to understand.

9 Close the Notepad program.

QUICK REFERENCE

TO EXPORT A TABLE TO AN EXTERNAL FILE:

1. IN THE DATABASE WINDOW, RIGHT-CLICK THE TABLE AND SELECT EXPORT FROM THE SHORTCUT MENU.

   OR...

   SELECT THE TABLE AND SELECT FILE → EXPORT FROM THE MENU.

2. SELECT A FORMAT FROM THE SAVE AS TYPE LIST AND THEN, IF NECESSARY, TYPE A NEW FILE NAME IN THE FILE NAME TEXT BOX.

3. CLICK EXPORT.

4. FOLLOW THE ONSCREEN INSTRUCTIONS OF THE EXPORT TEXT WIZARD TO EXPORT THE DATA.

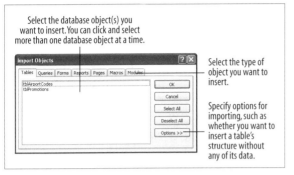

Select the database object(s) you want to insert. You can click and select more than one database object at a time.

Select the type of object you want to insert.

Specify options for importing, such as whether you want to insert a table's structure without any of its data.

Figure 11-8. The Import Objects dialog box.

Not only does the Import command insert information from other file formats, it also lets you import objects from other Microsoft Access databases. You can import tables, forms, reports, pages, queries, macros, and VBA modules from one Access database into another Access database. Inserting objects from another Access database saves you lots of time: Instead of creating a new object (such as a form) from scratch, you can import an object from another database and then modify it as needed.

In this lesson you will learn how to import an object from another Microsoft Access database.

1 Select File → Get External Data → Import from the menu.

Another way to import a database object is to right-click any empty area of the Database window and select Import *from the shortcut menu.*

The Import dialog box appears. Here you need to specify the Microsoft Access database that contains the object(s) you want to import into the current database.

2 Browse to your Practice folder and double-click the Promotions database file.

The Import Objects dialog box appears, as shown in Figure 11-8. The Import Objects dialog box looks a lot like the Database window—you click the tab that corresponds to the type of database object you want to import.

You can insert any type of database object—we'll try inserting a form.

3 Click the Forms tab.

Access displays all the forms in the Promotions database.

4 Click the frmPromotion form.

You can import more than one database object at a time—simply click the appropriate object tab(s) and select the database objects you want to select. When you're finished, here's what to do:

5 Click OK.

Access imports the frmPromotion form into the current database.

QUICK REFERENCE

TO IMPORT AN OBJECT FROM ANOTHER ACCESS DATABASE:

1. IN THE DATABASE WINDOW, SELECT FILE → GET EXTERNAL DATA → IMPORT FROM THE MENU.

2. BROWSE TO THE APPROPRIATE DRIVE AND/OR FOLDER AND DOUBLE-CLICK THE DATABASE THAT CONTAINS THE OBJECT(S) YOU WANT TO IMPORT.

3. SELECT THE DATABASE OBJECT(S) YOU WANT TO IMPORT AND CLICK OK.

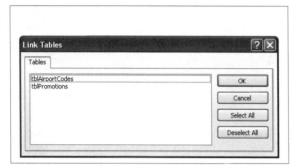

Figure 11-9. The Link Tables dialog box.

Another way that you can access information in another database is by creating a *linked table*. A linked table may sound a lot like an imported table, but there are some very important differences between the two:

- **Imported:** When you *import* a table, you copy data from a table in one Access database and place it in a new table in your database.

- **Linked:** When you *link* a table, the data stays in its original location. You can add, delete, and edit records in a linked table from within Access, but you can't change the table's structure. If the data in the original database changes, the changes will appear in your database too.

Many databases often use a *front-end* database file, which contains the forms, reports, and queries and is linked to a *back-end* database file, which contains the actual tables. Such designs work great when you want several users on several front-end databases to be able to access the same information in a single back-end database.

1 Select File → Get External Data → Link Tables from the menu.

The Link dialog box appears. Here you need to specify the database that contains the table you want to link.

2 Browse to your Practice folder and double-click the Promotions database file.

The Link Tables dialog box appears, as shown in Figure 11-9. All you have to do here is select the table(s) that you want to link to.

3 Click the tblPromotions table and click OK.

The dialog box closes and Access creates a link to the tblPromotions table. You can identify linked tables by their arrow. Let's try opening the linked table.

4 Click the Tables icon in the Objects bar, if necessary, and double-click the tblPromotions table.

Access opens the tblPromotions table. Though you can view, add, edit, and delete the records in the tblPromotions table, it remains in the Promotions database.

5 Click the tblPromotions table's Close button.

You can also create linked tables that access external information from such sources as dBase, Paradox, Fox-Pro, and SQL databases.

Figure 11-10. The results of a Microsoft Access query exported to a Microsoft Excel spreadsheet.

Access is capable of performing calculations on groups of records, but it can't hold a candle to its Microsoft Office 2003 counterpart, Microsoft Excel, when it comes to number crunching. An Excel spreadsheet is similar to an Access datasheet in many ways, with one important difference. Not only can you enter information in an Excel spreadsheet, but you can also easily add *formulas* directly into the spreadsheet grid—something you can't do in Access. It makes sense, then, that more people use Excel together with Access than any other program.

In this lesson you will learn how to create a Microsoft Excel spreadsheet based on an Access query.

1 Make sure that the Database window is displayed.

We will be using a query to create an Excel spreadsheet in this exercise, but you can also create spreadsheets based on tables and reports.

2 Click the Queries icon in the Objects bar and select the qrySales query.

Here's how to export the selected database object to Microsoft Excel.

3 Click the OfficeLinks button list arrow on the toolbar and select Analyze It with Microsoft Office Excel from the list.

> **TIP**
> *Another way to export an object to Excel is to select* Tools → Office Links → Analyze It with Microsoft Excel *from the menu.*

Microsoft Access sends the results of the qrySales query to Microsoft Excel, as shown in Figure 11-10. We won't spend much time working in Excel—this *is* a book about Access—but let's at least try adding a formula to the spreadsheet.

4 Scroll to the right if necessary, click in cell H2, type =G2*.9 and press Enter.

Excel multiplies the value in cell G2 by 0.9 (90 percent) and displays the results.

5 Close Microsoft Excel without saving any changes.

QUICK REFERENCE

TO EXPORT ACCESS DATA TO MICROSOFT EXCEL:

1. OPEN OR SELECT THE TABLE, QUERY, OR REPORT YOU WANT TO EXPORT.

2. CLICK THE OFFICELINKS BUTTON LIST ARROW ON THE TOOLBAR AND SELECT ANALYZE IT WITH MICROSOFT OFFICE EXCEL FROM THE LIST.

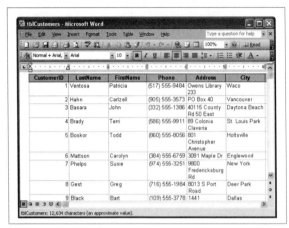

Figure 11-11. A Microsoft Access table exported to a Microsoft Word document.

If Microsoft Excel is the best tool for number crunching, Microsoft Word is definitely the best program to use for formatting and presenting large amounts of text. You can easily transfer records from a table or query using simple copy and paste commands or by using the Publish It with Microsoft Word command, found under the Office Links button on the toolbar. When records are transferred from Access to Word, they are formatted within the document as a Word table. This makes it easy to edit, sort, and format.

In this lesson you will learn how to transfer an Access table to a Microsoft Word document.

1 Make sure that the Database window is displayed.

Although we'll be using a table to create our Word document in this exercise, you can also create a document based on queries and reports.

2 Click the Tables icon in the Objects bar and select the tblCustomers table.

Here's how to export the selected database object to Microsoft Word.

3 Click the OfficeLinks button list arrow on the toolbar and select Publish It with Microsoft Office Word from the list.

 Another way to export an object to Word is to select Tools → Office Links → Publish It with Microsoft Office Word *from the menu.*

Microsoft Access sends the tblCustomers table to Microsoft Word, as shown in Figure 11-11. The results usually aren't pretty—but it's easy to fix this problem with some formatting and editing.

4 Close Microsoft Word without saving any changes.

QUICK REFERENCE

TO EXPORT ACCESS DATA TO MICROSOFT WORD:

1. OPEN OR SELECT THE TABLE, QUERY, OR REPORT YOU WANT TO EXPORT.

2. CLICK THE OFFICELINKS BUTTON LIST ARROW ON THE TOOLBAR AND SELECT PUBLISH IT WITH MICROSOFT OFFICE WORD FROM THE LIST.

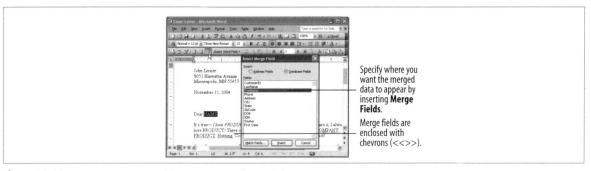

Figure 11-12. Inserting a Merge Field into a Microsoft Word document.

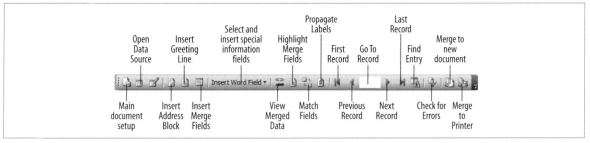

Figure 11-13. The Microsoft Word Mail Merge toolbar.

Ever wondered who at Publisher's Clearing House Sweepstakes types your name on the letters you receive on a weekly basis? Well, thanks to a process known as *mail merge*, creating these "personalized" letters requires no more effort than a few keystrokes. Mail-merge letters are used to send the same or similar documents to many different people at once.

To perform a mail merge you need two files:

- **A Main Document:** a Microsoft Word document that contains the text that is the same in all of the merged documents (also known as *boiler-plate text*).

- **A Data Source:** which contains the records that you want to insert into the merged documents. A Microsoft Access database makes a great data source.

In this lesson you will learn to merge information from Access into Microsoft Word.

1 In the Database window, click the Tables icon in the Objects bar, select the tblCompanies table, click the OfficeLinks button list arrow, and select Merge It with Microsoft Word from the list.

TIP

Another way to merge an object with Word is to select Tools → Office Links → Merge It with Microsoft Word from the menu.

The Microsoft Word Mail Merge Wizard appears and asks if you want to link the data to an existing Microsoft Word document or create a new Word document and then link the data to it. For this exercise you will be using an existing Word document.

2 Click OK to link your data to an existing Word document.

The Wizard prompts you for the name and location of the existing Word document.

3 Browse to your Practice folder, then find and double-click the Cover Letter document.

The Cover Letter document opens in Microsoft Word, as shown in Figure 11-12.

Now comes the most important part of the mail-merge process: You have to specify where you want to insert the information from the data source (or Access database) into your main document. You do this by inserting *merge fields*. Merge fields are where the information from your data source gets inserted into the main document.

4 Place the insertion point at the end of the date line and press Enter twice.

This is where you will place your first merge field.

5 Click the 🖹 Insert Merge Fields button on the Mail Merge toolbar, as shown in Figure 11-13, and select Name from the field list, click Insert, and click Close.

The Name field (from the Microsoft Access database) is inserted into the document. You may have noticed chevrons surround the field («»). The chevrons differentiate the merge fields from other text in the document.

6 Press Enter, click the Insert Merge Fields button, select Company from the field list, click Insert, and click Close. Press Enter, click the Insert Merge Fields button, select Address from the field list, click Insert, and click Close.

Move on to the next step and finish the address.

7 Press Enter, click the Insert Merge Fields button, select City from the field list, click Insert, and click Close. Type a , (comma) and press the Spacebar. Click the Insert Merge Fields button, select State from the field list, click Insert, and click Close. Press the Spacebar, click the Insert Merge Fields button again, select PostalCode from the field list, click Insert, and click Close.

Getting the hang of it? You can merge the information in the data source with the main document in one of four ways:

- **New Document:** Merges the data source with the main document and places the results in a single, new document. Each record in the data source will appear on a separate page. You can then save the new merged document.

- **Printer:** Merges the data source with the document and prints the results.

- **E-mail:** Merges the data source with the document and e-mails the results.

- **Fax:** Merges the data source with the document and faxes the results.

For this lesson, we'll merge to a new document.

8 Click the 🖹 Merge to New Document button on the Mail Merge toolbar, select the All option, and click OK.

Word merges the main document "Mail Merge Letter" and the data source "Mail Merge Letter Data" into a new document called "Letters1." The new merged document contains four letters—one letter for each record in the data source—that are separated with a page break.

9 Press Page Down several times to move to the next page of the document to view the second letter.

Notice that this letter uses data from the second record in the data source.

10 Close Microsoft Word without saving any of your changes.

Congratulations, you've performed a mail merge—a task many people consider to be one of the most difficult procedures in word processing.

QUICK REFERENCE

TO MAIL MERGE RECORDS WITH MICROSOFT WORD:

1. OPEN OR SELECT THE TABLE, QUERY, OR REPORT YOU WANT TO USE FOR THE MAIL MERGE.

2. CLICK THE OFFICELINKS BUTTON LIST ARROW ON THE TOOLBAR AND SELECT MERGE IT WITH MICROSOFT WORD FROM THE LIST.

3. SPECIFY WHETHER YOU WISH TO MERGE TO AN EXISTING WORD DOCUMENT OR IF YOU WANT TO CREATE A NEW WORD DOCUMENT.

4. PERFORM THE MAIL MERGE USING MICROSOFT WORD.

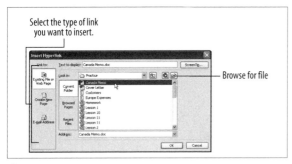

Select the type of link
you want to insert.

Browse for file

Figure 11-14. The Insert Hyperlink dialog box.

In this lesson, you will learn about how to use hyperlinks in Microsoft Access. A *hyperlink* can point to any file on your computer, on the network, or even on a Web page on the Internet. Whenever you click on a hyperlink, you jump to the hyperlink's destination (if it's available). A hyperlink is usually indicated by colored and underlined text. If you have ever been on the World Wide Web, you've used hyperlinks all the time to move between different Web pages.

Microsoft recognized the importance of the Internet and thus introduced the new *hyperlink field type* in Access 2003. You can use the hyperlink field to store clickable links to files on your computer or network or to Web pages on the Internet.

In this lesson you will learn how to use hyperlink fields to create links that point to files on your network or on the Internet.

1 Select the tblTours table and click the Design button.

First we need to add a hyperlink field to this table.

2 Click the first blank Field Name row and type Link. Click the Data Type list arrow and select Hyperlink from the list.

You've just created a hyperlink field!

3 Save your changes and then click the View button on the toolbar to display the table in Datasheet view.

Let's try adding a hyperlink to the Western Canada record.

4 Click in the Link field for the Western Canada record and click the Insert Hyperlink button on the toolbar.

Another way to insert a hyperlink is to select Insert → Hyperlink from the menu.

The Insert Hyperlink dialog box appears, as shown in Figure 11-14. This is where you will specify the name and location of the file or Web page you want to add as a hyperlink. If you know the location and name of the file or Web address, you can type it directly in the dialog box; otherwise, you can use the Browse button to locate the file.

5 Click the Browse for File button.

The Link to File dialog box appears and displays a list of files that you can use as the destination for your hyperlink.

6 Browse to your Practice folder, then find and double-click the Canada Memo document.

The Link to File dialog box closes, and the name and location of the Canada Memo is added to the Address box.

7 Click OK.

The dialog box closes and you return to the datasheet. Notice that the text "Canada Memo.doc" appears blue and underlined, signifying that it's a hyperlink. Let's see how our new hyperlink works.

8 Click the Canada Memo.doc hyperlink.

You immediately jump to the hyperlink's destination—in this case, the Canada Memo document.

⁝ NOTE ⁝ *If a dialog box appears, warning you that hyperlinks can be harmful to your computer and data, click Yes to continue.*

9 Close Microsoft Word without saving any changes.

You should be back in Microsoft Access, looking at the tblTours datasheet.

Once you create a hyperlink, you can easily edit it to change its title or target, copy it, or delete it by right-clicking the hyperlink.

10 Right-click the Canada Memo.doc hyperlink and select Hyperlink from the shortcut menu.

A shortcut menu with the most frequently used hyperlink commands appears. Here you could select "Edit Hyperlink" to change the hyperlink's target or "Display Text" to edit the hyperlink's title. Your

hyperlink is fine the way it is, so close the shortcut menu.

11 Click anywhere in the datasheet to close the shortcut menu. Close the tblTours table without saving any changes.

QUICK REFERENCE

TO CREATE A HYPERLINK FIELD:

1. DISPLAY THE TABLE IN DESIGN VIEW.

2. CREATE A NEW FIELD TO STORE THE HYPERLINKS.

3. CLICK THE NEW HYPERLINK FIELD'S DATA TYPE BOX, CLICK THE LIST ARROW, AND SELECT HYPERLINK.

4. SAVE THE TABLE.

TO INSERT A HYPERLINK:

1. SELECT THE HYPERLINK FIELD AND CLICK THE INSERT HYPERLINK BUTTON ON THE TOOLBAR.

   OR...

SELECT THE HYPERLINK FIELD AND SELECT INSERT → HYPERLINK FROM THE MENU.

2. EITHER SELECT A FILE YOU WANT (USE THE BROWSE BUTTON TO HELP YOU LOCATE THE FILE) OR TYPE A WEB ADDRESS FOR THE HYPERLINK'S DESTINATION AND CLICK OK.

TO EDIT A HYPERLINK:

• RIGHT-CLICK THE HYPERLINK AND SELECT HYPERLINK → EDIT HYPERLINK FROM THE SHORTCUT MENU.

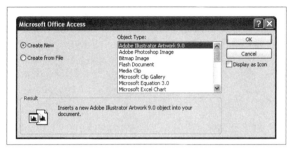

Figure 11-15. The Insert Object dialog box with the Create New option selected.

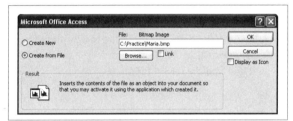

Figure 11-16. The Insert Object dialog box with the Create from File option selected.

Figure 11-17. In Datasheet view you normally can't see the actual OLE objects.

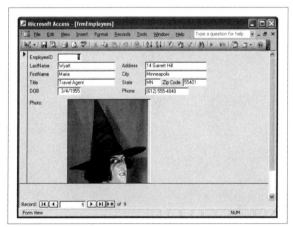

Figure 11-18. The inserted photo displayed in the frmEmployees form.

Perhaps the least understood of all fields, the OLE Object data type lets you store files created in other programs such as graphics, Excel spreadsheets, or Word documents. This lesson will give you some practice working with OLE object fields.

1 Select the tblEmployees table and click the Design button.

First we need to add an OLE field to this table.

2 Click the first blank Field Name row and type Photo. Click the Data Type list arrow and select OLE Object from the list.

You've created an OLE Object field!

3 Save your changes and then click the View button on the toolbar to display the table in Datasheet view.

Let's try adding an OLE object to the Maria Wyatt record.

4 Click in any field for Maria Wyatt, scroll to the right, click in the Photo field for the Maria Wyatt record (using the record selector as a guide), and select Insert → Object from the menu.

The Insert Object dialog box appears, as shown in Figure 11-15. You can create and then insert new objects by selecting the *Create New* option or you can click the *Create from File* option to insert an existing file. For this exercise, we already created and saved a photo, so you need to select the Create from File option.

5 Click the Create from File option.

The Insert Object dialog box displays the Create from File options, as shown in Figure 11-16. Here you will specify the name and location of the file you want to insert.

6 Click the Browse button.

Now you need to find and locate the file you want to insert into your document.

7 Browse to your Practice folder, then find and double-click the Maria.bmp file.

The name and location of the Maria.bmp file appears in the File box. Before we close the Insert Object dialog box, there is one more very important option we need to explore—the "Link" check box. The "Link" check box determines whether the OLE object is actually *embedded* within the database or merely *linked* to it. This is a rather difficult concept for most people—you might want to look at Table 11-2 for more on the differences between the two.

For this exercise, we want to embed the graphic within the database, so we'll leave the Link box unchecked.

8 Click OK.

The dialog box closes, and Access embeds the Maria.bmp picture in the Photo field.

The problem with working with OLE object fields in Datasheet view is that you can't see the actual OLE objects (see Figure 11-17). It's for this reason that you may want to use a form to work with OLE object fields.

9 Close the tblEmployees table. Click the Forms icon in the Objects bar, click the frmEmployees form, and click the Design button.

First we need to add the new photo field to the form.

10 Click the Field List button on the toolbar, if necessary. Click and drag the Photo field anywhere on the form.

> *TIP*
>
> *Another way to display the field list is to select View → Field List from the menu.*

Don't worry about where you place the Photo OLE object field or if it covers other fields—we're not striving for perfection here. As with any other form control, you can move and resize OLE object fields.

Let's see how the Photo field looks in Form view.

11 Click the View button on the toolbar to switch to Form view. Click the Next Record Navigation button until you find the record for Maria.

Yep! There's the picture! (See Figure 11-18.)

12 Close the frmEmployees form without saving any changes.

Table 11-2. Embedded vs. Linked Objects

Object Type	Description
Embedded (**Link box** not checked)	An embedded object is actually saved within the database. Databases with embedded objects are larger than databases with linked objects. The advantage of using embedded objects is that the objects are actually saved inside the database, so you don't have to worry about any attached files becoming lost or erased.
Linked (**Link box** checked)	A linked object is not saved in the database. Instead, a link contains information on where to find the source data file. The advantage of using linked objects is that if the source file is changed, the linked object in the database is automatically updated to reflect the changes.

QUICK REFERENCE

TO CREATE AN OLE OBJECT FIELD:

1. DISPLAY THE TABLE IN DESIGN VIEW.

2. CREATE A NEW FIELD TO STORE THE OLE OBJECTS.

3. CLICK THE NEW OLE FIELD'S DATA TYPE BOX, CLICK THE LIST ARROW, AND SELECT OLE OBJECT.

4. SAVE THE TABLE.

TO INSERT AN OLE OBJECT:

1. SELECT THE OLE OBJECT FIELD AND SELECT INSERT → OBJECT FROM THE MENU.

2. SELECT EITHER:
   CREATE NEW: TO CREATE A NEW OLE OBJECT FILE (YOU MUST SELECT THE TYPE OF FILE YOU WISH TO CREATE).
   CREATE FROM FILE: TO INSERT AN EXISTING FILE.

3. CLICK OK.

4. IF YOU SELECTED THE CREATE FROM FILE OPTION, BROWSE TO AND DOUBLE-CLICK THE FILE YOU WANT TO INSERT AND CLICK OK.

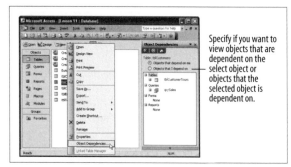

Specify if you want to view objects that are dependent on the select object or objects that the selected object is dependent on.

Figure 11-19. Right-click any Access database object and select Object Dependencies to view which database objects require the selected object and which database objects the select object requires.

Databases can often be complicated and interconnected. For example, a form might be based on a query, which in turn is based on a table. Deleting the query and your form won't work. So how do you keep track of all these interconnected database objects?

One of the most significant new features in Microsoft Access 2003 is its ability to view object dependencies. So, before you delete or rename a query, you can view every database object—every query, form, and report—that is dependent on that query. You can also do the reverse and view every database object that the query requires in order to function.

Here's how to view object dependencies.

1 Right-click any database object and select Object Dependencies from the shortcut menu.

Access displays which objects are dependent on the selected object, as shown in Figure 11-19. You can display two different types of information:

- Database objects that are dependent on the selected database object.
- Database objects that are required by the selected database object.

⸗ NOTE ⸗ Depending on how *Access is configured on your computer, a dialog box may appear, informing you that the* Track name Auto-Correct info *option has not been turned on. Click* OK *to enable this feature.*

2 Close the task pane and the database.

QUICK REFERENCE

TO VIEW DATABASE OBJECT DEPENDENCIES:

- RIGHT-CLICK ANY DATABASE OBJECT AND SELECT OBJECT DEPENDENCIES FROM THE SHORTCUT MENU.

Chapter Eleven Review

Lesson Summary

Importing Information

To Import Information from Another File into Access: In the Database window, select File → Get External Data → Import from the menu. Select the type of file you want to import from the Files of type list, browse to the appropriate drive and/or folder and double-click the file you want to import. Follow the onscreen instructions of the Import Text Wizard to import the data.

Exporting Information

To Export a Table to an External File: In the Database window, right-click the table and select Export from the shortcut menu or select the table and select File → Export from the menu. Select a format from the Save as type list and then, if necessary, type a new file name in the File name text box. Click Export and follow the onscreen instructions of the Export Text Wizard to export the data.

Importing Objects from Another Access Database

To Import an Object from Another Access Database: In the Database window, select File → Get External Data → Import from the menu, browse to the appropriate drive and/or folder, and double-click the database that contains the object(s) you want to import. Select the database object(s) you want to import and click OK.

Linking Information from an External Source

To Link to a Table in Another Database: In the Database window, select File → Get External Data → Link Tables from the menu, browse to the appropriate drive and/or folder, and double-click the database that contains the table you wish to link to. Click the table you wish to link and click OK.

Analyzing Records with Microsoft Excel

To Export Access Data to Microsoft Excel: Open or select the table, query, or report you want to export. Click the OfficeLinks button list arrow on the toolbar and select Analyze It with Microsoft Office Excel from the list.

Exporting Records to Microsoft Word

To Export Access Data to Microsoft Word: Open or select the table, query, or report you want to export, click the OfficeLinks button list arrow on the toolbar and select Publish It with Microsoft Office Word from the list.

Mail Merging Records to Microsoft Word

To Mail Merge Records with Microsoft Word: Open or select the table, query, or report you want to use for the mail merge, click the OfficeLinks button list arrow on the toolbar and select Merge It with Microsoft Office Word from the list. Specify whether you wish to merge to an existing Word document or if you want to create a new Word document and perform the mail merge using Microsoft Word.

Using Hyperlink Fields

To Create a Hyperlink Field: Display the table in Design view, create a new field to store the hyperlinks, click the new hyperlink field's Data Type box, click the list arrow, select Hyperlink, and save the table.

To Insert a Hyperlink: Select the hyperlink field and then click the Insert Hyperlink button on the toolbar or select Insert → Hyperlink from the menu. Either select a file you want (use the Browse button to help you locate the file) or type a Web address for the hyperlink's destination and click OK.

To Edit a Hyperlink: Right-click the hyperlink and select Hyperlink → Edit Hyperlink from the shortcut menu.

Using OLE Object Fields

To Create an OLE Object Field: Display the table in Design view and create a new field to store the OLE objects. Click the new OLE field's Data Type box, click the list arrow, select OLE Object, and save the table.

To Insert an OLE Object: Select the OLE Object field, select Insert → Object from the menu, select either Create New (to create a new OLE object file—you must select the type of file you wish to create) or Create from File (to insert an existing file), and click OK. If you selected the Create from File option, browse to and double-click the file you want to insert, and click OK.

Displaying Database Object Dependencies

To View Database Object Dependencies: Right-click any database object and select Object Dependencies from the shortcut menu.

Quiz

1. One of the most common and basic file formats used to import, export, and exchange information between different programs is:

    A. A JPEG file.

    B. A GIF file.

    C. A tab- or comma-delimited text file.

    D. A Microsoft Exchange-It file.

2. When you export a Microsoft Access table to an external data file, Access automatically includes the field names in the first row of the data file. (True or False?)

3. Which of the following database objects can you import from one Microsoft Access database to another? (Select all that apply.)

    A. Tables.

    B. Queries.

    C. Forms.

    D. Reports.

4. When you create a link to a table in an external database, Access imports the table into the current database. (True or False?)

5. The only way to export Access database information to Microsoft Excel is by saving it to an external file. (True or False?)

6. When you use the Publish It with Microsoft Word command to send information to Microsoft Word, the data appears in:

    A. A frightening dialog box that says "General Protection Fault."

    B. A comma-delimited text format.

    C. A tab-delimited text format.

    D. A table.

7. A hyperlink can point to: (Select all that apply.)

    A. A file on your computer.

    B. A file on a network.

    C. A Web page on the Internet.

    D. All of these.

8. Microsoft Access can import information from which of the following file formats?

    A. Excel workbooks.

    B. Comma-delimited text files.

    C. dBase database files.

    D. All of these.

9. You're building a database for your mail-order bride company. You want your table to include a field that stores the picture of your prospective brides. What field type would you need to use?

    A. Memo.

    B. OLE Object.

    C. Hyperlink.

    D. Access can't store graphics.

Homework

1. Open Microsoft Access, if necessary, and then open the Homework database.

2. Export the Insurance Claims table to a comma-delimited text file.

3. Create a link to the Employees table in the Lesson 1 database.

4. Create a Microsoft Excel spreadsheet based on the Science Test Answers table.

5. Transfer the Insurance Claims table to a Microsoft Word document. (If you're really inspired, change the document's Page Orientation in Word to Landscape so that the table fits on the page.)

6. Create a hyperlink in the Products table to the Maria.bmp file.**Hint:** You must first add a hyperlink field to the table.

7. Exit Microsoft Word, Microsoft Excel, and Microsoft Access.

Quiz Answers

1. C. Tab- and comma-delimited text files are the most common and basic type of file formats used to exchange information between different types of programs.

2. False. To include the field names, you must check the First Row Contains Field Names box (for an imported file) or the Include Field Names on First Row box (for an exported file) on the delimiter option screen of the Import/Export Text Wizard.

3. A, B, C, and D. Any of these Microsoft Access objects can be imported from one Access database to another Access database.

4. False. When you *link* to a table, the data stays in its original location.

5. False. You can export information to Excel by saving it to an external file—but you can also export it directly to Excel by clicking the Office Links list arrow and selecting Analyze It with Microsoft Excel.

6. D. When you use the Publish It with Microsoft Word command, information sent to Word appears in a table.

7. D. Hyperlinks can point to any of these items.

8. D. Access can import information from all of these file formats.

9. B. OLE Object fields can store objects created in other programs, such as pictures and graphics.

INDEX

Symbols

! formatting symbol, 138
! Input Mask character, 144
# formatting character, 136
# Input Mask character, 144
$ formatting character, 136
% formatting character, 136
& (ampersand) symbol, 180
& Input Mask character, 144
* formatting symbol, 138
* operator, 178
+ operator, 178
- operator, 178
, formatting character, 136
. , : ; - / Input Mask characters, 144
. formatting character, 136
.txt, .csv, 318
/ operator, 178
< (less than symbol), 137, 138
< = filtering operator, 103
< = operator, 69, 172
< filtering operator, 103
< Input Mask character, 144
< operator, 69, 172
= filtering operator, 103
= operator, 69, 172
> (greater than symbol), 137, 138
> = filtering operator, 103
> = operator, 69, 172
> filtering operator, 103
> Input Mask character, 144
> operator, 69, 172
? Input Mask character, 144
@ formatting symbol, 138
[] brackets, 180
[color] formatting symbol, 138
\ Input Mask character, 144
^ operator, 178
"ABC" formatting symbol, 138

Numerics

0 formatting character, 136
0 Input Mask character, 144
9 Input Mask character, 144

A

A Input Mask character, 144
a Input Mask character, 144
Access 2003
   closing and exiting, 49
   databases, converting, 87
   new features, 4
   starting, 6
Add to Group object shortcut menu command, 82
addition operator, 178
AddMenu macro action, 310
Advanced Filter, 104
After Update event, 305
Align command, 290
aligning text, 138, 282
.all file, 318
All tab (Properties dialog box), 222
Allow Additions property, 228
Allow AutoCorrect property, 224
Allow Datasheet View property, 227
Allow Deletions property, 228
Allow Edits property, 228
Allow Filters property, 228
Allow Form View property, 227
Allow PivotChart View property, 227
Allow PivotTable View property, 227
Allow Zero Length field property, 121
Always show full menus option, 10
ampersand (&) symbol, 180
AND/OR statements, 72, 104
Any Part of Field option (Match List), 97
Append Data to an Existing Table pasting option, 81
append queries, 198, 204
Apply Filter button, 103
ApplyFilter macro action, 310
area charts, 274
arithmetic operators, 178
arrow keys, 27
Auto Resize property, 227
AutoForm Wizard, 210
AutoFormat dialog box, 283
AutoKeys, 308
AutoNumber data type, 64, 128
   shortcut, 67

Colophon

Our look is the result of reader comments, our own experimentation, and feedback from distribution channels. Distinctive covers complement our distinctive approach to technical topics, breathing personality and life into potentially dry subjects.

Philip Dangler was the production editor and proofreader for *Access 2003 Personal Trainer*. Mary Brady, Marlowe Shaeffer, and Emily Quill provided quality control. Julie Hawks wrote the index.

The cover image of the comic book hero is an original illustration by Lou Brooks. The art of illustrator Lou Brooks has appeared on the covers of *Time* and *Newsweek* eight times, and his logo design for the game Monopoly is used throughout the world to this day. His work has also appeared in just about every major publication, and it has been animated for MTV, Nickelodeon, and HBO.

Emma Colby designed and produced the cover of this book with Adobe InDesign CS and Photoshop CS. The typefaces used on the cover are Base Twelve, designed by Zuzana Licko and issued by Emigre, Inc., and JY Comic Pro, issued by AGFA Monotype.

Melanie Wang designed the interior layout. Emma Colby designed the CD label. This book was converted by Andrew Savikas and Joe Wizda to FrameMaker 5.5.6 with a format conversion tool created by Erik Ray, Jason McIntosh, Neil Walls, and Mike Sierra that uses Perl and XML technologies. The typefaces are Minion, designed by Robert Slimbach and issued by Adobe Systems; Base Twelve and Base Nine; JY Comic Pro; and TheSansMono Condensed, designed by Luc(as) de Groot and issued by LucasFonts.

The technical illustrations that appear in the book were produced by Robert Romano, Jessamyn Read, and Lesley Borash, using Macromedia FreeHand MX and Adobe Photoshop CS.

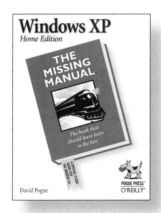

Related Titles Available from O'Reilly

Windows Users

Access Cookbook, *2nd Edition*

Access Database Design & Programming, *3rd Edition*

Excel Hacks

Excel Pocket Guide

Outlook 2000 in a Nutshell

Outlook Pocket Guide

PC Annoyances

Windows XP Annoyances

Windows XP Hacks

Windows XP Home Edition: The Missing Manual

Windows XP in a Nutshell

Windows XP Pocket Guide

Windows XP Power User

Windows XP Pro: The Missing Manual

Windows XP Unwired

Word Hacks

Word Pocket Guide, *2nd Edition*

Keep in touch with O'Reilly

1. Download examples from our books

To find example files for a book, go to:

www.oreilly.com/catalog

select the book, and follow the "Examples" link.

2. Register your O'Reilly books

Register your book at *register.oreilly.com*

Why register your books?
Once you've registered your O'Reilly books you can:

- Win O'Reilly books, T-shirts or discount coupons in our monthly drawing.
- Get special offers available only to registered O'Reilly customers.
- Get catalogs announcing new books (US and UK only).
- Get email notification of new editions of the O'Reilly books you own.

3. Join our email lists

Sign up to get topic-specific email announcements of new books and conferences, special offers, and O'Reilly Network technology newsletters at:

elists.oreilly.com

It's easy to customize your free elists subscription so you'll get exactly the O'Reilly news you want.

4. Get the latest news, tips, and tools

www.oreilly.com

- "Top 100 Sites on the Web"—PC Magazine
- CIO Magazine's Web Business 50 Awards

Our web site contains a library of comprehensive product information (including book excerpts and tables of contents), downloadable software, background articles, interviews with technology leaders, links to relevant sites, book cover art, and more.

5. Work for O'Reilly

Check out our web site for current employment opportunities:

jobs.oreilly.com

6. Contact us

O'Reilly Media, Inc.
1005 Gravenstein Hwy North
Sebastopol, CA 95472 USA

TEL: 707-827-7000 or 800-998-9938
(6am to 5pm PST)

FAX: 707-829-0104

order@oreilly.com
For answers to problems regarding your order or our products. To place a book order online, visit:

www.oreilly.com/order_new

catalog@oreilly.com
To request a copy of our latest catalog.

booktech@oreilly.com
For book content technical questions or corrections.

corporate@oreilly.com
For educational, library, government, and corporate sales.

proposals@oreilly.com
To submit new book proposals to our editors and product managers.

international@oreilly.com
For information about our international distributors or translation queries. For a list of our distributors outside of North America check out:

international.oreilly.com/distributors.html

adoption@oreilly.com
For information about academic use of O'Reilly books, visit:

academic.oreilly.com

O'REILLY®

Our books are available at most retail and online bookstores.
To order direct: 1-800-998-9938 • *order@oreilly.com* • *www.oreilly.com*
Online editions of most O'Reilly titles are available by subscription at *safari.oreilly.com*